D0788512

SHAKESPEARE AND THE
QUESTION OF CULTURE

EARLY MODERN CULTURAL SERIES

Ivo Kamps, Series Editor

PUBLISHED BY PALGRAVE MACMILLAN

SHAKESPEARE AND THE QUESTION OF CULTURE

EARLY MODERN LITERATURE AND THE CULTURAL TURN

Douglas Bruster

palgrave
macmillan

SHAKESPEARE AND THE QUESTION OF CULTURE

First published 2003 by PALGRAVE MACMILLAN™
175 Fifth Avenue, New York, N.Y. 10010 and
Houndmills, Basingstoke, Hampshire, England RG21 6XS.
Companies and representatives throughout the world.

PALGRAVE MACMILLAN is the global academic imprint of the Palgrave Macmillan division of St. Martin's Press, LLC and of Palgrave Macmillan Ltd. Macmillan® is a registered trademark in the United States, United Kingdom and other countries. Palgrave is a registered trademark in the European Union and other countries.

ISBN 0-312-29438-7 hardback
ISBN 0-312-29439-5 paperback

Library of Congress Cataloging-in-Publication Data
Bruster, Douglas.
     Shakespeare and the question of culture : early modern literature and the cultural turn / by Douglas Bruster.
          p.   cm.—(Early modern cultural studies)
     Includes bibliographical references and index.
     ISBN 0-312-29438-7 — ISBN 0-312-29439-5
     1. Shakespeare, William, 1564–1616—Criticism and interpretation—History.   2. English literature—Early modern, 1500–1700—History and criticism—Theory, etc.   3. Literature and history—England—History—16th century.   4. Literature and history—England—History—17th century.   5. England—Civilization—16th century—Historiography.   6. England—Civilization—17th century—Historiography.   7. Historicism in literature.   I. Title.   II. Series.
     PR2965.B78   2003
     822.3'3—dc21   2002028754

A catalogue record for this book is available from the British Library.

Design by Letra Libre, Inc.

First edition: February 2003
10 9 8 7 6 5 4 3 2 1
Printed in the United States of America.

for Liz

CONTENTS

ACKNOWLEDGMENTS

I am indebted to many friends and colleagues for their help with this book. My greatest thanks, as always, go to my wife, Elizabeth Scala, who has been my most demanding reader and intelligent critic. Together with our daughters Madeleine and Claire, and her mother Carole, Liz has been incredibly supportive of my endeavors in this project. I owe them all a debt that I doubt I will be able to repay.

At the University of Texas, I have been fortunate to experience a warm community of scholars whose support of this book has been exemplary. Mary Blockley, Eric Mallin, Timothy Moore, and Wayne Rebhorn, in particular, read various chapters here with care and sensitivity. A dream chairperson, James Garrison has also supported my research with a commitment that would surprise those who have not had the good fortune of working with him.

I have been grateful for the help of colleagues at other institutions as well, and regret that I cannot more fully chronicle my debts to them. Among those who have read and commented upon various pieces here are Joseph Black, W. Scott Blanchard, Michael Bristol, Mark Thornton Burnett, Stephen Cohen, Lisa Freinkel, Hugh Grady, Michelle Girard, Roland Greene, Jonathan Gil Harris, Kenneth Alan Hovey, Natasha Korda, Jesse Macleish Lander, Arthur Marotti, Ian Frederick Moulton, Janel Mueller, Michael Murrin, John G. Norman, Mary Beth Rose, Katherine Rowe, Winfried Schleiner, Jyotsna Singh, Tyler Smith, Elizabeth Spiller, Lisa Starks, Valerie Traub, Douglas Trevor, and William Veeder. Bruce Boehrer read the entire manuscript with a sensitive eye and uncompromising standards; for this I am extremely grateful. Matthew Greenfield, whose stimulating essay on "culture" I came upon late in the composition of this book, generously offered comments on the first chapter and the appendix. For his own part, Ivo Kamps has been an ideal editor. To all these I offer my sincerest gratitude.

Some of the chapters in this book have been published elsewhere in various forms. Throughout, I have attempted to incorporate the most recent criticism into my revisions of these pieces, as well as to make the relation between their arguments and the larger subject of this book clearer. An earlier version of chapter 3, "The Structural Transformation of Print in Late Elizabethan England," was published in *Print, Manuscript, Performance: The Changing Relations of the Media in Early Modern England,* ed. Arthur F. Marotti and Michael D. Bristol (Columbus: Ohio State University Press, 2000); chapter 4, "The Dramatic Life of Objects in the Early Modern Theater," has been published in *Staged Properties in Early Modern English Drama,* ed. Natasha Korda and Jonathan Gil Harris (Cambridge: Cambridge University Press, 2003); an earlier version of chapter 5, "Female-female Eroticism and the Early Modern Stage," was published in *Renaissance Drama* 24 (1993 for 1995); chapter 6, "Shakespeare and the End of History: Period as Brand Name," was published, in an earlier form, in *Shakespeare and Modernity: Early Modern to Millennium,* ed. Hugh Grady (New York: Routledge, 2000); an earlier version of chapter 7, "Shakespeare and the Composite Text: The New Formalism," appeared, under a slightly different title, in *Renaissance Literature and Its Formal Engagements,* ed. Mark David Rasmussen (London: Palgrave, 2002); and chapter 8, "The New Materialism in Early Modern Studies," appeared first in *Material Culture and Cultural Materialisms in the Middle Ages and the Renaissance,* ed. Curtis Perry (Arizona Studies in the Middle Ages and the Renaissance, vol. 5; Turnhout, Belgium: Brepols, 2001). I am grateful to these publishers for their generous permission to reprint.

On a more personal level, I am also thankful to the editors of the above collections. Not only have they supported my work, in each instance they provided comments and questions that made the essay in question much stronger. Because editing is typically a thankless business, I want to express special gratitude to them for their collegial help.

A NOTE ON TEXTS

Approximate dates for plays cited in this book are most often taken from *Annals of English Drama, 975–1700,* 3rd edition, ed. Alfred Harbage, revised by S. Schoenbaum and Sylvia Stoler Wagonheim (London: Routledge, 1989). Unless otherwise noted, all quotations from Jonson in this study are from *Ben Jonson,* ed. C. H. Herford, Percy Simpson, and Evelyn Simpson, 11 vols. (Oxford: Clarendon Press, 1925–52); those from Nashe are from *The Works of Thomas Nashe,* ed. R. B. McKerrow, 5 vols. (London: Sidgwick and Jackson, 1904–08); and those from Shakespeare are from *The Riverside Shakespeare,* 2nd edition, ed. G. Blakemore Evans et al. (Boston: Houghton Mifflin, 1997). I have modernized some of the spelling and punctuation in the passages quoted here.

SERIES EDITOR'S FOREWORD

Douglas Bruster's *Shakespeare and the Question of Culture* is a welcome addition to the Early Modern Cultural Studies series, and to cultural criticism in general, because it reinvestigates, from both a theoretical and from a practical perspective, the nexus between the categories of "the literary" and "culture." In *Shakespeare and the Question of Culture,* Bruster proposes an alternative to the Clifford Geertz–inspired "thick" description that characterizes much of New Historicist and other forms of cultural criticism. Bruster argues that, while "entertaining" because of its narrative qualities, "thick" description typically offers too narrow a slice of culture to give us a reliable sense of a culture's "representative beliefs, practices, and symbols." If "thick" description once was a much-needed corrective to the grand narratives of critics like E. W. M. Tillyard and social historians like Christopher Hill and Lawrence Stone, Bruster's case suggests that recent historical criticism has veered too far in the direction of the local and peculiar to be telling us a great deal about sixteenth- and seventeenth-century English culture as a whole. What Bruster offers instead is what he calls a "thin" description, a kind of criticism that, like a cinematic "deep focus," allows us to keep various places of culture in view simultaneously. Yet Bruster's approach is hardly a return to the narrative tradition that finds linear unity in entire epochs. Rather, he offers his work as a supplement to New Historicism's thick description by incorporating a broader range of contextual elements than New Historicism commonly employs. Beyond the powerful, yet narrowly meaningful, anecdote, Bruster frames his discussion of early modern culture with a consideration of genre, literary conventions and fashions, source texts, repertorial aims, habits, the use of props in the playhouse, and printing-house organization. Separate chapters on print culture in late-Elizabethan England, the dramatic objects of the theater, and female-on-female eroticism offer searching applications of the thin description method. One of several

the startling conclusions advanced by Bruster is that, contrary to a
prevailing view (among New Historicists), print culture is more concerned with the representations of "persons as objects of discourse"
than it is with expressions of the self.

The three remaining chapters are dedicated to an analysis of how
prominent critical schools, habits of thought, and critical key words
shape our literary readings. Bruster's aim here is to bring the same
kind of rigor and scrutiny to the reading of criticism that we commonly bring to the reading of literature. First Bruster turns his attention to the history and politics of two prominent literary terms
that are often used interchangeably—"Renaissance" and "early modern"—and argues that the concept of an "English Renaissance" is
largely an invention of American academia. In the final two chapters,
he turns to the promise of current trends in cultural materialism and
the new formalism. The cultural materialism under the microscope
here is not of the dogmatically Marxist variety, the kind that deals
with "monumental, almost glacial transitions in history" and large,
abstract concepts such as "social class, base and superstructure, and
ideology." Bruster is interested in a more nimble materialism that
centers on the actual material objects of daily life and the theater and
the place they have in culture. Likewise, Bruster finds much value in
the new formalism that no longer disregards history, and which once
again has brought issues of genre, convention, and style to the forefront—*and* investigates their relationship to the world outside the
text. While Bruster finds a great deal of promise in the efforts of the
new formalism, he also discusses their shortcomings, and concludes
his study with a simple, yet rarely asked, and all-important question:
Is it even possible to explain the relationship between text and context, between text and culture, between text and the world outside
the text? His answer will surprise many readers.

Ivo Kamps
Series editor

PREFACE

Because "culture" is such a confusing word, I should say at the outset what this book is not about. Concerned with Shakespeare and culture, and, necessarily, with some of the productive confusions that accompany this term, it does not try to tell a story about Shakespeare's life in relationship to his culture—a story, for example, whereby Shakespeare can easily become a Catholic, bee-keeping lawyer who served in the Low Countries, composing plays and poems in his spare time. Gentle or ungentle, Shakespeare is less interesting to me than what he wrote. Nor, on the other hand, is the "question of culture" meant to imply that this book argues for the centrality of Shakespeare's works to the education of those who aspire to culture, interpreted grandly. I will leave such arguments, pro and con, to those who feel more comfortable making them. Instead, *Shakespeare and the Question of Culture* examines how we read Shakespeare's works in relation to his own culture. It is one of my beliefs, though, that no study interested in this topic can examine Shakespeare's works in isolation: Shakespeare was one of many talented individuals writing for the acting companies of his day; contemporary writers of dramatic and nondramatic literature alike had perspectives that cannot be ignored if we wish to have a rich understanding of what was culturally possible, and culturally likely, in Shakespeare's England.

This examination spells "culture" with a small, rather than capital "c." Yet I remain interested in the variety of ways that we use this seemingly all-purpose word. In fact, this study begins from the conviction that while such variety of definition has fostered a diverse body of criticism, it is now time—perhaps past time—to take stock not only of where we have come with the cultural analysis of Shakespeare's works and early modern literature generally but of how we perform such cultural analysis in the first place.

My argument here involves three separate but related observations. First, I hold that, when defined as an extensive thing (consisting, for example, of widespread beliefs, practices, and symbols), culture is largely incommensurate with the limited number of literary texts from which we commonly adduce it. This is a fancy way of saying that culture is bigger than the books we tend to read. Although most critics would assent to this blunt truism, in practice its truth is less frequently followed. We often make large claims from small evidence and claims about culture from a relatively few cultural texts.

My second major observation dovetails with the first, and concerns the kind of criticism typically used to read cultural "texts": thick description. A borrowing from anthropology, thick description has become the most popular method of analyzing literary texts for their cultural content. I argue here that thick description is a fairly inefficient way of retrieving the cultural from literary texts; it remains an entertaining but problematic method of getting to culturally representative beliefs, practices, and symbols. If, as many feel, culture is indeed a text, we need to read more pages of culture's text than thick description commonly has us do.

Related to both of the preceding points, my third observation actually calls into question the larger relevance of cultural inquiry as practiced in this field: It is arguable that the culture we recover from literary texts is largely literary in nature. With the word "literary" here I mean to invoke not an idealized realm of transcendent masterpieces but the material resources that enable and affect the production and consumption of imaginative texts—texts that we often take as direct imaginings of their surroundings. This is not, of course, to maintain that there is nothing outside the text. Instead I assume that what *is* outside the text undergoes extensive mediation on its way in, and similarly from there to readers. Genres, conventions, icons, source texts, literary fashions, repertorial goals, habits, and personnel, printing-house organization: Each of these had an important, even "cultural" role in shaping literary texts of the early modern era.

The foregoing positions suggest that we need to modify the practice of thick description typically used in the cultural analysis of literature. Following an introduction that traces the rise of various kinds of cultural investments in Shakespeare and his contemporaries—from the belletristic to the new historicist and postcolonial—I present a brief for a "thin" mode of description. Such thin description looks to supplement, rather than replace, thick description's heightened amplification of detail; it aims to do so with a more deliberate approach to cultural elements. The aggregation of evidence; the determination, where possible, of that which is culturally representative; and the necessity of acknowledging context (including the scholarly conversation that contextualizes one's research)—all these go into a thinner kind of description than is usually practiced. Now, such thin description admittedly lacks the compelling narrative style of thick description. Yet the kind of focus that thin description helps to provide can benefit our criticism by allowing us, like audiences witnessing an instance of "deep focus" cinematography, to keep multiple planes of a culture in view without the abrupt editorial cuts between part and whole, anecdote and culture, that remain so characteristic of thick description.

As its section heading implies, the next part of this book uses thin description to analyze various aspects of early modern literary culture. Here I take up, respectively, a mode of writing, the career of stage properties in various early modern dramatic texts, and a sexual trope in early modern literature generally. Chapter 3 is the first of these, and addresses the remarkable confluence of highly "embodied" writing in late Elizabethan England. The pinnacle of what we often call the English Renaissance, the period from 1590 to 1610 witnessed the proliferation of works that put resonant identities and physical forms on the printed page with new intensity. We are used to thinking about this Renaissance through the expressive individual, through the lens, for example, of Stephen Greenblatt's *Renaissance Self-Fashioning* and its focus on significant and complex presentations of the self. What chapter 3's examination of embodied writing demonstrates is that the power of print during the height of the English Renaissance was more about the other than the self—at the very least, about writers' freedom to put others' bodies and identities onto the printed page. Whether in the form of satire, erotica, *à clef* writings, or controversial pamphlets, this intensified emphasis on persons as objects of discourse became a central feature of Elizabethan print culture. In fact, a thin description of the English Renaissance could very well define that Renaissance around, and on the basis of, this newly intensified handling of the personal in print.

A more literal kind of handling occasions chapter 4, which performs a thin description of stage properties in early modern drama. Extending the interests of a newer kind of materialism (discussed in chapter 8), critics have increasingly attended to the physical properties held by characters in early modern plays. That attention, however, has not translated into a larger portrait of such stage properties and their role in the early modern theater. The thick description of such objects as letters, handkerchiefs, and severed hands often gives us rich insights into the function of these particular objects but leaves us wondering about the larger place of such objects in the repertorial system. Analyzing the distribution of stage properties in the plays of Shakespeare and his contemporaries on a diachronic rather than—as is often the case with thick description—synchronic scale, I note significant tendencies in their appearance, tendencies that can be ascribed to both genre and date. What this thin description demonstrates is that, in the frequency with which they employ properties in their plays, dramatists were heavily influenced by the literary kinds in which they composed their plays and by trends that varied with time. For instance, from the late 1580s through the late 1630s the number of props called for by play texts declined at a fairly regular rate, although, as we will see, Shakespeare's own use of properties eventually resisted this pattern.

Where the two chapters preceding it propose various "genres" that have not been treated as such before—the genre of embodied writing and stage properties considered as a genre in their own right—chapter 5 takes up a particular trope in early modern dramatic texts: that of two female bodies imagined in erotic conjunction. With the recent publication of Valerie Traub's *The Renaissance of Lesbianism in Early Modern England,* and with the heightened attention that criticism has paid to issues of collaboration and friendship in early modern texts, many commentators have shown an interest in the utopian possibilities of a homonormative thematic in early modern literature—a thematic, in short, of same-sex partners expressing mutual affection in an equitable (and somewhat idealized) relationship. In this chapter I describe the way in which early modern texts, many of them dramatic works, often imagined pairs of female bodies in erotic situations neither affectionate nor mutually pleasuring but bound up, instead, with elements of coercion and hierarchy. These moments of female-female eroticism were rarely "for" the figures involved; more often they appear to have been presented for the voyeuristic pleasure of audiences and readers. Analyzing works by Shakespeare, Middleton, and others, I argue that to scrutinize the full array of representations of erotically paired women in this period is necessarily to abandon belief in any consistently idyllic or utopian function to them. Just as the aggressive handling of the personal in the embodied writing explored in chapter 3 worked to objectify the identities involved, these cultural representations increasingly objectified, manipulated, and even disempowered the female figures they addressed. Like the two chapters preceding it in this section devoted to "literary culture," chapter 5 emphasizes the intensively *literary* nature of the phenomenon it addresses.

The second section of this book turns from literature to literary criticism, taking a now-familiar liberty with the word "culture" in examining critical culture relating to early modern literature. My primary assumption in this section is that criticism stands to benefit from being itself the object of critical readings. I believe, in short, that the manner in which we read and interpret early modern texts can profit from undergoing the kind of scrutiny we typically give to literary works. Critical genres, styles, and key words influence our habits of interpretation and shape our portraits of literature and culture. As influences, these elements of critical culture bear examination, for what they reveal about critical practice can help to contextualize our research into the early modern period and lend nuance to our findings.

In chapter 6, accordingly, I examine two terms central to the field(s) addressed in this book (and already deployed in this preface): "Renaissance" and "early modern." Although it is clear that each of these ways of defining the period under study implies something quite different from what is implied by the other definition, many critics (including myself) who write on Shakespeare and literature of his time find themselves using these terms alternately, employing "Renaissance" in some venues and "early modern" in others. Where did these terms come from, and what are the implications of using one instead of the other? Was Shakespeare a "Renaissance" and not an "early modern" author, or vice versa? In this chapter I argue that the English Renaissance we know was largely an American invention of the first third of the twentieth century and was signally related to the creation of a literary canon and era subsequently known as the "American Renaissance." The phrase "early modern," in turn, came into widespread use in literary criticism only during and after the 1980s. Initially an offhand term derived from philology, where it describes an era in *linguistic* history, "early modern" has come to serve as a quasi-scientific term by which the disciplines of history and literary criticism can hail the past as a recognizably "modern" forebear of the present.

The pull of innovation in much recent criticism is indeed apparent from such terms as "early modern" and from such critical genres as "new historicism." The final two chapters of this book examine two such critical genres, neither of which is as well established as new historicism. Chapter 7 takes up what has been called the "new formalism" in early modern studies. As evidenced by various essays in the recently published anthology *Renaissance Literature and Its Formal Engagements* and elsewhere, the new formalism is a critical mode concerned with various "formal" elements of literary texts, from meter to vocabulary to genre, and with the relationship between such elements and larger issues and forces outside texts themselves. A brief way of describing the new formalism would be to say that this critical practice is the old formalism plus the new historicism. Such an unsubtle description leaves out volumes, of course, but hints at the new formalism's tendency to cast its net more broadly than did selected instances of formalist inquiry published earlier in the twentieth century. While it is dangerous to subscribe to stereotypes of the new criticism—stereotypes that can imply self-hypnotized critics believing that nothing existed other than the words of certain canonical short poems—it is clear that many works of literary criticism that can be identified as new formalist in nature have a greater interest than older formalisms did in the relationship between formal elements in a text and the world outside that text. To offer an instance of what such a newer formalism can accomplish, I posit in this chapter a material relationship between Shakespeare's *Henry V* (1599) and Nashe's *The Unfortunate Traveller* (1594) and explore the significance of that relationship for both a critical methodology—what is often called source study—and our understanding of these two writers' "politics."

The final chapter of this book takes up the "new materialism" in early modern studies. In recent years increasing numbers of critics have shown an interest in the material world of early modern England. From studies of clothing and household items to the larger ambitions represented in the title of *Material London, ca. 1600,* a newer kind of materialist criticism has become prevalent in the field. Whereas to many readers the term "materialism" conjures up images of marxist criticism concerned with monumental, almost glacial transitions in history—certainly with such large concepts as social class, base and superstructure, and ideology—this newer kind of materialism takes "matter" quite literally, focusing on physical objects and their cultural roles. Chapter 8 examines this decidedly post-marxist genre of criticism, arguing that its most promising aspects involve a return to the materialism of early modern England itself. That is, in contrast to the sometimes-abstract categories of traditional marxist criticism, this newer materialism, at its best, uses the language of the past to describe the function of the material in and for the world of early modern England. With these strengths, however, come certain weaknesses, among which is the tendency for the new materialism— like thick description—to be guided by the attractiveness and quiddity of the objects it seeks to interpret. As I argue in this chapter, sixteenth- and seventeenth-century authors theorized the material in ways that were often quite sophisticated; learning from their understanding of the material world can help us to avoid the seductions of transference that can be involved in the study of objects.

I conclude *Shakespeare and the Question of Culture* by asking whether cultural analysis, strictly conceived, is even possible. Hazarding that cultural study may be, among other things, one of the newest entries in a series of critical brand names, I suggest we use more deliberation in advertising the ability of our intellectual products to explain the relationship between the worlds in texts and the world outside them. To the study I have also appended a discursive etymology of "culture" aimed at supplementing my remarks about this term, and its range of meanings, throughout this book.

PART I

SHAKESPEARE AND CULTURE

CHAPTER 1

SHAKESPEARE AND THE
QUESTION OF CULTURE

Is Shakespeare a cultural author? On the face of it, this question has an easy answer. Shakespeare is everywhere in our culture. His works dominate the curriculum in literature departments; his plays are regularly and widely produced, including, in the past two decades, the appearance of numerous film versions; and artists continue to draw on his plays and poetry alike for their ballets, paintings, operas, musicals, and poems. Quotations from his works dot the public record, lending prestige and authority to those who quote them. Somewhat recently, an Anglo-American romance with Shakespeare—with his works, and with notions of greatness those works have come to embody—was celebrated with an Academy Award-winning film, *Shakespeare in Love*, a film that could have been titled *In Love with Shakespeare*. For their part, literary critics have encouraged this love affair, benefited from it, and have sometimes commented wryly on it. Noting the playwright's "extraordinary cultural stamina," Michael Bristol goes on to observe, simply, that "Shakespeare has made the big time."[1] For Marjorie Garber, Shakespeare's cultural role is best described with the language not of the celebrity marketplace but of the analyst's couch; Shakespeare has been and currently is "fetishized in Western popular—as well as Western high—culture," and functions as "the dream-space of nostalgia for the aging undergraduate (that is to say, for just about everyone)."[2] And if one believes Harold Bloom, Shakespeare is not only prominent in culture but was primarily responsible for it—inventing, as he did, our way of being "human."[3] A cultural author? Shakespeare is something like *the* cultural author for us.

As easy as its answer seems, there is a good reason to ask this question now. During the past few decades, and with increasing momentum, Shakespeare has become a "cultural" author for literary critics. He has become cultural, it is important to note, in a very specific way. Lately literary criticism has associated him prominently not only with our culture but also with his own. In contrast with various earlier observers who saw Shakespeare as "above the iron compulsion of space and time," recent commentators have chosen to see him as culturally significant in, for, and of his own time.[4] If Shakespeare is everywhere in our culture today, today's literary criticism has come to see Shakespeare's own culture as everywhere in his works. Clearly there is a distinction here between Shakespeare as a "hero" of his age and Shakespeare—particularly, Shakespeare's body of work—as a product of and commentary upon his times. *Shakespeare and the Question of Culture* takes up the latter image as it appears in recent criticism.

This "cultural Shakespeare" follows closely upon what has been called the "cultural turn" in the humanities.[5] Characterized broadly, and in terms of its affect on literary criticism, the "cultural turn" assumes a turn away from the analysis of works considered in isolation and toward the examination of texts in and as a product of their cultures. Sometimes this involves the consideration of cultures themselves as "texts." Such consideration has been shaped by the emergence of cultural studies in the academy, a multidisciplinary critical genre that dedicates itself to the examination of various cultural forms and practices—many of them previously considered to be too "low" for serious analysis.[6] Combined with the rise of cultural studies, the "cultural turn" has changed the way in which Shakespeare is read, even what and how his works mean for us.

To get a sense of the growing influence of the "cultural" in the study of Shakespeare, one could glance at how frequently the word "culture" has been used in a central journal of the field, *Shakespeare Quarterly*. The following figures represent a search of available back issues of *Shakespeare Quarterly* for items (including essays, reviews, and opinion pieces) containing the word "culture."[7] I offer these figures in part to confirm what could otherwise seem a subjective assertion and in part because it is one of this study's goals to reassert the usefulness of substantive warrants to cultural inquiry. The figures are grouped into units of five years, beginning with the journal's first issue:

Year	Items containing the Word "Culture"
1950–1954	23
1955–1959	35
1960–1964	33
1965–1969	41
1970–1974	24
1975–1979	69
1980–1984	82
1985–1989	121
1990–1994	152
1995–1999	244

A few words about these figures are in order. First, we should note that a blind search for terms has its limitations. For instance, the "culture" invoked by an essay in 1950 stands to differ radically from what is meant by the term in an essay of 2002 or today for that matter. This very difference, in fact, will be a focus of the latter part of this chapter. Second, some of the increase in quantity here comes from the journal's growth in size during the nearly half-century surveyed. *Shakespeare Quarterly* is a larger journal today than at its start, with more items in each number (hence more items that can contain the word "culture"). But even with the journal's growth, the obvious escalation of these figures suggests an increase in the frequency with which Shakespeareans mention "culture" (and cite works that do so), and demonstrates what most of them would willingly admit: that "culture talk" about Shakespeare and his works has grown considerably in the last few decades.

We could look to 1988 as the year in which "culture" became almost unavoidable in Shakespeare studies. It was in 1988 that David Sacks considered ten recent critical studies in a review essay for *Shakespeare Quarterly;* he titled his essay after what he saw as the central issue joining these studies: "Searching for 'Culture' in the English Renaissance."[8] That same year Stephen Greenblatt remarked, in his *Shakespearean Negotiations,* that his way of reading "plays by Shakespeare and the stage on which they first appeared" could be called "a poetics of culture."[9] It was also in 1988 that Leah Marcus closed her book, *Puzzling Shakespeare,* with the claim that "The Shakespeare we want is not a man, a set of describable data, but an 'ongoing cultural activity' or set of related, often competing, activities which need to remain open in order to retain their vitality."[10] That the notion of "culture" itself retained a vitality in Shakespeare studies is clear from

Albert Tricomi's wish, almost a decade after the above remarks had been published, that the new historicism be developed into something that we could rightly call "cultural historicism."[11] Moreover, in the substantial review essay "Recent Studies in Tudor and Stuart Drama" for the spring of 2000, Meredith Skura confessed to the "increasingly problematic" organizational categories we have inherited—those based, that is, on individual authors or genres—and pointed out that "what matters for most of the books reviewed here is not genre but how a text fits into the total dynamic of a given historical moment in a given culture."[12] Finally, testifying to the enduring popularity of the term, the convention of the Shakespeare Association of America that took place just prior to this book's publication held paper sessions with the descriptions "Negotiating Early Modern Popular Culture" and "The Cultural History of Emotion," with the Plenary Session being titled "Writing Cultural Biography."[13]

Shakespeare has clearly become "cultural" not only for our time but for his as well. How has this occurred? While there have been many studies of the centuries-long "setting up" of Shakespeare in Western culture—to borrow Michael Dobson's phrase—we rarely stop to ask how and why Shakespeare has been set up, in recent years, as cultural in relationship to his own time.[14] One reason for this is that a great deal of the field's self-consciousness has centered on the new historicism. A critical genre that makes central the historical material in and around literary texts, new historicism arose during the 1980s and has come to dominate the ways in which literature of the Elizabethan and Jacobean eras is discussed.[15] It is not exaggerating things to call the new historicism a revolutionary critical genre. Accordingly, much attention has been paid to the new historicism and to its methods of recovering historical material connected with literary texts. Less attention has been given to the way in which new historicism and other critical modes have cooperated with a profound change in our objects of inquiry, a shift in our attention from works of literature—literary "texts"—to culture itself seen as a text.

We have talked more about such criticism, it seems, than about what such criticism has helped to accomplish in our studies and classrooms. To begin examining Shakespeare and culture, therefore, it may be worthwhile to ask ourselves some basic questions. What effect has the cultural turn had on the way in which we read Shakespeare's works? What are we to make of the new, "cultural" Shakespeare it has produced? How should we "do" cultural criticism of his works? We could ask many other questions at this point, but for the moment I would suggest that such queries could be boiled down into one: How should we define the "culture" that we discuss in relationship to Shakespeare? Answering this question will give us a solid basis for exploring the "cultural turn" in Shakespeare studies. Such an exploration also will require us to look at what "culture" is and where, in turn, it has been.

To get to the most relevant senses of "culture" in Shakespeare criticism today, we can start with the major subentry for "culture" in the *Oxford English Dictionary* (*OED*)—a subentry whose very complexity, I would argue, reflects the variety of situations and topics that "culture" has been asked to attend to. In this fifth subentry, the *OED* begins by defining "culture" as what we would call "high" culture: "The training, development, and refinement of mind, tastes, and manners; the condition of being thus trained and refined; the intellectual side of civilization." Within the contexts of literary criticism today, this definition strikes one as old-fashioned, for it has been augmented, if not superceded, by major developments in sociology and anthropology. It is fair to say "old-fashioned" here because "culture" has been seen, with more and more frequency, to be an extensive phenomenon rather than (as this initial definition suggests) a potentially limited one. To many literary critics, "culture" is, in short, what pervasively *is* rather than what could be aimed for through refinement. Rather than the deliberate cultivation suggested by Latin *culta* (on which, please see the appendix), "culture" in this newer sense is that which happens to exist in a particular region at a particular time: a "natural" landscape or ecosystem, that is, as opposed to an artificially arranged and nurtured garden. Thus "culture" today often is defined as a situation that can be recognized and used by persons but that is largely outside their individual ability to alter. To be sure, the traditional sense of the word—the sense of the consciously tended garden—is still quite widely acknowledged. But this long-standing sense has given way, in prevalence, to those senses of "culture" that, arising in the last century and now predominating in Shakespeare studies, imply some kind of extension.

We can see this shuffling of place within the fifth subentry for "culture" in the *OED,* which, not incidentally, has a hard time distinguishing the various senses it asserts. The *OED* expands this part of the "culture" entry (sense "5.a.") by giving four subdefinitions (along with one subentry relating to the intentionally distorted, satirical spelling "cultchah" or "cultcher"). Significantly, it admits in two of these subdefinitions that they may not be distinguishable from the "refinement" definition of "culture" discussed above (that is, from definition "5.a."). These subdefinitions include, on one hand, ostensibly specialized use in anthropology and sociology, and, on the other, sense "5.b.": "A particular form or type of intellectual development. Also, the civilization, customs, artistic achievements, etc., of a people, especially at a certain stage of its development or history." So tangled here is the web of "culture" that the *OED* weaves—or perhaps more fairly, has tried to *unweave*—that, in the case of the anthropological and sociological senses, it is forced to confess, variously, that "In some contexts the meaning shades into an attribute of sense 5" and, in reference to sense "5.b.," that "In many contexts, especially in Sociology, it is not possible to separate this sense from sense 5.a."

By this point, it will be clear that such confusion is more than a reference work's understandable difficulty regarding emergent senses of a popular and changeful word. Apparent within this subentry, in fact, is something endemic to "culture" and its community of terms. Even as Latin *cultūra* bears witness to the difficulty of separating cultivator or cultivating faculty from the thing cultivated, the place of cultivation, and the attributes of cultivation, so too does English "culture" show the persistent difficulty of keeping distinct such things as, on one hand, a particular mode of civilization from the place where that mode exists, or, on the other, a training *in* manners from the state *of* manners that evidences that very process of training. Contrary to the implications of these *OED* subentries, however, the culprit is not sociology or anthropology but rather our desire to separate things that we have formerly insisted on combining. How to tell the process from the product? From the producing faculty, place, or agent? This is precisely what is involved in attempting to cull out and distinguish these various senses of "culture." And for the difficulty thereof, we have only ourselves to blame. Such reference works as the *Oxford Latin Dictionary* and the *Oxford English Dictionary* record merely the history of human ambitions for words. What sentences "culture" to participation in the most confused debates we are capable of generating is our own ambition of reference for it as well as the senses of "culture" that we have inherited.

We can therefore take "culture" to be a simple word with a long history of deliberately complicated use. I would suggest that one can hear at least five major senses of "culture" in Shakespeare and early modern studies today. This is not to say that there are not more senses obtaining or that the following definitions fully describe every occasion of the word's use. These five senses instead form something like chords on which variations of "culture" and "the cultural" are played: "Culture" as High Culture; "Culture" as Comprehensive Element; "Culture" as Synonym for "Society"; "Culture" as Segment of Social Life or Practice; "Culture" as International Identity. In the paragraphs that follow, I briefly discuss each of these before examining the larger role of "culture" in Shakespeare and early modern studies. Clearly these various senses deserve much more attention than I am able to give them here. By briefly defining them, I do not mean to caricature them or imply that they are commonly used in a simplistic fashion. On the contrary, what even brief explication reveals is how complicated the various situations are that "culture," in many of its current senses, has been asked to address.

Further, I should explain why "early modern studies" has been added to "Shakespeare studies" here. Some the following definitions invoke, in addition to studies of Shakespeare, scholarship on early modern literature and history. I call on these studies in part for their illustrative value, in part because I am convinced that any cultural inquiry related to Shakespeare's works must involve the works of his contemporaries, and in part because, as mentioned in connection with the "cultural turn," Shakespeare studies themselves have become exceedingly interdisciplinary—likely, that is, to draw on such disciplines as history and anthropology, among others. Finally, I should point out that, for convenience, I occasionally turn to titles of critical studies for some of my examples. I do so fully aware that these titles sometimes are chosen or shaped by presses rather than by the author or authors in question and that they sometimes differ, in their choice of words, from the writing in the books themselves. Yet because they are often the most recently and thoroughly considered words in a book, and because they advertise a book to the larger scholarly community, many times titles can tell us a great deal about critics' understanding of the field and about what they and their publishers wish their work to do.

"Culture" as High Culture

The first sense of "culture" we could define is "culture" as high culture. This sense parallels, if it does not exactly coincide with, the "refinement" sense from the *OED*. As I mentioned, it is seen by most Shakespeareans as an archaism, an old-fashioned sense that describes something no longer widely believed in (however much students, their parents, university administrators, and the general public may continue to endorse it). "Culture" as high culture is routinely connected with Matthew Arnold and his remarks in *Culture and Anarchy*

(1869). One often encounters a particular and well-known phrase represented as Arnold's definition of "culture": "the best which has been thought and said."[16] The word "civilization" could be offered as a potential synonym for this sense of "culture." To be fair to Arnold, however, we should notice that this resonant phrase truncates a more complex thought. "Culture," in Arnold's thinking, is as much a verb as a noun, and recalls the verbal senses of "culture" (for example, cultivating, rearing, training, improving) one may find in both Latin and English. The larger context of Arnold's remarks reads as follows: "The whole scope of the essay is to recommend culture as the great help out of our present difficulties; culture being a pursuit of our total perfection by means of getting to know, on all the matters which most concern us, the best which has been thought and said in the world."[17] Here "culture" is a *"pursuit"*; elsewhere Arnold calls "culture" *"a study of perfection"* and indeed seems to think of "culture" as the process and result of a person reading to keep good company, a company that includes Shakespeare, Vergil, and others.[18] Shakespeare, in fact, is the first writer of imaginative literature mentioned in *Culture and Anarchy*.[19] But we create something of a straw man when we conflate, as we so often do, Arnold's phrase "the best which has been thought and said in the world" with such things as lists of great books (including Shakespeare's works) and handbooks of "essential" cultural knowledge (which often mandate knowledge of Shakespeare's works).[20] Nevertheless, the sense of "culture" as high culture has been so widely identified with this phrase, and with Arnold, that we are not far wrong to invoke them for the purposes of definition as long as we remember that doing so repeats the very pattern one may see in the longer history of the word "culture": the steady conflation of a product ("high culture") with a process (the "pursuit" of culture).

"CULTURE" AS COMPREHENSIVE ELEMENT

A second sense of "culture" encountered in writing on Shakespeare and early modern England is as a comprehensive element. This comprehensive sense of "culture" has been defined as follows: "Culture consists of patterns, explicit and implicit, of and for behavior acquired and transmitted by symbols, constituting the distinctive achievement of human groups, including their embodiment in artifacts; the essential core of culture consists of traditional (i.e., historically derived and selected) ideas and especially their attached values; culture systems may, on the one hand, be considered as products of action, on the other as conditioning elements of further action."[21] Some background on this definition is in order. A version of it was written by Charles A. Ellwood for the *Dictionary of Sociology* in 1944. Prior to World War II and its settlement, in fact, the term "culture" enjoyed a popularity akin to, if not exceeding, its current vogue. As Adam Kuper points out, this level of "culture" talk diminished significantly during the 1950s through the 1980s, having perhaps been "interrupted for a generation by the ideological preoccupations of the Cold War."[22] So rife was the discourse of culture before 1950, though, that two anthropologists, A. L. Kroeber and Clyde Kluckhohn, tried to pin down this protean word through an exhaustive study of its origins and uses. Their landmark study, *Culture: A Critical Review of Concepts and Definitions,* originally appeared in 1952.[23] Surveying a wealth of disparate uses, they claimed to identify 164 discrete senses of "culture," most of which had appeared in the half century prior to the publication of their study. From these varying senses, Kroeber and Kluckhohn offered something like a master definition by revising and condensing Ellwood's entry for the *Dictionary of Sociology;* their revision comprises the definition just quoted. It gathers the major concerns yoked to the word by sociology and anthropology during the earlier twentieth century (the emergent senses that the *OED* tried to reconcile with its entry for "5.a.") and in the decades that followed. I call this the "comprehensive element" sense of "culture" to get at its pervasive nature. This sense refers to the *totality* of social life both "acquired" and "transmitted," as mentioned in the definition quoted above. And it differs from the "refinement" sense of "culture"—that of high culture—in appealing to the broadest range of "patterns," "behavior," "artifacts," "ideas," and "values."

"Culture" as Synonym for "Society"

Many would recognize the preceding sense of "culture"; another sense we often encounter is "culture" used as a general synonym for "society." In recent criticism, the word suggests a reference larger than the individual literary texts and archival documents examined. In the titles of such works as Carla Mazzio's and Douglas Trevor's *Historicism, Psychoanalysis, and Early Modern Culture* (2000), Catherine Belsey's *Shakespeare and the Loss of Eden: The Construction of Family Values in Early Modern Culture* (1999), and Mark Thornton Burnett's *Masters and Servants in English Renaissance Drama and Culture* (1997), "culture" takes up residence where, twenty years ago, one could have expected to encounter the word "society." For instance, had it been published prior to the 1990s, Lawrence

Manley's *Literature and Culture in Early Modern London* (1995) might well have followed the lead of L. C. Knights and standard scholarly nomenclature up to that time and been called *Literature and Society in Early Modern London*. Perhaps not surprisingly, a search of back issues of *Shakespeare Quarterly* for the word "society" reveals that it has always been prevalent in Shakespeare criticism but declined in frequency of occurrence in the journal during the early 1990s—precisely when "culture" began to experience its current popularity.[24] It seems no coincidence that, as the examples of titles from the second half of that decade may serve to indicate, at this time critics began substituting "culture" for "society" in their writings.

What is involved in "culture" being used as a synonym for "society"? This usage appears in part to be a bid for some kind of emergent rhetorical power. "Culture" not only has more cachet today than "society" but has absorbed the seriousness once possessed by that word. Historically, "society" and "culture" have had overlapping but distinct valences. A classic textbook on sociology provides the basic formula: "Society comes first and culture after."[25] Culture, that is, is what follows when humans have organized themselves socially, and it can indeed include, among many other things, the books that Shakespeareans take up. Thus one interpretation would hold the substitution of "culture" for "society" to be little more than truth in advertising: What we read is better defined as the product of society (that is, "culture") than as society itself. Another explanation could see, in the substitution, a distancing of critics from a key word (that is, "society") of political criticism—particularly marxist literary criticism, and particularly during and after the breakup of the Soviet Union, 1989 to 1991, when many academics rethought their allegiance to the Left. Whatever its cause, the substitution of "culture" for "society"—sometimes for "England" itself—has generated one of its most commonly encountered senses in Shakespeare studies.

"CULTURE" AS SEGMENT OF
SOCIAL LIFE OR PRACTICE

In a sense related to this use of "culture" for "society," but less ambitious in its scope, "culture" often is used to signify a segment of social life, practice, or experience. This fourth sense sometimes refers to a particular stratum of society, as in its early and influential deployment in the title of Louis B. Wright's *Middle-Class Culture in Elizabethan England* (1935). We see such usage as well in discussions of "popular culture" in early modern England, as in Leonard Ashley's

Elizabethan Popular Culture (1988) and Michael Bristol's *Carnival and Theater: Plebeian Culture and the Structure of Authority in Renaissance England* (1985). The example of these two titles suggests that "culture" may have become dominant in literary criticism only when it was understood to carry "popular" silently with it.[26] Critics also used "culture" to refer to a much smaller section of society, social practice, and social experience, as in J. W. Binns's *Intellectual Culture in Elizabethan and Jacobean England: The Latin Writings of the Age* (1990), in Peter Erickson's and Clark Hulse's anthology, *Early Modern Visual Culture* (2000), in Anthony Dawson's and Paul Yachnin's *The Culture of Playgoing in Shakespeare's England* (2001), and in Curtis Perry's *The Making of Jacobean Culture: James I and the Renegotiation of Elizabethan Literary Practice* (1997). Perry's text gives us an instance of "culture" that conveys the pervasive influence that a single individual, the monarch, had on literary practice in the early seventeenth century. "Culture" in this sense means no more and no less than the complex set of representations of and materials shaped by the king. And though its demographics therefore remain much more restricted than that implied by such phrases as "popular" or "plebeian culture," it has every bit as much authority as those phrases, for the materials it involves include many of the key texts of the early seventeenth-century literary canon. Likewise "culture" also can refer to a particular place and the variety of things (persons, practices, habits, and texts) associated with that place, as in *Spying and Court Culture in the English Renaissance,* the subtitle to John Archer's *Sovereignty and Intelligence* (1993). "Culture" in the preceding instances thus calls on the sense of "culture" as "society" that we have seen earlier, but restricts this sense to a particular social class, place, experience, or even—as in the case of Perry's *Jacobean Culture*—to a single person.

"Culture" as International Identity

The fifth major sense of "culture" in Shakespeare and early modern studies today refers to situations of cultural encounter—"culture," that is, as a set of national ideologies and practices that become glaringly visible in the juxtaposition of various peoples, beliefs, and habits afforded by colonial, military, and mercantile activities. This is the sense that Louis Montrose calls on in speaking of the "confrontation of alien cultures" in narratives of the New World and of "the projection into the New World of European representations of gender—and of sexual conduct, a distinct but equally *cultural* phenomenon."[27] More recently, Geraldo de Sousa has affirmed this sense of the cultural by placing Shakespeare's dramatic works "in the historical and anthropological context of Europe's colonial encounters and the large body of early modern ethnographic materials on alien cultural practices and on racial and gender difference."[28] Jyotsna Singh similarly defines the role of "culture" in early modern "narratives of the encounter" with the following observation: "While narratives of the English travelers/ writers such as Edward Terry reveal shared cultural/religious assumptions of the period, the Englishmen do not emerge as static allegorical entities, as agents of an incipient colonial ideology; but rather they frequently appear as complex historical subjects struggling to interpret a different culture that challenges the stable categories and assumptions of English cultural and (especially in Terry's case) religious identity."[29] It is important to note that the "encounter[s]" that Singh and others discuss sometimes make the various cultures they examine seem more unified and cohesive than they would appear were they looked at in comparative isolation. Significantly, Singh is careful to say that Englishmen are not "static," but she goes on to claim that their cultural and religious identities are "stable." This odd displacement is largely the result of a critic contextualizing cultures: As in photography, the wider one's focus, the more cohesive any objects within that focus become. That is, when examined over and against, say, "Indian" culture, or one of the various indigenous cultures of the subcontinent during the middle of the seventeenth century, Edward Terry's "English" cultural and religious identity may indeed appear to possess, as Singh alleges, "stable categories and assumptions." However, given that England had changed its national religion three times during the previous century and would behead its king amid a series of civil wars just prior to the publication of Terry's travel narratives, it is dangerous to trust that stability too far. In fact, this genre of criticism more often sees "culture" as essentially *un*stable. In most criticism concerned with cultural encounters, "culture" is less a stable entity than it is a national psyche full of tension and anxiety. The internal turmoil ascribed to this model of "culture" is revealed, in turn, primarily by encounters with an "other."[30] When criticism acts as analyst to the culture's patient, "culture" seems an error made visible only when undergoing the talking cure. Such "talking" is to be found, of course, in the records of a culture confronting, and confronted by, another culture. In the narratives of encounter they leave us, cultures betray their anxieties, antagonisms, and prejudices.

I have arranged the preceding five senses of "culture" in a rough chronology of their appearance in Shakespeare studies over the past century or so. Beginning with a no longer fashionable sense of "culture" as high culture (that is, elite, endowed, leisurely), we have traced a historical trajectory that has seen the enlistment of an anthropological sense of "culture" by historical scholarship, the casual replacement of "society" by "culture" in criticism generally, the particularizing interests of historicism in reference to such domains as "court culture" and "the culture of playgoing," and, finally, the cultural-studies use of "culture" to describe international encounters and exchanges. Following this trajectory of "culture," therefore, we also give ourselves an overview of the changing forms of scholarship concerned with Shakespeare and early modern England. This sequence—which, I should point out, is truer in outline than in particulars—includes belletristic criticism, historical scholarship and formalist criticism, new historicism, and cultural studies and takes us from the late nineteenth to the early twenty-first century.

What led to this sequence of senses? How do we explain what caused the meaning of the word "culture" to shift in this way? A responsible answer to this question would perhaps wind up giving a history of critical thought in the twentieth century. Even then it could risk providing only a more extensive description of the changing senses themselves. Yet given this difficulty, can we isolate any external factors that led to changes in the meaning of "culture"? Pressed to do so, we could gesture toward a variety of things that themselves make up a kind of cultural history behind the changing senses of the word. A list of such factors or influences could well include, among others: the increasing ease, affordability, and popularity of travel; the growing access to texts once available mainly in elite archives; a related diminution of the aesthetic status of canonical works through the mass production of affordable texts; the similar proliferation of academic publications and the diversification of topics afforded, and perhaps necessitated, by that very proliferation; the increasingly heterogeneous demography of both scholarly ranks and student populations; and the rise of interdisciplinary inquiry generally within the changing academy. Jet travel, electronically accessed databases, inexpensive paperbacks, the proliferation of scholarly writing, increasing heterogeneity of faculty and students, interdisciplinary work: Such factors are by no means discrete, of course; many of them are related to at least one or more of the other items tendered here. Together, they form a resume of academic life in the West that by now seems an inevitable record of our world. It makes up a very different catalogue, however, and a very different world, from what could have been anticipated in 1900 or even 1950. Along with a host of other factors intertwined with its items, it highlights some of the shaping influences on academic inquiry in the past generation.

These influences have helped change what "culture" means by re-placing a vertical hierarchy of status with a horizontal palette of dif-ference. We can better understand what is involved in such replacement, and in this sequence of senses, by considering various assumptions that have supported the move from hierarchy to differ-ence in Shakespearean "culture talk." Three such assumptions have special relevance. I give them in their broadest forms:

> *The most valuable product of a culture is its Art.*
> *Art is the best way of learning about a culture.*
> *The most interesting thing about art is the culture or cultures in it.*

Like the five senses of "culture" already explored, this set of assump-tions can be seen as a sequence. They detail a sequence, that is, of the basic ideologies supporting the past century of Shakespeare criticism. The first sentence, "The most valuable product of a culture is its Art," is an assumption that underpins a traditionalistic, even conservative point of view once prevalent in Shakespeare studies. It is a view one would connect with a belletristic understanding of literature and with the "refinement" sense of "culture" doubled by the word "civiliza-tion." To borrow Arnold's conceit, Shakespeare serves as the best company for a long voyage.[31] The second sentence, "Art is the best way of learning about a culture," is a point of view one would en-counter in a literary historian or a historicist critic of literature. Art re-mains a culture's most efficient way of registering its own assumptions, desires, fears, and struggles: in short, a kind of private journal of pub-lic matters. To continue our voyage metaphor, we could say that, under this point of view, art would be the best guidebook with which to learn about the distant culture toward which one was traveling. With the third statement here, "The most interesting thing about art is the culture or cultures in it," we move to the realm of cultural stud-ies and postcolonial criticism, perhaps the only modes of criticism that challenge the dominance of new historicism today. Under this as-sumption, art is not a traveler's boon companion or baedeker; it is in-stead the record of a traveler's encounter with an other. The history of the word "culture" itself could therefore be allegorized in terms of a voyage: at one time, "culture" was the best companion to accompany one on a voyage; it next became the guidebook that explained the place and people toward which one was sailing; finally, it has become a dramatic recollection of the encounter itself.

This set of claims is constructed with hyperbole: "most valuable," "best," "most interesting." Along with Raymond Williams's "*key-words*"—a grouping to which the word "culture" was central—these modifiers remind us how much is at stake in situations where the word "culture" is likely to appear. We use "culture" to imply and confer value, conveying quality as a positive attribute. Number also seems to be important. In this trio of assumptions, "culture" goes from being thought of as singular ("culture" as the height of civilization) to being thought of as plural ("English culture" contrasted with "Indian culture," and also "English cultures" contrasted with "Indian cultures"). Likewise, I have changed the capitalization of "Art"/"art" to reflect the relative importance given to it: in the first assumption, "Art" is akin to "the best which has been thought and said"; in the second assumption, "art" is still a rich thing, useful for information about the culture that produced it; in the third assumption, however, "cultures" are potentially the richest things—for their variety rather than their refinement—and artistic works the reservoirs or artifacts that hint at that variety.

As distinct as these assumptions seem, and as the explications here may imply, they are related in ways that we typically fail to recognize. For instance, while we have seen that they serve as the core ideological assumptions concerning "culture" in Shakespeare criticism during the twentieth century and beyond, the sequence they form is not one of replacement and exclusion. It is instead one of dialectic and interdependence. Indeed, the most important aspect of this interdependence for our examination of "culture" in Shakespeare studies comes with the unexpected relationship of the third assumption to the first. By this I mean that when we say that "The most interesting thing about art is the culture or cultures in it," we make a claim based directly on the anthropological insights associated with our second assumption—that is, that "Art is the best way of learning about a culture"—and indirectly, but tellingly, on our first—that "The most valuable product of a culture is its Art." But just how are these positions related?

To begin with, we could note that it is not surprising to find that a cultural-studies approach benefits from the resources of an anthropological one. As if recalling the *agon* of a classical tragedy, cultural-studies critics often take anthropology's interest in cultural content and "dramatize" its focus by studying cultures in conflict. Hence the encounters between New World peoples and the English—what Geraldo de Sousa calls "Shakespeare's cross-cultural encounters"—that are used in a variety of books and essays on Shakespeare's plays, from *Henry V* through *The Tempest*.[32] Yet although a cultural-studies approach is clearly indebted to anthropology for many of its terms and themes, it also is related to a more conservative understanding of "culture" through the anthropological approach's dependence on it. For instance, the second assumption ("Art is the best way of learning about a culture") draws on and is quite possibly incoherent without the "refinement" aspect of our first assumption, that "The most valuable product of a culture is its Art." I say "incoherent" here because the anthropological emphases of historicism assume literary texts to be the most efficient repositories of cultural energy. Rather than conveying the greatest values or pleasure—which a belletristic understanding of "culture" would assume of them—literary texts are held to convey the greatest amount of information about the cultures that produce them.[33] Because it relies on an anthropological model of culture, a cultural-studies approach to literary texts requires the same efficiency that its not-so-distant cousin, the belletristic approach, once claimed was literature's special attribute.

What differs, of course, is the content that literature is thought to convey. And here one could complain, with some justification, that an insurmountable divide exists between those who hold a belletristic understanding of literature and those who read literature in terms of cultural studies; between, that is, those who think of "Culture" and those who speak of "cultures." But what if we phrase our question another way and ask about the difference between, on one hand, someone who, using the word "culture," holds literature to be the most interesting or efficient carrier of X, and, on the other, someone who, using the word "culture," holds literature to be the most interesting or efficient carrier of Y? Put this way, the two endeavors' structural similarities are foregrounded. Obviously, the hypothetical parties described with these formulas would see themselves as having profound disagreements with their counterparts. Someone interested in a play like *Othello* for the music of its blank verse and the loftiness of its sentiments, for instance, could have little to talk about with someone for whom *Othello* is most profitably read for the cultural politics of its portrayal of race and ethnicity. And vice versa. I do not mean, therefore, to diminish the felt differences between these critical positions or to suggest that such differences have no real consequences in the world. Clearly they do.

When it comes to Shakespeare studies, however, these two positions—"The most valuable product of a culture is its Art" and "The most interesting thing about art is the culture or cultures in it"— have more in common than we typically are willing to admit. To see them as polar opposites rather than as variations on a common theme is to exaggerate the practices they support and rationalize. Regardless of which position we examine, the basic behavior associated with it is the same as the basic behavior associated with its counterpart. In each, scholars use a culturally valued book to make their way in the world. However critical Shakespeareans may be of its fictions, they rely on the First Folio for their profession. The book provides a living. Shakespeare may be said to be a "cultural" document, therefore, in much the same way that a holy text is "cultural." Scholars who make use of Shakespeare, that is, resemble religious functionaries (priests, rabbis, ministers, clerics, and others) who make their living in relationship to a sacred book. The force of such an analogy suggests that we use Shakespeare's works to make cultural arguments not because we have determined, through long study, that they have special cultural relevance for his own time but because they are culturally cherished in our own. We could push the analogy further and say that today "culture" is the equivalent of words like "grace" and "soul" to a religious age. It is abundant in, and a key word for, our more secular society in a manner that recalls the centrality of these sacred terms and similarly touches on the meaningful part of our life in the world. Such is the case not only because "culture" is, like "grace" and "soul," capacious and flexible, but because such capaciousness and flexibility allow writers to allude to abstractions—in our case, to complicated social, political, and historical formations that we cannot pin down—without the precision that would in turn complicate, and sometimes disable, such allusion.

And what about the function of the word "culture" in the doctrines of scholarly discourse today? To start to answer this question, and to examine the way in which we commonly arrive at a "cultural Shakespeare," I offer a paragraph from Christopher Pye's recent study, *The Vanishing: Shakespeare, the Subject, and Early Modern Culture* (2000). It constitutes an apologia for his title, topic, and set of texts:

> The chapters that follow approach the problem of the subject by pursuing intersecting paths through a range of materials and representational forms: pictorial as well as literary works; religious as well as secular material; high and low cultural phenomena, including witchcraft, anatomical treatises, the marvelous bric-a-brac of the "wonder cabinet." My choices are not intended to have a summary or even a

necessarily representative relation to early modern culture. Instead, in each instance I'm interested in teasing out those limit-points of symbolization where, I will argue, the cultural and sexual contours of the early modern subject come into view. My recurring literary focus will be Shakespeare. I would defend the emphasis heuristically: For any number of good and bad reasons Shakespeare amounts to a familiar "common ground." But that's probably just a way of saying it's the ground with which I'm most familiar. While I do feel that Shakespeare's texts offer a remarkably developed account of the subject and of the mechanisms of social and symbolic interpellation, I am certainly not claiming that they have a defining relation to modern subjectivity. At the same time, I would argue against the implicit sociologism of the assumption that one can come to terms with something like the problem of the subject through an empirically "representative" sampling. To argue (rightly) against claims for the universality of Shakespeare's work does not preclude the possibility that his work is at least as telling about, say, subject formation as anyone else's.[34]

This paragraph gathers a variety of issues relating to the "cultural" criticism of Shakespeare. Like most academic writing—mine included—it contains both honesty and bad faith, wants to have its cake and eat it too, and writes its way (rather than thinking its way) out of jams. Let me say at the start that Pye's work is intellectually engaging and takes a great many risks that enhance its mission. By focusing on this paragraph, I do not mean to unfairly single out its author; the paragraph could well have been written by any one of a hundred different literary critics or by a standing committee of the Shakespeare Association of America. That representativeness, in fact, is the point. As a paragraph, it typifies a certain tendency concerning "culture" in Shakespeare studies.

It is typical in part because the version of "culture" we get in Pye's book is much less expansive than is promised. Although Pye claims to have an interest in "high and low cultural phenomena," the "low" culture he examines consists largely of a sexual part of Michelangelo's *Last Judgment* and sections of *Hamlet*. Pye's definition of "culture" here is, in fact, like the "refinement" sense in the *OED* examined earlier. Less troubling than his declared interest in "low" cultural forms, however, is the awkward justification of his objects of study. Pye begins with a wry confession—"Shakespeare amounts to a familiar 'common ground.' But that's probably just a way of saying it's the ground with which I'm most familiar"—then follows up with a pat on his own back ("To argue (rightly) against claims for the universality of Shakespeare's work . . .") that just happens to jar loose a claim of his own: "does not preclude the possibility that his work is at least as telling about, say, subject formation as anyone else's." Rewarding himself for arguing "(rightly)" against claims that few of his colleagues in Shakespeare studies are guilty of making (claims, that is, concerning "the universality of Shakespeare's work"), Pye slips in the hope that Shakespeare's work may be "at least as telling" about his topic as anyone else's.

I said (wrongly) that Pye argues against a position that few take nowadays. Actually, he mocks it in passing. What he also decries here—three times, by my count—is what seems to be, to him, an equally troubling possibility: that something could be "representative" of early modern culture or one of its elements. Pye takes his stand against representativeness with the help of scare quotes and an "-ism": "At the same time, I would argue against the implicit sociologism of the assumption that one can come to terms with something like the problem of the subject through an empirically 'representative' sampling." Now, this is also less an "argument" than a claim: One can wait a long time in his book for an argument against "sociologism" (implicit or otherwise). But even more puzzling is Pye's anxiety (repeatedly expressed) about the "representative." He places the words in quotation marks, signaling that he has reason to disbelieve in them. He does not provide that reason. Nor is it easy to understand the logic by which Pye comes to his position against "sociologism" and empirical sampling. Perhaps there is no logic behind it. It could be, simply, that that kind of scholarship is less attractive to Pye: It is certainly less pleasurable to contemplate than a project that lets one write about works that have already brought one pleasure and piqued one's interest. I believe that, like most of us, Pye examines works that he wants to examine. Like most of us, too, he goes on to ascribe to them a "cultural" status he never demonstrates. His jab at the "representative" is perhaps a nervous attempt to forestall anticipated criticisms of his methodology. I should make it clear that I do not begrudge Pye (or anyone else) reading *Hamlet* and *The Last Judgment:* He has something to tell us about the representation of subjectivity in these and other early modern works. But I am suspicious of him dismissing, in a single sentence, an entire field (sociology) and a larger methodology of inquiry (empirical sampling), especially if the rationale for this dismissal is never articulated.

The best question to ask, however, concerns Pye's puzzling final sentence: "To argue (rightly) against claims for the universality of Shakespeare's work does not preclude the possibility that his work is at least as telling about, say, subject formation as anyone else's." My query here concerns the final clause about Shakespeare's work being at least as telling as anyone else's. Of this assertion, we should ask bluntly: "How would he know?" That is, how would Pye or any of us know whether Shakespeare's work is "at least as telling" about *anything* unless we read much more widely than this sentence suggests? This is where Pye's resistance to the notion of the "representative" and to the idea of extension and breadth in cultural research becomes most troublesome. Unless we are willing to admit that, by "culture," we mean merely a handful of things we like, how can we hazard claims without representativeness, without "sociologism," and without the "empirical sampling" that make Pye uneasy? Pye leaves it to a "possibility" that the texts he wants to examine are "telling" about his topic. He does not tell us, though, how he can tell this.

This is not only not an objective method of study, it is not something that inspires a great deal of confidence *as* a method. But I would offer that it is the method most prevalent in cultural criticism of Shakespeare today. However much I seem to be singling it out here, Pye's work features a contradiction typical of our field: a curious constriction of objects of study accompanied by an equally curious expansion of that study's purported reach. Although the culture advertised and theorized is often the anthropological sense of culture as a totality of beliefs and practices, the "culture" most concentrated on is—as is the case with Pye's book—the "refinement" sense of culture. Most of our work features an ingrained resistance to large constructs and totalities even as we often blithely employ these larger ideational units at liminal moments in our criticism: titles, introductions, transitions, and summary moments in our conclusions. We are "splitters" in our critical practice but "lumpers" in how we describe that practice.[35]

I began thinking about this simple word, "culture," and about the complex ways we use it when I found myself employing it in my critical writing as a synonym for "society." I will confess that I started to think about it even more after I used it in the subtitle to a book: *Quoting Shakespeare: Form and Culture in Early Modern Drama* (2000). As time went on, that is, I became less and less sure as to the word's exact meaning in that context. Now that I have used it in the main title of the present book and have spent the preceding pages exploring its various senses in Shakespeare criticism, I should make my own thoughts about "culture" explicit. Of the senses of "culture" presented in the preceding pages, I find the most consistently useful one to be the extensive sense found in anthropological writing. I prefer this extensive sense of "culture" because, while it is obviously the sense most open to criticism for its ambitions of reference, it is, to my mind, and perhaps because it *does* have these ambitions of reference, the most defensible of the senses examined here.[36] Speaking of "culture" as an ensemble of behavioral patterns, artifacts, ideas, and values means acknowledging a depth of difference between us and those sixteenth- and seventeenth-century persons who produced and consumed the texts that hold our attention even today. It is a difference evident in our classrooms, in students' responses to such texts, and correspondingly in the dense apparatuses (introductions, footnotes, glossaries, translations) accompanying many early modern texts in modern scholarly or teaching editions. It is also a difference that, even after years of studying such works as, for example, *The Book of Common Prayer, Songs and Sonnets,* or *King Lear,* one feels on a visceral level in reading this era's texts. The sometimes bewildering mental and social habits represented in these and many other works of the early modern period can strike us as alien, as profoundly "other." I begrudge no one the use of "culture" to refer to subcultures or even smaller units or locations of behavior. I use just such a smaller scale sense not only in the phrase "print culture" in chapter 3 but for two of this book's section headings ("Literary Culture" and "Critical Culture") as well. Yet for the extensive differences posed systematically by the world represented through early modern texts, the extensive sense of "culture" seems appropriate and worth our attempts to address.

Regardless of our definition, however, by this point a question may have arisen in the reader's mind. Why read Shakespeare—or any play from this period, for that matter—if what we are interested in is culture? Surely there are more objective ways, and more informative texts, to help us understand the culture of early modern England? Catechisms, parish registers, legal cases, conduct manuals, personal correspondence, state papers, diplomatic messages, graffiti—one could go on, of course, listing written resources for the investigation of "culture." And written resources are only part of the variety of items that could help us toward an archaeology of early modern culture. Painting, sculpture, clothing, embroidery, chamber pots, kitchen utensils, furniture—again the list could be greatly extended.[37] And although many of the preceding items—written and otherwise—have indeed been "read" by literary critics interested in early modern cultures, often (perhaps most often) they have been examined in conjunction with *plays* from this period, as if these items are ancillary things taken up ultimately to demonstrate the cultural materials already present in the dramatic texts at hand.[38] Which returns us to the question: Why read early modern plays if what we are interested in is early modern culture?

This question returns us to queries advanced earlier in this chapter, queries that can now be seen in another light. That is, in exploring the etymology of "culture," it becomes clear how difficult it is to keep distinct places, modes, processes, and products. "How to tell the process from the product?" it was asked, "From the producing faculty, place, or agent?" Returning to these questions we see that what had been cast as a potentially negative dilemma—how to separate things—now appears, at least potentially, to be a more positive situation—the *inseparability* of makers, making, and things made. And while I cannot pretend here to advance a unified theory of literature's relationship to culture, or even of the manifestation of culture within literary works, I can offer a few words about early modern drama's self-understanding of its relationship to culture.[39]

A *locus classicus* of the early modern playhouse's status as what I have called the "the dream screen of nascent capitalism" comes in John Lyly's prologue to *Midas* (1589).[40] I quote this document at some length to convey an extensive sense of its dominant conceit:

> Gentlemen, so nice is the world that for apparel there is no fashion, for music no instrument, for diet no delicate, for plays no invention but breedeth satiety before noon and contempt before night.
>
> Come to the tailor, he is gone to the painters to learn how more cunning may lurk in the fashion than can be expressed in the making. Ask the musicians, they will say their heads ache with devising notes beyond ela. Inquire at ordinaries, there must be salads for the Italian, picktooths for the Spaniards, pots for the German, porridge for the Englishman. At our exercises soldiers call for tragedies, their object is blood; courtiers for comedies, their subject is love; country-men for pastorals, shepherds are their saints. Traffic and travel hath woven the nature of all nations into ours, and made this land like arras, full of device, which was broadcloth, full of workmanship.
>
> Time hath confounded our minds, our minds the matter, but all cometh to this pass, that what heretofore hath been served in several dishes for a feast is now minced in a charger for a gallimaufry. If we present a mingle-mangle, our fault is to be excused, because the whole world is become an hodgepodge.[41]

Recently Robert Weimann has characterized this prologue as a signal meditation on the early modern theater's "world-picturing" abilities. As Weimann notes, "Lyly multiplies the efficacy of a coherent world-picture by setting out (in Martin Heidegger's sense of Vor-stellung) the picture before and in relation to an agency. This turning of the world into a picture of a representation answers a need for self-orientation and control in the face of a bewildering rate of change."[42] Indeed, Lyly's prologue situates the early modern playhouse in relationship to the very "world" it pictures, a "whole world" made up of a heady plurality of constituencies, including the international ("the Italian . . . the Spaniards . . . the German . . . the Englishman") and occupational ("soldiers . . . courtiers . . . country-men"). Plays answer the demands of, and attempt to "sati[ate]," such constituents: "soldiers *call for* . . ." and plays respond. Like Mercutio's account of the manner in which Queen Mab brings dreams to various social types in answer to those types' desires (*Romeo and Juliet,* 1.4.70–95), Lyly's version of dramatic "exercises" is one in which plays reply to audience desire—desire best understood in the plural. Indeed, in Lyly's account the "mingle-mangle" of early modern plays only correlates to the "hodgepodge" nature of the world to which playwrights, like tailors, painters, and musicians, marketed their wares and from which they drew their fashions.

If it is arguable that drama as a representational mode tends to possess the world-picturing quality that Weimann has pointed out in Lyly's prologue, the early modern theater in particular has left us plays unusually "thick" with the world around them.[43] National and international characters and locations combine with a copia of themes, ideas, and words to give us a representational array both unprecedented in earlier drama and unreplicated by later theaters. Along with the name of the playhouse itself, the sign imagined for the Globe Theater—Hercules bearing the world on his shoulders with the motto *Totus mundus agit historionem* ("All the World Goes to a Play")—stands as an exceedingly rich metaphor for the felt ability, of early modern plays, to capture the world, to represent the dazzling variety of people, actions, things, and ideas on the bare boards of its stages. Along with this Latin tag, the phrase *theatrum mundi*— which we could, following custom, translate as "the theater of the world"—reminds us of the ambitions of representation held by the platform stages of the early modern era. As if compressing the "stuff" of the world, and of experience of that world, into its plots, early modern drama offers versions of culture that seem to push their way into the pages of criticism. We could see the drama of the period as the most concentrated instance of the era's "compilation literature," a genre composed of such diverse but comprehensive forms as miscellanies, florilegia, and proverb collections.[44]

Early modern commentators recognized the drama of the day as a good medium for learning about other lands, peoples, and fashions—what we would call "culture." In fact, a German traveler, Thomas Platter, described London's playhouses as venues that substituted for travel. Having visited several theaters and animal baiting rings in the early fall of 1599, Platter remarked: "With such and many other pastimes besides the English spend their time; in the comedies they learn what is going on in other lands, and this happens without alarm, husband and wife together in a familiar place, since for the most part the English do not much use to travel, but are content ever to learn of foreign matters at home, and ever to take their pastime."[45] Others saw printed playtexts as offering useful information for those who—in distinction to Platter's *heimlich* playgoers—sought to travel internationally. In an essay entitled "A Method for Travell" prefacing his *A View of France* (1605?), Robert Dallington recommended that his would-be traveler read "history," "the Mathematics, discourses of war, and books of fortification." But prior to recommending this heavy curriculum, Dallington advises travelers to acquire linguistic fluency by reading plays:

> But for the cause alleged, I will presume to advise him, that the most compendious way of attaining the tongue, whether *French* or *Italian*, is by book, I mean for the knowledge; for as for the speaking, he shall never attain it, but by continual practice and conversation: he shall therefore first learn his nouns & verbs by heart, and specially the articles, and their uses, with the two words *Sum* and *Habeo:* for in these consist the greatest observation of that part of speech. His reader shall not read any book of Poetry at the first, but some other kind of style, and I think meetest some modern comedy.[46]

It is difficult to tell whether Dallington means "comedy" here in its general, modal sense (that is, as any kind of drama—surely the meaning of Platter's "comedies" [*Comedien*]), or, more particularly, in its generic sense. The distinction of "comedy" from "any book of Poetry" suggests the latter, as does, perhaps, his emphasis on "modern" in the phrase "some modern comedy." Presumably this qualifier recognizes the fact that languages—as well as manners, customs, and fashions—change over time, and the more recent the "comedy," the better its ability to prepare readers for travel. For Dallington, the modern traveler is well served by reading modern drama.

Critics today affirm Dallington's advice when they concentrate on the cultural "thickness" of early modern plays. To recent critics, drama of this period declares its own "*Sum* and *Habeo*" regarding the cultures it represents as well as the culture that gave it its being. Critics have read not just drama itself or the oeuvres of single playwrights, but individual *plays* as rich compendia of cultural energy and tensions. In his book *The Purpose of Playing: Shakespeare and the Cultural Politics of the Elizabethan Theatre* (1996), for instance, Louis Montrose uses *A Midsummer Night's Dream* (1596) to represent Elizabethan culture. Significantly, Montrose denies that he means for the play to have this function: "By addressing the cultural processes discussed in Part One from the exemplary perspective of *A Midsummer Night's Dream*, I do not seek to demonstrate that this particular cultural text is a *summa* of Elizabethan culture. Nor do I argue for the organic unity of either the culture or the text, but rather treat the text as a site of convergence of various and potentially contradictory cultural discourses."[47] One can quarrel with this denial, in part because Montrose's analysis relies heavily on *A Midsummer Night's Dream* to chart the shapes of Elizabethan culture. His monograph was constructed, in fact, from an extraordinarily influential essay originally published ten years prior to his book: "*A Midsummer Night's Dream* and the Shaping Fantasies of Elizabethan Culture. Gender, Power, Form."[48] His book revises and greatly extends that essay, to be sure, and adds a substantial theoretical and historical introduction to what he calls the "cultural politics" of the Elizabethan theater. (Montrose's analysis differs from Greenblatt's "cultural poetics" in its emphasis on association and institutions.) Yet despite this fleshing out, the play continues to dominate Montrose's presentation of Elizabethan "culture"; and it seems fair to say that, without Shakespeare's comedy, Montrose's book would not exist. *A Midsummer Night's Dream* may not be a *summa* of Elizabethan culture, but to Montrose's study it remains a *sine qua non*.

Clearly, the dilemma Montrose faces is a common one, involving (once again) the problem of representativeness. Logic tells us that the culture of early modern England must have exceeded any single text's ability to capture it. Absent a miraculous "book of knowledge" like the one Mephistopheles shares in *Doctor Faustus* (1592), we are left with parts of a vast and complex whole. Like so many who write on the cultural aspects of literary texts, Montrose understands literature to be especially revealing of this whole. For this very reason, the rhetorical figure of synecdoche has become the foundational trope of cultural inquiry. The *OED* defines "synecdoche" as "A figure by which a more comprehensive term is used for a less comprehensive or vice versa; as whole for part or part for whole, genus for species or species for genus, etc." In *The Arte of English Poesie* (published

1589), George Puttenham called synecdoche "the Figure of quick conceite," explaining that its allegorical method of figuration requires "a good, quick, and pregnant capacitie, and is not for an ordinarie or dull wit so to do."[49] As Kenneth Burke reminds us, the "'noblest synecdoche'" of all—what he calls "the perfect paradigm or prototype for all lesser usages"—can be found in that most Renaissance of doctrines, that of the identity of microcosm and macrocosm.[50] Critics who would never look on the early modern deployment of this paradigm with anything other than amusement— imagine the critical response, for instance, to a serious assertion that a person is "a little world made cunningly"—make similar use of this figure when they engage the *pars pro toto* function of synecdoche in their cultural studies of early modern texts and objects.

It may seem ironic that I have expressed a preference for the extensive sense of culture and then questioned those who would find just such cultural extensiveness in early modern plays. The irony may seem even deeper given my description of these plays as profoundly varied and heterogeneous documents—as extensive, that is, in what they present. I should make it clear, therefore, that part of what I am scrutinizing in this study is a truncation of process, a shortcutting, as it were, of the mediating aspects of literary form and production. Too often we take the plays' cultural "worlds" as doubles of the culture from which they come. There is more to literary representation than that, of course, and it is this "more" that we need to address before, and while, we make pronouncements about cultural content and processes in these dramatic texts. In the next chapter I propose one way of doing so. I argue that the "thin description" of literary texts— a process that involves reading widely in literary "culture"—will help us gain a more accurate picture of literature's relationship to the culture that produced it.

CHAPTER 2

DEEP FOCUS

TOWARD THE THIN DESCRIPTION
OF LITERARY CULTURE

Descriptions of culture as a totality occur infrequently today. In fact, changes to the form in which cultural research is presented hint at our diminished confidence in seeing culture "whole," or even extensively; we now tend to analyze culture not in book-length studies but in essays.[1] And such essays typically employ a critical genre of relatively recent origin: "thick description." Thick description can be said to have changed the way literary critics read and write. At the very least, thick description remains the form in which important changes to critical analysis and the presentation of research have been registered. Its popularity in Shakespeare studies surely comes from the special influence of new historicism on the field. In the preceding chapter I remarked that new historicism has been the dominant methodology in early modern studies for several decades. While some observers would see new historicism as a kind of ghost, a "moment in critical history that . . . is seen to be passing," even a "form of cultural and literary criticism that no one practices today except the founders," I believe that such characterizations overstate the case.[2] New historicism can be seen as a thing of the past precisely because so many of its assumptions and practices have become standard and hence less visible to us. One of these practices involves how new historicism is written. Arguably, its most profound effect on the field of early modern studies has little to do with history. Instead, what made, and makes, new historicism such an influential critical mode is its style, an important part of which is its use of thick description.

When Shakespeareans talk about analyzing Shakespeare and early modern literature—especially from a cultural angle—they often mention thick description, and positively so. For instance, reviewing a recent study of *King Lear* (1605), Edward Pechter writes that "we should all be grateful for the emphasis on contingency and thick description among the revisionist historians with whom [the author] identifies."[3] Likewise, Jane Donawerth, in an essay entitled "Teaching Shakespeare in the Context of Renaissance Women's Culture," observes that one of the first questions that confronted her as a feminist Shakespearean in the classroom was the following: "How could I teach undergraduate students to do 'thick description' of the historical contexts of the plays, analyzing Shakespeare as part of his culture, not universal author of culture?"[4] And finally, in her review of "Recent Studies in Tudor and Stuart Drama," Meredith Skura points out that "Clifford Geertz . . . has become almost indispensable for today's writers, who nearly all begin with thick description of their 'text' and whole-culture analysis of its function."[5]

To this point I have associated thick description with, variously, cultural criticism, the critical essay as a form, and new historicism. What is this popular, even "indispensable" thing? Because literary criticism often takes thick description for granted—indeed, for many critics thick description has become synonymous with an enlightened and nimble literary criticism—and because it is centrally involved in this chapter's argument, it will be useful to examine its genealogy. Unlike the survey of "culture" and its various meanings in chapter 1, a history of "thick description" reveals little by way of competing definitions: On the whole, people agree as to the term's meaning. Like cultural criticism, however, the practice of thick description has produced intense debates among critics. A history of the concept behind that practice therefore can help put debates over thick description into useful relief.

The term comes to literary criticism by way of anthropology—more specifically, from ethnography and (as Skura indicates) Clifford Geertz. But as Geertz himself acknowledges, it appeared first in two essays of the Oxford philosopher Gilbert Ryle; these essays were published in 1967 - 1968, and the anthropologist soon popularized the term.[6] To Ryle, "thick" and "thin" compose two general forms of description. Ryle gives the example of "[t]wo boys" who "swiftly contract the eyelids of their right eyes," and notes that this action can be described either as (1) a simple contraction of the eyelid (a "thin" description); or (2) a conspiratorial wink to an accomplice (a "thick" description).[7] Although Ryle associates thinness with simple, surface descriptions, and thickness with complex, deep descriptions, in the end thinness and thickness have less to do with the length or satisfactory nature of the description itself than with the areas of activity and experience being described. Thick descriptions, in short, elaborate the *context* of an event: the subject's motivations, intentions, and success at executing the intended action. Thin descriptions, by contrast, stress the plainer, objective facets of the event. Where thin descriptions could be characterized as generally nondiscursive, snapshot representations, thick descriptions involve a narration or story that sets out the process and situation of the activity and the pattern of motivations that first initiated it.

Ryle is careful to point out that any "thick" account of an action is neither reducible to the "thin" version nor to a second, independent activity but rather stands in an interdependent relation with it. Thus although these are somewhat loaded terms—terms that seem to place in opposition depth and complexity, on one hand, with surface and simplicity on the other—we should note that thick and thin are not absolutely opposed but rather relative points on an axis of complexity. Ryle is therefore careful not to champion the "thick" at the expense of the "thin." Reminding us that Euclid, in teaching his students complex geometrical proofs, may be described as "muttering to himself a few geometrical words and phrases, . . . [or] scrawling on paper or in sand a few rough and fragmentary lines," Ryle concludes: "This is far, very far from being all that he is doing; but it may very well be the only thing that he is doing. A statesman signing his surname to a peace-treaty is doing much more than inscribe the seven letters of his surname, but he is not doing many or any more things. He is bringing a war to a close by inscribing the seven letters of his surname."[8]

Ryle's "thick description" was popularized as a term in the introduction to Clifford Geertz's 1973 essay collection, *The Interpretation of Cultures,* and as a practice in the celebrated essay that closes that volume, "Deep Play: Notes on the Balinese Cockfight." As one could expect, thick description goes through some changes in its migration from the language philosophy of an Oxford don to the cultural inquiry of an American ethnographer concerned with Southeast Asia. Yet for Geertz, "thick description" remains more than a decorative term. It provides, instead, the very cornerstone on which he constructs his practice. For Geertz, "ethnography *is* thick description."[9] As he explains:

What the ethnographer is in fact faced with—except when (as of course, he must do) he is pursuing the more automatized routines of data collection—is a multiplicity of complex conceptual structures, many of them superimposed upon or knotted into one another, which are at once strange, irregular, and inexplicit, and which he must contrive somehow first to grasp and then to render. And this is true at the most down-to-earth, jungle field work levels of his activity: interviewing informants, observing rituals, eliciting kin terms, tracing property lines, censusing households . . . writing his journal. Doing ethnography is like trying to read (in the sense of "construct a reading of") a manuscript— foreign, faded, full of ellipses, incoherencies, suspicious emendations, and tendentious commentaries, but written not in conventionalized graphs of sound but in transient examples of shaped behavior.[10]

In this passage from the introduction to his study, and in *The Interpretation of Cultures* as a whole, Geertz's employment of thick description relies on some innovations to methodology that, although controversial (then and now) in the discipline of anthropology, have passed somewhat benignly into the theory and practice of literary criticism. Indeed, one of the most difficult things to convey to literary critics about the history of thick description is how revolutionary it was—and how controversial it remains—in its own field.

Geertz's work involves a profound reprioritizing of evidence and interpretation. Where conventional anthropology thought of observers amassing data while working from a vantage point interested in general truths and trends (we could note here Geertz's phrase concerning "the more automatized routines of data collection") and then extrapolating, from these data, useful and objective observations about a culture, Geertz's thick description follows out the implications of Ryle's interpretive practice and intuitively explores the "webs of significance" leading out from a particular event or practice. The metaphor here comes ultimately from Max Weber by way of Geertz, who remarks that, because "man is an animal suspended in webs of significance he himself has spun, I take culture to be those webs, and the analysis of it to be therefore not an experimental science in search of law but an interpretive one in search of meaning."[11] As this sentence suggests, Geertz's thick descriptions of culture give more weight to interpretation than had been the case in conventional ethnography, where chapters devoted to method and evidence sometimes were followed by hesitant evaluations and hypotheses offered under the modest banner of a "conclusion."

This new emphasis on interpretation strongly characterizes what remains the most famous thick description in any field, "Deep Play:

Notes on the Balinese Cockfight." Originally published in 1972, before its inclusion in *The Interpretation of Cultures*, this essay can be summarized as an examination of masculine identity and status in a Balinese village as represented in the ritual of cockfighting. This summary's grave inadequacy reveals itself to anyone who has read Geertz's essay, so rich are the piece's details, observations, and witty asides. Geertz's essay, in fact, is so much greater than the sum of its parts that it asks to be read as an artistic as well as a "scientific" document. The aesthetic effect of his essay was no accident; on the contrary, it obviously concerned Geertz. References, in "Deep Play," to such figures as Wallace Stevens, Arnold Schoenberg, Walker Percy—even Aristotle and Northrop Frye—speak to art's continuing presence to Geertz's attention as he thinks about his role as an interpreter.

Other innovations Geertz makes to methodology, in fact, relate to, where they do not derive from, this new emphasis on artistic interpretation and effect. We could tentatively understand these innovations to be combined in the following sentence: Cultures are themselves complex texts to be read; we are to read these complex cultural texts, in turn, the way critics read and interpret art (especially, perhaps, literary art). The familiar metaphor of culture as a text can be recalled from the excerpt already provided: "Doing ethnography is like trying to read (in the sense of 'construct a reading of') a manuscript—foreign, faded, full of ellipses, incoherencies, suspicious emendations, and tendentious commentaries. . . ." As important here as this metaphor, however, is a turn that Geertz makes when he aestheticizes not just culture but his own criticism. So thoroughly artful does he render the critical essay, in fact, that we are licensed to emend the preceding summary as follows: "Cultures are themselves complex texts to be read; in reading these complex cultural texts the way critics read and interpret art (especially, perhaps, literary art), we will benefit from lending our interpretations a corresponding and sympathetic artfulness of presentation." Although this is obviously a sentence Geertz did not write, the position it registers may not surprise those familiar with thick description's aesthetic impact. The artfulness of presentation is one reason people continue to interpret and critique Geertz's work; such artfulness is much less common with the scholarly efforts of many of Geertz's academic contemporaries.

Those who read "Deep Play" (I make recourse, once again, to the experienced reader precisely because this essay is by design irreducible) recognize immediately that they are being told a story. Thick description loves storytelling, especially beginning stories. Perhaps this is because beginnings offer up that moment when an artist, capturing an audience's attention, feels the excitement of control. Here, at any rate, is the beginning of "Deep Play": "Early in April of 1958, my wife and I arrived, malarial and diffident, in a Balinese village we intended, as anthropologists, to study. A small place, about five hundred people, and relatively remote, it was its own world. We were intruders, professional ones, and the villagers dealt with us as Balinese seem always to deal with people not part of their life who yet press themselves upon them: as though we were not there. For them, and to a degree for ourselves, we were nonpersons, specters, invisible men."[12] In paragraphs that have since been read by many thousands of students in various academic fields, Geertz recounts his and his wife's attendance at a village cockfight that happened to be interrupted by a government raid. He relates the details of their resulting flight (along with the other spectators at the cockfight) from the police as well as their subsequent acceptance into the Balinese village in a genial but compelling way.

Not until the second section of the essay, a section entitled "Of Cocks and Men," does Geertz, beginning again, give us something resembling the conventional opening to an academic study: the kind of beginning, that is, that intones "The purpose of this study is—" or "My topic here is—." When Geertz restarts his essay here by wryly noting that "Bali, mainly because it is Bali, is a well-studied place," proceeding to add relevant footnotes to scholarly works on "The Balinese Temper" and *Balinese Character*, we remember—with a combination, perhaps, of relief and resentment—how dull conventional academic writing can be. The delightful qualifier "mainly because it is Bali" is Geertz's way of winking at the reader, of having fun while initiating the motions of academic citation. At this point, however, after the engaging narrative that opens "Deep Play," we want less bibliography and more story. The production of this desire is no accident; on the contrary, it remains central to thick description. Telling stories perhaps traces ultimately to Geertz's conviction that culture is understood better as interrelated practices than as two-dimensional maps or sets of rules. From such a temporal dimension comes the narrativity of the thick-description essay itself. And with thick description comes aesthetic effect. Indeed, even more significant than Geertz's often-cited metaphor that "The culture of a people is an ensemble of texts" is his transformation of the *critical* (rather than *cultural*) text.[13] Much anthropological writing before Geertz soberly rehearsed facts; Geertz tells stories that make us believe, as readers of a novel believe, in the rich strangeness of Balinese village life. In place of the anthropologist as scientist, Geertz gives us the anthropologist as narrative poet. In place of the scientific text, Geertz gives us an aesthetic one.

Now, the preceding is obviously an abbreviated and inadequate account of thick description. I call it inadequate because it captures neither the experience of reading a thick description nor the disciplinary implications of a critical practice that has, for three decades now, proved both influential and controversial. Indeed, Geertz has had extremely vocal supporters and critics during this period. Because he anticipated some of the controversy he would inspire, the debate concerning his works and methodology has followed some of the lines he inscribed with his presentation of thick description in *The Interpretation of Cultures*. We could represent this debate as an argument over whether anthropology should be intuitive or rigorous, an art or a science, literary and qualitative or scientific and objective.[14]

Among Geertz's supporters are such anthropologists as Kenneth Rice, who in *Geertz and Culture* (1980) maintained that his subject's contributions to ethnography overshadow any problems of methodology relating to the practice of thick description.[15] Paul Roth, in turn, has argued that the "literary" nature of thick description does not invalidate it as an ethnographic practice; the charge that thick description involves "misrepresentation" is, to Roth, "plausible but epistemologically innocuous."[16] Alan Tongs has likewise supported thick description on a theoretical basis. Remarking the "continuing strength and fruitfulness of Geertz's interpretive anthropology," Tongs focuses on the shared meanings of a society to justify thick description's interest in the typical—an interest displayed, in thick description, through "strategic" generalizations about a culture.[17] On this side of the thick description debate stand those who feel that the interpretive gains thick description has made—what it has given us in terms of nuanced readings of cultures and cultural phenomena—more than outweigh any shortcomings of theory or method that it may display.

On the other side of this debate stand those who see thick description as an overly qualitative, even subjective, practice that, because it turns away from science to embrace the "literary," has little claim to anything more than the status of a diversion. Perhaps harshest among Geertz's critics is S. P. Reyna, who accuses the anthropologist of proposing to "replace science with gossip" and goes on to complain that "literary anthropologists know little, not because they have shown that little is knowable, but because they have chosen, without reason, not to know."[18] Others have been less brusque, but equally cautionary in their assessment of what Paul Shankman has called the "small industry [which] has grown up around the work of Clifford Geertz."[19] Writing on "Balinese Cockfights and the Seduction of Anthropology," for instance, William Roseberry has criticized weaknesses in the theoretical underpinnings of Geertz's "Deep Play" essay—in particular, the essay's artful confusion of agency and social process.[20] Similarly, Stephen Foster, in a 1982 review of Geertz's *Negara: The Theatre State in Nineteenth-Century Bali* (1980), finds that the book's methodology prompts nagging and unflattering questions: "How does the author arrive at his slick, symmetric formulations? What is the pathway between the 'data' and the meaning attributed to it?"[21] Not surprisingly, these questions concerning Geertz's ethnographical practice resemble the questions that many have asked about the critical genre that has popularized thick description in literary studies: new historicism.[22]

Ironically, just at the moment when anthropology fiercely debated the validity of thick description, literary study moved to embrace it. In a circular exchange—the type of which new historicism is fond of exploring—the literary-critical stance that empowered Geertz in *The Interpretation of Cultures* was "borrowed back," along with many of Geertz's cultural paradigms, by new historicists. When Stephen Greenblatt published *Renaissance Self-Fashioning: From More to Shakespeare* in 1980, for instance, Geertz was invoked as a progenitor of new historicism not only through citation but via Greenblatt's naming of this new literary-critical practice a "*poetics of culture.*"[23] In *Renaissance Self-Fashioning* as well as in such essays as "Shakespeare and the Exorcists" and "Fiction and Friction," Greenblatt draws heavily on Geertz's work, calling on Geertz as an authority, a disciplinary anchor as it were.[24] But these and other thick descriptions by literary critics make little or no mention of Geertz's profoundly controversial status within his own discipline of anthropology. I believe this is because Geertz's discipline mattered less to those who cited him than did his willingness to forgo disciplinary protocols to write in a personal and expressive manner. What new historicism saw in Geertz was a reflection of its own desire, a desire—as we will see—to interpret and impress through storytelling. As I have suggested, new historicists are perhaps more indebted to Geertz for the *style* of the thickly descriptive essay than for any of the various assumptions (for example, that culture is a "text") that accompany thick description. That style, once again, is intensively narrative, with the critic spinning a story that sometimes entrances its readers with accounts of things and events alternately wonderful, strange, violent, and odd.

Most recognizable about the style of thick description is how essays in this critical genre commence. We noted the importance of the opening to Geertz's "Deep Play" essay. That beginnings remain no less crucial to the thick descriptions of historically centered essays on Shakespeare and the early modern period can be seen from the following passages—each of which is the first sentence of an essay. The essays date from 1985 through 1999:

> Between the spring of 1585 and the summer of 1586, a group of English Catholic priests led by the Jesuit William Weston, alias Father Edmunds, conducted a series of spectacular exorcisms, principally in the house of a recusant gentleman, Sir George Peckham of Denham, Buckinghamshire.[25]

> In the autumn of 1599, Thomas Platter of Basle visited the London apartment of Walter Cope—gentleman, adventurer, and member of Elizabeth's Society of Antiquaries—to view Cope's collection of curiosities gathered from around the world.[26]

> In a Whitechapel neighborhood in London in 1610, at least seven women stood in the doorways of their seven houses, all "at work."[27]

> In 1615, while visiting Cambridge University, King James I attended a public debate between John Preston and Matthew Wren on the question of "whether Dogs could make syllogismes."[28]

Such openings invite us to listen to a story and, implicitly, to trust the teller of the story to execute and finish the tale (at the very least, an exploration of a topic) in an adequate and rewarding way. One could note the citing of dates: "Between the spring of 1585 and the summer of 1586"; "In the autumn of 1599"; "In a Whitechapel neighborhood in London in 1610"; "In 1615, while visiting Cambridge University." Such citation seems to assure us of the historicity of the issues examined in the essay that follows; it may speak as well to the critic's commitment to history. There is something particular, even peculiar, in the details of these initial events: "a series of spectacular exorcisms"; a "collection of curiosities"; the leading simultaneity of "at least seven women['s]" actions; the logical potential of canines. Such particularity can be said spectacularly to incite the reader's curiosity.

The compelling narrative style signaled by these beginnings is among the most well known and attractive aspects of thick description.[29] As taken up by new historicism, thick description is a masterful critical genre, one in which the critic gains our attention even

before announcing the topic of the essay itself; thick description goes
on to repay our attention (as did Geertz) with a cultural interpretation both *dulce et utile*. Among the other strengths of the thick description that one finds in new historicism and in criticism influenced
by it is its initial attention to detail. This focus on detail enables thick
description to follow the many strands of signification radiating outward from various cultural events, objects, and actors. Thick description also helps "freeze" our attention on a particular historical
moment, reminding us of the felt contingencies of the synchronic
and of the various, sometimes competing, factors that must have influenced the agency of individuals at these times.

New historicism is unimaginable as a methodology without thick
description. Yet not all thick description is employed by new historicists. The Shakespeareans quoted at the outset of this chapter testify
to the success of thick description, as both phrase and practice, across
Shakespeare studies. Were the phrase less inelegant, many of those
working in Shakespeare and early modern studies could be tempted
to call themselves "thick describers," for this is as accurate a term for
their interests and practices as "new historicism," "cultural poetics,"
or "materialism," and perhaps more exact than these terms in representing the form of much contemporary criticism. A thick description
in the field of Shakespeare or early modern studies typically begins
with an anecdote, event, or object that gives the critic an
Archimedean leverage into the larger cultural text that (the critic argues) may be accessed from that entry point.

Under the aegis of what could be called a "new materialism" in
early modern studies, it has become common to substitute an object
for an event (and the narration of such an event) in the thick descriptions of current criticism.[30] We could think of such objects as
something like firm places away from which critics push the boats of
their arguments: These objects provide a beginning to one's voyage,
to be sure, but in a slightly different way from the events of earlier
thick description. One such object appeared in Greenblatt's chapter
entitled "Resonance and Wonder" in his essay collection *Learning to
Curse* (1990).[31] Greenblatt begins this essay with a thing—"a round,
red priest's hat" found in "a small glass case in the library of Christ
Church, Oxford"—and uses this "artifact" to launch a series of remarks on the complex networks of circulation and exchange and the
"resonance" of various artifacts within these networks in every culture. (In Greenblatt's criticism, "circulation" is a trope derived sometimes from the human body, sometimes from currency systems, and
sometimes from electricity; that he ascribes to this object a "tiny

quantum of cultural energy" suggests that in this case he is thinking about the last.[32]) Greenblatt's analysis of the circulation of power and clothing "pushes off" from, and in that sense depends on, the quiddity of the hat. Its tangibility, no less than its strangeness, gives his essay its initial purchase and validation. As with the stylized narratives of the initial events described in the preceding paragraphs, the thick description of such resonant objects makes us feel the narrator's presence in the scene—a historical fiction that (however "factual") replaces what had been presented, by Geertz, as an anthropological "event" or truth.

Thick description remains popular among critics who may not consider themselves new historicists (and would perhaps not be considered as such by others), however deep their interest in history and culture. Such can be seen in a recent essay by Wendy Wall entitled "Why Does Puck Sweep?: Fairylore, Merry Wives, and Social Struggle."[33] Although it cannot be expected to represent all thick descriptions of early modern literature, Wall's essay does provide a good example of certain tendencies in thick description as practiced today. It also illustrates how the very form of thick description can shape a critic's argument (rather than, as some may expect, the critic's argument affecting the form). I will spend some paragraphs here examining Wall's essay, before returning to it later in the chapter. We will see, significantly enough, that "Why Does Puck Sweep?" winds up committing itself to positions that run antithetical to its author's own positions. Why does it do so? I would aver that thick description has a way of leading critics in directions of its own choosing, directions inherent to the critical form itself.

As its title implies, Wall's essay begins with a question about an object referred to in *A Midsummer Night's Dream* (1596). As Puck relates (to no one in particular) toward the close of the drama: "I am sent with broom before, / To sweep the dust behind the door" (5.1.389–90). Wall stops to question lines that most readers of the play (including me) have passed over without a second thought; her initial question leads, in turn, to others: "Why does Puck sweep? . . . [W]hy in helping to achieve this closure does the mischievous Puck play the role of housewife? Why does the reproduction of the social world, a goal at the very heart of romantic comedy, rest on a task usually too banal for representation—disposing of dirt left in domestic corners? Why introduce a homey image in a play concerned with the grand affairs of state or the chaotic force of the imagination, one situated, albeit loosely, in the remote world of classical Athens?"[34] Puck's sweeping, and Puck's broom—whether realized as a stage property during a production or merely mentioned by Puck—give Wall a firm item on which to center her argument, and the reader's attention, on a particular conjunction of topics, among them society, folklore, class, and gender.

Wall's thick description of Puck's sweeping and of this dramatic moment in *A Midsummer Night's Dream* leads to a significant examination of these topics and to a reading of *The Merry Wives of Windsor* (1597) as a kind of response-text to *Dream*. In addition to the broom, another object—the buck-basket from *The Merry Wives*—comes into play in the essay. I quote Wall's concluding paragraph in full:

> Taken together, these two Shakespeare plays reveal divergent ways in which the class-specific elements of fairylore could be taken to represent household and national relations. In the process, both plays expose the potential uncanniness of domesticity, the fantastical quality of everydayness that made submission to household tasks a precarious but formative activity. During a period when the household was seen as modeling and providing the training ground for political order, such an experiment had potentially important implications. Why would fairies be the logical finale for a plot about housewives and laundry? Why does Puck sweep? Thematically tied to a powerful popular lore, his broom, like the Fords' buck-basket, stubbornly recalls the material grounding for household relations as well as their vexed but critical place in the cultural imagination.[35]

As may be apparent even in the excerpts provided, Wall's essay uses a thick description of Puck's sweeping and the Fords' buck-basket to follow out the cultural "webs" that connect them and by means of which they are connected to larger issues and energies. Focusing on gender and domesticity, Wall moves gradually from these practices (sweeping, washing) and objects (a broom, a buck-basket) to concentric circles of society, culture, and nation founded on a vernacular, household-centered Englishness. We recognize the connections among these circles—are persuaded of their reality—in part because of our conviction as to the tangibility of the practices and objects realized in and by Wall's thick description.

I have spent some time examining Wall's essay in part because it makes a substantial contribution to Shakespeare studies, in part because it locates two of Shakespeare's comedies in relationship to a variety of complex cultural issues and forces, but mainly because it does so by means of thick description. Thick description, I will argue later in this chapter, essentially "takes over" Wall's analysis. Although some could see thick description as a thing of the past, an integral part of what Henry S. Turner has called a "now outdated New Historicism" and hence no longer a factor in the field, it is clear from Wall's essay and from many others, as well as from the Shakespeareans quoted at the beginning of this chapter, that thick description is very much a part of what Shakespeareans do when they talk about culture.[36] Whether one's primary interest lies, for instance, in colonialism, class, gender, sexuality, or the history of books, printing, and reading (among the many topics relevant to Shakespeare studies today), thick description is a popular way of exploring cultural themes. Thus although anthropologists have spoken of "paradigm exhaustion" relating to thick description, and although literary critics have announced the obsolescence of the new historicism that has promoted it, we can see that, far from disappearing from studies of Shakespeare and early modern literature, it has become the central means of reading these materials' cultural aspects. [37] Thick description remains a standard implement in the critical toolbox.

Not all tasks can be performed with a single tool, however, and sometimes the habitual reliance on (and apparent success of) a particular mechanism can blind us to its limitations as a means of accomplishing a task at hand. Such, I believe, is where we stand in relationship to thick description. Dazzled early by its utility and ease of application, we have been less than eager to notice its lack of fit for various duties we have used it to perform. Why should this be? Why, that is, have readers been slower to notice its deficiencies? I think part of the reason lies in thick description's aesthetic impact, an impact that depends on its "well-wrought" nature. Thick descriptions are no less pleasurable to write than they are to read, and the aesthetic dimension that has unfolded around such qualitative analyses of culture is perhaps doubly attractive to a generation of critics who have trained themselves to beware the formal seductions of literary texts. In that sense, the aesthetic—generally banished as an object of critical inquiry—has returned with ironic but uncanny persistence as a mode of critical inquiry itself. Here the aesthetic resides comfortably within critical narrative.

In addition to being a practice that has returned the aesthetic to criticism, thick description has become a thoroughly popular form of criticism, a form whose popularity can be explained in a variety of ways. Some can choose to see it, for instance, as a necessary revision of stale and falsely "objective" modes of academic inquiry. To others, it can seem a generational phenomenon, the critical genre of those who, having come of age in a changeful time that emphasized personal freedom, found in thick description an intellectually and politically liberating mode of expression. Still others can see it as a formal amalgamation, within literary studies, of new critical and historicist modes of inquiry. Perhaps each of these accounts holds some truth. However one wishes to define thick description or to chart its career in the academy, though, it seems clear that early modern studies needs to reevaluate thick description's role as a means of reading the "culture" in and around literary texts. If we define culture as an extensive phenomenon, a critical practice that concentrates—however intensively—on small parts of a culture will almost by definition be unsatisfactory as a method of representing the extension and variety of that culture. No book, no critical essay, surely, hopes actually to encapsulate a culture. But just as surely there are degrees of success for every critical endeavor that aims to address a topic or entity, however large and complex. For this reason, the following pages advance an argument for "thin description" as a needed supplement to the thick descriptions that currently drive our cultural studies. Even as Ryle pointed out the necessary interdependence of thick and thin description—whereby, for instance, we need to remain mindful of writing as both a simple and complex activity—I pursue thin description in the remainder of this chapter, and in the chapters that follow, as a practice that can enrich the ways in which we tend to read for cultural content.

Thin description, in brief, is more quantitative than qualitative—at least to the extent that it emphasizes reading widely in literary culture. By "widely" here I mean reading not only a canonical author writing at a particular time (for example, 1605) but many authors—canonical and noncanonical—writing at various times over the early modern period. Thin description thus looks first to aggregate evidence, to gather available information before coming to any conclusions about the culture toward which that evidence may gesture. Where thick description searches for a telling anecdote that can be used to represent larger issues and things, thin description seeks to amass evidence for its pronouncements about culture. Where a thick description begins the process of interpretation with a provocative detail, thin description first tries to "place" details in as large a context as possible. I will explore other aspects of thin description. Before I do so, however, I wish to reiterate that I am not advancing thin description as a substitute for thick description but rather as a critical genre complementary to it. We have learned too much from thick description to abandon it, or even to wish to do so; instead, we need to modify its role to better address the fullness of culture in the literary texts we study.

Problems with thick description could be boiled down to one word: "extensiveness." As we have seen, thick description replaces extensiveness of evidence with intensiveness of analysis. Geertz's critics in anthropology would say that thick description chooses qualitative over quantitative analysis. I believe that "extensiveness" better represents what remains at issue for thick description in the cultural study of literature; unlike anthropologists, literary critics have little by way of quantitative cultural analysis over and against which to measure the benefits and shortcomings of thick description. And while extensiveness thus offers a pointed challenge to thick description, it also remains an overarching category under which other reservations may be advanced. The following paragraphs set out some of my reservations concerning thick description under the three-part rubric of "Representativeness," "Quantity," and "Otherness." While I explore those reservations, I discuss features of a practice of thin description that could supplement our thickly descriptive cultural criticism.

REPRESENTATIVENESS

In its very trajectory the essay "Why Does Puck Sweep?" illustrates thick description. We saw that Wall's essay begins with a sweeping broom; its closing words, "the cultural imagination," affirm the telescoping process inherent to thick description. How do we get from a broom to a culture? Thick description commonly begins with small things and works, synecdochically, toward larger things—primary among them "culture." We could take a motto for thick description from Vergil's *Eclogues: sīc parvis componére magna sŏlēbam* (thus it was my habit to compare great things to small ones). To get thick description right, we should reverse the order here, beginning with *parva* rather than *magna*, for, almost by definition, thick description reads from small to large.

Traditionally, such analysis has occurred through the critical anecdote, a device that has come under considerable scrutiny in the past two decades.[38] Of the new historicism's penchant for the strategically deployed anecdote, Carolyn Porter asks: "If anecdotes cannot historicize . . . [,] what is their function in these analyses?"[39] I would wager that Porter knew the answer to this question before she asked it. New historicism uses anecdotes to make us feel that we know more than we actually do, to convey the feeling that a chapter or essay has captured "the real," and, perhaps most of all, to persuade us that the quaint or puzzling or violent situation indicated by the anecdote is representative of the larger culture—at the very least, of energies, themes, or tensions central to the culture of which it is a part. It is hard to say whether anecdotes like those the new historicism has employed have addicted critics to synecdoche or whether they are merely symptomatic of that addiction. Whatever the case, our interests in culture have combined with our training in literature to have us read culture and literature synecdochically, as possessing a "relationship of convertibility."[40] Almost by definition cultural criticism tends to move from small to large and to make generalizations about extensive matters by reading intensively.

One may be skeptical about such a relationship. Given the constraints of the essay form, it is almost impossible for thick description to demonstrate the reality of the connections it posits among various cultural issues, objects, actors, and practices. Absent such demonstrations, we may choose to question the importance placed on the anecdote or object. When is a broom just a broom? A basket just a basket? A hat just a hat? When is an exorcism a marginal thing, even an aberration, rather than an indispensable event by means of which one may understand a culture? When is transvestitism an exceptional rather than a typical or profoundly symbolic activity?

Readers of thick descriptions can have difficulty answering these questions, for thick descriptions—rather, the critics writing those descriptions—often are attracted to alluring anecdotes as a means of compelling their readers' interests, and usually decline to contextualize these entertaining anecdotes.[41] As Greenblatt confesses, "built into the new anecdotal process" is a combination of the anecdote's inherent attraction and the critic's ability to capitalize on that attraction: "one made good on one's choice by an act of will, or rather by an act of writing, an act of interpretation whose power was measured by its success in captivating readers."[42] The "scene" of thick description thus permits of many analogies. In some ways, for instance, thick descriptions seem like docents' lectures delivered to enraptured audiences before curious canvases in out-of-the-way museum corners.[43] Such an analogy captures the rhetoric of expertise and authority common to thick descriptions, as well as the obliging attention lent by their audiences. In presupposing a "given" and aesthetic object, however, the analogy misses the mark; thick descriptions routinely introduce the unusual, if not the unknown. Perhaps a better analogy would be to the more homely example of a particular literary genre. Wedded to the captivating opening, that is, thick descriptions may be said to possess the generic structure of the detective story. In thick description, as in the classic detective story, an unusual event or object introduces a mystery. The critic in thick description functions as the story's detective and narrator. When the police raid a cockfight in Bali, when an exorcism takes place, when we are introduced to a hat or a broom that had seemed ordinary but does so no longer, we want to hear the rest of the story, the solution to the mystery. We do not mind, therefore, being informed along the way that the story we are hearing is about much more than a cockfight, exorcism, hat, or broom. With thick description we "sign on" to a detective story and get a cultural analysis in the bargain.

The solution to the mystery of thick description's anecdote invites us to assume a larger relevance to the case at hand. The case implicitly becomes representative of the culture of which it is a part—at the very least, of highly significant aspects of that culture. In chapter 1 we saw Christopher Pye's skepticism over the "representative" and his eschewing of "empirical sampling" as a method of cultural inquiry. I pointed out that Pye does not account for his reluctance over these issues, and it is perhaps not hard to see why: While thick description relies on the implication of representativeness, it gets to the representative through intuition rather than aggregation and through narration rather than demonstration. As Geertz's critics in anthropology have been only too eager to point out, thick description remains a literary rather than a scientific methodology.

The aesthetic demands on the anecdote suggest that the primary debt it must pay is to the literary structure of the critical essay rather than to the culture of which it is a part. The demand to be captivating can therefore call into question the anecdote's stated function as representative item. Can an anecdote serve two masters well? Such a divided allegiance asks us to consider the relevance, for our understanding of thick description, of a popular legal adage: "Hard cases make bad law" (sometimes "Bad cases make bad law"). The larger context of the legal opinion from which this famous saying derives reads as follows: "Great cases like hard cases make bad law. For great cases are called great, not by reason of their real importance in shaping the law of the future, but because of some accident of immediate overwhelming interest which appeals to the feelings and distorts the judgment. These immediate interests exercise a kind of hydraulic pressure which makes what previously was clear seem doubtful, and before which even well settled principles of law will bend."[44] Legal tradition takes this maxim to refer to situations in which cases that, by precedent and legal reasoning, should be decided one way produce divergent results owing to what the justice calls here "some accident of immediate overwhelming interest which appeals to the feelings and distorts the judgment." Extrinsic factors (such as, for instance, the celebrity of plaintiff or defendant, the emotion or prejudice of judge or jurors) thus shape laws that stand to affect others in situations that lack those extrinsic factors. What the adage means by "bad law," therefore, is a legal code that derives from an unusual situation being applied to more typical ones. The "representative anecdotes" of thick description can be said to resemble "great" and "hard" cases in law in that they bring into play a range of extrinsic factors that can impressionistically—rather than rationally—shape our perceptions of a larger culture.

What claims can reason make on thick description? To begin with, thick descriptions prompt the questions Nelson Goodman posed in *Ways of Worldmaking* when he discussed the "fair sample": "What constitutes rightness or wrongness of . . . exemplification? When is a sample right?" Goodman's answer here involves the "projectibility" of the sample over the larger set from which the sample has been taken: "A sample fair in this sense is one that may be rightly projected to the pattern or mixture or other relevant feature of the whole or of further samples. Such fairness or projectibility, rather than requiring or guaranteeing agreement between the projection made and an actual feature of the whole or of further samples, depends on conformity to good practice in interpreting samples—that is, both in proceeding from sample to feature in question and in determining whether that feature is projectible."[45] To illustrate his point, Goodman gives us five boxes featuring equally sized representations of fabric swatches "cut from a bolt." The "material" in question consists of a series of parallel bars of varying widths and patterns separated by unprinted material. Because each of the five swatches is "cut out" at a different angle and location on the represented material, only one of the boxes (what Goodman would call a "fair sample") shows enough material for us to project what the whole bolt of fabric may look like (that is, it contains the whole of one set of bars and enough of another to suggest the larger pattern). And although—even within the fiction of the example—we could not know for certain what the entire bolt looked like, the box with the most information suggests invidiously that the other four samples provide inadequate if not misleading representations of the whole.

The lesson for thick description here concerns what Goodman calls "projectibility"—that is, the anecdotes and objects on which thick description relies have more than a narrative obligation to fulfill. Ideally, the critic who deploys them should work to ensure that the "thick" in thick description is not just a qualifier relating to his or her own stylistic powers. These anecdotes and objects should be verifiably "thick" with culture. Yet this is hardly an easy thing. How do we know when our anecdotes and objects can be safely projected as adequate representations of a larger entity? As "fair samples" of a whole?

QUANTITY

When Goodman cites "projectibility" as the basis for determining whether a sample is "fair," his very choice of words implies a particular understanding of culture. At the root of the verb *project* is the Latin *pro* + *iacere*, "to throw outward." We understand the force of the word, of course, in thinking about "projecting" a film, or statistical "projections"; for instance, of moving something outward (beams of light, numbers) from a definite point. To speak of "projectibility" in cultural inquiry is to describe a process by which we extrapolate what lies "outward" from the smaller sample we know. Importantly, it is also to lend a spatial dimension to that whole from which the sample is taken. Understanding an entity this way—whether a bolt of cloth or a culture—makes an enormous difference to the ways in which we imagine and analyze that entity.

Here it could be argued that thick description's sense of culture as a "web" provides us just such a spatialized metaphor; the web of culture, that is, extending outward in all directions. Yet I believe that the web's long and intersecting threads actually provide a more accurate metaphor of the narrative lines of thick description than of the culture and cultural phenomena that thick description purports to represent. In the thick description essay, the critic follows out one thread here, makes a right turn there, and travels at will along an intricate network of narrative possibilities. One thing that gets left out, however, is the size and shape of the web, for we are never told by thick description of the cultural web's circumference, design, its number of threads, or the distances and gaps between various of its elements. (Arachnologists, after all, will testify that there are many different kinds and shapes of webs.) Granted, a culture may be so vast and intricate a thing that only an estimate is possible. But thick description does not provide such estimates. We are asked to take on faith that culture *is* a web and to trust the thick description to navigate a representative portion of that web in an enlightening and responsible manner. In the end, therefore, the "web" of culture remains primarily a convenient metaphor for thick description; its convenience resides in the critic's never having to represent the culture from outside, or as a whole.

To invoke the "projectible," in contrast, is to understand culture as something that must be represented from outside, even as a region to be mapped. And although, as anyone who has glanced at an early modern map can attest, maps are about more than numbers, the quantification of distance through scale has long been an integral part of the science of mapmaking. How does quantification come into play in cultural analysis? To begin with, we could note that Goodman's representation of the "fair sample" involved five samples taken from an imaginary bolt of cloth. Had the pattern been closer together—say, a bolt of dotted cloth or gingham—fewer samples might have been required to obtain a "fair" sample. Had the pattern been, in contrast, more dispersed or intricate—a bolt, say, of paisley or tie-dyed cloth—more, perhaps many more, samples could be required. It is important here to recognize that Goodman's illustration depends on regularity in the examined material—in short, on its *pattern*. This notion of pattern remains central to any definition of culture. Raymond Williams has argued, for instance, that "it is with the discovery of patterns of a characteristic kind that any useful cultural analysis begins, and it is with the relationships between these patterns, which sometimes reveal unexpected identities and correspondences in hitherto separately considered activities, sometimes again reveal discontinuities of an unexpected kind, that general cultural analysis is concerned."[46] Williams makes a useful point here: asserting the existence of patterns in a culture—even defining culture through those very patterns—does not entail that we ignore "discontinuities" to those patterns. Neither should it mean, I wish to add, that we take norms or traditions for the "whole" of any culture. But at the same time, as Williams reminds us, the beginning of cultural analysis resides in *discovering* patterns. And it is thin description, rather than thick description, that provides us with our best tool for such discovery.

Thin description is good at revealing patterns in part because it embraces quantification as a useful tool. Where thick description likes to "taste" things and tell stories about them based on a small sample—the sometimes overelaborate rhetoric of wine-tasting seems an almost inescapable analogy here—thin description seeks to obtain as wide a sampling as possible before making pronouncements about culture. A culture, after all, is less like a largely uniform bottle of wine than it is like a banquet; cultures are likely to have varied tastes and consistencies. For this reason wide sampling—aggregation rather than hasty extrapolation—remains key to thin description. Such aggregation does not necessarily discredit thick description or call its interpretations into question. But gathering a great deal of evidence can, at the very least, help provide a meaningful context to the interpretations of thick description.

If thin description is indeed useful this way, why do we not encounter it more often in cultural studies of Shakespeare and early modern literature? Why has thick description proved so popular, that is, and thin description so rare? Sometimes the labor required by thin description seems to explain why it is performed less often than thick description. Thin description involves counting, and casting one's net as widely as possible. Doing this can appear, to critics, to be less rewarding than "close reading" a detail or anecdote that has already caught one's attention and seems in need of explanation. For an instance where the potential labor of thin description seems to have prevented a critic from recognizing its rewards, I would offer a quotation from a less recent work of criticism; the following passage evinces a profound skepticism concerning any extensive knowledge of a historical culture: "We cannot turn ourselves into Elizabethans; we should not fool ourselves by thinking we can. Even if we could, we should still have to ask which Elizabethans, for *Hamlet* cannot have meant the same thing to Burleigh as to Burleigh's cook, or to Jonson the poet and critic as to Gresham the merchant."[47] The critic here is Madeleine Doran, in *Endeavors of Art*. Doran is a formalist interested in literary history, and her book was published in 1964. But in this claim she could well speak for any of a number of current critics who are skeptical of totalizing images of culture.

To many critics today, culture is variety, whether national, linguistic, behavioral, or textual. Emphasis, in criticism, on the multiplicity of national identities (and complexity within these very identities), on the variety of religious, political, and sexual orientations and choices obtaining in the period, and on the numerous versions of various texts (including, famously, *Hamlet* [1601] and *King Lear*)—to name only a few subjects whereby variety has become a hallmark of culture—signals a profound change in the way we define culture.[48] In place of homogeneity and likeness, we look to acknowledge heterogeneity and difference. In the passage just quoted, Doran acknowledges the claim of variety and rightly insists on the forbidding complexity of early modern culture by making the simple observation that such a text as *Hamlet* would have meant various things to various readers. In her choice of texts Doran reminds us of Gabriel Harvey's sociological assertion—made during Shakespeare's own lifetime—that "The younger sort takes much delight in Shakespeare's Venus, & Adonis: but his Lucrece, & his tragedie of Hamlet, Prince of Denmarke, haue it in them, to please the wiser sort."[49] Like Harvey, Doran recognizes various groups, even strata, within early modern society; these groups would almost certainly have responded to literary texts in quite varied ways.

Yet in pointing out the existence of various kinds of early modern readers—a politician, a cook, a poet and critic, a merchant—Doran does not obviate inquiry as to their possible responses to *Hamlet* so much as she describes how large and formidable a task that inquiry would be. That is, in starting to list the various kinds of readings that *Hamlet* could garner, she begins a cultural catalog that would by definition remain unfinished and hence partial, but whose usefulness—even as an unfinished document—could well outweigh the partial picture it gives us.[50] I have called this list—"Burleigh . . . Burleigh's cook . . . Jonson the poet and critic . . . Gresham the merchant"—a "cultural catalog" but I could also call it a thin description. In beginning to pile up and enumerate various cultural actors, Doran—again, like Harvey nearly four centuries before her—asks us to see culture as an entity whose complexity is best understood, at the start of one's inquiry, through aggregation. Today we would notice certain signal absences from Doran's list, including, among other groups, women, middle-class citizens, and those outside of London. Despite these omissions, however, Doran's question—"which Elizabethans[?]"—licenses us to recognize that this kind of answer must be obtained, whatever the effort, should we wish to assert a "cultural" relevance to our findings. In terms of the question at hand, it is a desire not to "turn ourselves into Elizabethans" but rather to understand what kinds of responses Elizabethans had, and were likely to have had. To gain such an understanding, we must ask ourselves how many Elizabethans there were, as well as where and how they lived, and begin from there to draw our own map of Elizabethan culture. Thin description helps us to address the question of representativeness by providing grounds for estimating what happened or existed with regularity and/or extension in a given culture.

OTHERNESS

The process of accumulating as much evidence as possible—of aggregating material—puts us in a better position to evaluate cultures than thick description does. It helps us with cultural study not only by "mapping" the culture in question but by revealing varieties and tendencies within that culture. Some could argue that thin description lacks glamour and endorses drudgework for its own sake. Others may offer that it unnecessarily forestalls the act of interpretation crucial to any analysis. But the benefits of thin description more than compensate for the labor involved. In fact, thin description can help to address one of thick description's most profound, and least acknowledged, weaknesses: thick description's tendency to bypass, ignore, even suppress other issues and elements of the culture in question. Thick description focuses so quickly and with so much intensity that its "close-up" can miss other things in the scene. We can perceive one version of this oversight at the very beginning of the thick description essay, for it appears in the method's reluctance to acknowledge "otherness" in the critic's own field.

We have seen that thick description takes one of its strengths from style. The stylized voice of a critic leading us toward the solution of a kind of cultural "mystery" with confidence and intelligence remains among thick description's most attractive aspects. A colleague of mine once privately referred to Stephen Greenblatt as "an extraordinarily talented creative writer"—a remark intended, clearly, to point out the power of Greenblatt's prose even as it called into question the genre of his criticism. However sardonic, this characterization holds some truth when we assess thick description alongside traditional modes of academic writing. By "traditional" here I refer to a model of research that takes seriously scholarly conversations about a particular topic—the kind of research, that is, that begins with a statement of the topic, reviews the critical bibliography on that topic (or, where such does not exist, demonstrates a lacuna in critical discourse), and makes apparent one's differences from existing conclusions about the topic at hand.

Thick descriptions often pay their scholarly "dues," as it were, by citing relevant scholarship as the essay's argument unfolds. But as we saw in the "Deep Play" essay, and as is evident in many thick descriptions in early modern studies, there is in thick description a temptation to defer the payment of such dues, to place acknowledgment of others—where it is made at all—conveniently out of the way in notes. The attraction of thick description becomes clearer in this context. Traditional academic beginnings can seem quite mechanical and do not provide critics with the freedom they need for expressive writing. The routine of conventional citation—"I am interested in X topic; critics have said Y about it; I assert Z"—quite literally gets in the way of a good story. Thick description's good stories provide a great deal of pleasure to writers and readers. What brings much less pleasure is the scholarly template that involves citation of authorities on one's topic. Yet however formulaic the routine of declaring one's topic, the practice of acknowledging others' positions and stating clearly one's own position has a role larger than that of associational genuflection. It forces one's primary descriptions to be not of an anecdote or object but of both the research problem that one is addressing and the research conclusions that others have made. In describing a hat or an exorcism at the beginning of an essay, for instance, a critic makes a choice (conscious or otherwise) not to acknowledge others who have labored to reach conclusions about a problem or topic. The thick describer is thereby willing to participate in critical discourse, but mainly as someone who wishes solely to be heard. Because storytellers like to hold the floor, thick description somewhat uneasily accommodates itself to larger scholarly conversations.

The trade-off that readers are forced to make when confronted by thick descriptions is clear though rarely discussed. What we gain with thick descriptions is a more entertaining form of scholarship; thick description is, again, more elegant and playful than much research written in a conventional style. Further, its emphasis on interpretation can produce genuine insights into cultural materials both familiar and unfamiliar. Its defenders could argue that new historicism brings the past to life. But what readers lose with thick description is a sense of what thick descriptions "add up" to. That is, thick descriptions tend to be heavily satisfying and self-contained narratives (satisfying in part because they are so self-contained), but that satisfaction usually begins and ends with the prose of the thick description itself. Because the critics in question typically decline to "place" their remarks in relationship to an established conversation, what we hear are pleasant solos whose echoes soon fade.

Thick description has weaknesses that extend beyond questions of scholarly community and endeavor. The narrative impulse of thick description, for instance, can affect interpretation by blinding critics to other possibilities inherent in the cultural materials they take up. An extreme instance of this occurred with the hat that Stephen Greenblatt used for the beginning of his essay "Resonance and Wonder." Greenblatt's essay commences with a description of the hat and gives us a summary of the hat's provenance as related in a note card accompanying the hat in its display case. In a notorious review of the book in which this essay appeared, however, Anne Barton cited Greenblatt's version of the story told in that note card and then herself provided a summary of the story the note card in question actually tells. In contrast to Greenblatt's account, in which the note card relates a sparsely detailed story that allows one to speculate that the hat may have been Cardinal Wolsey's own, Barton points out that the note card provides a quite detailed account of the hat's provenance that does not support Greenblatt's speculations. For a variety of reasons, the story the note card actually tells is much less interesting than the mainly allegorical version that Greenblatt presents. In place of his broad-brushed narrative, for instance, the note card offers a very specific and somewhat boring story; this less interesting account undercuts the mythology retailed in "Resonance and Wonder," and disappointingly so. As Barton relates, "The elegance with which Greenblatt accommodates Wolsey's hat to a story about how the Reformation tried to dismantle the 'histrionic apparatus of Catholicism' by selling off papist vestments to the professional players makes one almost regret having to disturb it with the specificities of [the actual narrative on the note card]."[51] Barton's "regret" aptly captures the disappointment that can result when scholarly "otherness," whether in terms of citation or counterfactual details, intrudes on the leisurely narrative spell woven by thick description.

Although a man mistaking the facts of a hat provides what may seem an exceptional instance of thick description's tendency to pull critics into particular stories at the expense of other stories that could be considered, the very structure of thick description arguably promotes the quick occlusion of alternative possibilities. As readers, we are dropped down into a particular time, place, and topic by means of a thick description's controlling anecdote or object. So sudden and decisive is the beginning that we may not notice what we have given up merely by accepting the critic's narrative contract.

Critics also can lose out in this bargain by not noticing details or possibilities that do not square with the stories they intend to tell. This occlusion of alternative possibilities occurs in "Why Does Puck Sweep?" As I mentioned before, Wall begins with a little-noticed reference, by Puck, to sweeping. In a pattern characteristic of thick descriptions, Wall's essay begins with a detail and moves outward from it to larger issues in the culture at hand. Her prose, like the prose of any good thick description, makes not only the choice of detail but its explication seem natural. Why indeed should a fairy in a play "concerned with the grand affairs of state" invoke such a "homey image"? Why, at any rate, should "the mischievous Puck play the role of housewife?" Given the now-puzzling nature of the detail that Wall has focused on—a detail made puzzling, of course, through that very focus—we wish to have the mystery solved.

As I said before, Wall's solution to the mystery is smart and enlightening, and her notes responsibly take into account (as many thick descriptions do not) the wealth of research connected with its topic: fairylore in two of Shakespeare's comedies, in particular, and in early modern England generally. She gathers evidence from a variety of sources to show how fairies served as "magical footnotes to the materiality of the house" in many early modern writings.[52] But in making the initial association between Puck's sweeping and house-wifery—later she will call this reference Puck's "housewifely gesture at the play's end," and a subsequent section of the essay is titled "The Return of the Repressed Wife"—Wall quickly passes by possibilities that would change (although not discredit) the story she tells.[53]

One of these possibilities has to do with a history that many would call "literary" before calling it "social," although it happens to be both. By this I mean the admittedly mysterious history of the English Mummers' play, which, though recorded in textual form relatively late, may have existed in various forms before and during the Elizabethan period.[54] One of the tropes of the Mummers' play involved a figure speaking directly to the audience about sweeping. In a surviving play from Cinderford, Gloucestershire, the stage devil closes out the dramatic action with the following:

> *Beelzebub.* In comes I old Beelzebub and on my shoulder carries a nub and in my hand a dripping pan. Do you think I'm not a jolly old man?
> *This one walks in with a broom and sweeps round the room and says*
> . . . Money I want and money I crave:
> If you don't give us some money I will sweep you all to the grave.[55]

In another text, it is another devil figure who utters these ceremonial words:

> In come I, Little Devil Doubt
> If you don't give me money
> I'll sweep you all out.[56]

Such devils invoke sweeping at the ends of their plays as a ritualistic way of indicating the gathering up of money and the ordering of the performance space. When we remember that the term "mummer" appears to have originated in the practice of children with blacked faces ritualistically sweeping hearths in small towns and villages, the potential relevance of this folk genre to Puck's sweeping becomes clear.

Yet in rushing to identify sweeping with female labor, and the scene of sweeping with the domestic household, Wall—in a manner that departs from the sensitivity she has shown to issues of gender in previous research—overlooks other sweepers and another kind of house that would have been important to such an actor, playwright, and shareholder as Shakespeare. Sweeping was not confined to women in early modern England, nor is it so strongly gendered in Shakespeare's plays. As *The Taming of the Shrew* (1592) reminds us, a household that appears composed entirely of male servants still has a way of ensuring that its cobwebs are "swept" before the newlyweds' arrival (4.1.46–47). And Jack Cade describes himself as the broom that will remove corruption in the court when he declares, to the Lord Say, "I am the besom that must sweep the court clean of such filth as thou art" (*2 Henry VI* [1590] 4.7.32). "Besom," or broom, is a nonce-word in Shakespeare's plays, and we may feel initially that, to make his point, Cade is appropriating an item from the realm of Wall's "housewifery." Thus sweeping would be, to Cade, merely a metaphor borrowed from a world of female work he has only observed. Yet the play tells us that Cade is one of a number of "handicrafts-men" involved in the rebellion; this number includes a tanner, a butcher, a weaver, and, in Cade's case, a "shearman" (4.2.11; 21–28; 133). As "handicrafts-men," they can be expected to have labored in, where they did not own, workplaces that needed sweeping. A text from 1590, *Tarlton's News out of Purgatory*—mock published, interestingly enough, by "*an old Companion of his* [that is, Tarlton's], *Robin Goodfellow*"—testifies to this necessary act of maintenance in speaking of "a dirty malkin [that is, mop], such as Bakers sweep their Ovens withall."[57] We can assume that, when it was not done by bakers or shearmen, such sweeping often fell to the lowest-ranked members of these and other venues, the apprentices and servants.

We hear of men sweeping in a wide variety of early modern plays, from the "Broomeman" in Chapman's *The Gentleman Usher* (1602), to various references in Jonson's dramatic works. In *The Devil is an Ass* (1616), for instance, Fitzdottrell remarks that "I have one servant, / Who is my all, indeed; and, from the broom / Unto the brush: for, just so far, I trust him" (1.3.1012). Likewise, in a passage from *The Alchemist* (1610) cited by Wall, Subtle claims that he has rescued Face from a position of household drudge: "Thou vermin, have I ta'en thee, out of dung / So poor, so wretched, when no living thing / Would keep thee company, but a spider, or worse? / Rais'd thee from brooms, and dust, and wat'ring pots?" (1.1.64–67). Unlike London servants generally—where Face would be in a demographic added to significantly by numerous female servants—the metropolis's apprentices were, at this time, an overwhelmingly and perhaps exclusively male group.[58] Thus in *Henry VIII* (1613), when an anonymous character is describing a riot of apprentices, he not inappropriately invokes brooms in gauging the distance that stood between him and these apprentices: "They fell on, I made good my place; at length they came to th' broom-staff to me . . ." (5.3.53–55). Wall's analysis misses the possibility that Puck embodies something other than female labor, including the generalized (and perhaps unlocalized) labor of servants and apprentices. Why has she overlooked these male sweepers? Thick description's habits of quick, close, and intense focus may have led Wall here to accept a stereotype about the gender of work; instead of beginning with a general question about sweeping, she begins with an anecdote of a sweeper in order to move rapidly to another topic. The result, as with the hat in Greenblatt's essay, is that the real shapes of the alluring object get lost in the shuffle.

Yet Puck's sweeping could have a more specific valence. The playhouses in which *A Midsummer Night's Dream* was performed would of course need to be swept—the stage itself as well as the areas behind and before it. We should stop to ask, therefore: Who swept the early modern playhouses? Absent firm evidence, it is perhaps safe to assume that the assignment of such a menial task may have varied from year to year and from company to company. In Ben Jonson's induction to *Bartholomew Fair* (1614), it is an adult "stage-keeper" who is apparently assigned that task; as the Book-holder upbraids him: "Your judgement, Rascal? for what? sweeping the stage? or gathering up the broken apples for the bears within?" (Ind. 51–53). Elsewhere we hear that boys performed labor like this. In *Cynthia's Revels* (1600), for instance, Jonson has Cupid similarly upbraid Mercury for being "a lackey, that runs on errands for him [that is, Jove], and can whisper a light message to a loose wench with some round volubility, wait mannerly at a table with a trencher, and warble upon a crowd a little, fill out nectar, when Ganymede's away, one that sweeps the gods' drinking room every morning, and sets the cushions in order again . . ." (1.1.23–29). Jonson's play was acted in 1600 by the boys at Paul's, and the mythological veneer of the drama does little to disguise the metatheatrical interests announced by its own induction. Like one of these boy actors, Puck is a "lackey" given the task of sweeping the room: "*I am sent* with broom before . . ." We could note that Puck does not sweep out of any internal, household-centered impulse, but because he has been ordered to do so. Just as Ariel in *The Tempest* (1611) frequently reminds us of the status of the boy actor in the early modern theater, Puck may be seen as calling up a similar set of associations within the world of *A Mid-summer Night's Dream*.[59] Even where such a connection was not assumed, however, there would have been the unmistakable reality—given a performance in a commercial playhouse—of a structure that, like the household but not identical to it, also had doors and floors that needed to be swept.

Of course, nothing in the potential relationship of Puck's character to boy actor and the material edifice of the playhouse makes Wall's remarks about fairylore in early modern England untrue. Nor does the certainty that apprentices and servants of both sexes also swept. But such possibilities could change the implications of Wall's story; certainly they would enrich it. Together, they ask us to see the telescoping tendency of thick description as a pleasurable but problematic way of getting to "the cultural" in early modern literature.

The image of the telescope here betrays the fact that the preceding discussion has made more than occasional recourse to visual metaphors. The language of film, in particular, has helped structure some of my claims about thick description and cultural criticism. On the face of it, this fact may appear unremarkable. Concepts like "focus" and the "close-up" seem almost unavoidable when we wish to portray what we do when we examine (the phrase "look at" actually comes easiest here) cultural objects and issues. It is beyond the ability of this book, of course, to address the influence of the cinema and cinematic phenomena on the practice and rhetoric of criticism. But for various reasons—primary among which is thick description's own reliance on metaphors of visuality and focus—I believe that we can learn from even a brief consideration of cultural criticism's similarities to film.

Given an analogy whereby we take seriously such metaphors as "focus" and the "close-up"—an analogy, that is, of the thickly descriptive essay to a short film—what kind of insights can we draw? To answer this question, we could begin by taking up quasi-filmic techniques employed by thick and thin description, respectively. It is perhaps advantageous here to start with the latter, as thin description finds its most familiar double in an early and groundbreaking Shakespeare film, Laurence Olivier's 1944 production of *Henry V* (1599). The moment in question is the famous opening shot, a description of which I quote from the published screenplay: "*We see an aerial view of London, based on Visscher's engraving of 1600. Track back to show the City in long shot, then track in on the Bear Playhouse and then on to the Globe Playhouse, where a flag is being hoisted.*"[60] As those who have seen the film can attest, this description barely hints at the ingenuity and effect of what one sees in the film itself. Nothing in this version of *Henry V* has proven as memorable as this exhilarating opening shot, a shot neatly reversed in the closing moments of the film: "*Now dissolve to a long shot of London in 1600. The words: THE END: fade in and out of the sky above the city. The music stops.*" Olivier's camera here and at the film's beginning pointedly contextualizes an imaginary production of *Henry V* with what appears to be the Globe Playhouse's bustling urban environment.

What Olivier's production gives us in these "long shots" of early modern London can be analogized to an early version of thin description. In particular, these aerial views are an emergent version of what critical thin description means to provide in its emphasis on extensiveness. Just as thin description looks toward quantity rather than quality as its first line of interpretation, so does the long shot of "London" from above seek to place its object (the Globe Playhouse) within a large and dynamic context. In this way, these aerial shots from the 1944 *Henry V* are analogous also to the early, and inadequate, thin descriptions of a well-known British publication from the year before the film's release, E. M. W. Tillyard's *The Elizabethan World Picture* (1943). Tillyard's study of an intellectual and political paradigm he believed was omnipresent in Shakespeare's time gives us, like Olivier's aerial shots, a "background" against which to situate literature—in Tillyard's case, Elizabethan literature generally; in Olivier's, a production of a single Shakespeare play and the history it contains. The benefits of these long shots seem apparent: They help us to evaluate better the place and larger role of particular objects that we are interested in; their encompassing scope lets us perceive systems at work (a busy city, culture, or polity).

Their drawbacks are equally apparent. In stressing context over the particularities of content, these long shots flatten out and even erase details. In terms of Olivier's film, for example, we can tell little about the city in question save that it *is* a city until we get closer. In terms of the critical work, the familiar example here is Tillyard's citation of Ulysses' speech on order and degree from *Troilus and Cressida* (1602). Tillyard invokes this speech from a distance, as it were, without bothering to mention the speaker's cunning nature or instrumental purpose in uttering it—things known to readers and audience members "closer in" to the play. What was important to Tillyard was describing the speech as exemplary, putting it alongside similar statements concerning order and hierarchy to assemble a "long shot" of what Elizabethans thought.[61] The strength of his abbreviated book actually exposes the weaknesses of this larger and more extensive sense of "culture." *The Elizabethan World Picture*'s wide focus does not allow for the specific textures of things *within* the culture it examines, whether books, people, practices, or beliefs.

As we have seen, thick description tends to begin with close-ups of particular objects—the details that new historicism subsumes under "the anecdote." In Geertz's "Deep Play" essay, again, that anecdote consisted of a concentrated and frenetic event—the raided cockfight in Bali. Thick description shows us detail and lets us see the textures of individual things before we move toward larger frames of analysis. As a filmic example of thick description here, one could offer the various close-ups of action figures that occupy the initial sequence in Julie Taymor's recent version of *Titus Andronicus* (1593), entitled *Titus* (1999). At the beginning of Taymor's film we get a series of close-ups of various action figures that a boy is playing with. As Peter Donaldson argues, *Titus* itself relies heavily on a continuing series of visual tropes surrounding the commercial packaging of these very action figures and their "virtual" environments.[62] What *Titus* uses close-ups of these action figures to do, and what thick description accomplishes by its similar initial focus, is to join the particular to the general, the isolated to the pervasive. In Taymor's *Titus,* the action figures allow also for a progressive connection of things thought to be separate: of juvenile and adult aggressiveness (as well as that of the individual and society), of modern-day violence with that of the distant past, of civilization and barbarism. Thick description affords cultural criticism similar latitude. Whether it lights on a cockfight, an exorcism, a hat, or a sweeping broom, thick description's focus allows critics to establish and concentrate their topics. What follows such concentration is typically a process of editing that, in the cultural-studies essay, leads us from close-up to medium and long shots—from object, that is, to culture—and back again.

What thin description can add to such thick description is a useful context for its examination of detail. Staying within the rhetoric of film, one could say that thick description has left literary studies in need less of "deep play" than of "deep focus." By deep focus here I refer, of course, to the innovative mode of cinematography that, with increasing frequency from the early 1940s, allowed directors to capture foreground and background not sequentially but simultaneously. Familiar from Gregg Toland's remarkable cinematography for *Citizen Kane* (1941), deep focus allowed the camera to pick up various planes—foreground, middle ground, and background—and densely correlate objects within these spaces without editing cut-ins.[63] In contrast to conventionally edited sequences—which, for instance, might have narrated an encounter with a shot/reverse shot pattern—deep focus let viewers see these various planes at the same time and "place" their objects in relationship with one another.

I propose deep focus—and the thin description that can afford it—as an alternative to thick description's artful but sometimes misleading "cutting" from close to long shot. In contrast to traditional scholarship's initial establishment of its topic through a "location shot" representing existing criticism on the matter at hand and gradual progression toward detail by means of signaled steps, thick description begins with a fascinating close shot (a hat, a broom) and, after lingering on its object of attention, cuts quickly to a long shot of the culture as a whole. What thin description can add to our current mode of cultural criticism, therefore, is not only the middle ground that thick description tends to miss but, methodologically, a way of affording cultural details a less forced relationship to their surroundings. Such a *mise en scène* cannot come, of course, "naturally." Nor is it likely to be as pleasurable as thick description's stories. The deep focus that thin description can help to provide will doubtless break the spell of the heavily stylized thick description, and this is, as I have admitted, no minor loss. Yet I believe that it is a necessary loss if we are to pursue a more extensive view of the culture that Shakespeare and early modern literature represent.

As a prelude to the thin descriptions provided in the following chapters, I will say something now that I have not yet said clearly: The "culture" we read in Shakespeare and early modern literature seems largely *literary* culture. In chapter 1 I listed various ways of defining culture and indicated my preference for the extensive sense of culture common in anthropology; culture, that is, as "patterns, explicit and implicit, of and for behavior acquired and transmitted by symbols, constituting the distinctive achievement of human groups, including their embodiment in artifacts; the essential core of culture consists of traditional (i.e., historically derived and selected) ideas and especially their attached values." This definition anticipated and squares with Williams's assertion that cultural analysis must begin with a search for patterns.

As my discussion of thin description may suggest, a preference for this anthropological definition carries over to my thoughts about how to read for the cultural content in literary texts. I think it is important, however, that we do not conflate literature and culture, that we understand the representations of culture in literary texts, as well as the production and consumption of those texts, as inflected by the larger culture of which they are a part but with which they are not identical. Among my reservations about cultural criticism interested in early modern literature is that it sometimes forgets one of the primary ways in which literature is "cultural"—through literature's immediate and material contexts. To forget that literature came into existence in relationship to conventions of form and practice is to miss out on resources that can be important to our criticism even as they were important to the authors composing these texts. For their part, early modern plays were responsible, first, to what many today would call the "cultures" of playwriting and playing—to the business of composing and producing plays in the dynamic industry of the early modern theater.[64] Paul Yachnin has argued that the early modern playhouses comprised a "powerless theater" less interested in polemics than in legitimizing its own existence. In Yachnin's argument, we need to look closely at the interests of those who wrote and performed the plays and at how such interests may have shaped these dramatic texts.[65] Before it takes these plays as tissue samples of early modern English culture, criticism needs to scrutinize the mediating roles of convention and praxis. Things like genre; the shapes of the theatrical scene; the makeup and demands of various acting companies; the competition among rival repertories and theaters; shifting audience demographics; the availability and popularity of various printed "sources" for dramatic plots; the role of venues, performers, shareholders, buildings, audiences, specific historical events, and even individual patrons themselves considered as sources of these plots— these and many other "literary" matters must be considered as important influences on early modern plays. As influences, they do not necessarily come to us prior to, separate from, or in place of the cultural factors that recent criticism has stressed. But they nevertheless have a claim on these plays that cannot be subsumed into a larger, "cultural" interpretation.

As I have argued elsewhere, early modern plays, in particular, are tremendously derivative and composite documents, works that draw on a host of "sources"—social and textual alike—for their quiltlike composition.[66] We risk misunderstanding literature of all kinds when we ignore literature's composite nature. When thick description focuses on one detail, for instance, it can lead us to ignore the countless others that could be adduced. Further, when thick description emphasizes the synchronic, we lose out on the diachronic richness works contain. A thick description of *Hamlet* in terms of only the culture of 1600 - 1601 may have us forget that Shakespeare's drama itself seems to have been a revision of an earlier Hamlet play, that both plays participated in the new popularity of revenge tragedy, that this newly popular genre drew heavily on the Latin tragedies of Seneca emphasized anew in the Elizabethan grammar schools, that these schools flourished during the educational "boom" of Tudor England, and so forth.

Even in its brevity, this receding genealogy reminds us that literature is thoroughly cultural—shaped, as it is, by cultural factors. Yet a large part of literature's cultural aspect derives from elements of its production, including, importantly, other books. Genre, conventions, tropes, icons, stock characters, familiar themes and stories: All these and more contribute to what literature is. Insofar as such items are cultural, literature is indeed an extremely cultural thing. To the extent, however, that such things indicate patterns and assumptions that are more germane to highly particularized modes of expression—the epic, the lyric, revenge tragedy—than to verbal expressions generally, they ask us to consider whether any inquiry dedicated to reading the culture in literary texts can proceed without first assessing the very literary culture in and behind those texts. An intensively "literary" mode itself, thick description is good not only at entertaining readers, but also at persuading them that the anecdote has cultural extensiveness that exceeds its trivial appearance. It has been the aim of this chapter to demonstrate that this literary mode of analysis is quite partial, and, despite the *theatrum mundi* trope, that such partiality also characterizes literary representation itself. The thin descriptions of the chapters in the next section of this book attempt to show how we can more responsibly address the external culture in literary texts by first tracing the extensiveness of the internal, literary structures and vocabularies that shape its representations of the world outside its pages.

PART II

EARLY MODERN LITERARY CULTURE

CHAPTER 3

THE STRUCTURAL TRANSFORMATION OF PRINT IN LATE ELIZABETHAN ENGLAND

A thin description of early modern literature could characterize it simply as extremely personal in nature. During the closing years of the sixteenth century, in particular, English books became remarkably thick with the personal. It is now usual, of course, to evaluate literary works of this period in relationship to the self; "personal" in criticism concerned with the self typically refers to a new interest in subjectivity and inwardness.[1] Yet beyond this narrow conception of personal selfhood lies a more expansive personalism, one that unfolded textually in the production of books across various modes. From controversial pamphlets to Ovidian erotica, and from *à clef* poems to verse satire, an intensively familiar approach to others' bodies and identities—to their *persons* as objects of discourse—became a central feature of late Elizabethan print culture. The strong attraction of personal reference led many writers to ignore Gabriel Harvey's censorious creed of "no Liberty without bounds, nor any Licence without limitation."[2] Whether the liberties that these writers took served political comment, sexual titillation, or social positioning, readers could expect to find everywhere a more sustained and more graphic relationship between book and body. Works like *The Faerie Queene* (1590), *Venus and Adonis* (1593), and *Have With You to Saffron-Walden* (1596) offer familiar instances of this relationship. We could understand the sense of "personal" in such texts as denoting less the self than the "other" and bodies rather than consciousness; it indicates an emphasis on the external, the *trans*personal, and that which is between rather than within.

So widespread was this emphasis, in fact, that the works it affected can be seen as belonging to a developing genre that we could call *embodied writing*.[3] Embodied writing may be defined provisionally as a kind of text and a textual practice that, increasingly during the 1590s, put resonant identities and physical forms on the printed page. By "body" in "em*bodied* writing" I refer to the direct, sensuous, or satirical description of persons; sometimes these constitute descriptions of imaginary bodies and sometimes descriptions of the bodies of actual Elizabethans whose social and political identities proved of concern. Embodied writing aggressively drew real and imaginary figures into print for potentially indecorous handling. This writing often described the body in detail, through graphic treatment of physical appearance and body parts. And where its descriptions could involve such mythological personae as Diana, Ganymede, and Corinna, embodied writing also incorporated real bodies under fictional names. Such names as "Stella," "Horace," and "Vanderhulke," for instance, transparently covered those persons whose identities the social relationships of the texts betrayed. Granting a bodily presence to fictional characters, and a fictional identity to real bodies, this writing mediated the imaginary and the actual in its bodily address.

We are most familiar with embodied writing through its appearance, alternately, in the sensuous, "body-wanting" blazons of erotic verse and in the rough handling of antagonists in satirical works.[4] Dissimilar on the surface, these forms possess a common liberty of expression in relationship to the body, a liberty that characterizes texts of various modes in this period. While instances of embodied writing typically are explained in relationship to classical, Renaissance, and vernacular models—to such forms as Old Comedy, Ovidian narrative, flyting, *effictio,* the *débat,* and the Petrarchan lyric—for a number of reasons late Elizabethan texts share as much with similarly "embodied" works of this time as they do with generic predecessors.[5] Indeed embodied writing was enabled most strongly not by earlier forms, but by the confluence, in the late Elizabethan era, of such factors as the profound reorientation of authority in England following the Reformation; a subsequent and extensive habituation to print; the ambitions of a younger generation of writers eager to ply this familiarity with the printed word; and, perhaps most important, the dynamics of the commercial playhouses, which offered this generation vivid models for the imaginative, and public, representation of persons.

Writing shaped by these forces tended to collapse the traditional distance between bodies and texts and, in doing so, brought about important changes in the cultural status of print. Partly through the agency of the late Elizabethan "best-seller," persons merged with characters, and books became entwined with their authors. These authors more openly addressed others' bodies and identities, borrowing various capabilities from the painter, anatomist, mimic, litigator, and barber surgeon. Readers of the last years of Elizabeth's reign came, in turn, to assume a more intimate connection between person and page. With this change to the general horizon of expectations, a significant, more public discursive venue became available in and through the field of print. Thus what we tend to define primarily as a moment of "golden" or expressive literature emphasizing the self may be better grasped as a period during which literature itself, and print culture generally, underwent a structural change that facilitated the radical expression of otherness. To trace the contours of this shift is to begin to understand not only the role that literature took in the personalization of print but how a new emphasis on the personal in works of the late Elizabethan era articulated a nascent public sphere. By offering a thin description of the era's aggressively embodied writing, therefore, this chapter explores a major transformation to the print culture of Shakespeare's day, a transformation that has important implications for our understanding of the larger culture of early modern England.

The rise of embodied writing was roughly circumscribed by a pair of well-known social dramas. The first of these, the Martin Marprelate controversy, began almost accidentally in the late 1580s and soon escalated into a vitriolic pamphlet war concerning the foundations of power in England.[6] Martinist pamphlets harshly criticized the prevailing form of church government and, as part of their critique, came to attack specific individuals. Before this unlicensed activity was suppressed, its libertine wit had harassed the Elizabethan church and state to such an extent that it formed, in the words of Robert Weimann, the "greatest popular scandal" of the era.[7] The second of these events is the also scandalous "poetomachia," or satire wars, that occupied many poets and playwrights in the years 1598 through 1601. The satire wars took place on stage, in the "War of the Theaters," as well as in formal verse satires and epigrams. These satiric exchanges were punctuated by the notorious "Bishops' Ban" or "Satire Ban" of June 1, 1599, in which the Archbishop of Canterbury and the Bishop of London listed books, some satirical, some obscene, some controversial, some historically oriented, to be variously called in and burned, no more published, or allowed only on strict examination. Although this chapter seeks to demonstrate that the Marprelate controversy and the satire wars actually were part of a continuum, the two events offer useful markers for a period that introduced lasting changes to the relationships among early modern readers, writers, and texts.

The Marprelate controversy bordered the development of embodied writing and strongly influenced it. Where personal invective had always been a staple of controversial writing, flourishing in the Latin polemics of the Reformation, the vernacular nature of the Marprelate publications ushered in a new era of *ad hominem* reference.[8] The sharp goads of Marprelate publications like *Hay any Work for Cooper* (1589) and *An Almond for a Parrot* (1590) made explicit personal address—address with a political purpose—a more likely quantity for writers of fiction. The personal reference surrounding Falstaff/Oldcastle in Shakespeare's *Henry IV* plays (1597) and Broome/Brook in *The Merry Wives of Windsor* (1597), for example, occurred in the abusive, flyting atmosphere the controversial pamphlets had nurtured. With its street-cry title, *Hay any Work* lampoons Thomas Cooper, Bishop of Winchester, and in more than one place engages mocking personal satire: "Parson Gravet, Parson of St. John Pulchre's in London (one of dumb John's boosing mates) will be drunk but once a week. But what then? Good children should take links in a cold morning, and light them at his nose, to see if, by that means, some part of the fire that hath so flashed his sweet face might be taken away. This were their duty, saith T. C., and not to cry 'Red Nose, Red Nose!'"[9] Such address was often as aggressive as it was explicit: The title page of *A Countercuff Given to Martin Junior* (1589) lauds the success of its author's past retorts and "the clean breaking of his staff upon Martin's face."[10] As the gleeful undertone of this phrase and the mocking details concerning William Gravet's red nose suggest, entertainment proved a powerful weapon on both sides of the exchange. In John Dover Wilson's famous characterization, Martin Marprelate was a "disciple both of Calvin and Dick Tarlton"—having learned, that is, from both the religious reformer and the famous Elizabethan clown.[11]

Yet although the controversy would briefly spill over to the popular stages, an even stronger link with the theaters of the 1590s and after came with the loosening of inhibitions regarding personal satire.[12] So customary had personal reference become by the middle of the first decade of the seventeenth century, for instance, that writers saw fit to inoculate their texts against *à clef* interpretations. In the prologue to *All Fools,* published in 1605, George Chapman speaks of the threat of "personal application" in contemporary stage plays.[13]

Likewise, in the epistle prefacing *Volpone,* published two years later, Jonson defensively asks "what publique person" he has provoked, "Where have I been particular? Where personal?"—before indicting those who "care not whose living faces they intrench, with their petulant styles."[14] And Thomas Dekker alludes similarly to dangers associated with embodied writing when *The Gull's Horn-Book* (1609) points to the possibility of a writer "that hath either epigrammed you or hath had a flirt at your mistress, or hath brought either your feather or your red beard or your little legs, etc., on the stage."[15]

Dekker's sentence aligns three experiences: being addressed by an epigram; suffering someone having a "flirt at" one's mistress; and being mocked on stage by actors who represent one's idiosyncrasies. At first glance, these may seem different experiences. They are joined, however, by a manipulative, even threatening relationship to the body. The epigram and stage caricature pose threats to the body of Dekker's gull by representing it elsewhere. Someone who has had a "flirt at" one's mistress has insulted her in an obvious way, threatening one whose reputation would reflect upon the gull.[16] Neither mistress nor gull is secure. For even as the mistress's body appears related to yet dangerously separate from the gull, so does the gull's body seem open to appropriation in both epigram and stage play: It may be flouted on stage with its "red beard" and "little legs, etc." The open nature of the stage made such embarrassment a decidedly public threat. Not coincidentally, therefore, did statements like Dekker's and those of Jonson and Chapman come in the wake of the poetomachia, an episode in which at least two of the former were involved and that not only increased the license that writers took but itself evolved from an earlier social drama. We can draw a direct line, that is, from the *ad hominem* of the Marprelate works to the emetics administered to rival writers in the satire wars of the late 1590s and early 1600s. Horace/Jonson's purge of Crispinus/Marston in *Poetaster* (1601) remains only one of a host of violent literary fantasies that, in seeking to remedy the excesses of identifiable persons, found their immediate models in the turmoil of the Marprelate controversy.

As the Bishops' Ban testified by collocating the satiric, the political, and the erotic, in this genre the importance of the body transcended incidentals of domain and mode. Arguments that hold, variously, that the ban concerned itself primarily with satire, or primarily with erotica, or primarily with controversy miss the point: Covering works of controversy, satire, English history, anti-feminism, and the erotic, the Bishops' Ban addressed works that took liberties with bodies considered either above mention or above certain kinds of mention.[17] Ian Frederick Moulton observes, in this regard, that "works thought of as ribald or licentious were not differentiated from politically subversive or heretical works, but were included in a broad range of material which could seduce the innocent."[18] What most defined this range of material and rendered these texts seductive was an unprecedented openness concerning the body. All the works involved in the ban were seen as transgressive, and they were all transgressive in their embodied familiarity. One could say that the Bishops' Ban "knew" something about the transformation of print culture that we have yet to perceive. During the 1590s, writers and printers alike had experimented with topics and ways of addressing those topics that ignored traditional boundaries, mingling sacred and profane, poetry and politics. Frequently the body itself served as the topic of both statement and objection. For instance, when in his *Virgidemiae* (1597) the protestant Joseph Hall criticized Robert Southwell for his catholic poems, *Mary Magdalen's Funeral Tears* (1594) and *St. Peter's Complaint* (1595), he did so not out of doctrinal differences but on the basis of the alleged profaneness of these poems. What Hall meant to criticize can be seen best, perhaps, in Southwell's Counter-Reformation emphasis on Christ's body. His Peter sensuously blazons Christ's eyes in the manner of a sonneteer of the 1590s: "The matchless eyes matched only each by other / . . . / The eye of liquid pearl, the purest mother"; "These blazing comets, lightning flames of love."[19] Hall objected to Gervase Markham's *The Poem of Poems, or Sion's Muse* (1596) because Markham seemed to make Solomon "a newfound Sonnetist, / Singing his love, the holy spouse of Christ, / Like as she were some light-skirts of the rest."[20] Hall's displeasure here centers on the sheer *familiarity* of Southwell and Markham with their subjects, their lewd and embodied handling of otherwise sacred material.

While Hall assumes that sacred topics should be above the overly personal treatment of literary forms like the blazon, the Marprelate controversy had opened gates that would not soon be closed. Hence Nashe's politically explicit *Almond for a Parrot* gave way, during the 1590s, to his sexually explicit poem, *The Choice of Valentines*. And thus did the mild pornography of works like *Hero and Leander* (1593/98) and *Venus and Adonis* (1593) follow the license of the Marprelate publications by exchanging the political for the erotic. Such erotic writing replaced the pamphlets' antagonists with arousing mythological bodies and the stings of controversial satire with a more playful, if equally licentious and satirical, relationship to the physical. Although these erotic narratives participated in a tradition springing from Ovid's *Metamorphoses*, poems of the 1590s have an explicitness absent from such earlier Ovidian work as Thomas Lodge's *Scilla's Metamorphosis* (1589). One of the reasons for such a difference is the climate of satire that the Marprelate pamphlets had helped to generate. Satirical works accustomed writers and readers to a sadistic treatment of the body that enabled the bolder erotic, even pornographic visions of the 1590s. The "witty subversiveness" of late Elizabethan erotic narratives eventually culminated in John Weever's *Faunus and Melliflora* (1600), which grafts an account of satire's origins onto a conventional erotic story.[21]

We can see this convergence of satire and sexuality in many of these erotic narratives' blazons. Marlowe's poem, for example, is celebrated for its sensual handling of the myth. He enlivens Leander's swim with a description of an amorous Neptune, who, as a god of water, steals kisses from Leander and is said to "dive into the water, and there pry / Upon his breast, his thighs, and every limb, / And up again, and close beside him swim, / And talk of love."[22] Shakespeare's Venus is similarly explicit in her equally notorious self-blazon as a "park" in which Adonis, as deer, can graze upon her mountains, dales, the hills of her lips, or lower, "where the pleasant fountains lie."[23] Of this poem Thomas Freeman wrote, in 1614, "Who list read lust, there's *Venus and Adonis* / True model of a most lascivious lecher."[24] Contemporaries gave support to this assessment by focusing on Venus' explicit blazon when quoting this poem in their works and commonplace books.[25] Although Nashe's own pornographic poem would remain in manuscript, others ventured into print such daringly erotic works as *Pygmalion's Image* (1598) and *Salmacis and Hermaphroditus* (1602), texts whose attraction came as much from the scandal of their bodily address—from their indecorum itself—as from the indecency of the bodies they represented. This liberated approach owed its conditions of possibility both to Marlowe and Shakespeare and to the productive chaos of the Marprelate years before them.

But if the Marprelate controversy served as an instructive episode for writers of this era, such authors as Thomas Nashe and John Lyly—enlisted by the authorities to respond to Martin—demonstrate the contributions that literature made to the rise of embodied writing. Lyly's skills in *à clef* writing had become apparent in such dramas as *Endymion* (1588) and *Midas* (1589), which may have been one reason for his selection as controversialist by the church. Literature of this era was never distinct from surrounding forms, but it offered inflections on the body that others did not. Thus while such *à clef* poems as *Willoby his Avisa* (1594) and *Caltha Poetarum* (1599) evoke real individuals in their allegorical fictions, including individuals at the highest levels of the Elizabethan church and government, they do so with an often-sensual portrayal of the body that readers would not expect in more explicitly political writings. The treatment of the body in such works depends on the hallmark trope of lyric poetry in the late Elizabethan era, the blazon. Along these lines, one could notice Hall's criticism of Markham for resembling a "sonnetist" in his familiar treatment of a decidedly spiritual topic. The mutual influence of, on one hand, such literary forms and devices as the blazon, satire, epigram, and Ovidian epyllion, and, on the other, more traditionally political forms like controversy and libels, prompts us to recognize that embodied writing had a number of textual sources even as it connected various domains through the personal.[26]

This emphasis on the personal within texts was accompanied by significant external changes. During the later Elizabethan era, contemporary authors and their works attained a status they had not before enjoyed; this status, in turn, affected the relationship between person and print as characters, authors, and books became much closer to each other and sometimes interchangeable. This is particularly visible in relationship to the late Elizabethan "best-seller," a term used here to describe authors and books alike. The 1590s produced a concentration of writers who, in any given year, had a number of titles printed and of works that went through five or more editions before Elizabeth's death.[27] To be sure, there had been salient if scattered examples of the best-seller before. We could take Lyly and his *Euphues* texts, and Robert Parsons's *Directory,* as harbingers of this phenomenon in the 1580s. (And, as we will see, Lyly's achievement was significant to the rise of embodied writing in many ways). In the last decade of the century, however, what before had been confined to isolated books and authors became widespread; even as the total number of imprints remained relatively stable, certain authors and texts experienced a heady popularity.[28] As the examples of Parsons and Lyly may indicate, religious and literary authors and writings formed the bulk of these. That the "literary" here includes several of Southwell's devotional works speaks to the early 1590s publication of texts by figures—puritan, protestant, and catholic—who would later become involved in larger religious controversies. Correspondingly, best-selling religious texts came from a variety of positions. For instance, Leonard Wright, a participant in the Marprelate controversy on the side of the prelacy, saw his *A Summons for Sleepers* go through five editions from 1589 to 1596, and

Thomas Playfere, who eventually became chaplain to King James, also had a work gain five editions: his *A Most Excellent and Heavenly Sermon,* published from 1595 to 1597.

But it would be two puritan authors, William Perkins and Henry Smith, who most clearly demonstrated the novel status of selected books and authors. Perkins had three "best-sellers" during this era: *Armilla Aurea* (*"The Golden Chain"*), which went through ten editions (English and Latin), from 1590 to 1597; *A Treatise Tending Unto a Declaration Whether a Man Be in the Estate of Damnation or the Estate of Grace,* seven editions, 1590? to1600; and *The Foundation of Christian Religion,* six editions, 1590 to1601. The publication history of Smith's works was even more striking. Spurred, perhaps, by his early death in 1591, the books of "silver-tongued Smith," an extremely popular divine, sold in amazing numbers during the 1590s.[29] Smith had five best-sellers in this period, mainly editions of his sermons: *The Sermons of Henry Smith, Gathered in One Volume,* eight editions, 1592 to 1601; *A Sermon of the Benefit of Contentation,* seven editions, 1590 to 1591; *Six Sermons Preached by Master H. Smith,* seven editions, 1592 to 1599; *The Wedding Garment,* six editions, 1590 to 1591; and *The Trumpet of the Soul,* five editions, 1591 to 1593. The total number of imprints under each of these authors' names during this period is also extraordinary. While Perkins had a total of fifty-one imprints from 1590 to 1599, Smith had eighty-one imprints published—including twenty-nine during 1591, the year of his death. In this year Smith's works account for over 11 percent of *all* English imprints. And with Perkins' five imprints in 1591 the two authors were responsible that year for over a quarter of all publications of a religious nature, with over three times as many imprints as of the Bible and the Psalms put together. Clearly this pair of authors enjoyed an astonishing popularity.

That the best-seller was an extensive phenomenon can be seen when one examines, in addition to the status of these religious writers, the prominence, during the 1590s, of certain literary authors and texts. Best-selling literary texts of this era include Shakespeare's *Venus and Adonis,* seven editions, 1593 to 1602; Samuel Daniel's *Delia,* five editions, 1592 to 1598; Michael Drayton's *England's Heroical Epistles,* five editions, 1597 to 1602; Thomas Kyd's *The Spanish Tragedy,* five editions, 1592 to 1603; Thomas Lodge's *Rosalind,* five editions, 1590 to 1604; Thomas Nashe's *Pierce Penniless,* five editions, 1592 to 1595; and Robert Southwell's *Mary Magdalene's Funeral Tears,* five editions, 1591 to 1602, and his *Saint Peter's Complaint,* six editions, 1595 to 1602. Like the popularity of Henry

Smith's works, the attraction of Southwell's two texts, and of Sidney's *Arcadia*—which saw five editions from 1590 to 1605—must have derived in some part from their authors' early deaths. As Arthur Marotti suggests, during this period the "corpse of the author and the *corpus* of the work were in closer imaginative proximity."[30] The examples of Sidney, Smith, and Southwell hint that this proximity could spur canonization. Such, in any case, had come quickly: Sidney had died in 1586, and Southwell was executed in 1595, during the popularity of *Mary Magdelane's Funeral Tears* but before the success of *Saint Peter's Complaint*. Parallel in another way to Smith's works here were two very popular books: Robert Greene's *Quip for an Upstart Courtier,* which saw six editions in 1592 alone, and John Harington's *Apology,* with five editions in 1596.[31] As is clear from the preceding titles, many of the works that have since achieved canonical status were eagerly received in their own time as well.

Even as such books came to be especially desired by readers of the 1590s, various literary writers also began to experience a new prominence. Beginning in 1591, the year in which Henry Smith's works appeared in such surprising numbers, we find Robert Greene with six imprints of various titles. In 1592, the year of his death, Greene had eighteen editions of twelve different titles in print, and Thomas Nashe, four imprints. In the years 1593 and 1594 Greene again occupied printers with three and four imprints, respectively. Southwell, whose execution had occurred early in 1595, had six imprints brought out that year. The following year, in 1596, Harington had eleven imprints, all entries in his *Ajax* "series": *The Metamorphosis of Ajax, An Anatomy of the Metamorphosed Ajax,* and *An Apology* (to which was joined, also that year, two editions of the pseudonymous *Ulysses upon Ajax,* not by Harington). Lodge, too, had five imprints in 1596. In 1597 Nicholas Breton had four imprints, and in 1598 Shakespeare had seven—six editions of four dramatic titles, and *The Rape of Lucrece.* But 1599 was especially notable for best-selling authors, with John Davies and Shakespeare each having six imprints, and Greene, who had been dead for over half a decade, five imprints. Davies's titles that year included *Nosce Teipsum, Hymns of Astrea,* and the composite *Epigrams and Elegies;* Shakespeare's, *1 Henry IV, Romeo and Juliet, Venus and Adonis* and the composite *Passionate Pilgrim.*[32] In 1600 Nicholas Breton had seven imprints, six of these consisting of his *Pasquil* series: *Pasquil's Mad-Cap* (two times published), *Pasquil's Fool's-Cap* (two times published), *Pasquil's Mistress,* and *Pasquil's Pass, and Passeth Not.* In 1600 eight imprints by Shakespeare were published: seven editions of six dramatic titles, and *The*

Rape of Lucrece. The works of Breton and Shakespeare would again be popular in 1602, when they saw six and five imprints, respectively. By this time, however, the literary "boom" of the 1590s had begun to subside, and hereafter few writers would experience the intensive popularity that many writers had earlier enjoyed.

The titles and publication figures in the preceding paragraphs help establish the outlines of a new development in print culture during the later Elizabethan era. Such numbers describe a popularity new in its extension and new in its stress on contemporary authors, both alive and recently deceased. In its depth and breadth, this popularity worked to solidify authorship as an essential category for Elizabethan readers and writers. Along with the internal changes that embodied writing had brought about, print culture was shaped by the best-seller's emphasis on contemporary authors and their works, which often put their identities in close focus. These identities were shaped also by writers and printers, who labored to increase the attention given to individual authors and books. R. B. McKerrow has said of John Weever's *Epigrams* (1599), for example, that, "with the exception of the *Palladis Tamia* of Francis Meres, there is, I think, no single work of so early a date that contains references by name to so many Elizabethan writers of the first or second rank."[33] To which E. A. J. Honigmann responds by suggesting that such was hardly an accident: Weever and Meres "belonged to the same group—one that adopted new methods of publicising contemporary writers, and in particular other members of their own group."[34] Such efforts were far from unsuccessful. At the end of Elizabeth's reign we perceive for the first time a significant number of readers and publishers placing as much importance on who had written a work as they did on what was in that work. We also observe them supporting individual works and clusters of titles in a way that, prior to this time, had been confined to selected works like Lyly's *Euphues* texts.

If these two titles of Lyly's were harbingers to the best-sellers of the 1590s, they also played a part in the rise of embodied writing by inaugurating a textual celebrity. As we will see, this celebrity implied embodied characters and even texts. From 1578, when *Euphues, the Anatomy of Wit* was first published, through 1595, there passed no two years during which either it or its sequel, *Euphues and his England* (1580), was not printed. The immediate effect of these texts can be seen in the rush to "hail" them, evident in such titles as Greene's *Euphues his Censure to Philautus* (1587), and his *Menaphon: Camilla's Alarum to Slumbering Euphues* (1589); in Lodge's *Rosalind: Euphues' Golden Legacy* (1590), and his *Euphues' Shadow*

(1592); and in Arthur Dickenson's *Arisbas: Euphues Amid his Slumbers* (1594). Lyly's texts were so frequently printed and cited that one could see them—one could see "Euphues"—in readers' hands and booksellers' stalls with predictable regularity during this period. So present were these texts and Euphues to the reading public of their day that it remains no exaggeration to call Euphues the first textual citizen of early modern London, an artificial person whom one could expect to meet with some frequency in this rapidly expanding metropolis. More than a passing curiosity, this embodiment has serious implications for our understanding of print culture in early modern England, as Lyly's significance comes not in these texts' unprecedented popularity but in an effect of such popularity.

While the stylistic vogue of "Euphuism" is perhaps too well known to need recounting here, we could consider the context in which Gabriel Harvey first used the term. Harvey coined the word "Euphuism" in his *Four Letters* (1592), whose gossipy subtitle speaks tellingly to the personalism of embodied writing: *Four Letters, and Certain Sonnets: Especially Touching Robert Greene, and Other Parties, by him Abused; But Incidently of Divers Excellent Persons, and Some Matters of Note*. In the Third Letter Harvey turns his full attention to Thomas Nashe, with whom, owing to their energetic, entertaining, and thoroughly regrettable personal feud, his name would forever be remembered. Harvey celebrates his chief advantages over Nashe: maturity and discretion. Nashe, he reminds us, was once a student auditor at Cambridge who had beheld Harvey in his full glory as a lecturer. What has Nashe done since, Harvey asks, rhetorically, "excepting his good old *Flores Poetarum,* and Tarlton's surmounting Rhetoric, with a little Euphuism, and Greeneness enough, which were all pretty stale, before he put hand to pen? I report me to the favourablest opinion of those that know his Prefaces, Rhymes, and the very Timpany of his Tarltonizing wit. . . ."[35] In this short and vital passage Harvey converts the names of figures—Euphues, Greene, and Tarlton—into, respectively, nouns ("Euphuism," "Greeneness") and an adjective ("Tarltonizing"). But what stands out in addition to this concentration of neologisms is the passage's easy use of identities as things. What are we to make of these strange commodities: Euphuism, Greeneness, and Tarltonizing wit? And by what warrant does Harvey imagine them *as* things?

An initial answer could point to the fact that all three bring to mind popular figures with whom readers and audiences would associate apparently idiosyncratic *styles:* with Euphues, a highly artificial rhetorical pattern; with Greene, a "canicular" scurrility based in the cony-catching pamphlet; and with Tarlton, a libertine wit deriving its energy from familiar address of its object and audience.[36] In this way Harvey's reading of the situation of print in the early 1590s would seem to anticipate Buffon's *Le style est l'homme même,* but with reversed order: *L'homme est le style même.*[37] What this paraphrase misses, however, and what we elide in calling Euphues, Greene, and Tarlton "figures" is the license Harvey takes in equating a literary character and a text with real individuals. Perhaps even more audacious than his distilling of the human into a thing is his use of a thing—the printed creature of "Euphues," books and character—in parallel with the human. Harvey thus leaves us with a riddle: When is a literary creature like a person? To which our earlier survey of publications figures leads us to respond: When public desire, reading habits, and the printing press combine to make it so. As we have seen, Euphues became so present to the reading public that he, the *Euphues* texts, and the style they fostered were as known to many Londoners as were Greene and Tarlton. Like the "Greene" of countless title pages and the "Tarlton" of recent and fond memory (he had died in 1588), "Euphues" gained his cultural identity by being dispersed among his admirers. The best-seller gave life to authors, characters, and texts.

The slipperiness of identity in Harvey's description relies on a sequence of transactions: If the heavily autobiographical character of Euphues can be said to have translated Lyly's person into fiction, that character also was translated into the narratives condensed in the *Euphues* titles, which in turn came to stand in for a style of rhetoric associated with the character and books—"Euphuism." We could illustrate the chain of metonymy as follows:

Lyly → Euphues → *Euphues* → "Euphuism"

Shorter patterns of relationship take us from a kind of writing to "Greeneness" and from a genre of humor to "Tarltonizing." Motivating these chains of metonymy was the sheer popularity of the figures involved. "Greeneness" could be identified in part because Greene's books existed in great numbers. Harvey accordingly seems to be speaking not to a coterie of readers but to a reading public. That this public was, of course, limited by social position and literacy is apparent in Dekker's reference to "Arcadian and Euphuized gentlewomen."[38] Yet, as the impersonal process of the verbal form ("Euphuized") and the yoking with Sidney's best-selling *Arcadia* may also serve to indicate, it was a public. These adjectives describe readers influenced by texts so widely read that Dekker is under no compulsion to say what he means by "Arcadian" and "Euphuized." Thus where a nineteenth-century critic saw *Euphues* as commencing "the literature of the drawing room" in England, it is more accurate to say that Lyly's texts made "drawing-room" manners and language public, bringing them to an audience larger than Lyly or anyone else had imagined possible.[39]

Given life by the printing press, Euphues haunted the works of Greene and his contemporaries. The historical "moment" of the Harvey passage quoted above was, again, one that hailed *Euphues* in the titles of various books by Greene, Lodge, and Dickenson. Addressing this pattern of reference in his study of Lyly, G. K. Hunter calls it "a completely superficial cashing-in on the manner or the name."[40] It is hard to dismiss this assessment, for these works do deploy "Euphues" in their titles as advertisement, and possibly in a misleading manner. But in seeing such quotation negatively—this remark occurs in a chapter called "The Victim of Fashion"—Hunter fails to notice that it signals one of Lyly's most prominent legacies and an important contribution to the rise of embodied writing. Following the success of *Euphues,* best-selling works often featured characters who became, first, independent of, then identified with, their authors.

Among these works were Greene's "cony-catching" pamphlets, Harington's *Ajax* books, and Breton's *Pasquil* sequence (completed in 1602 by *Old Mad-Cap's New Gallimaufry*). Harvey associates the cony-catching pamphlets so closely with Greene that he refers to the latter as "Greene the Conycatcher."[41] Breton, on the other hand, often addresses the readers of his *Pasquil* series in the persona of Pasquil. And because he appeared so frequently in print, Pasquil, like Euphues, acquired a more tangible identity than most literary creations. Some twenty years later the names of Breton and Pasquil would be synonymous to Ben Jonson, whose "Execration upon Vulcan" refers to "Nicholas Pasquil."[42] Similarly, when in 1598 Robert Joyner set out to satirize John Harington and the notoriety of his *Ajax* works, he did so by writing an epigram for Harington *as* "Ajax," making little distinction in the poem itself among Harington, his *Ajax* books, and the ever-present privy, or "jakes," lying behind Harington's title.[43] Harington returned the favor by later referring to Joyner as "Itis"—the title of the latter's collection of epigrams and satires.[44] It seems no accident, therefore, that when John Weever penned *"Ad Gulielmum Shakespear"* in his *Epigrams* (1599), he not only executed it in the form of a fourteen-line sonnet with the

"Shakespearean" rhyme scheme (the only poem with this form in the collection) but in it mentions both *The Rape of Lucrece* and *Venus and Adonis,* the latter a Shakespearean best-seller.[45] Weever goes on to conclude that although Shakespeare's characters initially seemed "got" by "*Apollo* . . . and none other," one eventually perceives them to be the writer's own offspring: "They burn in love thy children *Shakespeare* het them, / Go, woo thy Muse more Nymphish brood beget them."[46] "[H]et" means "heated." Shakespeare's creative fire, the image implies, helps to "beget" characters on his personal Muse. Like the other best-selling authors whose characters took on a life outside their texts, Shakespeare is described as responsible for yet separate from his creations.

For persons to merge with characters and for books to be conflated with their authors is perhaps not surprising to readers of this era's texts, for during the 1590s many controversialists ridiculed their opponents by name and writers of satire often would conceal the objects of their aggression with a nearly transparent disguise. But the phenomenon of the best-selling author and text goes beyond the satiric and allegorical traditions that the Elizabethans inherited and, along with embodied writing generally, speaks to a profound, even structural transformation of print. The making of an author's style into a thing (and the naming of that thing after the author); the celebrity of authors and the textual celebrity of characters who seemed to exist outside their works; the intensive familiarity of recent books and titles; these books' familiarity with bodies and identities: All suggest a personalization of print that changed what and how printed matter meant. Everywhere a new fluidity between person and thing characterized the relationship between authors and books, between characters and persons, and between readers and books.

One of the signal results of this fluidity involves what we could call the nascent "public sphere" of late Elizabethan England. The term "public sphere" usually is reserved for later eras, of course, and as such often describes a common space of rational intellectual and political discourse—a space sometimes identified with physical locations such as the German *Tischgesellschaften* (learned "table societies"), French salons, and the coffee houses of eighteenth-century England.[47] However, scholars have begun to question the received location of the public sphere in terms of both place and time. Traditional definitions have stressed bourgeois conversational settings, neutral places in which persons meet to exchange views. But new insights to the role of print as a medium for the articulation of controversial views ask us to recognize a sphere of public expression that preceded, and in some ways enabled, these later conversational settings. Indeed, where the standard chronology would see the public sphere as a decidedly post-Enlightenment phenomenon, some scholars have posited the existence of a dynamic public sphere in England from at least the 1620s onward, solidifying especially during the Interregnum.[48] David Norbrook, for instance, speaks of the "massively uneven development of the public sphere in the seventeenth century and beyond," observing that "It is not the case that after 1640, or after 1695, there suddenly was a securely established public sphere."[49] Yet while Norbrook is right to call our attention to the public sphere of early seventeenth-century England, even his emphasis on the 1620s is too late to account for the public aspects of print that characterize texts of the 1590s and after. For it was then that the energies of the Marprelate controversy joined with various historical forces to radically expand the discursive potential of print, sounding out the limits of a meaningful public space. Into this space came controversial writers like Nashe and Harvey, explicitly erotic texts, bestselling works such as Greene's cony-catching pamphlets and Harington's *Ajax* books, and such newly embodied characters as Lyly's Euphues and Breton's Pasquil.

But while the personalism connected with such authors, texts, and characters asks us to revise our chronology of the public sphere, the embodied writing of this era suggests that we modify inherited notions of the public sphere in qualitative ways. We need to define the public sphere, for instance, in terms of more than physical sites of conversation, rational political discourse, and polemic responding to social and political crises, as the roots of these later formations can be traced in part to the radical, sometimes ludic expressivity of the 1590s. As we have observed, in vaunting the personal this expressivity often disregarded conventional notions of status and bodily integrity. If standard accounts of the public sphere see the disregard of rank as one of its constituent features, the leveling aspects of embodied writing—in which a satirist could mock an equal, or even his better, and in which a writer of erotic verse could salaciously emblazon a goddess queen—can be seen as an enabling condition of "social intercourse that . . . disregarded status altogether."[50] The idea of convention is key here, as the events and texts of this period speak to a cultural shift in early modern England that began the displacement of long-standing patterns of respect. This shift involved a general movement from cooperation and the habit of obedience to calculation and competition—a movement, in short, toward modernity. As a phenomenon, this shift was most visible, during the later

1590s and early 1600s, in responses to indecorous practice. The use of "public sphere" to describe the directions of print culture at this time is therefore justified not only by the complex ways in which embodied writing prepared for the expressions of the mid- and later seventeenth century and after but by the censoring impulses that printed material of the late Elizabethan era elicited from the political authorities. Subtending the ban on satire, on controversy, on the erotic, and even on unapproved English histories was a response to the putative confusion of spheres: The private had been made public through the medium of print, changing how the space of the public was defined.[51]

The nascent public sphere of the late Elizabethan era involved identity and decorum more than rationality or policy, and was often irreverent rather than somber. In providing a space for otherwise ordinary individuals and their voices, however, it functioned as a pivotal site for an emergent segment of English society. This public space, again, came into being when writers publicized hitherto private bodies and identities, including their own. Some of these had been out of bounds through long-standing traditions that precluded familiar handling of the aristocracy, others through prudence based on moral decorum. But perhaps more important than the transgression of these boundaries was the unmistakable presence, in print, of individuals from the middle orders of early modern society.[52] Earlier, such atypical works as John Stubbes's *A Gaping Gulf* (1579) and the anonymously published *Leicester's Commonwealth* (1584) offended precisely because they dealt with individuals at the highest level of Elizabethan society. Increasingly, the consequential bodies in printed material of the later Elizabethan era were from inconsequential origins. Of the hundreds of names that followed the formulaic "To," "*Ad*," or "On" of the epigram tradition in the 1590s, for instance, many, if not the majority, involve those whose social status would have precluded significant mention in print several decades earlier. The same could be said of the personal allusions to middle-class writers in plays like those of the *Parnassus* Trilogy (1599–1603) and in many other topically inclined works.

The public sphere that works of the 1590s began to establish was highly theatrical in nature, having at its base a focused playfulness and the public theaters themselves. If Harvey's reference to Euphues and Greene springs from a personalism that licensed readers' attention to paper bodies, his invoking of Tarlton both recalls an older social type, the licensed jester who bonds "lord and lown" and reminds us that the amphitheater playhouses (where the rough music of Tarlton's

"Timpany"-wit endeared him to the Elizabethan public) were arenas of celebrity and public discourse. During the 1590s, publishers found that readers were eager to buy the plays they had seen and heard in London's theaters. Beginning in 1593–1594, texts of public theater plays began to make up an increasing percentage of literary publications. By the first decade of the seventeenth century, they would sometimes constitute over 20 percent of all literary publications and over 5 percent of all titles published. The popularity of this comparatively novel kind of publication has a significant place in the history of embodied writing, for the printing of dramatic scripts made available to the reading public words that it could associate with specific actors, some of them celebrities. However accurate, the anecdote in John Manningham's *Diary* that details Burbage's and Shakespeare's erotic rivalry—Burbage appointed to visit an enamored citizen under the name of "Richard the Third," Shakespeare, anticipating him, sending word that "'William the Conqueror' was before Richard the Third"—testifies to the fact that public playing had generated a "star" system.

What we forget in the coincidence of these names, however, is how closely the jest depends on the recent popularity of the history play. Burbage had doubtless played Richard the Third, and Shakespeare may well have been associated with the one surviving play to feature William the Conqueror.[53] In any case, public playing had made celebrities of certain actors, and the printed play texts that began to appear in great numbers in the 1590s would have offered readers a record of lines they could connect with real bodies on the platform stage. Humorous testimony to this effect comes in Richard Corbett's "Iter Boreale," a poem written shortly before Burbage's death. Describing a journey through England, Corbett relates that one of his hosts, "full of *Ale* and *History*," makes a telling mistake in his rehearsal of the Battle of Bosworth Field:

>   Why, he could tell
> The inch where *Richmond* stood, where *Richard* fell:
> Besides what of his knowledge he can say,
> He had Authentic notice, from the Play;
> Which I might guess, by must'ring up the Ghosts
> And policies not incident to Hosts:
> But chiefly by that one perspicuous thing,
> Where he mistook a Player, for a King.
> For when he would have said "King *Richard*" died,
> And call'd "a horse, a horse," he, "*Burbage*" cried.[54]

The Host's reported confusion of Burbage with Richard, mistaking "a Player, for a King," is precisely what an acting company would have hoped for, of course, during any production of the play. But the lingering identification of actor and role was something that the printing of play quartos made especially likely. Those who purchased *Richard III*, for instance, would possess a version of what they had heard specific actors speak in London's playhouses: these the lines of Richard Burbage, those the lines of Will Kemp, still others the lines that Shakespeare had spoken on stage. Their voices would have seemed dried in ink.[55]

In much the same way, the bodies of playwrights themselves came to be identified with particular voices or styles. As James Shapiro has argued concerning the question of influence among early modern playwrights, a developing sense of authority, voice, and canonicity formed a prelude to the War of the Theaters at the turn of the century. The sharp parody in such satirical plays as *Cynthia's Revels* (1600), *Satiromastix* (1600), and *Poetaster* (1601) depended on a heightened "sensitivity to the distinctive voices of individual dramatists."[56] Paradoxically, this sensitivity was augmented by the collaborative nature of dramatic authorship. Playwrights became deeply aware of the differences between their own styles and the styles of potential rivals—even, perhaps especially, those with whom they worked most closely—and "struggled to locate themselves relationally" by parodying other dramatists.[57]

Nowhere is this kind of positioning more familiar to modern readers than in the "upstart Crow" passage from *Greene's Groatsworth of Wit* (1592). This "first published notice of Shakespeare in London" comes, the text's most recent editor points out, as "a remarkably bitter outburst . . . apparently provoked by envy at the success of a player turned playwright."[58] Although Henry Chettle is most likely the primary author of this text, its personal satire seems entirely consonant with the atmosphere of embodiment that surrounded Greene, from his citation of Euphues and his self-allegorization as a prodigal poet to his best-selling pamphlets and literary reputation. This well-known passage grounds its general resentment of others in the theatrical business by warning a friend about a particular individual: "Yes trust them not: for there is an upstart Crow, beautified with our feathers, that with his *Tiger's heart wrapped in a Player's hide,* supposes he is as well able to bombast out a blank verse as the best of you: and being an absolute *Johannes fac totum,* is in his own conceit the only Shake-scene in a country."[59] Although much about this notorious passage still occasions debate, it

offers several clues to its primary mystery, the identity of the un-
trustworthy upstart who has strutted onto the theatrical scene. The
more apparent of these clues, though, has overshadowed a less obvious mechanism in the passage. Where "Shake-scene" clearly brings
to mind "Shakespeare," the passage already has identified its target
by quoting his words. In mentioning this individual's "*Tiger's heart
wrapped in a Player's hide*," that is, our author is revising a line from
York's diatribe against Queen Margaret in Shakespeare's *3 Henry VI:*
"O tiger's heart wrapped in a woman's hide" (1.4.137). Because a
version of this play was first published in 1595, three years after
Groatsworth, the author of this pamphlet is appealing to what must
have been, for many readers, playhouse memories. The chain of associations this quotation therefore depends on involves more than a
simple triangulation of pamphlet-author, reader, and object of
ridicule. For even if Shakespeare himself acted the part of York, the
allusion includes others, and other experiences, in its "embodiment"
of Shakespeare.

We may recall Harvey's distillation of "Euphuism" as we trace this
process of embodiment. The author of *Groatsworth* points at Shakespeare, and does so to an ideal reader who may have heard Shakespeare's play in person or had other access to information about the
play or quotation. If the former, the *Groatsworth* writer could be seen
as assuming the following sequence of agents and events. The dia-
gram charts the "history" of the quotation, from playwright to play,
to actor, to audience member, to pamphlet:

(Shakespeare) Playwright ➔ Play Text ➔ Actor: "O tiger's heart[!]" ➔
Playgoer ➔ *Groatsworth*

But we have to reverse this process to get to the "upstart Crow" the
Groatsworth Author derides, and only when we do so may we realize
how complex the allusion is. For although Shakespeare might have
acted the part of York, a number of things still would have come between the pamphlet and him: the playhouse, the character (and, assuming another actor, the actor's body in whom the quotation would
have been given voice), the paper from which the actor would learn
these lines, even the fact that Shakespeare wrote these lines.
Groatsworth imagines a canny reader who has shared its author's experiences of public spaces in London and who would recognize the
pamphlet's paraphrase as a strategic misquotation of a production in
one of the public theaters. *Groatsworth*, further, seems directed toward a reader used to libels, controversial pamphlets, satires, and *à*

clef narratives—used to reading as much for the identities on the page as for the plot.

The paper tiger to whom *Groatsworth* points shows how embodied writing licensed readers to imagine licentious authors. Even as others' bodies began to appear more often and more graphically on the page, however, readers began to associate printed matter with authors' bodies. To return to the emetic that Horace administers to Crispinus in *Poetaster*—a transparent fantasy of Jonson's in which he cures Marston of his verbal excesses by making the dramatist vomit his strange words—we see that Jonson locates the problem in Crispinus/Marston's body, and the solution in curing that body. In an age fascinated by neologisms, the deployment of newly acquired words could well prove a mark of distinction. And as Jonson's satire shows us, often these words seemed foreign matter. Yet increasingly during the 1590s readers considered words and style an intractable part of an author's body. In Harvey's distillation of "Greeneness," for example, readers are assumed to have had enough access to and familiarity with a writer's works to identify what Harvey perceived as a quintessential property of Greene's style—to connect Greene's body with the body of his works through some habit of composition, stance, or favorite subject. It is perhaps a combination of these that Shakespeare posits as a personal marker in Sonnet 76, when he asks himself "Why write I still all one, ever the same, / And keep invention in a noted weed, / That every word doth almost tell my name, / Showing their birth, and where they did proceed?" (ll. 5–8). This "noted weed" or familiar garb is the *dispositio* of the poetic speaker's invention, the arrangement in his verse of his material. So familiar is this arrangement, the sonnet relates in an exaggeration meant to show the poet's devotion, that even the poem's words seem to carry birthmarks and to point toward its author.[60] His style, *semper eadem*, gives him away.

Belief in the power of a work to name its author grew during the late Elizabethan era. "Style" came to be seen as only sometimes a conscious decision but "many times natural to the writer," something the author often "holdeth on by ignorance, and will not or peradventure cannot easily alter into any other."[61] The words here are George Puttenham's, from his *Arte of English Poesie*, and it is also in this work that we encounter a revealing myth concerning the identity of authors and their texts. We could call this the *hos ego* myth after the catchphrase by which it would be known during the early modern era. Puttenham tells us that once, when Vergil had composed a distich praising Augustus and had set it upon the palace gate, another writer—a certain "saucy courtier"—saw how much these anonymous lines were admired and took credit for them, receiving a "good reward" from the emperor. Angered at the fraud his modesty had enabled, Vergil returned the following night and "fastened upon the same place this half meter, four times iterated":

> *Sic vos non vobis*
> *Sic vos non vobis*
> *Sic vos non vobis*
> *Sic vos non vobis*

No one could make sense of this, and, having baffled the court, Vergil returned and wrote above these four half-lines "*Hos ego versiculos feci tulit alter honores,*" or "These verses I did make, thereof another took the praise."[62] He then finished the four *Sic vos non vobis* half-lines with corresponding complaints from laboring beasts and insects; "So you not for yourselves," Vergil writes: oxen pull the plow, sheep bear wool, bees gather honey, and birds build nests. Like these toiling creatures, he suggests, poets find themselves robbed of their labor's fruit. Puttenham tells us that to clinch his case the poet "put to his name *Publius Virgilius Maro.*" If Vergil's authorship of the earlier distich is implied by the content of his poem, his authority is demonstrated by his ability to finish it when others could not, an authority consolidated with the inscription of his name.

Articulated by Phaer and Twynne in their edition of *The whole xii books of the Æneidos* in 1573, the *hos ego* myth was represented in texts with growing frequency toward the end of Elizabeth's reign. After appearing in Puttenham's *Arte of English Poesie* in 1589, it figured also in Joseph Hall's *Virgidemiae* in 1597 and in the Second Part of *The Return from Parnassus* in 1603. As in this gossipy, satiric play, Hall's use of the phrase calls on the larger story of plagiarism and authority associated with Vergil's rise to cultural notice. In the second satire of Book Four, Hall ridicules the embarrassment an aspiring young gentleman feels for his father and their common, laboring-class roots:

> Could never man work thee a worser shame
> Than once to minge thy father's odious name,
> Whose mention were alike to thee as leave,
> As Catch-pol's fist unto a Bankrupt's sleeve;
> Or an *Hos ego* from old *Petrarch*'s sprite
> Unto a Plagiary sonnet-wright.[63]

The mere "minge," or mention of his father's name ("Lollio," which is, of course, his own), serves as an uncomfortable reminder to the young gallant of something he would rather forget. But just as the *Groatsworth* passage would have its reader believe that borrowed feathers are recognizably alien to the borrower, so does it seem, to Hall, that debts will out: Even as this name returns to remind the young gallant of the source of his money, a "bankrupt" will find himself apprehended and a "plagiary sonnet-wright" will be admonished by the ghost of Petrarch, who hails the thief with the two words that declare the subject (*ego*) and object (*hos*) of literary ownership.

The *hos ego* myth maintains that an umbilical cord links authors and their writings. In the "original" story Vergil's completion is based on content and style, whereas by Hall's time it seems oriented more toward stylistic borrowing. In this way the *hos ego* story illustrates changes in beliefs about what texts were, as during the period under focus a number of readers began to hold that the best way to determine authorship was to search for internal rather than external evidence. That is, where traditionally the political authorities would search for publisher and printer, interrogating individuals to ascertain provenance, during the 1590s and after we see a more forensic approach to the issue of authorship: If authorities had earlier been tempted to coerce those associated with the printing and distribution of dangerous anonymous texts, at the end of Elizabeth's reign readers suggested putting pressure on the *style* of those texts as a way of determining who wrote them. As one could expect, the anonymity of the Marprelate publications figured centrally in this development.

In 1595 the Reverend Matthew Sutcliffe published a pamphlet whose very title indicates the revolving-door progress of that controversy: *An Answer unto a Certain Calumnious Letter Published by Master Job Throckmorton and Entitled 'A Defence of J. Throckmorton Against the Slanders of Master Sutcliffe' Wherein the Vanity Both of the Defence of Him Self and the Accusation of Others is Manifestly Declared by Matthew Sutcliffe.* In this pamphlet Sutcliffe, who wrote in support of the system that had rewarded him with multiple benefices, points at Throckmorton as the real author of the Marprelate tracts— or rather, claims that the tracts themselves point at Throckmorton. As Sutcliffe contends, not only did the manuscript of *More Work for Cooper* (in the possession of which the printers Valentine Simmes, Arthur Tomlyn, and John Hodgkins had been arrested in 1589) feature Throckmorton's handwriting and interlinear corrections, but "the style is so like to Job Throckmorton's talking and writing, that as children do declare whose they are by the lineaments of their visage and proportion of parts, so these libels do bewray their natural father by the frame of the words and sentences, and such draughts as can proceed from no other author."[64] A few pages later Sutcliffe continues: "the phrase and manner of writing—which are a certain indice and sign of the Author's affections—doth declare from whence the book did come: so scurrilous, wicked and railing stuff could come from no other than Throckmorton." Sutcliffe concludes that Throckmorton is Martin Marprelate: Because both his handwriting and his very manner of speaking and writing ("the frame of the words and sentences") confirm his authorship of *More Work,* the boast in that text that its author is Martin Marprelate proves that Throckmorton (and not John Penry or any other of the alleged conspirators) was responsible for the Marprelate tracts.[65]

The warrants for stylistic identification here seem highly subjective. Is there, as Sutcliffe claims, and as modern critics who engage in the statistical analysis of literature maintain, something about "the frame of the words and sentences" of texts that shows a trained eye that a work "can proceed from no other author"? It was Harvey's contention, after all, that however identifiable "Greeneness" and "Euphuism" and "Tarltonizing wit" were, Nashe had been reproducing them in *his* writings. And at another point Harvey accuses Greene of "Tarltonizing" too.[66] A similar irony appears in *Groatsworth*'s borrowing from Shakespeare to claim that Shakespeare had first borrowed from others. Literary identity, like literary property, depends on ownership, and only things that can be stolen can be said to be owned. Ironically, the surest proof of the developing notion of authorship and literary property during this period was its continued discourse of plagiarism. But such a metaphysical approach to authorship misses the realities of writing and politics: the fact that authors, printers, and publishers faced severe punishment for producing certain texts and competed with each other for prestige and money; and that it mattered to readers who had written particular books. Without accepting the basis of Sutcliffe's attribution, therefore, we can notice the confidence that he displays in his ability to discern an idiosyncratic *style*—and to trace that style to an author's other texts and to a manner of speech. Style is both the man and the text.

Sutcliffe's anatomy of the style of *More Work* offers an understanding of the printed word more forensic than rhetorical. Its relationship to empirical method, in fact, may be seen in a story told by Francis Bacon. In his *Apology* for Essex, originally published in 1604,

Bacon tells us that once when Queen Elizabeth encountered a particular text and "would not be persuaded, that it was his writing whose name was to it, but that It had some more mischievous Author, and said with great indignation, that she would have him racked to produce his Author, I replied 'Nay Madam, he is a Doctor: never rack his person, but rack his style; let him have pen, ink, and paper, and help of books, and be enjoined to continue the story wherein it breaketh off, and I will undertake, by collecting the styles, to judge whether he were the Author or no.'"[67] Bacon sets himself up as a literary detective able to determine whether two examples of "style" come from the same author. His pride in his ability to "judge" authorship, though, stops short of Sutcliffe's claim of an organic relationship between text and author, for authorship is instead a craft, with pen, ink, paper, and "help of books" all contributing to the final product. But if the author's body is spared the rack, his style is not: The physical apparatus of torture gives way to method; and what may once have taken place between bodies, with a book as object, now takes place between a reader and a book, with the author's body as object. Retelling the *hos ego* myth from inside the Court, where an Elizabethan Vergil faces another kind of reward, Bacon replicates also Sutcliffe's confidence in stylistic identity.

Their belief remains indicative of the larger reorientation of bodies and print described in the preceding argument. The historical context of Bacon's anecdote reminds us how much about print culture had changed during the last few decades of Elizabeth's reign.[68] English citizens who can be imagined as having left their country prior to the Armada would, upon returning after Elizabeth's death, doubtless recognize the basic forms of works published in their absence. But assuming they had had no contact with English publications during the decade and a half they had been away, they just as certainly would be surprised by the profusion of embodied texts greeting them upon their return. As readers they could be expected to notice a number of things that had happened in and to texts during the last years of Elizabeth's reign. Most remarkable to them could have been the way in which print had adopted practices and topics that had before this mainly characterized manuscript forms, like libels and erotic verse.[69] These readers would encounter many explicitly erotic texts, the license behind which had in addition underwritten many of the *ad hominem* sallies in both the Marprelate controversy and the satire wars. Such readers might have noticed too an emphasis on contemporary authors, something evidenced in a cadre of best-selling authors and texts. These readers might have been surprised to find a closer connection between artificial personae—"paper bodies"—and real ones. The notoriety of personae such as Euphues and Pasquil was accompanied, finally, by an entrenched star system in the public theaters, where actors were enjoying a celebrity that they had not possessed some fifteen years earlier.

How did this situation come about? What lay behind the development of embodied writing described in many of the preceding changes? This kind of writing undoubtedly had many sources, including the changeful political climate under an aging Elizabeth.[70] We also should consider among these sources "the increasingly litigious character of late Elizabethan society and the adversarial bias of contemporary rhetorical training."[71] To these we could join the ways in which certain literary genres of the 1590s represented "alternative form[s] of ethical innovation in response to the disorienting effects of urbanization on traditional values."[72] But among the overdetermination of sources here, four in particular stand out. First among these is the momentous change in the roles and sources of authority in England following the Reformation. As Robert Weimann has argued, the Reformation profoundly altered the relationships of power, authority, and representation in early modern England and drastically affected venues and modes of expression. Such authors as Sidney, Nashe, and Lyly "had to cope not only with the wider horizon of international traffic and exchange but also with a largely unsanctioned diffusion of signifying activities."[73] We already have noted that many of the best-selling authors and texts diverged from the middle way of the Elizabethan settlement. From Perkins and Smith to Parsons and Southwell, and from *The Golden Chain* to *St. Peter's Complaint,* print culture of the 1590s bore witness to the Reformation's fragmentation of consensus. The Marprelate controversy, again, proved crucial to what followed, for in the creation of an alternate place for the utterance of deeply held beliefs, it helped form a nascent public sphere for meaningful expression and debate. Texts published in the decades following the Marprelate controversy often took advantage of the license it had extended. Where the Reformation can be said to have multiplied the positions that believers could occupy, embodied writing—including Spenser's *Faerie Queene,* more overtly political allegories like *Caltha Poetarum,* and even devotional works like *Mary Magdalen's Funeral Tears*—put many of those positions onto the printed page.

The importance given to reading following the Reformation leads us to the second of the primary sources of embodied writing, the general habituation to print. By the end of Elizabeth's reign, no one living would be able to recall a time when the printing press had not existed, and few would ever have known anyone who could remember such a time. The Elizabethans had become thoroughly familiar with print, and the printed page with it. As Christopher Hill suggests, they were soon to become, if they were not already, "the people of the Book."[74] Thus where the Reformation can be rightly described as "the story of great books," it was also the story of those books' readers and of the surprising variety of texts from which they had to choose.[75] John Foxe prefaced his *Actes and Monuments* with an apology for adding yet another text to what he saw as "an infinite multitude of books": "considering nowadays the world so greatly pestered, not only with superfluous plenty thereof, but of all other treatises, so that books now seem rather to lack Readers, than Readers to lack books."[76] Foxe was not alone in feeling that the "gift of printing" had thoroughly altered English culture. We hear echoes of his sentiment in Spenser's description of Errour in *The Faerie Queene*, for instance, where the monster's vomit is "full of bookes and papers" (1.1.20.6). This would seem to concern more than Catholic propaganda, for Spenser's indictment of this "floud of poyson" displays a reluctance over quantity as well as content. Indeed the following year, in 1591, the Epistle Dedicatory of *Martin Mar-Sixtus* believed itself justified in saying "We live in a printing age," and seven years later John Florio half lamented what he called "this our papersea."[77] The flood of books that these authors describe had accustomed people to reading, and during the 1590s writers, printers, and readers began to refashion what had become ordinary. As Matthew Greenfield has argued, the sometimes cacophonous medley of styles in pamphlet culture of the 1590s developed "as the solution to the *emergence* of a public—a public which read in a new way."[78] Responding to readers who read extensively as well as intensively, writers were forced to adjust their practice in this new era of books and reading.

Many of these writers came from a group that assumed an energetic role in the development of embodied writing. Anthony Esler has identified a "significant younger generation" of Elizabethan subjects who, born in the 1560s, rose to prominence in the 1590s, and it is this generation that remains largely responsible for much of the embodied writing in the later Elizabethan era.[79] Members of this younger generation came to London from Oxford and Cambridge, where satiric revues and epigrams prevailed, and where an emphasis on Latin models (flourishing also in the Tudor grammar schools) and the agonistic forms of humanist controversy helped shape the aggressive style of embodied writing.[80] They came from London's own Inns of Court, where disputation was a keynote and where explicit literary treatment of the body seemed rather the norm than the exception.[81] Coming also from various of England's counties, from which London and its "commonwealth of wit" seemed a center of opportunity, members of this younger group both competed among themselves and pushed against the boundaries they had inherited.[82] We can most clearly observe this generation, and the generational division it faced, when we examine the disparity of ages of those involved in the Bishops' Ban of 1599. The mean age of the known authors covered by the ban is around thirty (or twenty-seven if Harvey is, as Nashe might have preferred, counted an outsider); whereas if we average the ages of the men who issued the ban, Richard Bancroft (Bishop of London) and John Whitgift (Archbishop of Canterbury), along with that of their sovereign, Queen Elizabeth, we get a composite reader over sixty-three years of age.[83] This disparity of ages gives us a hint as to why one may rightly describe the outlook of the Elizabethan younger generation as less "aspiring" (Esler's word) than *despairing*. Not only did a scarcity of patronage and the pressures of the literary marketplace lead to widespread discontent among this group (one could note, for instance, the abundance of "malcontent" figures in literature during and after the 1590s), but the apparent hegemony of an older generation—especially what has been called the "paranoia of the establishment"—seemed a bar to its social progress.[84] Much embodied writing resulted from this generation's frustrations, resentments, and ambitions.

Yet it would be the public playhouses of London that most continually influenced the genre of embodied writing examined in this chapter. These theaters can be said to have provided both a space for public expression and a continuing metaphor for its representation. Actors and playwrights alike enjoyed an informal license to represent influential figures, the workings of statecraft, and issues of moment— and all in a venue that used the body to expand received limits on discourse. Actors were indeed "the abstract and brief chronicles of the time" and in their playing testified to an age "grown so pick'd that the toe of the peasant comes so near the heel of the courtier, he galls his kibe."[85] Hamlet prefaces his famous description here by saying it is a phenomenon "this three years I have took note of," a probable allusion to the embodied sallies of the satire wars, if not the War of the Theaters in particular. These theaters were as important conceptually as they were in practice, for the idea of the stage remained central to many notions of community during the early modern era. Nashe's inflection of the *theatrum mundi* trope in his preface to the 1591 edi-

tion of *Astrophel and Stella,* for instance, asks readers to "turn aside
into this Theater of pleasure, for here you shall find a paper stage
strewed with pearl, an artificial heav'n to overshadow the fair frame,
and crystal walls to encounter your curious eyes, whiles the tragicom-
edy of love is performed by starlight."[86] The "paper stage" he assigns
to the following sonnet sequence itself could appear to suggest a private theater or performance place. But the unlicensed movement of
Sidney's sequence (hitherto a comparatively private document) from
manuscript to print asks us to see this "Theater" as a public space, the
relationship between its manuscript readers and readers of its printed
form analogous to the relationship between private- and public-the-
ater audiences. And even as theaters drew on the growing sense of authorship and the embodied writings of the 1590s for some of their
energy, so too did print display its indebtedness to the theaters in its
representation of the public. Hosting millions of visits by playgoers
during the early modern era, purpose-built structures like the Globe,
the Rose, the Curtain, and the Swan formed sites of public discourse
and offered, through their familiar repertories, a personal celebrity not
wholly dependent on the court or connected with the church.

To be sure, the plays performed there seemed to make little hap-
pen; they led, that is, to no immediate political action, such as a rebellion or the expulsion of an ambassador, and were in this sense
"powerless."[87] But they held power of another sort. With their "liberty" and "license" they offered a place for the common handling of
otherwise uncommon ideas and provided models for the familiar
representation of identities. As we have seen, the influence was mutual. Presenting historical as well as fictional characters, dramas fostered the kind of personalization that embodied writing would
exercise. Thus when we consider Thomas Middleton's 1624 play, *A
Game at Chess*—in its intricate though direct allusion to contemporary personages and issues, perhaps the most notoriously embodied
text of the early modern era—we will not be surprised to find that
Middleton had learned the details of his craft during what he himself had called the "angry satire days" of the late 1590s, when his
own *Microcynicon, or Six Snarling Satires* was prohibited by the
Bishops' Ban on the first day of June in 1599. The daring, *ad
hominem* politics of *A Game at Chess* initially could seem confined to
the theater where the play took life and was, not long after its unprecedented popularity, silenced as a theatrical production. But the
following year its clever, embodied satire found new life in print.
And during the remainder of the seventeenth century, the license of
what an eighteen-year-old Middleton had understood as "satire
days" developed into a more mature and enduring liberty.

CHAPTER 4

THE DRAMATIC LIFE OF OBJECTS
IN THE EARLY MODERN THEATER

καὶ γὰρ πρὸς ἄψυχα καὶ τὰ τυχόντα ἔστιν ὥσπερ εἴρηται συμ-
βαίνει, καὶ εἰ πέπραγέ τις ἢ μὴ πέπραγεν ἔστιν ἀναγνωρίσαι

... *for indeed, [recognition] may take place in this manner*
through lifeless things or chance events, and one may recognize
whether someone has or has not done something.

—Aristotle, Poetics 1452a34–37

Sometime you shall see nothing but the adventures of an amorous
knight, passing from country to country for the love of his lady, en-
countering many a terrible monster made of brown paper, and at
his return, is so wonderfully changed, that he cannot be known but
by some posie in his tablet, or by a broken ring, or a handkircher or
a piece of a cockle shell, what learn you by that? When the soul of
your plays is either mere trifles, or Italian bawdry, or cussing of
gentlewomen, what are we taught?

—*Stephen Gosson,* Playes Confuted in Five Actions

The early modern playhouse in England was a theater of easily held
things. Hand-held objects figured centrally in plays of all genres
there, not just the dramatic adventures of "amorous knight[s]" that
Stephen Gosson derides. Indeed, one of the clearest departures that
early modern playwrights made from Aristotle's precepts came in the
ready employment of those "lifeless things" that the *Poetics* goes on

to criticize when used as a means of recognition.[1] So common was this practice, in fact, that our memories of many early modern plays involve images of characters holding things. With Shakespeare, for example, *Hamlet* (1601) can suggest a man contemplating a skull; *Antony and Cleopatra* (1607), a woman with an asp; *Romeo and Juliet* (1596), a young woman with a dagger. Sometimes this link between character and prop is so strong that certain objects can gesture toward a drama, character, and scene: a severed finger may call to mind De Flores in the third act of *The Changeling* (1622); a skewered heart, Giovanni in the final scene of *'Tis Pity She's a Whore* (1632). The endurance of such images—often aided by contemporary and subsequent printed illustrations—helps us to understand why Gosson would claim that, from a spectator's point of view, the "soul" of many plays resided in their objects.

Criticism devoted to these objects usually has come in a few established modes. One approach, influenced by the study of iconography, has built on the visual status of familiar hand props. Thus the skulls of *Hamlet* and *The Revenger's Tragedy* (1606) are explained in relationship to the memento mori tradition, the severed hands of *Titus Andronicus* (1593) as icons of political agency, and the heart and dagger of *'Tis Pity* alongside baroque and Neoplatonic imagery.[2] Another critical vein springs from the study of metaphor and signification; this approach examines what one critic has called "the language of props," seeing hand-held objects as "the realization of the verbal image in dramatic terms."[3] Because such objects often are related to the body, and may be the focus of characters' desires, they sometimes are described in psychoanalytic ways—the handkerchief of *Othello* (1604) being the classic site of this approach.[4] Still another critical genre explores the manner in which such props reveal social relations in the dramatic worlds they help define or resonate with other issues of their texts' historical moments. Criticism in this mode might take up, for example, the viol of *The Roaring Girl* (1611) for what it can tell us about the operation of gender in this play, or the severed head of Macbeth as an object rich in cultural symbolism.[5]

Yet while these approaches often shed light on important aspects of early modern plays, just as frequently their helpfulness has been limited by several factors. The first involves the matter of focus: In many instances of the critical traditions just outlined, insights are restricted by the particular objects under discussion. As with the thick descriptions examined in chapter 2, the close focus of essays on specific objects can be limiting. Such analyses can teach readers a great deal about specific objects in specific plays; however, the insight they lend often is confined to the prop in question. Because hand props were prevalent in all dramatic genres of the era, and because the "same" prop appears in many plays, over time, a critical approach that concentrates on single props, in single plays, can unnecessarily limit our understanding of such props' significance; this seems especially true in relation to audiences and playwrights who were familiar with numerous plays.[6] Success also can hamper these critical traditions. Thus while a strongly iconographic, or strongly semiotic, or strongly cultural materialist inquiry may illuminate hand props in the early modern theater and purport to explain them, the roles that such objects assumed were multiple and routinely elude those who press forceful claims about theatrical objects in relation to select domains of experience.

What criticism of hand props in the early modern theater most attests is our lack of a general account of such objects, an account in relation to which more specific claims could be measured. This chapter aims to provide such an account. Offering a thin description of hand props in early modern plays, this chapter necessarily declines the narrow focus that has characterized so much criticism of theatrical objects to date. Yet by describing hand props in a broader way, it seeks to lend this critical detail a context that will deepen our understanding of the materiality of the early modern playhouse. The following paragraphs locate hand props in relation to the array of physical objects appearing on the early modern stage and survey a variety of contemporary records that mention hand properties; they then explore the relationships among these properties, the dramatic genres of the era, and the playwrights who employed them. Among the questions this chapter addresses: What general truths can we offer about the number, kinds, and roles of hand props in early modern plays? What influence may genre, author, venue, and historical moment have had on these quantitative and qualitative issues? How did contemporaries describe and account for these props? And how may the answers to such questions affect our understanding of the plays and playhouses of early modern England?

A variety of things appeared on the otherwise bare stages of early modern England, from actors and costumes to scenic decorations, signs, and hand props. Their "thingness" may be more or less apparent, depending on both the production in question and our definition of a thing. We can qualify the preceding questions, therefore, with still others: How should we define a theatrical object? What do hand props have in common with bodies, costumes, and larger properties, and how do they differ? Objects in the theater can be defined in many ways, of course. As Shoshana Avigal and Shlomith Rimmon-Kenan have suggested, a theatrical object can become so by being

- either inanimate or capable of becoming inanimate;
- transportable or placed so as to enable the actors to move around it;
- deprived of intentionality: the object is manipulated but cannot itself initiate discourse;
- either multifunctional, or different from its everyday use, or completely non-utilitarian except in its technical theatrical function;
- capable of "furnishing" the "stage-space" and acting as mediator between the actor's body and this space;
- seemingly mimetic and referential;
- artificial, "fabricated," unnatural;
- artifact, capable of being evaluated with the help of such aesthetic criteria as are used in the plastic arts[7]

Most of these aspects relate objects closely to the human. Actors transport objects, and objects are placed in relation to actors. Objects imitate and refer for humans and are fabricated, used, and evaluated by them. It is also true, however, that such objects help to define human subjects through their felt difference: If an object is that which is for a subject, we are subjects because we are not—perhaps not *only*—objects. Thus do the above descriptions, which set out to define theatrical objects, wind up telling us about theatrical subjectivity: in particular, that it often is established in relation to objects.[8] It was perhaps partly in response to such dependency that the *Poetics* criticized dramatic recognition deriving from trivial properties. By defining human relations through the inanimate, such recognition worked to blur the distinction between person and thing. It therefore threatened to challenge the sharp boundaries that Aristotle sought to establish in describing tokens as *apsuka,* or "lifeless."[9]

  Granting the thoroughly material nature of the early modern stage and the fact that objects can seem quite vital, how may we justify a concern with hand props? How do they differ from other things in the theater? Hand props of course share with costumes, bodies, and scenic devices the condition of being "materially realizable on stage in three dimensions." And all these things possess a certain "mobility," a capacity to acquire various states, shapes, and meanings within the context of the theatrical production.[10] On stage a living body may seem to become an inanimate one; a shoe can signify a personal relation; a lone tree, a garden. And, like hand props, costumes and items of apparel can be acquired, exchanged, altered, and discarded, frequently changing in significance as this occurs. Yet if hand props in early modern drama—what we could define as "unanchored physical objects, light enough for a person to carry on stage for manual use there"[11]—shared the essential nature of these other objects, they differed in an important way, by having more mobility than costumes, bodies, and larger properties. Because they are detached and easily held, they are more easily transferred from one character, play, and genre to another. Much like coins and other units of currency, hand props testify by their size and portability to an open potential. They can be variously possessed, traded, lost, found, concealed, and evaluated. This ability allows them to relate characters to each other and to larger elements in their dramatic worlds as well as to qualify those relations more fluidly than can such larger properties as costumes and scenic devices.

It is precisely this fluidity that ensured that hand props would steadily disappear from discourse concerning the stage. If we imagine a sequence beginning with the plays themselves, then including bills and inventories, descriptions of productions, and, finally, formal criticism of these plays, what becomes apparent is that the number of hand props diminishes as one moves from play and theatrical records to criticism. Where a play easily can contain thirty or more hand properties, a playhouse inventory will list only a fraction of these, an account or illustration of a production fewer still, and critical essays (when they mention properties at all) commonly only one.[12] Close focus on certain resonant properties has, ironically, worked to limit our understanding of these and other objects. We need to read against this tendency to recover the range of props in and their importance to early modern drama. To do so, we should examine the ways in which properties have disappeared from view and determine why they have done so.

We can begin with contemporary bills and other lists of expenses connected with theatrical productions. A record detailing the most basic theatrical materials appears in the "emptions and provisions" for the Christmas entertainments at court in 1572, which lists expenses incurred by a "propertymaker" named John Carow in relation to such objects as "A nett for the ffishers maskers," "wooll to stuf the fishes," "speares for the play of *Cariclia*," "A tree of Holly for the Duttons play," "13 Arrowes," "A palmers staf," "A desk for farrantes playe," "A vyzarde for an apes face," "A keye for Janus," "A Monster," "Dishes," and "Egges counterfet vii doozen."[13] Such a list is as close as we may come to a document that acknowledges, as fully as the plays themselves, the drama's use of and dependence on various materials. Of course, in some ways a list like this is even more thorough than a dramatic text in that it catalogs physical objects whose use the play's fiction may not make explicit. Thus, besides the wool used to stuff fishes, the bill submitted by the property-maker Carow includes such items as "syxpeny nayles," "three peny nayles," "twopeny nayles," "Tackes," and "hoopes for the monster"—things not only not specified in dramatic texts but that a playwright or show organizer might never have considered when writing or producing a drama.[14]

Objects typically make their way onto the page in direct relation to their value to the one who writes that page. Because it is probable that Carow first purchased the materials for the above items himself (and most likely submitted the bill within a short time of fashioning them), he had reason to detail his expenses fully. Nails were well worth itemizing, as were visors, staves, and arrows. We gain the benefit of this detail because they were important expenses to Carow. On the other hand, some documents pass over such detail because they contain items of a much greater value, with the expensive forcing out the less valuable. Here we may consider a transcript of Philip Henslowe's list of stage properties. Henslowe originally recorded this list in his "diary" under the heading: "*Enventary tacken of all the properties for my* Lord Admeralles men, *the* 10 *of Marche* 1598."[15] This list comes in the context of other inventories, and of payments throughout Henslowe's diary, related to costumes. The early modern theater was, of course, thoroughly invested in the display of clothing.[16] The Elizabethan eye was attracted to sumptuous dress to a degree that can be hard for us to imagine, and early modern playhouses were careful to satisfy the many playgoers who wished to see sumptuous costumes. Thus Henslowe's inventory of physical "properties" from 1598 should be seen in the context of the most important property in Henslowe's theatrical business: not actors, playwrights, play texts, or hand props, but clothing. More valuable than other properties, clothing largely supplants notice of other theatrical objects throughout his diary.

Even as Henslowe's mention of what we could call "harder" properties pales in comparison with the attention paid to costumes, however, so does he give little notice to the more ordinary properties—and especially the smaller ones. This list mentions approximately eighty-four objects and groups of objects (a precise count is made difficult by Henslowe's tendency to record a type of object—say "iij tymbrells"—alongside a less generic property: "j dragon in fostes"). The following is a representative selection of its contents:

> *Item,* j gowlden flece; ij rackets; j baye tree
> *Item,* j wooden hatchett; j lether hatchete.
> *Item,* j wooden canepie; owld Mahemetes head.
> *Item,* j lyone skin; j bears skyne; & Faetones lymes, & Faeton charete; & Argosse heade.
> *Item,* Nepun forcke & garland[17]

As this sampling makes apparent, Henslowe stresses special things, objects related to particular characters and plays. Within a few lines, for instance, one finds references to Mahomet, Phaeton, Argus, Neptune—even, in light of "gowlden flece," Jason and Medea (and, perhaps, Hercules); and what may involve Dekker's *Phaeton* (1598), the anonymous *Mahomet* (1588), and *Jupiter and Io* (1597), among other dramas. And while over half the objects that Henslowe records (forty-four of eighty-four) could be defined as hand properties, very few of them are ordinary or unremarkable.

On the contrary, Henslowe's inventory primarily records objects that, if lost, stolen, or damaged, would require special fabrication to replace. It makes no mention of such smaller and everyday objects as purses, documents, jewels, toothpicks, and coins. In his extended analysis of Henslowe's diary, Neil Carson relates that

> Almost as surprising as the presence of so many large properties [in Henslowe's accounts] is the inexplicable absence of some small ones. There are, for example, no chairs or benches in the inventory, nor any tables, trenchers, or mugs for the numerous banquet and tavern scenes in Elizabethan drama. The seventeen foils (while certainly more than the four or five mentioned by the chorus in *Henry V*), seem an absolute minimum to present believable battle scenes. There are none of the letters and purses regularly required in plays of the period, nor is any mention made of books, writing materials, and other objects needed for "study" scenes. It would seem that the inventory is only a partial list of the Company's resources. Many of these smaller items were probably kept backstage or supplied by the actors.[18]

It could be argued, following Carson, that the small size of such objects entailed they be kept in a separate place—for instance, a locked chest or chests in the playhouse's wardrobe. If their existence was recorded at all, perhaps it was noted in a list that has not survived. Recently, however, a more intriguing suggestion has been advanced by Natasha Korda, who, exploring the relationship between Henslowe's pawnbroking and his theatrical investments, proposes that the absent properties may have been supplemented by unredeemed items in the pawn accounts.[19] As a pawnbroker, Henslowe could be expected to have had a surplus of the ordinary objects missing from the diary's lists. Because a company would not need a property maker to fashion them, these objects would likely be absent from any bill; they would merely have been borrowed from another of Henslowe's businesses. Whatever the explanation for their absence, one truth remains: However important they were to the function of the plays, these more ordinary objects were not included in what Henslowe's list calls "*all the properties for my* Lord Admeralles men."

Their absence would be less noteworthy here were it not part of a larger pattern. We hear even less about hand props, for instance, in contemporary descriptions of dramatic performances, although the exceptions are familiar. The account of *Twelfth Night* (1601) that John Manningham recorded in his diary in 1602 mentions the letter that Maria counterfeits to fool Malvolio, and likewise Simon Forman's memories of *Cymbeline* (1609) include Iachimo's theft of Imogen's bracelet.[20] Significantly, each of these instances involves some kind of transgression. We could take it as a given, in fact, that objects customarily appear in such accounts when they are involved in some breach of decorum or audience expectation. The induction to *A Warning for Fair Women* (1599), for example, complains of those plays that feature "two or three like to drovers, / With taylers bodkins, stabbing one another."[21] Here the difficulty is over the triviality of the entire production, from actor to property and, in the famous lines just prior to these, diction: "skreaming like a pigge half stickt, / And cries *Vindicta*, revenge, revenge." Instead of swords— appropriate to a dramatic spectacle—the actors are said to bear weapons small enough to be mistaken for "bodkins."[22] Other instances where a breach of decorum appears to have made props more remarkable include Thomas Platter's description of a play in which a "servant proceeded to hurl his shoe at his master's head"; Ben Jonson's sneer at spectacles in which "egges are broken" (apparently when thrown at others); and Sir John Chamberlain's gossipy hearsay to the effect that the King's Men had obtained Gondomar's cast suit and litter for their scandalous production of *A Game at Chess* in 1624 (these representing objects larger, of course, than the hand properties of our other examples).[23] An allusion to a stage fool who will "twirle his Bawble" in Thomas Goffe's *The Careless Shepherdess* (1619) may nod to the potential indecorum associated with fools' bawdy actions, for baubles (fools' clubs or instruments) were often material for indecent jests.[24] Fools were expected to have baubles, which often served as an extension, if not mark, of their characters. And this near identification of character and thing typically was solidified in the many visual representations of dramatic performance and of characters and situations associated with the theater.

If objects found their way into the gossip of social records when they were involved in indecorous actions, they were most often portrayed in visual representations when they upheld decorum of character. In early modern illustrations, hand properties seem not the exception but the rule. Perhaps this was because such properties helped identify a character and scene and more fully embodied a play. Perhaps it was owing also to a certain *horror vaccui* when it came to figures' hands: Illustrators preferred that hands be used for gestures, or rest on something, or grasp an object, rather than remaining empty. Whether we explain this tendency through content (through what a hand held) or process (through the fact that a hand was doing something), illustrations connected with the early modern stage routinely feature characters holding things.[25] The visual representations that R. A. Foakes gathers in *Illustrations of the English Stage 1580 - 1642* feature approximately seventy props in figures' hands. (There are more properties when one counts worn weapons, hats, and other items worn on the body, or objects on tables accessible to these figures.)[26] Most of these held props in the relevant illustrations are weapons and objects of authority. The weapons include swords, daggers, halberds, lances, pikes, staves, mauls, and crossbows. Although many of these weapons convey authority, there are also scepters and orbs (particularly in representations of Elizabeth), which remain authoritative without the direct threat of violence. Besides such props, dramatic illustrations also feature objects more firmly grounded in the routines of everyday life, such as food, utensils (goblets and knives), books, papers, letters, pipes, snuff boxes, lights, fans, canes, crutches, and hats.

In some illustrations, hand props work to identify the figure. For instance, the book and staff on the title page of the second quarto of Marlowe's *Doctor Faustus* (publ. 1616) join with a doctor's gown and hat, a magic circle, and an impish devil to tell us that the main figure is the title character. Likewise a cane or walking stick in the 1658 quarto of *The Witch of Edmonton* (1621) helps identify old "Mother" Sawyer. Hand props similarly confirm the identities of characters on the title page of Henry Marsh's collection of drolls, *The Wits, or, Sport upon Sport* (1662, 1673), where such figures as Falstaff and Antonio (the latter from *The Changeling*) are identified both by their names and by such physical accoutrements as costume and prop: The "Changling" wears a fool's cap and has a hornbook dangling from his wrist; Falstaff is dressed in clothing redolent of Shakespeare's time, and his identity is fleshed out not only by a protruding stomach but by the cup he holds aloft—a confirming symbol of his epicurean character.[27] Perhaps no illustrated prop is more clearly a token of a character's identity, however, than the bracelet that an almost nude Bateman displays in a woodcut published with William Sampson's *The Vow Breaker* (1636).[28] The object in question is a kind of "charm bracelet" from which hangs half of a piece of gold that Bateman and Anne, his beloved, had divided between them as a love token. Bateman, having been away as a soldier, returns from the wars on the very day when Anne has married another man. In the woodcut, Bateman is pointing to the bracelet and saying "Thinke on thy promise alive or dead I must and will injoy thee."

The marking of this bracelet as the living symbol of Anne's "promise" also marks Bateman as her intended; the bracelet contains within itself their history together and the grounds of his present and future actions. One could say that the bracelet is a miniature "plot" or summary of the play's action. Much like the tokens that Gosson derided in the epigraph to this chapter, it does more than trivial objects are commonly thought capable of doing. It is this function that evokes the intensive commentary that such objects have drawn. What Aristotle, Gosson, and Thomas Rymer after them responded to is, in part, the indecorum of recognition deriving from the trivial and, in part, the irrationality of fictions that define human relations through small properties. As Rymer complained in his well-known indictment of *Othello*, "So much ado, so much stress, so much passion and repetition about an Handkerchief!"[29] To critics of this orientation, reducing social relationships to the level of trivial, "external" things makes no sense.[30]

Yet where these commentators could appear the exception (in that their emphasis on decorum and reason may seem too strict), they established the pattern that most later criticism has followed. In writing about Desdemona's handkerchief, or *Hamlet*'s skull, that is, critics follow in the footsteps of Rymer, Gosson, and Aristotle. It is difficult to avoid repeating these commentators' rationalism because analysis often is drawn to moments of the irrational—to sequences in plays, for instance, that cross the boundaries of reason, and so call for dispassionate analysis. Thus a concentration of social or psychological energy on a seemingly trivial object appears to be "fetishism" (the sustained exaggeration of an object's value or importance), which in turn begs for critical rationalization. We are drawn to the handkerchief and to the skull not only because the characters in these plays are drawn to them but in part because we feel they should not be.

Significantly, this moralistic evaluation of objects begins not with critics but with the plays themselves. One could compare Hamlet's incredulous "This?" in response to hearing that a skull belonged to someone he once knew—upon which he addresses it, asking

> Where be your gibes now, your gambols, your songs, your flashes of merriment, that were wont to set the table on a roar?
>
> (5.1.182, 189–91)

with Vindice's famous apostrophe to the skull of Gloriana, his beloved:

> Does the silkworm expend her yellow labors
> For thee? For thee does she undo herself?
> . . . . . .
> Does every proud and self-affecting dame
> Camphire her face for this? and grieve her maker
> In sinful baths of milk, when many an infant starves,
> For her superfluous outside—all for this?
>
> (3.5.71–2, 83–6)[31]

In these well-known passages, we hear variations on a single rhetorical question concerning the lack of fit between the object at hand and a complex set of memories and truths separate from, if related to, the object. There is an edgy surprise behind the utterances: How could such a vital, irrepressible body be reduced to so unremarkable an object? Why do Nature, society, and individuals waste resources on such hollow vanities?

This kind of dramatic moment sees hand props at their most resonant. Time slows as the speaker, like Bateman pointing toward his bracelet, directs our attention toward the object. Not coincidentally, it is precisely such moments that draw the most critical attention. In fact, one could offer no better example of a "reading effect": the process by which a structure in a literary text uncannily shapes, in its own image, critical accounts of that structure or text. As Shoshana Felman defines this phenomenon: "The scene of the critical debate is thus a *repetition* of the scene dramatized in the text. The critical interpretation, in other words, not only elucidates the text but also reproduces it dramatically, unwittingly *participates in it*. Through its very reading, the text, so to speak, acts itself out. As a reading effect, this inadvertent 'acting out' is indeed uncanny: whichever way the reader turns, he can but be turned by the text, he can but *perform* it by *repeating* it."[32] Felman's description of the "reading effect" has a great deal to teach us about object criticism. Insofar as we "read" the same objects that dramatic characters read, and read them in similar ways, the criticism we produce runs the risk of being more an effect than an analysis of such texts. In our continual concern with a select few properties in early modern drama, we can be seen as performing these texts, participating, like the plays' characters, in their scenes of wonder. Therefore, if we are to avoid asking the same kinds of questions that a play's characters ask (and possibly getting the same answers that they do), we need to work against the selective focus displayed in speeches such as those just examined. Plays are full of objects, and while many of these objects fail to draw extended notice from the plays themselves, they remain integral to their dramatic worlds—not despite but because of their ordinariness.

To return to the primary question that began this chapter: What general truths can we offer about the number, kinds, and roles of hand props in early modern plays? We should start by establishing what is known about hand props. Much of our objective knowledge about the broad range of hand props in early modern drama derives from Frances Teague's *Shakespeare's Speaking Properties*. A major virtue of Teague's study is that it includes, in its appendixes, figures relating to properties in plays written by Shakespeare (excepting *The Two Noble Kinsmen* [1613]). Her first appendix offers a detailed property list for each drama. The second divides these properties into categories and calculates the distribution of properties across the plays. Although the chapters of Teague's book offer many insights about the function of stage properties in Shakespeare's plays, the figures in these appendixes are for the most part underutilized. Because these figures are the first hard data concerning hand properties in any body of early modern plays, it will be useful here to listen to what they tell us.

We could begin with numbers. How many hand props appeared in Shakespeare's plays? Teague counts the props in the thirty-six Folio plays and in *Pericles* (1608). She records them on their first appearance only and omits references to costumes, unless they come to function as a property—such as, for example, Osric's hat and Troilus's sleeve. Teague's figures suggest an average of thirty-four properties per play.[33] We see thus that Shakespeare's plays used more props than actors. (T. J. King estimates that the principal parts in most plays of the late-Elizabethan and early Stuart eras would have required around fourteen actors, ten men and four boys, with other personnel hired to fill in the few remaining lines and roles).[34] If we still needed a reason to take the function of props in early modern drama seriously, the fact that the typical play in such a grouping employed more inanimate things than actors as their "performing objects" would seem to give us our warrant.[35] This was not true for every play, of course. Some plays, especially shorter ones, had fewer props than actors. To make comparisons with plays of various lengths, therefore, it will be helpful to find out how many properties were likely to occur in units both shorter and longer than Shakespeare's average play. The calculations could be made as follows: If we average the through line numbers of Shakespeare's plays, we come up with a composite play of around 3,018 lines, or a text approximately the length of *All's Well That Ends Well* (1602). Given the typical frequency of properties across all of Shakespeare's plays, we could expect approximately 11.26 properties per every 1,000 lines.

What kinds of props made up these numbers? Teague offers six categories: lights; weapons or war gear; documents; riches or gifts; tokens of characters; and "other." Were a typical Shakespeare play to exist, it would contain at least 1 light (for example, torch, candle), three rewards (moneybags, coins), six documents (letters, proclamations), five tokens of identity (crowns, gloves, rings, scepters), six weapons, and nine "other" or miscellaneous objects. (The numbers here total less than thirty-four because of rounding). Of course, no play is typical in this way, because genre strongly influences both the number and kind of props a play uses.[36] Regarding genre, tragedies tend to have the most props, histories the second greatest number, and comedies the least. The numbers, on average: tragedies, 11.48 props per 1,000 lines; histories, 10.6 props per 1,000 lines; comedies, 8.43 props per 1,000 lines.

The romances pose a special problem. Although romances have a higher frequency of props than the comedies, *Pericles* remains something of an anomaly, with almost double the number of props as its companion romances. Figures for the romances are as follows: *Pericles,* 19.14 per 1,000 lines; *Cymbeline,* 10.21 per 1,000 lines; *The Winter's Tale* (1610), 8 per 1,000 lines; *The Tempest* (1611), 11.53 per 1,000 lines. Acts 1 and 2 of *Pericles,* usually thought non-Shakespearean, have a frequency of 23 props per 1,000 lines, whereas if we inspect acts 3, 4, and 5 of the play, most of which is traditionally ascribed to Shakespeare, we find a lower frequency, of 16 props per 1,000 lines. Some, though not all, of this density of props in the first two acts of *Pericles* involves the parade of knights in 2.2, each of whom bears a device on his shield. This procession recalls the practices of an earlier moment in the early modern theater, when, in histories and romances alike, spectacular displays of arms and colors were common.[37]

Genre affects not only the number but the kinds of props appearing on stage. It is apparent, for instance, that certain kinds of properties serve as generic signals: A lute or a hobby-horse could signal a comedy, a skull or a dagger, a tragedy. And knowing the genre of a play can lead one to expect it to feature certain properties. We can perceive this in table 4.1, which draws on Teague's figures to show both the composite and generic distribution of properties across her six categories. The figures in boldface show percentages higher than the mean.

Some of these figures confirm what we might have surmised about the plays: Shakespeare's comedies, for example, feature more "rewards" than do his histories and tragedies. However, several facts may surprise us. The comedies employ more documents than do the other genres—surprising in that critics usually emphasize writing and writings in the tragedies and histories.[38] A typical comedy, however, features more documents than a tragedy and a history play combined. Comedy's emphasis on interpersonal relationships, and the tendency of comedic characters to express their desires in letters and poems, help to explain this feature. Consider the four male lovers and their individual "papers" in 4.3 of *Love's Labor's Lost* (1595) or the various letters that the lovers exchange in *The Two Gentlemen of Verona* (1593).

Table 4.1 **Distribution of Props in Shakespeare: Composite and by Genre (in percentages)**

Plays	Lights	Rewards	Documents	Identity Tokens	Weapons	Other
Composite	3.2	10.33	19.79	16.1	21.55	29
13 comedies	2.7	**18.61**	**27.62**	10.81	16.21	24
10 histories	1.6	5.67	16.48	**25.1**	**22.7**	28.37
10 tragedies	5.4	7.37	18.18	12.53	**25.06**	**31.44**
4 romances	2.17	**11.59**	14.49	15.21	21	**35.5**

Source: Based on figures from Frances Teague, *Shakespeare's Speaking Properties.*

We may not be surprised to find that Shakespeare's histories use more identity tokens (usually objects of authority and rank) and weapons than the average or to find that his tragedies rely even more heavily still on weapons. On the whole, it is the tragedies' use of weapons—daggers, swords, rapiers, and cudgels—that accounts for their greater frequency of props. But the tragedies also heavily use lights, a fact that reminds us how many of these plays unfold mainly at night. In contrast, the history plays take place largely during the day and have the fewest lights of any genre.

Like his comedies, Shakespeare's romances employ a higher than average percent of rewards yet differ from the comedies in their comparative paucity of documents. In fact, the romances use fewer documents than any of the other three genres. We could understand this, first, as a function of how the romances present desire (that is, in a more chaste way than do the passionate poems and letters that characterized Shakespeare's comedies in the 1590s) and, second, as a function of alienation in the romances: The emotional reconciliations at the ends of *Pericles, Cymbeline, The Winter's Tale,* and *The Tempest* depend in part on the fact that characters have been profoundly divided from each other, not communicating through letters to the same extent as characters in the comedies. *The Tempest,* which has no letters, epitomizes this tendency. Stranded on an island, Prospero seems unable to send letters; after the storm has delivered his enemies and friends to him, he does not need to send any.

Because Shakespeare changed his generic emphasis during his career, pronouncements about the effect of chronology on the frequency of properties in his plays can be dangerous. Nonetheless, certain observations are valid. If we were to graph the frequency of properties in Shakespeare's plays, we would see something like a shallow V over the course of his career. That is, beginning with many props in the early 1590s, we witness a gradual diminishing through the following decade. Early plays like *Titus Andronicus* (21 props per 1,000 lines) and *2 Henry VI* (1590) (15.5 props per 1,000 lines) have comparatively many props when examined in the context of similar tragedies from later in the 1590s and early 1600s. *Hamlet,* for instance, has 10.24 props per 1,000 lines, and *Henry V* (1599) has 7.7 props per 1,000 lines—a much lower frequency than Shakespeare's earlier history plays and tragedy. After this decline in frequency, we see a significant increase beginning about 1605, when such tragedies as *King Lear* (1605) (16 props per 1,000 lines), *Macbeth* (1606) (17.4 props per 1,000 lines), and *Timon* (1607) (17.64 props per 1,000 lines) approach and exceed the frequency for tragedies of the 1590s, and when a collaborative history play, *Henry VIII* (1613), exceeds the frequency for all history plays, with 17.61 props per 1,000 lines. *Henry VIII* recalls the heavy use of things in the "drum and trumpet" shows of the late 1580s and early 1590s, and nostalgically re-creates that environment—perhaps even with a surplus of things.

What might have caused Shakespeare to vary the frequency of props over the course of his career? Genre alone cannot account for the variation, as plays written between 1598 and 1605 tend to have fewer props than plays of the same genre written before and after this period. We have already seen that *Hamlet* and *Henry V* have fewer properties than, respectively, *Romeo and Juliet* and *Titus Andronicus* and seven earlier history plays. The middle comedies also have fewer properties than earlier comedies. For instance, *Much Ado About Nothing* (1598) (6.33 props per 1,000 lines), *As You Like It* (1599) (5.36 props per 1,000 lines), and *Measure for Measure* (1604) (5.1 props per 1,000 lines) can be compared with such earlier works as *The Merchant of Venice* (1596) (13.5 props per 1,000 lines), *The Merry Wives of Windsor* (1597) (13.55 props per 1,000 lines), and *A Midsummer Night's Dream* (1596) (9 props per 1,000 lines). Clearly the decline in numbers was apparent across various dramatic works and did not occur because of changes in Shakespeare's generic preferences.

How, therefore, to explain it? Venue may seem to offer a solution. For the first "Globe" plays so considered—*Henry V*, and *Julius Caesar* (1599) (9.9 props per 1,000 lines)—have fewer properties than earlier instances of their genres. And *As You Like It* has noticeably fewer than either *The Merchant of Venice* or *The Merry Wives of Windsor*. Did the move to a "new" playhouse cause a reduction of the props called for in Shakespeare's plays? Even if we answered this question in the affirmative, such an explanation would not be the entire story. The move from the Theater to the Globe occurred during 1599, and a noticeable decline in property use appears in *Much Ado About Nothing*—commonly, though not universally, dated 1598/99. Also, the King's Men leased the Blackfriars for indoor performances in 1608—again, after Shakespeare's use of properties had begun to increase. It may be, therefore, that this variation is evidence of a response to alterations in audience tastes and in the company's taste in audiences, which the change in venues signaled. That is, rather than being the cause of such variation, these changes of place were, at least in part, an effect of the same cultural and aesthetic forces that produced changes in property use. Causality, in this account, was overdetermined: Properties not only signaled larger theatrical changes but were themselves changed by, and had a role in shaping, those transformations.

Such a description would also remain consonant with thematic changes in Shakespeare's plays. Broadly stated, during the late 1590s and early 1600s his plays center increasingly on individuals, psychology, and character and less on the sometimes superficial stories of nations and factions. With Prince Hal, Brutus, and Hamlet, a shift toward the interiority of the later tragedies has occurred. More of a play's time is spent with fewer characters—in short, sieges give way to soliloquies, polity to the personal. If we compare the props in the first acts of *Titus Andronicus* and *Hamlet,* for example, we find that the early tragedy includes "colors," "swords for Saturninus's party," "swords for Bassanius's party," "crown," "coffin covered in black," "laurel wreath," "Titus's sword," "four sons' swords," "Titus's palliament—white cloak," "patrician swords," "chariot," and "Titus's crest." *Hamlet,* in contrast, offers us exactly half this number of properties: "seats," "ghost's armor," "Marcellus' partisan," "Claudius's letter to Norway," "Hamlet's tablet," "Hamlet's sword."[39] These lists are a study in contrast. The props of *Titus Andronicus* seem those of a playwright utilizing display to its maximum advantage and perhaps for its own sake. A coffin competes with a chariot, and a laurel wreath with a crown for the audience's eye. *Hamlet,* on the other hand, is quite spare. Its properties seem to follow the action, arising out of it rather than providing the action's reason for being. The same is apparent if we contrast the two props in *Henry V*'s first act— a throne and tennis balls —with the various swords, letters, armor, petitions, colors, robes, and halberds in the first acts of earlier history plays. With their respective assertion and denial of his authority, the throne and the tennis balls help to establish the play's interest in Henry's character, whereas the assortment of props in earlier history plays indicates nothing if not the dispersion of dramatic interest across various characters and factions.

If during the last years of the Elizabethan era Shakespeare increasingly stressed the tragedic or heroic individual, and in so doing departed from the early plays' larger groupings of characters and the objects that identified them, another kind of shift may have been responsible for the increase in his plays' use of properties after 1604. Where the first half of his career witnessed a shift from spectacle to speech, the second half saw a return to spectacle, as his generic emphasis moved from history plays and comedies to tragedies and romances. All plays, of course, use more properties when they show instead of tell. Dumb shows, for example, rely heavily on props to convey their information. We have to look no further than the prop-intensive dumb show in *Hamlet* for a silent language that speaks through properties:

> *Enter a King and a Queen very lovingly, the Queen embracing him and he her. She kneels and makes show of protestation unto him. He takes her up and declines his head upon her neck. He lies him down upon a bank of flowers. She, seeing him asleep, leaves him. Anon come in another man, takes off his crown, kisses it, pours poison in the sleeper's ears, and leaves him. The Queen returns, finds the King dead, makes passionate action. The pois'ner with some three or four mutes come in again, seem to condole with her. The dead body is carried away. The pois'ner woos the Queen with gifts; she seems harsh and unwilling awhile, but in the end accepts love.*
>
> (3.2.135 s.d.)

Crowns, a bank of flowers, poison, gifts. Increasingly after the accession of James, such silent language came to influence Shakespeare's dramatic practice, as the spectacular nature of courtly shows displaced some of the intensively verbal copia that had been his trademark during the late 1590s and early 1600s.[40] Similarly, we know that during this period the way Shakespeare described playgoers changed. As Andrew Gurr points out, "From 1600 onwards, Shakespeare abandoned the idea of an auditory in favour of spectators."[41] What we may be witnessing in the decline and rise of Shakespeare's use of props, therefore, are larger changes in the nature of his plays and in the desires of the audiences for whom he wrote. An intensively visual theater of the late 1580s and early 1590s was temporarily affected by verbal preferences in the late 1590s and early 1600s, which in turn gave way to practices influenced by the spectacles of the Jacobean court and by audiences oriented toward those spectacles.

While within Shakespeare's career we see a double movement in the frequency of hand props, in early modern drama as a whole the narrative is more straightforward. Using the same principles underlying the examination of Shakespeare's plays, an original survey of twenty non-Shakespearean dramas from approximately 1587 to 1636 helps contextualize the Shakespeare figures even as it shows a discernible pattern in the use of hand properties across early modern plays.[42] We can begin with the figures for seventeen plays by various authors and in various genres presented in Table 4.2.

This table reveals a number of things. Regarding numbers, playwrights' use of hand props was close to that of their contemporaries. Those plays written during the period in which Shakespeare was active approximate his practice in relation to hand props. And his con-

Table 4.2 Frequency of Props in Non-Shakespearean Plays, 1587–1636

Play	Approximate Year	Total Lines	Total Props	Props Per 1,000 Lines
The Spanish Tragedy	1587	2,625	42	16
The Battle of Alcazar	1589	1,591	35	22
The Jew of Malta	1589	2,385	28	11.74
Woodstock	1592	3,218	56	17.4
Edmund Ironside	1595	2,063	21	10.18
Every Man in His Humour	1598	3,074	30	9.76
All Fools	1601	1,858	15	8.07
Sejanus	1603	3,146	19	6.04
A Trick to Catch the Old One	1605	2,139	17	7.94
The Revenger's Tragedy	1606	2,534	24	9.47
A King and No King	1611	2,665	17	6.37
The Devil Is an Ass	1616	3,235	20	6.18
Women Beware Women	1621	3,311	25	7.55
The Roman Actor	1626	2,282	17	7.45
The Picture	1629	2,672	20	7.48
Perkin Warbeck	1633	2,539	20	7.87
The Royal Slave	1636	1,665	7	4.2

temporaries' practices are also equivalent to one another: Middleton's practice in *Women Beware Women* (1621) is close to that of Massinger in *The Roman Actor* (1626), which in turn is much like that of Ford in *Perkin Warbeck* (1633). Indeed, the second important thing this table tells us is that there was a general decline in the number of hand props used. Before 1603, no play listed has a frequency of fewer than 8 props per 1,000 lines; after 1606, there is no play listed with a frequency *greater* than 8 props per 1,000 lines. George Peele's *The Battle of Alcazar* (1589) features the greatest frequency of props, a number that includes, like *Titus Andronicus,* a potentially embarrassing array of such props as swords, chariots, whips, knives, drums, and brands. And although the frequency here may seem inflated because of the comparative brevity of the play (1,591 lines), Peele very well might have employed even more props to illustrate his dramatic tableau had the play been twice its length.

Plays written in the late 1580s and early 1590s employed the most hand properties—a truth confirmed by similarly high frequencies in Shakespeare's early plays. Thus even a late history such as *Perkin*

Warbeck has a frequency closer to other plays from the 1620s and 1630s than to a history play from the late 1580s or early 1590s. A comedy such as *The Jew of Malta*, from 1589, features more properties than comedies written ten, fifteen, and forty years later. And *The Spanish Tragedy* (1587) likewise has a greater frequency of properties than all the tragedies written after it on Table 4.2. Seen over nearly half a century like this, the frequency of hand props appears to have been more greatly influenced by historical moment than by genre. And despite the temporary increase we have seen in Shakespeare's practice after the accession of James, with the shift from Tudor to Stuart we are witnessing an overall decline in the frequency of hand properties in plays.

One cause of this decline may have been a reduction in the numbers of actors and roles in early modern plays. The expansive tableaux of all genres in the 1580s and 1590s (for instance, the parade of characters even in the comedy of *Love's Labor's Lost*) entailed numerous figures entering and exiting the audience's view; many of these figures carried hand properties. Such an explanation would dovetail with scholars' accounts of the "large" plays and repertories established in London during the 1580s and early 1590s, a phenomenon explored by Andrew Gurr, David Bradley, T. J. King, and Scott McMillin, among others.[43] Gurr points to the establishment of the first "large" acting company in 1583 (twelve sharers rather than eight in the Queen's Men), a fashion that had become the norm by the early 1590s and that influenced the writing of "large" plays (mainly chronicle histories) until 1593/94. After this, the ambitions of these "large-capacity" companies—and, accordingly, the number of roles in the plays they staged—declined as the plague and travel and economic pressures brought home to the companies the difficult realities of their augmented size.[44] By the time Cartwright pens *The Royal Slave* (1636), the sprawling organization of the Elizabethan repertories had given way to smaller acting repertories accustomed not to the expansive plebeian amphitheaters but to the more restricted spaces of the hall playhouses.[45] Fewer actors generally meant fewer roles, which in turn reduced the quantity of hand props required. In itself, though, the reduction of roles explains a decline in number but not in frequency. The decline in frequency may have come from a diminished need to differentiate characters from one another: With fewer "group" scenes, there is less need to mark characters by means of such an identifying property as, for instance, a banner or shield.

Three plays examined fell out of the specified range and make up something like a distinct "genre" of drama in their infrequent use of—and, in one case, reference to—hand props. The plays in question are Daniel's *Philotas* (1600–4), Jonson's *Catiline* (1611), and Elizabeth Carey's *The Tragedy of Mariam* (1602–8). Daniel's play came under the auspices of the Queen's Revels, and Jonson's play was acted by the King's Men. Carey's text is a "closet" drama, never meant to be acted, and is included here for precisely that reason: to suggest how frequently a dramatic text not connected to the theater could be expected to call on hand properties in imagining a dramatic world. Using the same criteria employed in the previous tabulation, we see that *Mariam* has a frequency of 2.76 props per 1,000 lines, which is almost exactly like *Philotas*, with 2.81 props per 1,000 lines, and only slightly below *Catiline*, which has 3.11 props per 1,000 lines. Taken as a group, these plays are remarkably spare in their use of properties, calling on fewer than half the props of any play in Table 4.2. Such plays could be said to constitute a nontheatrical dramatic genre, one devoted more to political philosophy than to popular entertainment.

There are several reasons *Catiline* may have been "damned" when first staged in 1611, but surely first among these is its essentially untheatrical nature.[46] *Catiline* gradually metamorphoses from a drama into a collection of speeches. No one better realized this than Jonson, who, in his letter "To the Reader in Ordinairie" prefaced to the first quarto in 1611, remarked that "you commend the two first Actes, with the people, because they are the worst; and dislike the Oration of Cicero."[47] The division Jonson draws here is significant, for the first two acts of *Catiline* contain most of its props, 7 of 11, with a frequency of just over 7 props per 1,000 lines—very close to the other non-Shakespearean plays on Table 4.2. However, after act 3, properties disappear entirely from the play, and it turns into a series of long speeches without the familiar attraction of objects to engage the audience's eyes. This is not to say that *Catiline* failed because it had no properties after its third act. Yet it is clear that, at the same time he turned his back on the world of things, Jonson forgot what helped to make plays successful on the early modern stage.

We could take Jonson's reluctance over properties in *Catiline* as indicative of a larger trend in his thinking about the stage and society. Jonson's tension with the stage is a staple of criticism. However, we are often reluctant to say what specifically about the stage led to this tension. As Jonas Barish has argued, Jonson retained a special animosity toward theatrical stuff, the stage objects and material practices that made the early modern theater what it was:

When it came to stagecraft, [Jonson] rejected with equal vehemence all the varieties of theatrical claptrap most cherished by Elizabethan audiences: fireworks, thunder, and ordnance, the raising of ghosts from the cellarage and lowering of gods from the hut. In the course of his feud with Inigo Jones, Jonson also ridiculed such newer and more esoteric wonders as the *machina versatilitas*, or turning device, and the *machina ductilis*, or tractable scene, both of them among the admired playthings of the court theater. One common factor in all these dislikes . . . is that "they were all directed against scenes, lights and machines which moved before the spectators' eyes" and were hence "most likely to distract attention from the spoken word."[48]

Barish's observation asks us to consider *Catiline*'s second half less in relation to the theater than to the pulpit, where few if any props would have distracted the audience from the speech in question. We can sense just such a reluctance over the objects of theater in Shakespeare's middle period, when a larger antitheatrical sentiment shaped by both satirical verse and the poetomachia of the late 1590s/early 1600s may well have affected his use of props in his plays. When Hamlet remarks, for instance, that he has "that within which passes show," we need to remember the theatrical context of his statement, which completes a sentence that begins: "These indeed seem, / For they are actions that a man might play," and likewise ends with a nod to the costumes of grief in mentioning "the trappings and the suits of woe" (1.2.83–86).

Thus far we have discussed how many hand props were used, of what kind they were, and in which genres they appeared. It is worth asking a different kind of question now, one concerning not the numbers and kinds of stage properties but the *roles* of objects in plays of the sixteenth and seventeenth centuries. We could start by observing that plays of the later 1590s and early 1600s often show an intensive interest in particular properties. This interest seems similar to the process of the poetic blazon so popular during the 1590s and may borrow from it. We could compare Hamlet's and Vindice's meditations on the skulls they hold with any of a number of aggressive treatments of faces and bodies in late Elizabethan poetry and even with such a passage as Marlowe's "Was this the face that launched a thousand ships / And burnt the topless towers of Ilium?"[49] In such passages the Elizabethans' inquisitiveness is at its most apparent, as is their almost childlike habit of restlessly pushing against *things,* both animate and inanimate, to define themselves.

Elsewhere I have argued for a historical shift in the function of hand properties, tracing a marked liveliness to these objects during the late-Elizabethan and Jacobean eras. The role that properties took progresses, between (approximately) 1590 and 1620, with props serving not only as floating signifiers between characters (signs, for example, of such things as marriage, chastity, and social position), but also as legitimate objects of interest in and of themselves. What we see in the transition from early Elizabethan drama to later Elizabethan and Jacobean drama is that, while in the earlier plays what had been important was where props *were* (with this character, for instance, as opposed to being in the possession of another character), the later plays show an interest in the integrity of the properties— whether, for instance, the property is clean or pure. "Shifting its attention from semiosis to subjectivity, the drama began to explore the reified basis of personal relations even as it tended, with more and more frequency, to personify commodities, according them a life of their own. Identity thus came to be inscribed *in,* instead of *by,* these objects."[50] This chapter's analysis of the frequency of props has shown that the moment of this shift—best represented in Shakespeare's works by *Hamlet, Troilus and Cressida* (1602), *Twelfth Night,* and *Othello*—saw the playwright exploring the "life" of objects even as he reduced their number in his plays. It is as if the price of focusing on a central object or objects (a sleeve, a handkerchief, a skull) were presenting the audience, his actors, and himself with fewer objects to consider.

<hr/>

I began this chapter by pointing out that criticism of hand props traditionally has confined itself to selected modes and has been limited by this selective focus. One of the things that our thin description of props has suggested is that there existed a fluidity between person and thing on the early modern stage; this, in turn, served as one spur to the moralizing criticism of objects that has long been part of both dramatic texts themselves and commentary on those texts. We have seen that objects seem to "stand out" from their surroundings when they are involved in some breach of decorum and usually receive attention when they contravene expectation. It has been my claim, though, that to pay attention to objects only in these circumstances, and on the plays' terms, is to repeat rather than analyze these texts.

Like the dramas of his contemporaries, Shakespeare's plays call for more props than actors. Shakespeare's use of hand props changed significantly: Plays written at the beginning of his career have more props than those written between 1598 and 1604; plays written after

1604—most probably under the influence of Jacobean taste for spectacle—resume the pattern established early in his career. The fifteen non-Shakespearean plays scrutinized tell a larger story. Although genre is an important determinant of the kinds (and, to a lesser extent, the quantity) of props a play will employ, historical moment most affected the number of props in a dramatic text. From the late 1580s through the 1630s, the number of props in early modern plays decreased at a steady rate, using fewer and fewer props but at the same time increasing their pressure on these props and on the putative difference between the animate and the inanimate.

Such changes—none of which would have been visible through a thick description of a particular prop or play—seem to indicate a cultural shift in what the theater was and in what, and how, plays acted there meant to their audiences. A theater that had established itself as a commercial entity through the display of objects found its voice and gradually put some of those objects behind it as the next century unfolded. When its actors were themselves put aside with the closing of the playhouse doors, however, the early modern theaters must have recognized that they, as well as their actors, had more in common with those objects than had once been imagined.

CHAPTER 5

FEMALE-FEMALE EROTICISM AND THE EARLY MODERN STAGE

Comment un dramaturge pouvait-il traiter d'un sujet qui n'existait pas?

—*Nadia Rigaud*

Can a woman take so much delight in hearing of another woman's pleasure taken?

—*"Bellamy," in Brome's* A Mad Couple Well Match'd

The last two chapters have sought to demonstrate how convention and trend can shape literature, including what is often read as literature's "cultural" content. Such cultural content, I argued earlier, is sometimes read in virtual abstraction from the important contexts of literary making. No less than the thin descriptions of chapters 3 and 4, then, the interpretations of this chapter aim to show the importance of what I have called "literary" culture—the roles that tradition, composition, materiel, and context play in giving various literary texts their themes, structures, vocabularies, and ideologies. Although it may seem innocuous, an emphasis on works' discursive contexts—contexts that often are strongly literary in nature—can place one's interpretations into divergence, if not debate, with readings that stress sociological links and political implications.

This chapter puts special pressure on the concept of literary culture in taking up an erotic trope in early modern literature. Because the erotic, sexuality, and sexual orientation have become so pivotal to identity today, we sometimes encounter a critical eagerness to find in early modern representations of sexual behavior and identity an unmediated representation of the real. That is, the variety of the sexual in early modern texts—a variety extensively chronicled by Gordon Williams's *A Dictionary of Sexual Language and Imagery in Shakespearean and Stuart Literature*—offers a wide field of practices, possibilities, and identities to explore.[1] My argument here is that we may benefit from attending to various traditions—many of them literary in nature—that affected this variety of representation in early modern works.

The particular trope this chapter explores is the erotic pairing of female bodies in early modern literature. Until fairly recently, to speak of female homoeroticism in the early modern era has been to speak in the negative: thus not only the anachronism of "lesbian" as a category, but also the relative invisibility of female homoerotic desire and the seeming nonexistence of practice on that desire. In the last several decades, however, a growing chorus of voices has established that female homoeroticism was far from unrecognized in the early modern era. This research includes Judith Brown's history of a "lesbian" nun in Renaissance Italy; essays on Donne's provocative verse epistle, "Sappho to Philaenis," by James Holstun, Janel Mueller, Paula Blank, and Elizabeth Harvey; Nadia Rigaud on "l'homosexualité féminine" in Richard Brome; and Harriette Andreadis's research into Sapphic representations during and after the seventeenth century.[2] To this bibliography we could add Laurie Shannon's recent study *Sovereign Amity: Figures of Friendship in Shakespearean Contexts*, which in the course of an argument about friendship examines various relationships between female characters in early modern literature.[3] Most recently, however, our knowledge of the topic has been advanced by Valerie Traub's *The Renaissance of Lesbianism in Early Modern England*. Traub has consolidated discussion of the topic in a monumental examination of early modern representations concerned with affection, bonds, and sexual activities between female figures. If earlier studies have responded to the "anxieties of anachronism" that continue to haunt inquiry into the history of sexuality by demonstrating resonant, though scattered, instances of female homoeroticism in early modern literature and society, Traub's work dispels such anxieties with its persuasive rationale for locating this subject at the forefront of inquiry into sixteenth- and seventeenth-century sexualities.[4]

However salutary these studies have been, they have tended to stress affirmative aspects of female homoeroticism—aspects almost by definition subversive of patriarchy and the repressive codes it can foster. While understandable, this partiality—what we could, following Shannon's title, call the sovereignty of "amity" in sexually oriented criticism—has in some cases given us a limited picture of the erotic as it pertains to female bodies in cultural representation.[5] For instance, by foregrounding relationships in which pleasure appears not only mutual but outside hierarchies of rank and power, much of the criticism dedicated to female homoeroticism in the early modern era has idealized the erotic. An example of this tendency is Harriette Andreadis's recent study, *Sappho in Early Modern England,* which at one point expresses interest in a "more sexually evasive yet erotically charged language of female friendship [used] to describe female same-sex intimacy."[6] Andreadis skillfully steps from lesbian discourse to a discourse of friendship back to "same-sex intimacy," intimacy disguised, ostensibly, through a subterranean "double discourse" necessitated by watchful authorities. More problematic than the positing of coded language that a perceptive modern reader may decode is the blending of sex and friendship within this paradigm. Certainly reclaiming a tradition of affective and reciprocal eroticism among females would add compelling nuances to a period otherwise notorious for its constriction of female roles and desires as well as for its misogyny generally. But to emphasize mutuality can limit our understanding of the complexities of the erotic, in and out of texts. As Suzanne Moore has reminded us in a different context, when we say that representations of sex "should be soft-focus, sentimental and loving," we overlook how sex remains "bound up with power, dependency, dominance and submission."[7] Indeed, we have learned from the "sex debates" in lesbian theory itself precisely how complicated pleasure, desire, and the implications of sexual practices are.[8] And while our paradigms of eros obviously differ in ways from those of previous times, we stand to learn from these recent theoretical positions concerning the idealization of sexuality.

To deepen our understanding of the erotic in early modern England, we need to consider instances and aspects of female-female eroticism that have so far been ignored. I propose the term female-female eroticism, in fact, as a means of widening the scope of what follows. With this term I mean any instance, imaginary and otherwise, of females in a conjunction perceived as erotic by one or more of those involved and/or by third parties. In the range of terminology possible for an inquiry into eroticized relations among female bodies—from "lesbian" to "homosexual," "homoerotic," and "homosocial"—"female-female eroticism" has the paradoxical benefit of inclusiveness. As I show in the last section of this chapter, the flexibility of this term is necessary to describe instances—prevalent in the drama—of triangulated eroticism in which a female seduces, coerces, or suborns another female for heterosexual sex, gratifying all the same certain desires of the seducer. At the far end of the spectrum, too, stand scenes in which the manipulation of one female character by another seems designed to excite playhouse spectators in relations not unlike those found in contemporary pornography.[9] In these scenes the "eroticism" in female-female eroticism is produced by characters but is not necessarily for them.

If, as I argue here, early modern drama offered many representations of female-female eroticism, we must remember that the relations of production in the professional theater were dominated by men. Thus, answering Nadia Rigaud's (ironic) rhetorical question— "How could a playwright treat a subject that didn't exist?"[10]— means not only acknowledging the existence of female-female eroticism as an available topic but imagining many others involved in its production and circulation, from playwrights, actors, and audiences to printers, editors, and readers. It also will mean thinking about how desire and the erotic are channeled inside and outside dramatic fictions. While we will observe, for instance, that female-female eroticism is more prevalent in early modern literature than currently believed, this chapter also illustrates that eros among female characters often was cathected through male desire. Erica Rand has pointed out that "sexual scenarios in cultural production do not secure their tethers in any way that is either absolute or obvious to all."[11] Following the tethers of various texts and their equally varied audiences, we typically find them more heterogeneous than might be expected. The commercial theaters, of course, intensified this heterogeneity. To write for diverse audiences and to play for them means that no scene of eros remains cloistered from differently oriented desires; entered into such public representation, the erotic is invariably for and about others.

Eroticism related to paired female bodies in the literature of early modern England is more complicated than our current understanding allows. Throughout this chapter I focus on male-produced fantasies of such eroticism rather than homoerotic practice. We can better understand these fantasies, I will show, by discerning the elements of a larger myth of female-female eroticism, a myth made from both classical and contemporary narratives. The elements of this myth form a story from which individual instances derive, sometimes differing in important ways. The first part of this chapter, therefore, establishes the assumptions that made up a central story of female-female eroticism in early modern England and suggests why these existed and how they interrelated. Then, in readings of passages from canonical and noncanonical literature, dramatic and otherwise, I trace a crucial divergence from one strain of these assumptions, a divergence that complicates a simple picture of desire and the erotic. In contrast to other venues, the sixteenth- and seventeenth-century stage rarely imagines mutually pleasurable erotic relations among the female bodies it represents. What it imagines instead are erotic and eroticized relations consonant with current narratives of heterosexuality, with potentially unequal levels of power and pleasure.

If drama on the commercial stage does not often imagine female homoerotic practice, perhaps I should begin by saying where such imaginings took place. Many readers are familiar with the voyeuristic scene that transpires in the Bower of Bliss in Book II of Spenser's *The Faerie Queene*. In this episode, Guyon watches "Two naked Damzelles" "wrestle wantonly" and then for his pleasure, in a fountain of "richest substaunce" (II. xii.60–69). In early modern England, suggestions of sexual practice among females gravitate strikingly toward such coterie discourses, and only there do we find its most radical, positive expression. For instance, as Janel Mueller has demonstrated, in "Sappho to Philaenis" Donne provides an "affirmative representation of lesbian sexuality" and "goes to lengths unparalleled in his time to personify the lesbian love of his Sap[p]ho as both sexually active, and emotionally and morally positive."[12] Donne's Sappho pens a richly erotic love letter to her beloved, arguing for the superiority of lesbian love: "Men leave behind them that which their sin shows" (l. 39); "between us all sweetness may be had" (l. 43).[13] The character Sappho also relates that, during autoeroticism, she imagines their bodies as one: "touching my self, all seems done to thee" (l. 52). Mueller's description of this poem's radical structure of feeling is accurate. But the form that Donne's efforts took raises questions about the cultural work the poem may have performed. Like most of Donne's poetry, this verse epistle circulated early in manuscript. As Arthur Marotti reminds us, "Generally, only close friends, patrons, and patronesses had limited access to the poetry Donne wrote."[14] Its influence even after it was printed in 1633 remains difficult to determine. It is hard to tell, for example, what the

poem may have meant to the aristocratic woman who took the part
of Sappho in Davenant's *The Temple of Love* (1635)—a part apparently unconcerned with Sappho's sexuality—to her companion actors, to the audience for the masque, and to the larger society of early
modern England. Because Sappho was known, in England, almost
exclusively through Ovid's *Heroides,* it is perhaps not surprising to
find her mentioned in comparatively select discourses.[15] In their most
radical form, suggestions of female homoeroticism appeared in
venues that offered freedom to experiment. Speaking to coterie audiences and readers, texts like "Sappho to Philaenis" enjoy a license
to imagine erotically that more popular works lack.

The imaginative freedom that a coterie audience provides—as well
as the limitations of the mode—characterizes the Coleorton masque
of 1618 (most likely written by Thomas Pestell), which makes a
strong statement about the cultural desirability of female homoeroticism.[16] This masque was written, as David Norbrook points out, "at
the height of the Jacobean controversy over women" and at one
point responds to the misogyny of the current debate.[17] In this work
six women masquers representing various virtues appear just prior to
a sarcastic comment by Favonius, who deliberately misreads them:
"What have we here? a metamorphosis! Men transformed to women!
this age gives example to the contrary."[18] After an interval the six
masquers descend, and, as the manuscript reports, "while they pass
to the dancing place was Sung this" (here excerpted):

> Brave Amazonian Dames
> Made no count of Mankind but
> for a fit to be at the Rut.
> free fire gives the brightest flames;
> Men's overawing tames,
> And Pedantlike our active Spirits smother.
> Learn, Virgins, to live free;
> Alas, would it might be,
> women could live & lie with one another![19]

Men overawe and, "Pedantlike," smother the "active Spirits" of
women. The solution this song imagines—however unattainable or
impermissible it appears—is a community of "free" women who
might "live & lie with one another!" Like Donne's verse epistle, this
song voices its utopian longings to a coterie audience: We know the
date and venue of what seems to have been a single performance, the
names of most of the players, and the primary audience of this

masque at the Beaumonts' residence at Coleorton, Candlemas night.[20] It is difficult to imagine the radical wish of the last lines quoted here appearing in a pamphlet or other popular work of the time. Difficult, for this optative relies on many factors that the printed page could not hope to duplicate, from the class locations of its audience to the physical location of the masque itself. With "Sappho to Philaenis," the Coleorton song remains a rare positive fantasy of female homoerotic practice.

Literature of the time more often imagines women in erotic conjunction in less utopian terms. When figured in texts of the period, coterie and otherwise, female-female eroticism typically appears in relationship to a set of assumptions underlying a cultural myth. I suggest that these included the following, here phrased in modern terms:

1. In erotic attraction, beauty is more important than biological sex.
2. Likeness—of body, age, temperament, and situation—attracts.
3. Sex-segregated institutions and spheres enable same-sex eroticism.
4. Female-female eroticism is a phase in the past—classical, national, and personal.
5. Female-female eroticism involves those who differ from each other in age, rank, power, and experience.

The first four assumptions descend from the general to the specific, from what could and did include heterosexual and male homoerotic attraction to the specificity of female-female eroticism as a thing of the past. If erotic attraction springs from beauty, likeness was shown to focus that attraction; sex-segregated institutions and spheres, further, enabled acting on this desire. Because early modern England had few such institutions and spheres, and as a way of diffusing threats that female homoeroticism could raise, texts frequently locate it in the past. As we will note, these first four assumptions often cohere into an idealized scenario of female-female eroticism: mutual attraction of beautiful "twins" in a separate place at an early or earlier time.

However, with the last assumption—that female-female eroticism involves difference—we have an important divergence. These differences included varying levels of social rank, age, experience, and power. Where idealizing assumptions about female-female eroticism stress the affirmative aspects of a relationship between equals, this accent on potential differences of erotic partners introduces issues of power and frequently coercion. Mirroring patriarchal society in monstrous terms, the resulting scenarios render the erotic a commodity for others even as one desiring female body manipulates another. These scenarios are often triangular and sometimes sadistic. After scrutinizing how the affirmative myth functions, what its elements are and how they interrelate, we will examine the difference-based assumption and how it affects portrayals of female-female eroticism. For, strong as the affirmative myth was, versions of a less idyllic eroticism are equally prevalent.

One of the most important assumptions behind portrayals of female-female eroticism from this time, and the first on my list, holds that beauty overrides traditional constraints on the choice of a beloved. That is, a lover's beauty counted more than her sex. Such thinking, again, was by no means sex-specific in this, an era comparatively obsessed with physical beauty; several proverbs current at the time speak to its force: "Beauty draws more than oxen" and "Where beauty is there needs no other plea."[21] Because it concerns the draw of beauty and provides a classic site for the affirmation of female-female eroticism as well as for its denial, we should consider here the story of Iphis and Ianthe in the ninth book of Ovid's *Metamorphoses,* a story that Lyly would dramatize in his *Gallathea* (1585). In the translation of George Sandys, Iphis, who, disguised as a boy, has fallen in love with Ianthe, bewails her predicament with an analogy—rather, the lack of one:

> No Cow a Cow, no Mare a Mare pursues:
> But Harts their gentle Hinds, and Rams their Ewes.
> So Birds together pair. Of all that move,
> No Female suffers for a Female love.
> O would I had no being!
>
> (ll. 730–34)[22]

The use of the animal kingdom here is meant to prove the unnaturalness of female-female eroticism. But it quickly reminds Ianthe/Ovid of an instance in which the division between human and animal was breached. At least Pasiphae, Ianthe laments, could satisfy her lust for a bull with Daedalus's contrivance: "she pleas'd her blood; / And stood his errour in a Cow of wood" (738–39). For Iphis, however, the unnatural equals the impossible: "Can art convert a virgin to a boy?" (744). If beauty has overcome traditional boundaries—"Where beauty is there needs no other plea"—the sameness of their bodies seems to make sexual union impossible.

In creating this impossibility or paradox to be solved by divine contrivance, however, Ovid winds up showing that nature itself is unnatural. To deny, teasingly, their ability to satisfy each other, the poet needs to have Iphis and Ianthe erotically attracted. For this he relies on the potent attraction of beauty. *Gallathea* tells us that either Gallathea or Phyllida could be thought "the fairest and chastest virgin in all the country," which means that one of them must be sacrificed to Neptune to assuage the god (1.1.42–43). And they initially desire each other because of their "beautiful" and "fair" aspects (2.1.45, 62). This beauty, in turn, is part of why their fathers dote on them—something that leads others to accuse them of incestuous desire (2.1.5–9, 4.1.37–42, 5.3.10ff). While beauty levels boundaries that cultures set on the basis of biological sex, this sequence insinuates, it also works to erase other lines of division. But *Gallathea* places most emphasis on the mutual draw of beauty between Gallathea and Phyllida. Whether explained purely in terms of facial beauty or in relation to Olivia's "fivefold blazon" in *Twelfth Night* (1601) of Viola/Caesario's "tongue . . . face . . . limbs, actions, and spirit" (1.5.292–93), "beauty" remains an unquestioned locus of desire. This is a common trope: Mutual attraction based on beauty characterizes female-female eroticism in, among other plays, *As You Like It* ([1599]; 3.5.113 ff.) and *A Mad Couple Well Match'd* ([1639]; 2.1.119–20).

The myth of female-female eroticism in England at this time draws on Ovid's beautiful equivalence to frame the erotic through tropes of twinning and substitution—acute forms of our second general assumption, the attraction of likeness. Through these figures affection becomes affinity, with the latter verging on absolute identity and the fiction of beautiful sameness. As Laurie Shannon reminds us, the contemporary discourse of friendship would be crucial to narratives of these relationships. Laurens Mills has also pointed out that the theme of friendship so central to the literature of the time drew heavily on a classical tradition that found new extension through humanist scholarship. Although Mills held that this theme, in which the "exchange of personalities that results logically from the identity of two friends"—the "one soul in two bodies" trope—was rarely expressed in relationship to friendship between women,[23] several speeches on close female friendship have acquired canonical status in recent criticism of early modern drama: Helena's "double cherry" speech to Hermia in *A Midsummer Night's Dream* ([1596]; 3.2.195–219) and Emilia's speech concerning her and Flavina's past in *The Two Noble Kinsmen* ([1613]; 1.3.54–82). In these speeches, "twin" characters stress the innocence and purity of their affectionate relationships even as they insist on the pleasure that physical proximity brought them.

Our third assumption appears when writers employ these narratives of proximity in relationship to all-female institutions or spheres and the closeness they afford. Similar passages from various travel narratives available in England detail with some explicitness how the freedom offered by the Turkish baths was thought to promote sexual activity. In Thomas Washington's 1585 translation, from the French, of Nicolas de Nicolay's *Navigations into Turkey*, and in Busbequius's Turkish letters, the institution of the same-sex public baths facilitates erotic relations among women.[24] England had few institutions of this kind, yet we know of the existence of boarding schools for young women aged five to sixteen, starting at least by the 1670s and increasing in number rapidly after that.[25] Carroll Smith-Rosenberg has argued in an influential essay concerned with a later historical period that these institutions, usually preparing girls and young women for marriage, brought females into close emotional and sometimes physical relationships with each other.[26] It is perhaps not surprising that, given the proliferation of female boarding schools in England during this time, we find a pornographic fantasy of female-female eroticism in such a school in *Erotopolis. The Present State of Betty-Land* (1684). The author (anonymous in the publication) fantasizes about what happens in these female boarding schools— what he calls "those Houses of Female Instruction" in "Betty Land" (which, as James Henke points out, is sometimes England and sometimes the female body).[27] He speaks of *"Boarding-Schools,* kept by a certain sort of she-Creatures that will pretend to be whatever you will have them to be. . . . If you will have them to be she-*Centaurs,* she-*Centaurs* they shall be, of which there appears not a little probability, for in these places it is, that the young Shepherdesses first learn the Art of Horsemanship and Horse-play, first riding one another, and then in a short time after, riding quite away with some Shepherds or other, to the great Consolation of their Parents."[28] Like the Turkish baths, the "Boarding-Schools" of Betty Land enable sexual contact. But they also give male writers an explanation for and limit on female homoeroticism. Graduated, the students "rid(e) quite away" with men. Imagining female-female eroticism as the product of places rather than persons allows the author to lessen its ramifications. Thus homoeroticism is, "in these places," a stage in a schoolgirl progression toward heterosexuality.

This points to the fourth assumption in the cultural myth we have been unfolding: namely, that female-female eroticism is a phase in the past—classical, national, and personal. Indeed if *Erotopolis* satisfies it-self that its "Shepherdesses" will ultimately ride "quite away with some Shepherds or other," literature after the Reformation also imagines places where no such progression was implied. Andrew Marvell's "Upon Appleton House" (1650–52), for example, locates female-female eroticism in the convents of England's Catholic past. In this poem, Marvell works to justify contemporary ownership of an estate appropriated from the church at the Reformation. One of his justifications springs from the transgressive sexuality he ascribes to the convent. A nunnery on this land hosts a struggle, between Mar-vell's historical Fairfax and a "smooth(-)Tongue(d)" nun, for Fair-fax's beloved. This experienced nun is described as having "sucked in" his beloved with promises of variety in bed companions.[29] She says that

> Each Night among us to your side
> Appoint a fresh and Virgin Bride;
> Whom if *our Lord* at midnight find,
> Yet Neither should be left behind.
> Where you may lie as chaste in Bed,
> As Pearls together billeted.
> All Night embracing Arm in Arm,
> Like Crystal pure with Cotton warm.

(ll. 185–92)

The nun's invitation clearly echoes that of Marlowe's "Passionate Shepherd." It would have been hard for a contemporary reader not to hear the Marlovian pull of the lines; the nun's invitation is a richly secular attempt at seduction.[30] But like Ralegh's Nymph, a moralis-tic Fairfax responds by saying that "I know what Fruit their Gardens yield, / When they it think by Night conceal'd. / Fly from their Vices" (ll. 219–21). As is true with the poem generally, these words are framed in terms of the land and buildings of the Fairfax estate. Marvell uses the pre-Reformation nuns' nighttime "Vices," in fact, to justify the contemporary ownership of the property.[31]

Marvell imagines a past as well as a place for female-female eroti-cism. According to Traub, in Shakespeare and other dramatists "'feminine' homoerotic desire was granted signification only *after* it was rendered insignificant" and was "figurable . . . in terms of the al-ways already lost."[32] To this calculus one could add the remoteness of Sappho in Donne and other early modern authors. "Past" here also concerns character, for, as Traub notes, this period's drama tends not only to locate female-female eroticism in the youth and/or past of female characters—most frequently identified as, then, virgins—but relies on it as and for something that the heterosexual could displace.[33] Thus the progression of Betty Land's students. And thus Helena emphasizes her and Hermia's "school-days friendship" in *Dream* (3.2.202); she laments that such friendship appears outdated in a well-known question: "And will you rent our ancient love asunder, / To join with men in scorning your poor friend?" (3.2.215–16). The insistent anteriority of the female homoerotic found uncanny testimony during the early months of the Restoration, when, on June 29, 1660, Humphrey Moseley, a royalist publisher of belles-lettres, entered several play titles in the Stationers' Register, including one ascribed to Shakespeare titled *Iphis & Iantha, or a marriage without a man*.[34] The sense of things former and missing often associated with female-female eroticism finds no better example, perhaps, than this apparently lost Renaissance play.

To this point we have traced interrelated commonplaces about female-female eroticism. These assumptions and motifs function as elements in a larger cultural myth—one that, again, involves erotic attraction of beautiful "twins" in a separate place at an early or earlier time: Helena's "ancient love." The telescoping quality of these assumptions, I argue, comes from the desire to portray female-female eroticism as narcissistic, anterior, and incidental—a step toward mature heterosexuality. Joined this way, they underwrote what Traub has called elegiac, "femme-femme" scenarios of the erotic.[35] Examples in Shakespeare's works include scenes between Rosalind and Celia in *As You Like It*, Marina and Philoten in *Pericles* (1608), Helena and Hermia in *Dream*, and Emilia and Flavina in *The Two Noble Kinsmen*. The charged relationships in these pairs prompt Traub to query why critics have been slower to take up female-female desire, "why we assume that the images of 'a double cherry' and of 'Juno's swans . . . coupled and inseparable' are qualitatively different, somehow less erotic, than the 'twin'd lambs' of Polixenes and Leontes in *The Winter's Tale*."[36] Traub is right about these speeches' eroticism. Yet careful examination shows that their erotic content exceeds the relationships they describe and even escapes the speakers themselves. As we will see, this discrepancy actually forms a precondition of audience arousal in such scenes and is one reason we must expand our definition of the erotic where it pertains to paired bodies in this way.

Characters involved in these relationships report them as utopian, decorous, natural, and positive; an absolute identity between friends prompts a platonic merger fantasy of making "one soul in bodies twain." On another level, however, these speeches can invite carnal imaginings. This is explicitly so, of course, in Donne's "Sappho to Philaenis," where the punning "mutual feeling"[37] depends on the physical likeness of two female bodies:

> My two lips, eyes, thighs, differ from thy two,
> But so, as thine from one another do;
> And, oh, no more; the likeness being such,
> Why should they not alike in all parts touch?
> Hand to strange hand, lip to lip none denies;
> Why should they breast to breast, or thighs to thighs?
>
> (ll. 32, 45–50)

We have here an important slipperiness between likeness and contact. Imaginings of practice arise with observers (here Donne and Sappho) who literalize the principle that likeness attracts. These observers interpret apparently metaphysical questions of beauty, identity, and likeness as questions of body, place, and contact. So even bodies imagined together in terms of spiritual pleasure can be paired otherwise in other imaginations. Proximity thus offers a ribald potential as, like Sappho herself, readers and audiences imagine a female pair in erotic conjunction—a pair that effectively becomes a single sex object for the imaginer.[38]

To see how this slipperiness functions, we could examine part of Emilia's speech in *The Two Noble Kinsmen*. Describing her bonds with Flavina, for instance, Emilia recounts how

> The flow'r that I would pluck
> And put between my breasts (O then but beginning
> To swell about the blossom), she would long
> Till she had such another, and commit it
> To the like innocent cradle, where phoenix-like
> They died in perfume.
>
> (1.3.66–71)

The imagery here is remarkably sensual, despite—or perhaps because of—her insistence on the word "innocent," which she uses three times in her larger speech at regular intervals: lines 60, 70, and 79. Indeed, this careful reiteration of innocence seems to solicit an imagining *not* innocent—one that pictures the girls' twinned bodies erotically. What I have described in relationship to Donne's Sappho lyric as a slipperiness between likeness and contact operates here as well. Surely Emilia takes great, even physical pleasure from their relationship; this is the point of the speech. Yet where Sappho's sensuality emanates for as well as from her eroticism, and where Spenser's "naked Damzelles" know of their sexual appeal to others, Emilia does not recognize the erotic potential of her speech. When an audience hears of the flowers placed between the "like innocent cradle(s)" of Emilia's and Flavina's breasts, I would argue, there is an erotic charge to her speech that depends on the pair's not realizing the implications, for others, of the sensuality she describes. We could find a telling analogy here with the innocent Susanna of the apocryphal tradition. Tessa Watt has shown that Susanna's story was extremely popular during the late sixteenth and early seventeenth centuries, appearing in many ballads, pictures, and wall paintings. Influenced then by Ovidian eroticism, the story's deep appeal, Watt suspects, "lay in the image of naked Susanna washing herself in the orchard, an object of fantasy which probably titillated the viewers of Renaissance paintings on the theme just as much as it did the wicked elders whose lechery was supposedly condemned."[39] Like viewers of the Susanna story, I believe, Emilia's listeners receive a thrill that depends precisely on the innocence she ascribes to their bodies. If her speech is erotic, it is erotic for the audience rather than for her.

With this kind of third-party arousal, we have come to the point where the insufficiencies of a uniform model of female-female eroticism have become apparent. Simply put, too many individuals of varying orientations and desires were involved in producing and consuming these texts for their representation of the erotic to be univocal or ideal. Even Donne's "Sappho to Philaenis," when read in the context of a contemporaneous pornographic text like Nashe's *Choice of Valentines,* can be seen as a work that would have aroused a variety of readers; indeed it was most likely written for this purpose, among others. However affective and close female-female relationships were portrayed, they were always open to the erotic appropriation I have described. Yet relationships among female characters themselves are sometimes represented, in early modern texts, as being more appropriative than gentle. This is the difference, in short, between the world Emilia depicts and that which Marvell imagines when he has Fairfax allege that the experienced nun is attempting to seduce a young woman. While the mutual, femme-femme mode proved influential, therefore, early modern plays more often emphasized differentials of power, experience, and pleasure in scenarios of female-female eroticism.

That these scenes involved characters who differ from each other in such matters as age, rank, power, and experience constitutes the fifth and last of the assumptions set out earlier. These scenes occur most often in tragedies—in contrast to the idyllic relationships that tend to characterize comedy and romance—and it is worth keeping in mind the determining role of genre in establishing their tenor. This assumption of difference contradicts other notions about female-female eroticism and calls into question the idyllic femme-femme scenarios that our central cultural myth sponsors. These external differences sometimes find parallels in ascribed differences *within* characters. Writers often explain powerful women, for instance, as mannish and otherwise between comfortable identities. Categories like "Amazon," "hermaphrodite," "virago," and "changeling" help account for ostensibly unnatural behavior. Lear's "Down from the waist they are Centaurs, / Though women all above." (4.6.124–25) and Jonson's "Madame Centaure" in *Epicoene* (1609) anticipate the passage from *Erotopolis*, quoted previously, concerning those "she-*Centaurs*" who instruct and oversee the "Shepherdesses" that ride one another. All three instances seek to explain sexual desire and aggression through unnatural anatomy—by creating a "phallic" woman. And while a woman who takes assertive erotic initiative may be focusing on a male lover, in many plays aggressive female characters manipulate and coerce other female characters.

A story foundational to scenes of aggressive eroticism between "female" characters was the myth of Callisto and Jupiter. This story, told in book 2 of Ovid's *Metamorphoses,* inspired many early modern painters and poets.[40] Ovid's version of the myth relates that Callisto, a nymph of Diana's (and thus devoted to chastity), became the object of Jove's lust. Disguising himself as Diana, Jove first groped then raped Callisto; when she becomes pregnant, and that pregnancy is discovered, Callisto is rejected by Diana, punished by Juno, and converted into a constellation by Jove. The myth of Callisto betrays a tendency not only to imagine an active and a passive division in any erotic and/or sexual encounter between women, but to understand that division as essentially a male/female one, with the more aggressive member of the pair somehow "male" at base. The story of Callisto was dramatized on the English Renaissance stage in Thomas Heywood's *The Golden Age* (1610), which shows Jupiter as a phallic intruder into an otherwise stable place of eroticized "sport and play" among Diana's nymphs.[41] Yet with many other plays, the aggression we see in Heywood's Jupiter appears in female characters.

Thus we often find seduction scenes formed around an experienced and otherwise powerful seducer and a less powerful, sometimes passive seduced character. These relationships are, again, not infrequently associated with a male/female division—agency, power, and experience commonly portrayed as masculine. (Horace's phrase "mascula Sappho" [*Epistles* 1.19.28] sometimes was applied to Sappho's sexuality rather than her poetic mastery.) In *The Roaring Girl* (1611), Mistress Gallipot relates that some claim Moll Cutpurse is "a man, and some, both man and woman," to which Laxton replies, "That were excellent: she might first cuckold the husband and then make him do as much for the wife!" (2.1.209–12).[42] Perhaps the strongest statement of sexual aggression as masculine comes in the obscene political pamphlet, *Newes from the New Exchange* (1649/50), ascribed to Henry Neville. A woman-by-woman libel of what the title page calls *The Commonwealth of Ladies*, this pamphlet seems a product of the new freedom of the press occasioned by the Civil War and anticipated in the "embodied writing" that chapter 3 of the present study explores. Neville turns eventually to Lady Margaret Hungerford[43] and what we would call bisexual experiences:

> Now, as a brave * *Woman-man-of-mettle*, heigh for my *Lady Hunger-ford*. Since Sir *Edward* is in Heaven, the fittest *mate* for her upon Earth, must needs be *Annis-water Robin*, For they may fit one another by turns, and be beholding to no body. This *Lady* over-rid and excarnated, no less than three of her women in her husband's lifetime; and hath left no part of four *Gentleman-ushers* visible in the world, but their *periwigs;* but the fifth scapes yet, and may perhaps for a twelve-month.[44]

A note printed in Neville's margin explains the asterisked *Woman-man-of-mettle* as: "*Supposed a hermaphrodite." Likewise the pamphlet imagines that Lady Hungerford would be compatible with "*Annis-water Robin*"—apparently an actual seller of anise-seed water, thought to be a hermaphrodite.[45] Whether intentional, the deep pun on "beholding to no body" tells the story of the passage, in terms of both openness of object-choice and lack of concern for that object once chosen. Riding three of her "women" as the Shepherdesses of *Erotopolis* are said to ride each other, Lady Hungerford "excarnated" them—stripped their flesh (*OED*)—through the friction of sex.[46] Her "women" are her servants, sexually and otherwise. It is apparently impossible for the author of *Newes from the New Exchange* to imagine scenes of female homosexuality associated with Lady Hungerford—even as it is apparently impossible for him to think of scenes of sex between her and her "*Gentlemen-ushers*"— without imagining her an active, even predatory figure. Rather than

mutually pleasuring femme-femme eroticism, therefore, the relationships here are thoroughly implicated in differences of power and
authority.

The differentials of power behind what Neville describes as sex between people of unequal degree underwrites dramatic sequences in
striking ways. These sequences portray female desire and sexuality as
aggressive and manipulative, and often one-sided. In them, female
characters use other female characters, sometimes in relation to heterosexual sex and desire. Many of these scenes stress a "for-others"
aspect of the erotic within the dynamics of the dramatic plot itself.
We have already seen an instance of this in Emilia's speech. And while
the appropriation that I held was likely to characterize audience response to these speeches had obvious drawbacks, in many plays an
immediate physical danger marks literal instances of appropriation in
scenes of prostitution, "bawd" eroticism, and sexual aggression.

An early, disturbing scene of this type involves Tamora and
Lavinia in *Titus Andronicus* (1593). Perhaps the most transgressive
female character in the canon of Shakespeare's plays, Tamora vio-
lates the sexual and racial taboos of her dramatic world, ultimately
bearing the child of Aaron the Moor. Various characters call her
"Semiramis," identifying her with the sexually notorious, crossdressing Assyrian queen—a queen whose martial activities helped
render her a legendary symbol of the aggressive hermaphrodite.[47]
Shakespeare refers to such power when he has the Lord of the Induction in *The Taming of the Shrew* (1592) characterize Semiramis
in terms of her control over her bed and, by extension, her sexuality: "We'll have thee to a couch, / Softer and sweeter than the lust-
ful bed / On purpose trimm'd up for Semiramis" (Ind. 2.37–39).
As both Aaron (2.1.22) and Lavinia (2.3.118) notice, Semiramis's
transgressive reputation provides an apt analogy for Tamora's actions and speeches in this play.

What could be described as a limit case of desire occurs when Tamora discusses the imminent rape of Lavinia with her sons Demetrius
and Chiron:

> *Demetrius.* This minion stood upon her chastity,
> Upon her nuptial vow, her loyalty,
> And with that painted hope braves your mightiness;
> And shall she carry this unto her grave?
> *Chiron.* And if she do, I would I were an eunuch.
> Drag hence her husband to some secret hole,
> And make his dead trunk pillow to our lust.

Tamora. But when ye have the honey we desire,
Let not this wasp outlive, us both to sting.

(2.3.124–32)

Perhaps unmatched in Shakespeare's work for its grisliness, this scene also sketches one of the more complicated triangulations of hostility in drama of this time. The Romans have sacrificed Alarbus, Tamora's oldest son, for which she wants revenge against the pious Romans Bassanius and Lavinia (daughter of Titus, who sacrificed Alarbus); and she suborns her sons to murder Bassanius by lying to them. Called "Semiramis, nay, barbarous Tamora" by Lavinia (118), Tamora is eager to stab her, but is stopped by Demetrius and by Chiron, who proposes to rape Lavinia on the corpse of Bassanius.

The beginning of Tamora's response is blunt: "when ye have the honey *we* desire" (emphasis added). "Honey," it should be stressed, is highly sexualized elsewhere in Shakespeare's works. Venus's "A thousand honey secrets shalt thou know" in *Venus and Adonis* ([1592–93]; l. 16), and Hamlet's "honeying and making love / Over the nasty sty" ([1601]; 3.4.93–94) clearly support Eric Partridge's definition of "honey" as "the sweets of sexual pleasure."[48] Significantly, each of these instances involves experienced, even (if we are to believe Hamlet) uninhibited female characters: Venus and Gertrude. Yet it would be the use of "honey" in a rape narrative—the contemporaneous *The Rape of Lucrece* (1593–94)—that has most bearing on Tamora's line. For there Tarquin says "I know what thorns the growing rose defends, / I think the honey guarded with a sting" (ll. 492–93). Lucrece too says, "My honey lost . . . a wand'ring wasp hath crept, / And suck'd the honey which thy chaste bee kept" (836, 839–40). What does it mean that, before the rape of Lavinia, Tamora calls on the same image that Tarquin uses before raping Lucrece? *Titus* can be said to have Tamora share responsibility for the rape: she suborns her sons into sadistic revenge, denies Lavinia's repeated pleas for mercy, then says that this sexual violence against Lavinia is their mutual "honey."

But how could a woman desire—and enjoy vicariously—the rape of another woman? This is exactly what Lavinia asks, begging Tamora to find the essential quality of womanhood in her—a quality Tamora disclaims (135 ff.). It may also have been a question that a compositor of the Second Folio asked in 1632, for there the line just quoted reads "But when ye have the honey *ye* desire" (emphasis added). What may have been an instance of the first "ye" sticking in the compositor's head also could have been a conscious decision to correct a perceived mistake. How could Tamora, after all, derive pleasure from the rape of Lavinia? What, we may ask, *is* the status of her "we"? The scene as well as the play helps answer these questions. If we recall the complexity of the relations of power, desire, and antipathy among these characters, the proxy or secondhand pleasure that Tamora promises to take from the rape becomes clearer. Tamora shows how variously tethered these desires and acts are when she tells her sons "see that you make her sure" (187), and "use her as you will; / The worse to her, the better lov'd of me" (166–67). This last remark is telling. Where Chiron promises to use Bassanius's corpse as "pillow to our lust," Tamora locates her pleasure—and perhaps, by implication, her body—in this situation as well. Joined to Lavinia through her sons, she is also joined to her sons through a rape whose sadistic "honey" is sweet in proportion to the pain that sexual violence brings Lavinia.

This economy of pain, violence, and pleasure is quite disturbing. It also makes the price of one female character's desire and power the body of another. We need to remember that it is in the work of a male writer that a female character—in this case Tamora—is portrayed as deriving pleasure from a rape. Yet to decide that such pleasure is therefore unworthy of our attention means emending "we" to "ye" in the phrase "honey we desire," hence limiting what a female character like Tamora desires—and, perhaps, should want. The audience and readers of plays like *Titus* consisted of women and men, girls and boys—individuals free to empathize and identify with Tamora as well as Lavinia, with Chiron as well as Bassanius, and with Aaron as well as Titus. And even letting stand the category of the "hermaphrodite" or the "unnatural," perhaps it was exactly such unnaturalness, such behavior contrary to prevailing social norms, that attracted heterogeneous audiences to this circuit of aggression.

Tamora's once-removed assault on Lavinia speaks to the importance of misogynistic triangulation in female-female eroticism in this aggressive mode, of pleasure derived indirectly. Especially important in such triangulation were bawds, both professional and amateur. As procurers of women for men, they typically seduce these women. Professional bawds also have the further incentive of profiting from the sexual work of their subordinates; the bawds' desires, therefore, often merge with the wants of those men they sell sex to, making it difficult to extricate their desire for their customers' money from those customers' desire for sex. That is, to the extent that a bawd depends on the satisfied desires of her male customers for her income, she looks at these women with and through her customers' eyes. The successful bawd must relate herself to women in a manner similar to how a customer will. When this involves—as it often does—physical proximity of the bawd and her "object," texts commonly eroticize the conjunctions.

We find clear evidence of such eroticism in the exploitative relation between "Bawd" and Marina in *Pericles*—an overwhelming contrast to the "femme-femme" Marina/Philoten relationship. Bawd, a professional, attempts to coerce Marina into prostitution. Early in their encounter Bawd concerns herself with what she calls Marina's "qualities" (4.2.46), ordering Boult—in the presence of Marina herself— to "take you the marks of her, the color of her hair, complexion, height, her age, with warrant of her virginity, and cry, 'He that will give most shall have her first.' Such a maidenhead were no cheap thing, if men were as they have been" (4.2.57–61). Bawd recognizes what men want: "if men were as they have been." The way she talks about and to Marina, in fact, implies that she has internalized this point of view. Left alone with her, Marina becomes the object of Bawd's seductive assurances as to the "pleasure" she shall have as a prostitute, and Marina eventually stops her ears. Then she responds as Lavinia had to Tamora: "Are you a woman?" (4.2.82). Like Lavinia, Marina is confronted with a sexually experienced, even predatory figure. Her category crisis is similar to Lavinia's also: How could a woman, she may be seen as asking, relate herself to me and my body in this fashion?

Marina's and Bawd's exchange after this accents the role of power in their relationship:

> *Bawd*. What would you have me be, and I be not a woman?
> *Marina*. An honest woman, or not a woman.
> *Bawd*. Marry, whip the gosling, I think I shall have something to do
> with you. Come, you're a young foolish sapling, and must be
> bow'd as I would have you.
>
> (4.2.83–88)

Bawd's metaphors for Marina—"gosling," "sapling"—are of the young and supple. She positions herself to discipline her new sex worker, to "whip" her and "bow" her. Later in this scene Bawd turns to Marina, saying "Come, young one, I like the manner of your garments well" (133–34), only to return to her appraisal of Marina as an object when she remarks to Boult: "When nature fram'd this piece, she meant thee a good turn" (139–40). Just how would Bawd "have" Marina? If the final answer is "pliable to the customers," that pliability involves, at least to Bawd, disciplining Marina and bowing Marina to her will. So while this seems ultimately "for" the customers, it should be remembered that Bawd's desires are not wholly separate from theirs. Mingled through the cash nexus, these desires agree in taking Marina as their object.

This intermingling of desires proves central to Thomas Middleton's scenarios of female-female seduction. Gratiana's seduction of Castiza in *The Revenger's Tragedy* (1606), Livia's seduction of both Bianca and Isabella in *Women Beware Women* (1621), the attempted seduction of the White Queen's Pawn by the Black Queen's Pawn in *A Game at Chess* (1624), and the seduction of Diaphanta by Beatrice-Joanna in *The Changeling* (1622) all reveal Middleton's fascination with the erotic manipulation of women by other women. Why should women seduce other women, and what does it look like when it happens? These questions doubtless fascinated the playwright, for he returns repeatedly to scenes of manipulative female-female eroticism. Many of Middleton's powerful female characters have sexual experience and control their own bodies. They also show interest in and attempt to control the bodies of other female characters. Although they try to seduce less powerful characters into heterosexual intercourse, the scenes of seduction themselves often have an erotic content that makes that intercourse appear almost an afterthought.

Indeed, behind the chessboard arrangement and manipulation of desire in his plays, Middleton eroticizes female-female contact while having it function "for" adulterous heterosexuality. We could take as example here Livia in *Women Beware Women,* perhaps the most powerful of Middleton's characters and, with Tamora, arguably among the most powerful female characters in early modern English drama. She describes herself as experienced, almost cynically so: "I have buried my two husbands in good fashion, / And never mean more to marry" (1.2.50–51). This experience, I would argue, enables her to seduce both Isabella and Bianca—it takes one dead husband for each woman Livia helps seduce, seduction predicated on a sexual displacement or equivalency. Middleton is so interested in female characters seducing other female characters, in fact, that he has Livia come to Bianca only after persuading Bianca's mother-in-law through what Livia calls "tongue-discourse" reflecting their mutual "Experience in the world" (2.2.152–53). Significantly, when Livia at various moments describes her linguistic ability, she uses images that closely relate her body to the bodies of other female characters. In an aside after deceiving Isabella—Livia has convinced her that she is really no relation to her uncle, and can sleep with him—Livia says:

"Who shows more craft t' undo a maidenhead, / I'll resign my part to her" (2.1.178–79). The metaphor is both theatrical and bodily: Livia's "part," that is, remains both her role as a bawd or go-between and that part which makes her so strong in this play—her tongue.

This image hints that Livia has undone Isabella's maidenhead with her "part" or tongue. Another passage makes this connection in an even stronger way. Here Livia claims that "I could give as shrewd a lift to chastity / As any she that wears a tongue in Florence: / Sh' had need be a good horsewoman, and sit fast, / Whom my strong argument could not fling at last" (2.1.36–39). The final metaphor may come from jousting; it could also refer to Livia's argument as horse. With "lift," we are perhaps asked to visualize a scene in which Livia's strong tongue, one that can lift chastity, becomes an argument/jouster/horse that can similarly throw a "horsewoman." The conjunction, noted earlier, between tribades and horses/centaurs may support this conceit on a deep level. Whatever its source, Middleton describes Livia's seduction as itself a competitive act, an act that—through the arrangement of bodily puns and images—possesses an erotic charge. As spectators of her various gamelike seductions, audiences are in a position to delight in Livia's success. In this way the triangulation includes two third parties: the men for whom Livia seduces women and the audience members who may enjoy her efforts in and of themselves.

Nowhere, however, did Middleton make the potential excitement connected with female-female seduction so explicit or physical than in the seduction of Diaphanta by Beatrice-Joanna in *The Changeling*. This seduction and the subsequent virginity test Beatrice performs on her maid appear to have been based on a real event, and it will be useful here to compare what happens in the play with it. For reasons that may become clear, Middleton had a long-standing and ambivalent fascination with Frances Howard (1592 - 1632), daughter of the earl and countess of Suffolk. Howard had been married to Robert Devereux, the third earl of Essex, when she was thirteen and he fourteen. Immediately after the marriage, Essex went abroad, and Frances stayed at court. Eventually she had a notorious affair with Robert Carr, the king's favorite, and, when her husband returned to England in 1610, she filed for an annulment on the grounds of nonconsummation of their marriage. This "nullity" suit occasioned a scandal of enormous proportions, partly because the king himself worked strenuously, and without subtlety, to overcome the objections of his officials. Before their marriage Howard and Carr would poison Sir Thomas Overbury in the Tower; along with the nullity suit, this action would earn

Howard a permanent place in Middleton's imagination as a model for strong, if misguided, female characters like Beatrice.[49]

To "prove" her virginity, Frances Howard appeared to submit to a physical examination by a group of sixteen matrons and gentlewomen.[50] This jury found her virginity intact, thus facilitating the annulment. Yet rumors held that Howard had substituted in her place a young virgin wearing identical clothing and veiled, ostensibly for modesty.[51] On the basis of such rumors, Middleton appears to have constructed the virginity test and substitution in *The Changeling*, written the year Carr and Howard were themselves released from the Tower for their part in Overbury's murder. Beatrice's predicament is remarkably like that of Howard, which implies that Middleton was deeply concerned with the power of women in his time and that his plays were speaking to and about real issues as well as individuals.[52]

Having lost her virginity to De Flores, Beatrice seeks a substitute for Alsemero's chemical virginity test and for a subsequent "bedtrick" on their wedding night. At a loss, Beatrice sees her maidservant Diaphanta, whom earlier Jasperino has described as sexually attractive. Beatrice says in an aside: "Seeing that wench now, / A trick comes in my mind; 'tis a nice piece / Gold cannot purchase" (4.1.53–55). In referring—however metaphorically—to Diaphanta as a "piece," Beatrice calls on the rhetoric of female objectification, a rhetoric we might assume male. The word *piece* as used here comes from "piece of flesh." Partridge defines it as "A girl (or a woman) regarded sexually," deriving one of his examples from *Pericles*, where Boult, referring to Marina, tells Bawd "I have gone through for this piece" (4.1.43).[53] And we have already heard another instance when Bawd refers to Marina, in her presence, as "this piece." Beatrice's desire to find a female body to use parallels Bawd's, as does her language in describing this body as an object. Yet Beatrice remains in every sense a bawd figure for herself, seducing Diaphanta to represent her own body in the dark with Alsemero.

It also proves crucial for Beatrice herself to subject Diaphanta's body to Alsemero's virginity test, so that she, Beatrice, can watch the results and imitate them (4.1). When Beatrice insists on putting Diaphanta's virginity "Upon an easy trial," Diaphanta responds in an aside: "She will not search me, will she, / Like the forewoman of a female jury?" (4.1.99–101). This would have formed an obvious allusion, for contemporary audiences, to the physical examination that ostensibly had established Howard's virginity. Unlike that "search," however, Middleton stages this examination for a playhouse audience. Even without a large audience, however, the chemical test

Beatrice administers—one that she has stumbled across, and realizes will be tried on herself—is in every way invasive. Persuaded to drink a vial of mysterious liquid, Diaphanta responds with the precise symptoms a virgin, in this test, should exhibit; phrased by the book Beatrice has discovered, "'twill make her incontinently gape, then fall into a sudden sneezing, last into a violent laughing" (4.1.48–50). There is something inescapably lewd about Diaphanta's body opening "incontinently" and making noise for Beatrice. As Marjorie Garber has argued, we can see this testing spectacle as symbolic of Beatrice learning to "fake it," counterfeiting a series of expected reactions that simulate orgasm.[54] That Beatrice is by this time sexually active with De Flores seems to make little difference: She needs to know what Alsemero will expect of a virgin, and she can learn this, apparently, only by first seducing then testing a virgin herself, only by seducing then watching a female body in an unfeigned reaction.

Where Alsemero and Jasperino take voyeuristic confidence in the apparently natural response of Beatrice's body to the chemical contents of "Glass M" (4.2.130 ff.), the audience recognizes that they see only what Beatrice herself has produced and observed after buying Diaphanta's virginal body. Beatrice watches a female body respond to a stimulus she, Beatrice, has administered. What does it mean to watch Beatrice experiment with Diaphanta's body this way? By assuming, if only to subvert, the position of men here, Beatrice effectively places herself in the sexually controlling role Alsemero assumes he will take with her. Insofar as the seduction and bodily testing of Diaphanta are activities associated, in this play, with males and wedding-night sex, Beatrice's actions directly concern the erotic. But they concern mainly the mechanical details of erotic performance—a pleasurable show of sexual pleasure, a show that is perhaps especially pleasing to heterosexual men. Whereas Livia has her "part" perfect, Beatrice is still learning hers. So in contrast with Livia, she seems hardly to enjoy her exercise of power. That this enjoyment, such as it is, remains left to the audience hints that the misogynistic triangulation of female-female eroticism in this and other Middletonian seductions is with the paying customers in the playhouse itself.

Beginning with Donne's Sappho and femme-femme eroticism, we have traced arrangements of bodies and desire in texts that include figures like Neville's Lady Hungerford, Shakespeare's Tamora, and Middleton's Livia and Beatrice-Joanna. Our thin description of female-female eroticism has moved from mutual pleasuring to apparently one-sided pleasuring to a sadistic and triangulated form of bodily relations. If in Donne's poem female bodies seem to be strongly for each other (though, as I have argued, these conjunctions are always susceptible to, even for, an aroused appropriation), in Neville one female body seems to be for another. In contrast, the Shakespeare and Middleton plays examined manipulate female bodies primarily for the audience. Likewise we move across a spectrum from few to marked differentials of power, rank, age, and experience. As we go from the practice of female-female eroticism—that is, from physical contact—to no physical contact between females, we also go from mutual pleasure to its absence and even to pain. So while we have seen powerful female characters manipulate others, to follow cultural representations of female-female eroticism along this spectrum is to see various female bodies increasingly objectified, manipulated, and disempowered.

What can we learn from instances of such objectification? They show us, I believe, that we cannot easily separate, from the potentially carnal imaginings of readers and audiences, the impulses that led authors to write arousing scenes and descriptions of paired female characters. And while it could be argued that the manipulation of female characters by other female characters functions as a figure for their misogynistic exploitation by males, in as well as outside of texts, I would offer that it is precisely the misogyny of writers that leads them to give certain female characters wants and abilities—including the ability to manipulate—they might not otherwise have been granted in literary representations. Apparent even in the title of *Women Beware Women,* with its vicious circle of the imperative, for instance, is Middleton's bind: how to make women fear each other without making them dangerous? And how to make them dangerous without making them powerful and desiring? Similarly, Neville's misogynistic fantasy of Lady Hungerford "excarnat(ing)" her female servants acknowledges, with Donne's poem, that a woman could take sexual pleasure in another woman. Whatever his motivation, for Neville to suggest that a contemporary practiced what Donne's Sappho advocated is important testimony of the sexually imaginable. And in another example, the very scene we may find emblematic of a patriarchal heterosexuality—Alsemero's jealous desire to know and control Beatrice's body by testing it—already has taken place between Beatrice and Diaphanta. The coercion we may associate with men appears in a female character who manipulates another female character's body. Are we to take this as indicating a false consciousness on Beatrice's part? Situational resourcefulness? Middleton's ambivalent fascination with Frances Howard and her sexuality? We will not find the answers to these questions until we recognize them as worth asking.

As *The Changeling* makes clear, female-female eroticism in the drama of early modern England is almost invariably connected with the spheres and interests of other sexualities. This play also reminds us that desire and the erotic are often transgressive—too often, I have argued, to enlist them in narratives that, emphasizing mutuality, would lessen our understanding of how power and danger marked the erotic on and off the early modern stage. For every positive figuration of female-female eroticism like that of "Sappho to Philaenis," we have fantasies concerning such predatory characters as the smooth-tongued nun of "Upon Appleton House." For every idyllic relationship like that between Marina and Philoten, we have many versions of manipulative eroticism like that which transpires between Marina and Bawd. So although recent criticism concerned with female homoeroticism and with same-sex friendship has uncovered instances of strongly affective relations, we need to place such instances within a wider range of early modern literature as well as within a broader understanding of the erotic in and among characters, actors, audiences, and readers. To do so is to ensure that our understanding of the topic is as complex as female-female eroticism itself was in the drama of early modern England.

PART III

CRITICAL CULTURE

CHAPTER 6

SHAKESPEARE AND
THE END OF HISTORY

PERIOD AS BRAND NAME

What's in a period name? Had Juliet had asked the question this way, her answer could well prove satisfying to Shakespeareans today. As a group, Shakespeare critics face a similar dilemma when deciding whether what they read is "Renaissance" or "early modern" literature. For some time now, "Renaissance" has dominated the critical culture of Shakespeare studies. But its popularity and cachet do not stop there: "Renaissance" is everywhere we turn. As I write this chapter, in fact, the current telephone book in Austin, Texas, lists more than a dozen "Renaissance" businesses—firms or institutions, that is, that call themselves "Renaissance _____." These concerns include a computer store, a women's hospital, a hotel, a builder, a senior living community and beauty shop, a glass company, and a pest control service (this last perhaps an ironic match for a word that promises rebirth). In this context, "Renaissance" is an all-purpose modifier that seems to assure us of the quality of services rendered. A business using "Renaissance" in its name—for instance, "Renaissance Stone Design"—shares a family resemblance with "Prestige Roofing," "Deluxe Carpet Cleaners," "Classic Pizza," and "Elite Electrolysis and Waxing," all listed in the same telephone book.

The modifiers of these businesses are at once interchangeable and vital. However empty of meaning, however effortlessly contrived, and however poorly they describe the business in question, they are central to these firms' identities and testimony that presumption remains the largest asset of contemporary business. We could say that these names succeed not in spite of but because of their indecorum; as claims made against an account that society never balances, what they advertise is less any quality of service than the freedom to boast.

The word "Renaissance" always has been more claim than reality. And although its prevalence in business and in academic writing may suggest that it always has been with us, "Renaissance" as a period label is of relatively recent origin. Its use in relationship to *English* history and literature is more recent still. While we instinctively think of Shakespeare as a writer of the Renaissance, we could say that he became a Renaissance author not through taking up a pen in the late 1580s or early 1590s, or even when writing the major tragedies of the early 1600s. Instead, Shakespeare became an author of the English Renaissance primarily in the 1920s, when it first became common to speak of an "English Renaissance" at all.

However recent this term, the tenure of Shakespeare as a "Renaissance" playwright has lately come under pressure from other ways of placing him in history. As the present book attests, it is becoming more common to call Shakespeare and his contemporaries "early modern" authors, a label that emphasizes those things about this period of English history and its culture that survived to define the "modern." If "English Renaissance" has a deceptively short lineage, "early modern England" is even newer as a term to describe and define a historical period. Used by English historians since the early 1960s, it was taken up by literary critics only since the mid-1980s. Although it lacks the glamour of "Renaissance," "early modern" has its own implications, ones that bear examination.

Knowing something about when and why "Renaissance" and "early modern" came into use puts us in a better position to understand their role in the field and, correspondingly, the field itself. More than an academic exercise, an inquiry of this nature shows us, first, that "periods" themselves have periods—that is, that terms invented to describe the past come into use, and experience their greatest popularity, in identifiable segments of time. Through its interest in the weight of these key words as they fall into discourse, such an examination also helps to define the status of value and belief in current criticism of Shakespeare.

This, therefore, is the subject of this chapter: the names we give to the era of Shakespeare and his contemporaries, the genesis of those names, their influence on the way we interpret the past, and their significance for understanding the "Shakespeare" we live with. My argument is that, as used in literary criticism today, "Renaissance" and "early modern" imply more than they actually say, or are capable of demonstrating; neither term is based on a well-considered account of what a period is or its defining contours and boundaries. Both are more typically extensions of the naming practice seen in the examples of "Renaissance" businesses found in any telephone directory: labels that seek to suggest qualities in objects, practices, persons, and times that do not obviously possess them.

AN AMERICAN "ENGLISH RENAISSANCE"

Those who write on the literature and history of the 1500s and 1600s have at their command a range of terms for defining the time that relates to their object of interest. Among these are numerical markers: Someone may write, for instance, of the sixteenth- or seventeenth-century lyric, or of pamphlets of the 1590s or 1620s. The seeming objectivity of these descriptors is given a personal thickness in such terms as Henrician, Elizabethan, Jacobean, and Caroline, and a larger, familial import in such terms as Tudor and Stuart. These terms share something with century and decade labels in that, while adding personality to the mix, they offer fairly uncontroversial chronological boundaries. Other terms that involve events include "Reformation" and "post-Reformation," "pre–Civil War" and "pre-Restoration."

The most popular terms for discussing the era indicated by this range of labels, once again, are "Renaissance" and "early modern." Chances are good that any new book or essay relating to this era will use one of these terms. It is just as likely, though, that few such works will explain why they use the terms they do or explore the implications of using them. We should start, therefore, by looking at when these terms initially appeared.

The term "Renaissance" first came into use during the nineteenth century. Most readers are familiar with its appearance in Jacob Burckhardt's landmark *Civilization of the Renaissance in Italy,* published in 1860.[1] It was advanced before this, however, by Jules Michelet, in 1855, in the seventh volume of his *Histoire de France,* titled *La Renaissance.*[2] Although Michelet framed the "Renaissance" as a European phenomenon, throughout the latter half of the nineteenth century the term and concept were increasingly used in relation to Italy and, to a lesser extent, France. Historians and critics were reluctant to speak of an "English Renaissance" because England lacked a rich history in the plastic arts of painting and sculpture, because it lagged behind much of Europe in architecture, and because its liter-ature—the mode of cultural expression for which later commentary would most credit England—was seen as having reached maturity only late in the sixteenth century, well after the continental Renais-sance was held to have occurred.

Ironically, two French scholars, Hippolyte Taine and J. J. Jusserand, appear to be first to write of the "English Renaissance": Taine in *Histoire de la littérature anglaise* (1863–64) and Jusserand in *Histoire littéraire du peuple anglaise* (1894, 1904).[3] Scattered uses of this phrase cropped up thereafter. In 1895, for instance, Mandell Creighton, Lord Bishop of Peterborough, published his Rede Lec-ture (delivered earlier that year), titled *The Early Renaissance in Eng-land*.[4] Perhaps under the pressure of the continental Renaissance's earlier date, Creighton tries, in this lecture, to show a *fifteenth*-century Renaissance in England, one that centered on court poetry and the revival of learning. However, Anglo-American critics gener-ally avoided this usage as it pertained to any century of English his-tory. As late as 1920, for instance, Hyder Rollins could publish *Old English Ballads, 1553–1625*, a title that would seem anachronistic in several ways only a decade later.[5]

These last two instances call for a brief discussion. This chapter re-lies heavily on titles of books and essays to identify trends in the use of "Renaissance" and "early modern." It is important to note, there-fore, that the titles of works often diverge from the nomenclature of the arguments they advertise. Indeed, in several works discussed here, critics use one term in a title and another, or others, in the body of their works. For instance, in the first sentence of his 1936 article, "Symbolic Color in the Literature of the English Renaissance," Don Cameron Allen intoned: "The indebtedness of the so-called Renais-sance to the Middle Ages increases with every new investigation of their relationships; and one is often led to wonder if the term 'Re-naissance' is not a misnomer and if one would not be right, if one re-ferred to this period as 'the later Middle Ages.'"[6] There are many possible reasons for the kind of divergence seen here, from a critic's dissatisfaction with a term, a natural tendency toward synonyms, and the "house style" of a particular journal or monograph series, to an attempt to capitalize on current fashion or public taste. These last possibilities may explain Allen's title: Whatever scruples he had con-cerning the term, they did not prevent him from going on to publish five influential books with the word "Renaissance" in their titles.

Beginning in the early 1920s, "English Renaissance" was increas-ingly adopted as a period term.[7] For instance, in an essay in *Studies in Philology* (1920), Thornton S. Graves employs "Elizabethan" and "pre-Restoration" interchangeably, but not "Renaissance"; by 1922, however, he is contributing a review essay (soon to become a regular feature in that journal) titled "Recent Literature of the English Renaissance." Later in the same number Graves also published an essay that uses "Elizabethan" in the general sense but does not use "Renaissance."[8] Similarly, where Louis B. Wright would use the term "pre-Restoration" and "Elizabethan" interchangeably in an essay issued in 1928, three years later, in 1931, he would publish two essays in *Studies in Philology* using the phrase "English Renaissance" in their titles, most likely at the journal's request.[9] Wright's most influential publication, in fact, would be titled *Middle-Class Culture in Elizabethan England* (1935), in the preface to which he wrote: "For want of a better term, I have followed the conventional practice of using the word 'Elizabethan' to describe the period beginning with the accession of Elizabeth and ending with the Puritan Revolution in the 1640's."[10]

Use of "English Renaissance" became more common as the 1920s progressed—and not only in *Studies in Philology*. By 1929, and throughout the 1930s, scholars would use this term with unmistakable boldness. We see this in such works as J. William Hebel and Hoyt H. Hudson's influential anthology, *Poetry of the English Renaissance* (1929); Martha Hale Shackford's *Plutarch in Renaissance England* (1929); Lily B. Campbell's "Theories of Revenge in Renaissance England" (1930/31); George T. Buckley's *Atheism in the English Renaissance* (1932); Israel Baroway's "The Bible as Poetry in the English Renaissance" (1933); and H. O. White's *Plagiarism and Imitation during the English Renaissance* (1935).[11] The phrase "English Renaissance" had become routine in scholarship by the mid-1930s. Since that time, of course, it has obtained what appears to be permanent acceptance in the titles of such publications as *English Literary Renaissance* and *Renaissance Drama*, the latter of which focuses on but is not exclusively devoted to English plays of the sixteenth and seventeenth centuries.

As we have seen from its use in commerce, the word "Renaissance" suggests a quality that such descriptors as "sixteenth century," "Reformation," and even "Elizabethan" do not. Like an attractive box or embellished label, "Renaissance" adds prestige to things, scholarship included. This embellishment also was occurring outside the pages of academic writing in the first half of the twentieth century. At the same time that the idea of an "English Renaissance" was being solidified in scholarly usage, Americans were hard at work constructing the prestigious myth of the English Renaissance in imaginative works. Of course, "Renaissance" texts and figures had long been a staple of both English and American culture; Shakespeare's plays, in particular, have been important to American culture for almost as long as it has existed.[12] But in the 1920s and 1930s, a broad and intensive interest in literature of the sixteenth and seventeenth centuries constituted a kind of "double renaissance": an efflorescence, in relationship to England, of a period concept (that of the Renaissance) that was itself held to signify the renewal or rebirth of earlier ideas, forms, texts, and energy. The English Renaissance we know is largely an American invention that coalesced during the 1920s and 1930s.

During this time, Americans called the English Renaissance into being through a culture-wide pattern of invocation. The term made its formal debut between the world wars in the titles of literary works that quoted or otherwise alluded to Renaissance works, in revivals of that era's plays, in books and films set in Elizabethan times, in radio programs centering on the stories of that period, and in institutions and scholarly works devoted to its literary heritage. Related to the Modernist tendency to quote resonant literary passages in its poetry—the obvious example being *The Waste Land* with its dense weave of references—this pattern of invocation involved a focus on prestigious individuals and texts from sixteenth- and seventeenth-century England.

America in the 1920s and 1930s fostered what Joan Shelly Rubin has called the "making of middlebrow culture," which originated in an impulse to enlighten an interested citizenry by means of "improving" works. [13] This impulse led to the diffusion of popularized literature and ideas in such formats and agencies as the Book of the Month Club, in radio programs and discussion groups, in colleges' extension programs in the humanities, and in publication series dedicated to the intellectual betterment of the average reader. The "English Renaissance" fashioned at this juncture of American history, therefore, unfolded in an environment peopled by authors, publishers, and producers striving to make otherwise elite works available to general audiences.

This phenomenon left its mark in many places. For instance, such titles as *Look Homeward, Angel, The Sound and the Fury,* and *For Whom the Bell Tolls*—only a few of the many works of this period to quote English Renaissance texts in this manner—packaged their narratives as "high" art, as literature to be taken seriously, by invoking already canonical texts. During this period there was also an intensive interest in the English Renaissance as a source of filmed "costume dramas." These included not only the well-known adaptations of Shakespeare in 1935's *A Midsummer Night's Dream* (Warners) and 1936's *Romeo and Juliet* (MGM) but also such films as *The Private Life of Henry VIII* (1933, London Film Production), *Mary of Scotland* (1936, RKO), and *The Private Lives of Elizabeth and Essex* (1939, Warners), which took the stories of English history (however loosely adapted) as their source.

Behind this interest in the English Renaissance appears to have been a desire to legitimate modern letters and American culture by casting them as the rightful inheritors of English forerunners. As Hugh Grady and Richard Halpern have pointed out, invocations of Shakespeare were central to both artistic and critical Modernism during the first half of the twentieth century.[14] Sometimes these invocations implied a "parallel lives" theme worthy of Plutarch, a formation by which American efforts were joined to English precedents in an attempt to bridge time and geography.

Perhaps nowhere was this tendency so explicit as in a series of textbooks published by Noble and Noble beginning in the 1930s. This series, called *Comparative Classics,* paired "modern" works by Eugene O'Neill, Maxwell Anderson, and others with "classic" works, meaning those from the classical era and from the English Renaissance. Among other texts, Milton's "Minor Poems" were published with modern descriptive verse, *Macbeth* with O'Neill's *The Emperor Jones, Romeo and Juliet* with Rostand's *Cyrano De Bergerac,* and *Hamlet* with both Euripides' *Electra* and O'Neill's *Beyond the Horizon.*

If Eliot's patterns of quotation in *The Waste Land* implicitly ask readers to compare the modern present with the past, a past Eliot often represents through the English Renaissance, Noble's *Comparative Classics* series turns this request into a schoolroom exercise. Appended to the twinned plays *Julius Caesar* and Anderson's *Elizabeth the Queen,* for example, is a collection of questions, positions, and topics that teachers can put to their students. These include the following:

- Point out three things in *Julius Caesar* that were made necessary by stage limitations.
- Show two ways in which *Elizabeth the Queen* is more free.
- Compare the two plays as to the historical truth of the principal characters, Elizabeth and Caesar.
- Compare Anderson's Fool with any of Shakespeare's Fools. Who supplies the place in *Julius Caesar?*

- "What Private Griefs"—A Comparison of the Plotters:—Brutus and Cassius vs. Cecil and Raleigh.[15]

The edition is careful to insist that students note the differences between Renaissance and modern plays. But in the end the "comparative" principle and format of the series undermine the historicist impulse, proving that we compare things that we believe essentially alike.

At work in this series, and in the larger movement it represented, was not an unqualified admiration of masterpieces across the ages, regardless of their time of composition. Instead, it was an attempt to join the modern present with certain resonant moments in literary and cultural history: classical Greece and the European—especially, the English—Renaissance. Throughout the 1920s and 1930s American artists and scholars worked to solidify apparent links connecting these special eras in Western history, with America somehow the logical descendant of these elevated cultures. We see this in the foundation of institutions dedicated to the study of earlier literatures and history, such as the Folger Shakespeare Library and the Huntington Library. The cornerstone of the Folger was laid in 1930, and the Huntington published its first *Bulletin* in 1931. Scholars would use these libraries, and draw on some of the ideology they represented, to construct not only an "English Renaissance" but an American one as well.

The term "American Renaissance" is a familiar one by now. Coined in F. O. Matthiessen's famous study, *American Renaissance: Art and Expression in the Age of Emerson and Whitman* (1941), it refers to the flowering of American letters in the mid-nineteenth century in the works of such authors as Melville, Hawthorne, Emerson, and Whitman.[16] Matthiessen's book continues to be one of the most influential studies of American literature; in the wake of the book's influence, the "Renaissance" he describes can, like the "English Renaissance," seem self-evident. But because this "American Renaissance" is, as a term and concept, so clearly attributable to a single person, Matthiessen's idea has been criticized for its role in the formation of an elitist canon of American literature.[17] What his critics have not acknowledged, however, is that his "American Renaissance" followed, and can be seen as a product of, the "English Renaissance" that was being constructed in America by many scholars and artists of the time. Matthiessen's graduate work and first book concerned "Elizabethan" literature. In fact, the title of this 1931 book, *Translation: An Elizabethan Art*, speaks to his interest in the way one culture can "translate" the energies of another.[18]

The constructive power of the "English Renaissance" also appears to have made itself felt in the scholarship of Willard Thorp, a Princeton University professor of English. His doctoral thesis of 1926 was entitled *The Triumph of Realism in Elizabethan Drama, 1588–1612*.[19] During the 1930s and 1940s, Thorp's interest in literary "realism" shifted from the Elizabethan era to the "American Renaissance." Like Matthiessen, Thorp's scholarship figured importantly in setting up the canon of American literature. Thorp published, in 1938, *Representative Selections* of Melville's writings, and in 1947, edited *Moby-Dick* for Oxford University Press. Trained as scholars of what was increasingly called "English Renaissance" literature, Thorp and Matthiessen both contributed to a scholarly movement that translated an English Renaissance into an American one.

EARLY MODERN

Recently the phrase "early modern" has begun to replace "Renaissance" in literary criticism relating to England. Seemingly a simple phrase, "early modern" betrays some of its complexity even in the understated tension between its components: "early," which takes time in one direction, and "modern," which leads it in another. This tension remains an integral part of what "early modern" is, and does, in the study of Shakespeare and his contemporaries. Like a hand with index finger extended, "early modern" points to the past with one finger while three others aim squarely at the here and now.

Since its adoption by the field, "early modern" has performed a variety of functions. It serves, variously, as a slogan by which one may advertise the newest critical wares (in the words of Heather Dubrow, it remains a "badge, a ready way for scholars practicing contemporary modes of criticism to distinguish themselves from their predecessors and recognize one another"[20]); as an assertion about a larger sequence of history that—owing to the specific frame implied by the word "early"—is rarely demonstrated in the pages of criticism unconcerned with modernity as a whole; and, in its capacity as an assertion seldom proved, as an antidote for fears about presentism and anachronism.

When did "early modern" first come into use? To answer this question, we need briefly to examine the genesis of the "modern" period in historiography. In a sensitive discussion of periodization relating to the sixteenth and seventeenth centuries, Margreta de Grazia looks to Hegel's *Philosophy of History* as a text central to the setting up of the "modern" in historical consciousness.[21] She outlines the "decisive break," for Hegel, occasioned by the fifteenth century, and made irrevocable by the Reformation, Martin Luther, and Protestantism's transfer of spiritual authority from institution to individual. Following Hegel, such figures as Karl Marx, Jules Michelet, and Jacob Burckhardt helped establish the idea of an epochal divide, an idea centering on "their identification of the emergent period with heightened consciousness."[22]

While historians always had been willing to write about broad eras, with the *Annales* school in the twentieth century came a new explicitness, both in theory and practice, of what it means to conceive history in terms of such expansive time frames. The historians affiliated with the journal *Annales* often embraced what Fernand Braudel famously called *la longue durée*.[23] As opposed to the histories that unfolded out of political events or the efforts of powerful individuals, Braudel was interested in larger subjects and larger units of time. His research would involve, for instance, not only Spain or Italy but "the Mediterranean and the Mediterranean world" (1949); we see a similar scope in the translated title of *Civilization and Capitalism, 15th–18th Century* (1981–84).[24] Widely credited (along with others of the *Annales* group) for revolutionizing the study of history, Braudel was explicit about his debts to Marx, whose genius, Braudel held, "lies in the fact that he was the first to construct true social models, on the basis of a historical *longue durée*."[25]

By 1957, the example of the *longue durée* had begun to make itself felt across the channel in one of England's leading historical journals, *History* ("The Journal of the Historical Association"). In its February number that year, *History* began dividing its book reviews by means of period categories. These categories included "Medieval," "Early Modern," and "Later Modern." Significantly, the books reviewed in the "Early Modern" section in 1957 all employed older nomenclature and generally concentrated on the influence of political figures in history. Among the books reviewed were Cyril Falls's *Mountjoy: Elizabethan General* (1955), Conyers Read's *Mr. Secretary Cecil and Queen Elizabeth* (1955), D. H. Wilson's *James VI and I* (1955), R. T. Petersson's *Sir Kenelm Digby* (1956), and J. W. F. Hill's *Tudor and Stuart Lincoln* (1956).

It would not be until the mid-1960s that, bolstered by the examples of broad periodization at use in the work of the *Annales* group, younger historians concerned with the social history of sixteenth- and seventeenth-century England began referring to "early modern England" in the titles of their works. An important event in this chronology was the 1965 Past and Present Annual Conference, the

focus of which was "Social Mobility." Two essays from this conference were published in the April 1966 issue of *Past and Present:*
Lawrence Stone's "Social Mobility in England, 1500–1700," which
uses "early modern" in the body of its argument but not in its title;
and Alan Everitt's "Social Mobility in Early Modern England,"
which uses this period label in its title but not in its argument.[26] The
provisional nature of "early modern" here is apparent not only from
its tentative use but from the fact that, two years earlier, in his *Past
and Present* essay "The Educational Revolution in England,
1560–1640," Stone had spoken of his task as being that of "the historian of a pre-nineteenth-century society."[27] Only a decade later,
this would seem an occasion for which use of the phrase "early modern" was not only appropriate but nearly obligatory.

Stone and Everitt take great pains to justify their nomenclature,
explaining exactly what (to their minds) was "modern" about "early
modern England." For Everitt, social changes that merit our attention included "the dramatic effects of the enclosure movement, the
rise in prices, the dissolution of the monasteries, the progress of commercial farming, the expansion of London, the development of transport, the increase of population, and the catastrophe of the Civil
War."[28] Interested more in social class than in agriculture, Stone sees
English society as experiencing a "seismic upheaval of unprecedented
magnitude," one that led to the transformation of the "status hierarchy" of the sixteenth century to the "loose competitive status ag-
glomerations to which we are accustomed today."[29] To Stone,
England was "early modern" as a result of the following events and
conditions: the price revolution, changes in land ownership, urbanization, increasing specialization, a growing bureaucracy, greater
physical movement of people, increased litigation, expansion of educational opportunity, and greater commercial activity. Both Everitt
and Stone are careful to point out that the "modernity" they describe
was neither uniform nor pervasive; it was, instead, an unevenly emergent aspect of social life.

The notion of "early modern England" had so caught on with a
subsequent generation of historians that by the middle and late
1970s it would appear in the titles of such studies as Keith Thomas's
"Rule and Misrule in the Schools of Early Modern England" (1976);
Joan Thirsk's *Economic Policy and Projects: The Development of a Consumer Society in Early Modern England* (1978); and J. A. Sharpe's
Defamation and Sexual Slander in Early Modern England (1980).[30]
To my knowledge, the first work of literary criticism to employ the
phrase "early modern England" in its title was Annabel Patterson's

Censorship and Interpretation: The Conditions of Writing and Reading in Early Modern England, published in 1984.[31] Because her study has made an important contribution to the field, and because it appears to have led others to speak of "early modern England" in their criticism, Patterson's understanding of the phrase merits scrutiny here.

One thing to notice about Patterson's title is its authoritative resonance. Its subtitle, in particular—*The Conditions of Writing and Reading in Early Modern England*—seems confident and objective, almost as if representing a genre of inquiry separate from literary criticism. In this, it followed the clinical title of Barbara Lewalski's *Protestant Poetics and the Seventeenth-Century Religious Lyric* (1979), a title that may be said to read like the cover of a policy briefing.[32] The intentional sobriety of this latter title was pointed out by William Kerrigan and Gordon Braden, who argue that it marks the beginning of a "revolution in critical fashion": "In place of 'Christian' we find the sectarian precision of 'Protestant', and in place of 'humanism' with its strong epochal ring, we find the timeless 'poetics.' Instead of the evocative 'Renaissance,' we have the flatly denotative 'Seventeenth-Century,' with which nobody will bother to quarrel."[33] As we will see, the "revolution" that Kerrigan and Braden hold Lewalski to have spurred was continued by Patterson, whose use of "early modern" would be widely adopted by literary critics.

Patterson's main objective in *Censorship and Interpretation,* as she states in her introduction, is "to break down the barriers between academic discourse and 'real' issues, by recovering for inspection and inquiry that stage in European culture when all the major European powers were themselves emergent nations, engaged in a struggle for self-definition as well as for physical territory, and when, in consequence, freedom of expression not only was not taken for granted, but was a major subject of political and intellectual concern."[34] This sentence is both a summary of the book's topic and an apologia for the term "early modern." Referring to the early modern as a "stage," Patterson quickly gains the benefit of a developmental narrative. Indeed, in its very style this sentence reveals the microprocessor-like speed associated with the function of "early modern" in literary criticism. That is, "early modern" couples with incredible quickness two things at a great distance from one another. This sentence proposes, for instance, a highly specific project—"inspection and inquiry" into history through a set of sixteenth-, seventeenth-, and eighteenth-century literary texts—as a solution to a general, present-day problem, "the barriers between academic discourse and 'real' issues." In doing so, the sentence races past us a set of undemonstrated claims, offering them as fact: "that stage in European culture when all . . . and when, in consequence . . . a major subject. . . ." Like "early modern" itself, the syntax of this long sentence is stretched taut to cover a variety of times and topics.

In contrast to those of the historians examined in preceding paragraphs, Patterson's definition of the "early modern" is a thin one; it centers on the idea of the nation-state and, in particular, the nation-state's relationship to freedom of expression. Perhaps because of literary criticism's traditional pursuit of single themes, this thinness is almost always part of its uses of "early modern." Connecting the theme of freedom of expression in the twentieth century with analogous formations in sixteenth- and seventeenth-century English texts, Patterson's argument sees the past as both prologue to the present and also much like it. As did the "parallel cultures" myth of the English Renaissance earlier in the twentieth century, Patterson's early modern paradigm gives readers of old books the comfort of feeling at home in the past by allowing them to see it as a version of the present.

It would take four years from her book's appearance for the field to adopt Patterson's usage. The year 1988 was the turning point, in fact. Before this, for example, such critics as Stephen Greenblatt and Jean Howard had used the word "Renaissance" in relationship to English literature of the sixteenth and seventeenth centuries: We can see this in Greenblatt's *Renaissance Self-Fashioning* (1980), and (as editor) *Representing the English Renaissance* (1988) and Howard's "The New Historicism in Renaissance Studies" (1986).[35] During and after 1988, however, each critic would use the phrase "early modern" in their titles: Greenblatt in *Learning to Curse: Essays in Early Modern Culture* (1990), Howard in "Crossdressing, the Theater, and Gender Struggle in Early Modern England" (1988).[36] Howard's first sentence in this essay—"How many people crossdressed in Renaissance England?"—uses the older period term, as does the body of the article itself. But in her next book, in 1994, she would adopt the newer descriptor in both her title—*The Stage and Social Struggle in Early Modern England*—and her text.[37]

"Early modern" gained such acceptance in literary criticism by the early 1990s that significant discussion of the term itself began to occur. In 1992, Leah Marcus started an essay on the subject by asking "What manner of beast is early modern studies?" before contrasting the latter with "Renaissance" studies in the first full-fledged examination of the two terms.[38] The following year, in 1993,

Frances Dolan would publish in *PMLA* an essay concerning "the Face-Painting Debate in Early Modern England," which occasioned a series of letters to that journal's "Forum."[39] Like Marcus's essay, this brief exchange highlighted key tensions between competing models of history and interpretation, models broadly associated with "Renaissance" and "early modern."

This "early modern" exchange began in 1994 when Crystal Dowling wrote to challenge Dolan's employment of the term, arguing that Dolan's use worked to hide the historical divergence of her evidence. As Dowling pointed out, "all the attacks on face painting that Dolan quotes range from 1583 to 1616 whereas all the defenses come from 1660 and 1665."[40] Dowling's insight touches on something that many scholars of the period recognize: There is something of a "break" or "rupture" in representations of gender and sexuality during the later seventeenth century, with the period after 1660 featuring more texts with recognizably "modern" concerns and positions. Dolan replied to Dowling's concern over "early modern" by saying that this term was "more helpful in enabling me to attend to similarities in gender constructions from the late sixteenth century to the end of the seventeenth" and that she welcomed "the sweeping view permitted by the category 'early modern.'"[41] Later that year, Heather Dubrow contributed to the same venue a thoughtful meditation on problems arising from the newly popular "early modern." These problems included, to Dubrow, the tendency of "early modern" to keep the Middle Ages an "Other" (a problem also, she pointed out, with "Renaissance" as a period term), its tendency to overemphasize the reach of capitalism and to underemphasize regional differences and, largely, to neglect religion.[42]

Dolan's reply to Dubrow expanded on her earlier answer (to Dowling), and contains four observations that have special relevance here:

1. "I think it is significant that many scholars . . . use a range of periodizations, adopting whichever one best suits the project at hand . . ."
2. " . . . instead of a new consensus (*early modern*, for instance) replacing an old (*Renaissance*), the possibilities are proliferating."
3. "This multiplicity and the concomitant necessity of choosing mean that it is necessary to reflect constantly on periodization."
4. " . . . juggling is always involved in creating (rather than discovering or describing) periods and their literatures."[43]

Much of what Dolan says here is uncontroversial. Most critics (including me) do use "a range of periodizations" in their work, and such terminology has indeed proliferated. What makes these remarks relevant is that, for the most part, they represent mainstream thinking about how we write criticism. And it is in this typicality that we see the major difficulties that spring from "early modern."

We could begin by noticing the instrumentality of the term. As spelled out in Dolan's reply, "early modern" is, like other period terms, a tool rather than a truth. Offering too casually the view that periods are created rather than discovered or described—as if, for instance, Reformation England were merely a creation of A. G. Dickens in 1964—Dolan puts critics in a largely rhetorical world, and the world of the past largely in the rhetoric of critics. Much of her position, in fact, offers a consumerist celebration of choice; we may recognize in her phrase "the possibilities are proliferating" a genre of advertising that eagerly promises abundance without consequence. And where Dolan suggests that "this multiplicity and the concomitant necessity of choosing mean that it is necessary to reflect constantly on periodization," we can sense a claim that is true only if circular. Expansion of choice, in itself, does not mean reflection on the objects chosen. On the contrary, a persuasive argument could be made that the multiplicity that Dolan embraces means that critics will reflect *less* frequently, and *less* deeply, on the issue of historical and literary periods.

In her confusion of selection with reflection, Dolan foregrounds the manner in which criticism has become detached from belief. Noticeably absent from her remarks is any sense that one term could be truer than another or even that a critic could believe this to be the case. Where period designations are concerned, we are left as enlightened agnostics: all the labels are constructs; none is perfect; each has its proper time and place. As I have indicated before, I am not unsympathetic to the dilemma that produces such a belief. But I also sense that such a belief has potentially dangerous consequences for our criticism. While the refusal to commit often is held to be an intellectual virtue, it is also, in its supple instrumentality, a potential concession to the lure of opportunity. When belief gives way to occasionalist use of language, for instance, what we write about literature is in peril of being seen as an empty gesture toward the elusive rewards of the academic market. "Early modern" risks, in this sense, being seen as part of a critic's professional wardrobe: a fashionable item with which to accessorize one's ensemble of words, an ambitious phrase that draws on the power of appearance.

"Early modern" often seems produced as much by the social formations of the present as by those of the past. That the designation frequently speaks to the professional lives of those who use it has been addressed by Michael Dobson, who, in a characteristically insightful review of four critical studies of Shakespeare and early modern literature, discerned "an important shift in perceptions of Shakespeare's position within his culture, and indeed of that culture's priorities":

> Rather than being first and foremost a Stratford bourgeois preoccupied with dowries and second-best beds, the Bard who emerges from these studies is an assiduously networking professional, and one, furthermore, whose courtly aspirations and connections aren't to be taken lightly. Consequently, the Elizabethan England these books persuasively depict is far closer in spirit to the Rialto and its serious money than to Windsor and its merry wives. Its literary and political circles are peopled by upstarts and would-be cosmopolitans, marketing their humanist skills across patronage networks which, structurally hostile to the domestic, operate in a dangerously ambiguous space somewhere between the professional, the amicable and the erotic. In this culture favours are reciprocated in cash, in books or in kind; rival factions exchange information among themselves by letter and in closets; while sycophants and sexually available apprentices rub shoulders and scratch backs with confidential secretaries and common players. It is a culture preoccupied with status and with clothes, in which an internally inconsistent patriarchy is always under threat but always in place: a culture, nonetheless, in which certain outstanding women, partly or wholly cross-dressed à la Portia, can achieve a sexily masculine success. It is a culture, in short, which bears striking resemblances to the one that developed in the Eighties around the annual conference of the Shakespeare Association of America.[44]

The sting at the end of this paragraph is a deserved one. Although it is not shocking to see critics creating a Shakespeare in their own image, it is surprising to see how little consciousness there is, in criticism, of that very reflexiveness. Given the term's sober, somewhat marxist origins in the writings of British social historians, for instance, it is ironic that "early modern" has become a popular brand name among American Shakespeareans. But such an irony extends past the fact of its adoption and into the details of its usage.

As we have noted from its use in Patterson's *Censorship and Interpretation*, "early modern" is less a replacement of "Renaissance" than its structural equivalent. If "Renaissance" connotes value through the trappings of aristocratic culture, "early modern" offers up the self-serious attitude of the technology age. It is bathed in the gleaming light of the computer monitor—one difference between "Renaissance" and "early modern" essays being that many of the former were written in longhand or on typewriters, whereas most of the latter have been written on computers. The difference is indeed cosmetic, and importantly so. As Marjorie Garber has suggested, the greatest aesthetic change in contemporary editions of Shakespeare—the switch from Roman to Arabic numerals as markers of acts and scenes (by which, for instance, I.ii becomes 1.2)—derived from the example of Marvin Spevack's *Harvard Concordance to Shakespeare* (1973), which used Arabic numerals in its entries. What effect did the choice of Arabic numerals have on Shakespeare studies? Computers, of course, have been set up to function with Arabic rather than Roman numerals. Where Spevack's choice was made for him by the desire to generate his concordance via a computer, that choice itself encouraged subsequent scholars (many of whom used his *Concordance*) to give their references to Shakespeare's texts using the same system.[45] In this way, changes in technology have encouraged changes in the look of contemporary editions of Shakespeare's texts. Inasmuch as the latter reinforce our sense of an "early modern" Shakespeare, we have modern technology and the sensibilities it encourages (rather than Shakespeare) to thank for the modern appearance of his texts.

Another of the ironies surrounding "early modern" involves its relationship to issues of social class. Often credited with helping us pay attention to subordinated groups in history, "early modern" seems at times to advertise historically emergent, privileged habits and interests on the American coasts. While it may be unfair to hold "early modern" to be a term of the California freeway, the New York subway, and the analyst's couch, a term through which the culture of the British isles in the sixteenth and seventeenth centuries is inflected through ways of life on Manhattan island in the twentieth and twenty-first, it is clearly a designation that confesses an interest in the past's contemporary utility.

THE LAST SHAKESPEARE IN HISTORY

My remarks on the presentist attraction to Shakespeare ask for some explanation. Let me begin by saying that two unspoken truths about "early modern" underlie literary criticism relating to England. Both are worth stating here, not only because they have gone unsaid but because they figure centrally in the question of period labels that this chapter has explored.

The first is that what most makes this literature "early modern" is not any of the things that critics normally offer in defense of the term. Not, that is, a new interest in questions of nationality, subjectivity, race, exploration, or gender. That these things are as "new" as is often claimed is a point of debate: Medievalists can fairly describe the same as important features of many of the texts they study.[46] Instead, what makes the works of Shakespeare, Sidney, Nashe, Jonson, Wroth, and Donne "early modern" is a thing so integral to our criticism that we rarely talk about it: the English language. English literature of the sixteenth and seventeenth centuries can be called "early modern" because the English language had by that time entered its modern state. As Baugh and Cable remind us, "we attain in this period to something in the nature of a standard, something moreover that is recognizably 'modern.' The effect of the Great Vowel Shift was to bring the pronunciation within measurable distance of that which prevails today. The influence of the printing press and the efforts of spelling reformers had resulted in a form of written English that offers little difficulty to the modern reader."[47] This modernization of written and spoken English is what allows us to label texts from the sixteenth and seventeenth centuries "early modern." Because they give us less "difficulty" than the works of Chaucer, Langland, Gower, and the *Pearl* Poet, they seem chronological neighbors in a way that the writings of these earlier authors do not. We should observe that the first uses of "early modern" in relation to England came not from historians or literary critics but from philologists. In this regard, we could note Arvid Gabrielson's "Early Modern English I/r (+ cons.)" in the 1930 number of *Studia Neophilologica* and E. J. Dobson's "Early Modern Standard English" in the *Transactions of the Philological Society* in 1955.[48] "Early modern English" thus preceded and enabled "early modern England" as a period term, and also as a quantity: Without the modern "feel" of its language, literature of this period would be more difficult to posit as the anticipation of our own concerns.

The reason Shakespeareans almost never discuss language in this context is that doing so means giving away the game, confronting the fact that what we do depends less on our commitment to various ideas and causes than it does on a book of such incredible articulation that it could be dubbed the speech manual of modern culture. I am referring, of course, to the First Folio. This 1623 text brings us to the second unspoken truth about "early modern" studies relating to England: They would not exist without this great work of early modern English. "Shakespeare"—by which I mean Shakespeare's writings and the host of associations those writings have generated over the centuries—is the center from which countless studies of "early modern" texts and phenomena take their being. However scientifically these projects are described, they would have far fewer readers were it not for Shakespeare's well-spoken plays and poems and the hold the latter have had on our culture. Although "the Age of Shakespeare" sounds trite as a designation, in signaling who pays the piper of our academic tune it is perhaps more honest than "early modern," which is honest (about its presentism) in only an unconscious way.

It is to Shakespeare's language—more specifically, to the articulation of his plays and poems—that we must look in order to understand the importance of periodization trends relating to the sixteenth and seventeenth centuries. "Shakespeare" has become something like the mouthpiece of Western culture in English, an eloquent representative of the age of speech in a society of the spectacle. Yet even as the "talk" of his works makes them stand out to us, our growing predilection for the visual has put pressure on the way we teach them. I offer a small example of the sway of the visual from my own experience teaching Shakespeare's works: At my university, more and more classrooms are being outfitted with elaborate (and, perhaps needless to say, extremely expensive) technologies that allow—even pressure—instructors to teach literature by means of projected films, illustrations, and outlines. A large, locking master-console contains not only a VCR and DVD player, but also a PC with an internet connection; an overhead projector effectively transforms the classroom into a screening room. This technology makes it more likely that instructors will have visual experience (including films, film clips, and web images) a central component of their courses. This is more likely where I teach because instructors who "show movies" typically receive higher figures on their student evaluations (which, in turn, can translate into a greater likelihood of an instructor receiving a raise) than instructors who work primarily or exclusively with the printed word. I do not believe that such is confined to any single college or university, nor that my experience with the increasingly pervasive role of the visual is at all unique. Like our culture generally, our educational institutions have become addicted to looking.

As we become increasingly swayed by the power of the visual, Shakespeare stands out to us like an uncanny reminder of a faculty we have already lost. He does so in an ever more singular fashion, as if his works hold a monopoly of well-spoken English. No longer a supremely gifted writer working in a time and place remarkably rich in literary talent, he is instead a figure in whom the precedents of his craft and the efforts of his contemporaries have been collapsed. Such condensation of status and value has produced a "Shakespeare industry" both inside and outside the academy. However justified the attention generated through the operations of this industry, it has worked to change the way we write about Shakespeare's works. And this change is not necessarily for the better. An interest in Shakespeare that leads us to ignore the achievement of his contemporaries, for instance, is regrettable. And where "early modern" sometimes is held to be a corrective to this tendency—by democratizing our objects of study—in casting the traces of Shakespeare's time as harbingers to our own, this period concept has effectively done the opposite. Gradually erasing any associations of his era ("Tudor," "Elizabethan") and replacing them with first an aristocratic ("Renaissance"), then a quasi-scientific label ("early modern"), we have accelerated the process by which a man has become his words, and those words have become, in turn, valuable and even value itself.

This estrangement is a necessary step in the commodification of Shakespeare's eloquence: Shakespeare has become, through our period labels, the costume in which we have most recently cloaked the vitality of his language. We say "early modern Shakespeare," therefore, as if it is merely one more Shakespeare in an infinite sequence. But it is precisely this admission of sequence—a sequence without content, only difference—that testifies to what we could call the end of Shakespearean history. Absolved of any integrity of relation to a particular time or place, these sequential Shakespeares signify only in relation to each other and only by declining to mean. The "ever new" Shakespeare is, in this perpetual newness and constant circulation within the commercial and educational institutions of our culture, always the same.

CHAPTER 7

SHAKESPEARE AND
THE COMPOSITE TEXT

THE NEW FORMALISM

Earlier I maintained that a thin description of early modern literature could well begin by pointing out the intensively personal nature
of that era's texts. In addition to this emphasis on the personal, literary works of the early modern period in England tend to be unusually copious—thick, that is, with "stuff," including quotations of
other texts, as well as descriptions of and references to material from
the world outside their pages.[1] Such copia often has attracted the attention of critics interested in the cultural contexts of early modern
literature. As was observed in chapter 2, however, the literary and social materials of various texts are typically important, in these critical
modes, not as sources of the texts in question but rather as potential
sources for critical thick descriptions thereof. I maintained there that
these descriptions have become almost a separate literary genre in
their own right. Obviously, the field has benefited a great deal from
the cultural turn in literary study and from the thick descriptions that
have accompanied this turn. But one of the things that get left out
by thick description's interest in literary contexts is the relationship
between newer forms of criticism—criticism usefully gathered by the
coinage "cultural historicism"[2]—and an older kind of formalist criticism that served as an unspoken, and perhaps unconscious, model for
it: source study.

Much of what is currently practiced under the name of historicism
and cultural criticism is actually a modified version of source study.

For several decades now, this apparently old-fashioned mode of criticism has served as an unacknowledged template for the newer kinds of inquiry into early modern literature and culture. Recognizing their relationship to source study will help us understand some of their limitations as well as some limitations traditionally attributed to source study. Only by understanding their shortcomings can we adapt these critical modes to account more fully for the composite nature of early modern literature. This is particularly true, I believe, in relation to plays from Shakespeare's era—plays whose "worldliness" often comes from the worlds of other books, and whose "culture" is thus often strongly literary in nature.

One reason for asking how sources relate to literary form and, by extension, to the practice of formalism in literary criticism is that source study typically is seen as a critical subgenre of its own. As an approach, source study seems unlike formalism in that it can be as interested in a work's prehistory as it is in that work's ultimate form. Conventional wisdom sometimes compounds this problem by associating formalism too closely with the ahistorical—defining it, that is, as the study of a frozen text, a work of literature that exists for us as a verbal object outside time. Few formalist inquiries actually embody this stereotype, of course: Such topics as prosody, genre, metaphor, philology, and rhetoric have complex histories that affect their appearance in literary works, and most critics respond to these histories when practicing formalist criticism.

The histories to which formalism attends reveal source study's affiliations with formalism. Just as a formalist study of a text may focus on the relation between elements of that work's form and prior instances of theory or practice relevant to the topic under examination—for example, a particular rhetorical trope in a text, previous instances of that trope, its apparent functions, and comments on its use and import—so does source study remind us that texts are fashioned, that they are fashioned with extant materials, and, further, that these materials have histories of their own. Source study is a formalism, then, not only through its interest in the parts that make up a textual whole but also through its sensitivity to the histories of those parts.

THE NEW FORMALISM

Yet if, in its attention to the elements of a literary text, source study *is* a variety of formalism, how can we hope to describe it as anything more than an antiquated practice? Whether called source study, *Quel-*

lenforschung (*Quellenstudien*), or *le critique de génèse,* it remains one of the oldest modes of literary criticism. How can it be seen, then, as novel in any way? And what, for that matter, is so unprecedented about formalist study of literature today that it could justify such a collective label as "the new formalism"?

We can start to address the question of source study's innovations by defining this larger critical genre. New formalism could be defined as follows: a critical genre dedicated to examining the social, cultural, and historical aspects of literary form and the function of form for those who produce and consume literary texts. As this definition suggests, the new formalism sees language and literary forms—from the single-lettered interjection "O" to the stanza, the epic battle, and epic itself—as socially, politically, and historically "thick." Instead of relying on literary texts primarily for anecdotes or synecdoches of the real, the new formalism seeks to understand texts—and their mediated relations to the external world—by scrutinizing the cultural work that forms do, the symbolic capital attached to specific forms, and the choices available to authors and others involved in the production of texts.

As it pertains to criticism of literature in early modern England, the designation appears to have been coined by Heather Dubrow in the title of a special session at the December 1989 meeting of the Modern Language Association: "Toward the New Formalism: Formalist Approaches to Renaissance New Historicism and Feminism." The following year, in the conclusion to *A Happier Eden: The Politics of Marriage in the Stuart Epithalamium,* Dubrow noted both the ahistoricity of some new historicist and feminist criticism of the 1980s as well as the marked lack of attention to language and form in these and other methodologies. She went on to argue that "the interplay between texts and their cultures can best be explicated through another kind of interplay, the dialogue between some of the questions posed by the new historicism and some of the methods employed by New Criticism, linguistics, and formalism."[3] Building on this observation about historicism's role in supplementing the concerns of formalist criticism, one could say that the new formalism is "new" not only in its expanded notice of the cultural valences of literary form but also in its proximity to and qualification of the new historicism.

The late 1980s and the 1990s saw the publication of a number of formalist studies that, directly and indirectly, responded to the aformal directions of new historicism. In addition to Dubrow's book on epithalamia, studies that might be characterized as contributing to a new formalism include (in chronological order) Annabel Patterson's *Pastoral and Ideology* (1987), Ann Baynes Coiro's *Robert Herrick's Hesperides and the Epigram Book Tradition* (1988), Joshua Scodel's *The English Poetic Epitaph* (1991), David Quint's *Epic and Empire* (1993), Mary Thomas Crane's *Framing Authority* (1993), Kevin Dunn's *Pretexts of Authority* (1994), Dubrow's *Echoes of Desire* (1995), Ann Moss's *Printed Commonplace-Books and the Structuring of Renaissance Thought* (1996), Judith Anderson's *Words That Matter* (1996), Patricia Parker's *Shakespeare from the Margins* (1996), Daniel Fischlin's *In Small Proportions* (1998), Lynne Magnusson's *Shakespeare and Social Dialogue* (1999), and the anthology, edited by Mark David Rasmussen, entitled *Renaissance Literature and Its Formal Engagements* (2002). To be sure, few if any of these authors announce a group identity with other formalists. Some may not welcome the identification of their work as "formalism" at all. But whether taking up words, tropes, figures, or genres, all helped renew a critical approach that had lagged in popularity, and most did so by stressing the social and political implications of literary form. Each of these studies understands form as possessing significant agency before, during, and after literary composition. Each sees form as not only a valid but an overwhelmingly compelling object of inquiry.

A variety of the new formalism has concerned itself with literary sources. In this critical subgenre, sources function in a more complex manner than previous criticism had allowed for. Robert Miola speaks to the changing assumptions behind this critical development when he notes that the traditional tendency, in source study, to "rely almost exclusively on verbal iteration as proof of influence" has given way to a model of source that is "plural rather than singular, encompassing and allowing for a wide range of possible interactions between sources, intermediaries, and texts."[4] Recent source studies that engage literary sources and, by addressing the social and political implications of borrowing, ask us to revise our stereotypes of this practice include Andrew Gurr's "Intertextuality at Windsor" (1987), Claire McEachern's "Fathering Himself: A Source Study of Shakespeare's Feminism" (1988), G. Harold Metz's edition of *Sources of Four Plays Ascribed to Shakespeare* (1989), Miola's *Shakespeare and Classical Tragedy: The Influence of Seneca* (1992), his *Shakespeare and Classical Comedy: The Influence of Plautus and Terence* (1994), Eric Mallin's chapters on *Hamlet* and the plague, and on *Twelfth Night* and the Anjou affair, in his *Inscribing the Time: Shakespeare and the End of Elizabethan England* (1995), Frank Whigham's chapter on *Arden of Faversham* in *Seizures of the Will in Early Modern English*

Drama (1996), Heather James's *Shakespeare's Troy: Drama, Politics, and the Translation of Empire* (1997), Stephen Lynch's *Shakespearean Intertextuality: Studies in Selected Plays and Sources;* Richard Knowles's essay, "Cordelia's Return" (1999), Grace Tiffany's "Shakespeare's Dionysian Prince: Drama, Politics, and the 'Athenian' History Play" (1999), and John Klause's "New Sources for *King John:* The Writings of Robert Southwell" (2001).[5] Gurr represents the expanding definition of "source" in noting that the search for the sources of *The Merry Wives of Windsor* (1597) "becomes . . . more complicated when it looks for echoes that are not specifically verbal, that are not overt, and that simply resonate the need of the two companies [playing in London in the mid- to late-1590s] to follow each other's fashion in playmaking. Subjects, plots, even the alignment in politics, religion or social questions begin to join the verbal parallels as examples of a writer's response to the intertextual activities of the time."[6]

THE SOURCES OF CULTURE

New formalist accounts of early modern literature in England emphasize these social and political dimensions of form—dimensions, in Gurr's words, that are "not specifically verbal"—in large part because the field in general has embraced the cultural context of literary works. In this emphasis, such studies respond to the profound transformation of literary criticism since the late 1970s. Arguably the greatest disciplinary change during the twentieth century came in its last two decades, when—spurred by the new historicism, by feminist criticism, and by cultural materialism—a predominant concern with the structure and aesthetics of literary works gave way to a predominant interest in the relations of these works to the times, places, and persons who worked to produce them and for whom they were produced. As the appendix to this book shows, criticism of the 1980s and 1990s reproduced the trajectory that Raymond Williams described when he noted the change in the meaning of "culture" during his life: an earlier sense of culture as "high culture" (what Williams called "the teashop sense") was being replaced by our current sense of culture as "a whole way of life."[7] Formalist studies have merely responded to a growing conviction in the field that the "culture" of literary texts is less that of their literary heritage than that of their larger environment.

This conviction has produced a revolution in the objects of criticism, for, as we have noted, critics have moved from examining books toward examining culture. If before the 1980s books often were understood to be among the most significant products of their culture (indeed transcending their culture, in some instances), more recently we have embraced a notion of culture in which books are only one kind of object among many that should be scrutinized. Among the objects an expanded pattern of inquiry takes up are not only non-"literary" texts (such as, for instance, pamphlets and speeches) but items of material culture generally (such as embroidery and clocks), social practices (such as rituals and customs), and events (cases at law, social dramas). Obviously, this shift has had both supporters and detractors. Those who most strongly support it, for instance, point to the way this change in critical focus has opened up a host of cultural objects to our view, placing literature itself in a context richer than that afforded by a grand tradition of literary masterpieces. Those who find this critical revolution problematic sometimes note that these same literary masterpieces have an uncanny way of appearing in even the most politically "radical" research—that great literature provides the symbolic capital that underwrites such criticism—and that most critics are not well trained in the methodologies by which they seek to write cultural history.

This last reservation is worth exploring: Not that this critical revolution has replaced the literary text with the "text" of culture, but that, in so doing, it has left largely unchanged the procedures by which the relevant text is analyzed. That is, in moving from literary text to culture *as* text, many critics have retained the principles and methodology of literary analysis they were taught—which means, in most cases, the principles and methodology of formalism pressed into service via thick description. What is too seldom observed in discussion of the changes in the field over the past few decades is that the new historicism, and much cultural inquiry, owes as great a debt to formalist criticism as the new formalism does to it.

To demonstrate this relationship without forcing any single critic to be its exemplar, I would like to take the liberty of discussing an imaginary book. This addition to an academic publisher's booklist is titled *Pursued by a Bear: Representations of Russia in Early Modern England*. Although I have made up this title, it seems not at all inconceivable that a study like this may soon be written and published; certainly it sounds worth reading. Such a study would begin by noting the underacknowledged relationship between Russia and early modern England. It would castigate scholars for having almost willfully overlooked this relationship and chide those who have noticed it for not adequately differentiating the various peoples and subcultures of early modern Russia. This study would help make its case by examining strong commercial and political links between Russia and England at the time. It would quote relevant correspondence and pamphlets. Later chapters would survey literary representations of Russia. We could expect a chapter devoted to Russians in Shakespeare: *Love's Labor's Lost* (1595), for instance, and *The Winter's Tale* (1610). But the topic would also take one through many other plays (among them, *The Travels of the Three English Brothers* [1607], *The Four Prentices of London* [1594], and *The Loyal Subject* [1618]) as well as through prose fictions and poems. The study would conclude, of course, by suggesting that to neglect the importance of Russian themes and concerns to early modern England is to misapprehend English culture.

In place of "Russia" in this example we could supply any number of categories: from ethnic, national, and religious identities to social customs, body parts, and other physical objects. Many books and essays have followed the pattern I describe and have done so by employing various of the preceding categories. What I want to show with this hypothetical monograph is that, like much historicism and cultural inquiry today, it is essentially a source study. Instead of investigating, say, the sources of *Love's Labor's Lost*—in which "Russia" would perhaps be a contributing element, along with many others—this study takes the culture of early modern England as its text and argues that Russia is a significant and underacknowledged source of that text. Instead of taking a book as its central object, this study reads parts of books themselves as the sources of a larger cultural text. Critics have reversed the objects of the procedure, then, but have left the procedure intact.

IMAGES OF SOURCE STUDY

The connections between source study and cultural inquiry are so seldom recognized because source study has acquired a negative reputation in the field. There is perhaps no better proof of its low status than that offered recently by *The Norton Shakespeare* (1997). Earlier editions of Shakespeare that sought to be "complete" in some way— here G. Blakemore Evans's *Riverside* and David Bevington's Harper-Collins edition come to mind—almost invariably included a section detailing Shakespeare's literary sources. Along with lists of characters, chronologies, first-line indexes to the poems, and selected critical bibliography, Shakespeare's sources were held to be as indispensable to a "complete works" as was a royal genealogy.

But although *The Norton Shakespeare* has a chart of the kings and queens of England, it omits a separate section on sources, preferring to mention them in passing in the editors' prefaces to the individual plays. In place of a section that might be called "Shakespeare's Sources" or "Shakespeare's Reading," the volume's general editor, Stephen Greenblatt, entertains readers with three imagined events that may have affected Shakespeare's later writing. These events are Shakespeare's possible attendance at, respectively, official cere- monies in which his father might have taken part; a royal progress and parliamentary elections; and a Catholic exorcism.[8] That Green- blatt understands these fantasized primal scenes as sources of the plays is clear from the way that he introduces them: "Even in ordi- nary mortals, the human imagination is a strange faculty; in Shake- speare, it seems to have been uncannily powerful, working its mysterious, transforming effects on everything he encountered. It is possible to study this power in his reworking of books by Raphael Holinshed, Plutarch, Ovid, Plautus, Seneca, and others. But books were clearly not the only objects of Shakespeare's attention; like most artists, he drew upon the whole range of his life experiences."[9] By substituting these imaginary events for the lists of books and ex- cerpts from books that other editions traditionally have provided for their readers under the heading of Shakespeare's "sources," Green- blatt illustrates the way in which historicism and cultural inquiry have expanded our notion of what counts as a possible source of lit- erature. What Greenblatt summarizes as "the whole range of [Shakespeare's] life experiences" is most often defined not bio- graphically but *culturally*. In addition to books, that is, things like weather, riots, marriages, diplomacy, the plague, cases at law, royal proclamations, economic fluctuations, trade disputes, social contro- versies, changes in fashion, religious conflicts, hangings, personali- ties, shipwrecks, wars, marital infidelities, and accents may be seen as contributing to a literary text.

Of course, none of these potential sources was unknown to tradi- tional scholarship—to "old historicism"—which, if it is to be faulted, tended to go even further than Greenblatt in its speculative identifi- cation of the sources of Shakespeare's plays.[10] By "old historicism" here I am referring to a genre of criticism that seeks to identify the social material that has gone into the composition of literary texts. Instances of old historicism include John Dover Wilson's "Martin Marprelate and Shakespeare's Fluellen" (1912), Lilian Winstanley's *Hamlet and the Scottish Succession* (1921), Edith Rickert's "Political Propaganda and Satire in *A Midsummer Night's Dream*" (1923),

Frances Yates' *A Study of "Love's Labour's Lost"* (1936), Henry Paul's
The Royal Play of "Macbeth" (1950), E. C. Pettet's "*Coriolanus* and
the Midlands Insurrection of 1607" (1950), T. W. Baldwin's *On the
Compositional Genetics of "The Comedy of Errors"* (1965), and B. N.
De Luna's *Jonson's Romish Plot* (1967). These studies are alike in
holding that the plays they examine directly incorporated identifiable
figures and social events—from King James and social insurrections
to the Gunpowder Plot—into their represented worlds. In this way
"old" and "new" historicisms share a conviction that literature is intensively worldly. Yet old historicism differs from its newer incarna-
tion in that it never overlooked books as crucial, and interesting,
sources of literary texts.

The Norton Shakespeare is not alone in finding literary sources un-
fashionable. The (new) New Arden editions of Shakespeare, as at
least one commentator has observed, tend not to include significant
examples of a play's literary sources. Reviewing the third series'
Antony and Cleopatra (1607), *King Henry V* (1599), and *Titus Andronicus* (1593), Barry Gaines points out that "No longer is a generous selection of source material included in appendixes; thus
Antony and Cleopatra lacks excerpts from Plutarch, and *Henry V*
lacks excerpts from Holinshed."[11] What makes the simultaneous exclusion of literary sources from these editions less than surprising is
the reputation that traditional source study has come to possess with
a new generation of editors. Even as source study provides the model
for some of the most exciting kinds of cultural study practiced today,
it is widely held to be an anachronistic mode of literary criticism.

Although a general sentiment about source study is that it remains
bookish and irrelevant, there exist more pointed criticisms of it as a
mode. These include the following, which we could introduce as
Reasons to Avoid Source Study:

1. Some authors do not seem to use sources significantly.
2. Authors always change the contexts of what they borrow.
3. Authors make sources unnecessary precisely by using them.
4. Source study distracts us from what is on the page in question.
5. Source study, in its emphasis on books, doesn't allow us to
   treat social themes, such as gender, race, and social class.
6. Source study is forensic, even prosecutorial.
7. The greater the influence on a text, the less visible is that influence in a text.
8. Source study privileges those who have access to large libraries
   and archives.

To respond to these claims, it may prove helpful to offer some of my own. I will start by saying that while various forms of expression, from painting and sculpture to dance and architecture, can be said to "quote" previous instances of their form, the verbal basis of literature makes it especially open to source study: When repeated across various texts, words and phrases can help identify more certainly which sources an author used. But even with literary works, source study is far from an exact science. Source study necessarily depends on the objects it examines; not every work of literature, or every genre, or every period of literary history, for instance, lends itself to an examination of sources. Source study tends to be a productive way to read plays of the English Renaissance because the authors of these plays were particularly aware of literary tradition and tended to read widely in the works of that tradition and in the writings of their contemporaries. Dramatic works of this period were, in turn, profoundly heterogeneous, often containing within their pages a rich picture of the cultural world they were written to please.

These claims are by no means original, and most are far from controversial. In themselves, however, they work to counter some of the criticisms listed above. For instance, the criticism that some authors do not make particularly significant use of sources does not apply to most early modern authors and certainly not to most early modern playwrights. Dramatists of this period routinely looked to printed materials in their search for stories, characters, ideas, situations, words, and phrases. Making recourse to a wide range of source materials, they necessarily changed the contexts of what they borrowed. It is through this change of contexts that such authors made the sources more, rather than less, necessary to our understanding of their texts (the second and third criticism in the list). In changing the contexts of these materials, the playwrights show us paths not taken and more lucidly foreground those ultimately decided on.

Criticisms 4 and 5—that source study distracts us from what is on the page in question, and that, in its emphasis on books, it prevents us from treating social themes—would seem to cancel each other. One says, for instance, that "close reading" is the most desirable approach to a work of literature; the other, that a work's cultural and historical milieus are most important to its interpretation. Each of these criticisms speaks from the vantage of an effective mode of reading, and, although in potential opposition, these modes deserve to have their positions addressed. Source study indeed takes our attention away from what is on the page we read. It seems even the antithesis of close reading. Yet this diversion from the page or pages at hand need not be permanent or disabling. As was pointed out above, in adding other contexts to the texts, passages, and words in question, source study can enrich, rather than diminish, them. By providing these alternate contexts, source study can help us read more closely what is on the page.

The criticism that traditional source study prevents us from treating social themes is true only if one accepts two assertions: first, that traditional source study examined only books as sources; and second, that books themselves are not the repository of intensively social themes. This first assertion does not withstand much scrutiny, for, as I have pointed out, the "old" historicism routinely sought sources in the world surrounding the texts it took up, and recent instances of historicism and cultural criticism have drawn heavily on source study for some of their materials. The second assertion—that books do not contain social themes—cannot be assented to, logically, at the same time that one reads literature for these social themes. That is, if we see literature as incorporating and responding to its environment, we also must admit that when literary texts borrow from other texts, they are incorporating (in however mediated a way) elements from social environments that merit our attention. And while authors often borrow from older sources that do not seem to enclose a synchronic "truth" about their culture at the moment of the text's composition, borrowing is itself a social practice that can tell us a great deal about the older materials that help make up every culture, whether books of the Bible, passages from Ovid, ethnographic details from travel narratives, chronicles of the reigns of English monarchs, or Greek idylls. Source study thus helps us overcome the narrow synchronic window through which new historicism typically chooses to view literature's relation to the surrounding world.

Criticisms 6 and 7—that source study is forensic, even prosecutorial in nature, and that the greater the influence, the less visible that influence is in a text—are perhaps among the most serious of those on the list. Each has to do with problems of evidence and proof. It will help us evaluate their merit if we examine strong versions of these claims. I turn first, therefore, to G. W. Pigman III, who, in an essay titled "Neo-Latin Imitation of the Latin Classics," suggests that critics who sense they have found relationships among texts (through imitations of models, quotations, and echoes) may well be noticing coincidental uses of language. Pigman goes on to elaborate this position:

> At first sight the proposition that neo-Latin imitations are more difficult to identify and interpret may well sound absurd, for a computer

which had been fed the Roman poets and almost any collection of Renaissance neo-Latin verse could spit out line after Renaissance line with some phrase from an ancient poem. But actually, that is the heart of the problem: what do we do once we have our massive print-out of similar and identical phrases? It is impossible to believe that all of the repetitions are conscious, much less significant, and often a reader, deafened by the roar of the echo chamber, feels incapable of finding a signal in all that noise. I would hazard the guess that a large proportion of the repetitions is due to coincidence and unconscious reminiscence—large enough, in any event, to raise doubts about "imitations" and "borrowings."[12]

What makes this passage relevant to our examination of source study is that it deals with difficulties of evidence relating to verbal recurrence. The problem, for Pigman, is that we have so much information that it can remain meaningless. His imaginary computer program overwhelms our senses: "spit out line after Renaissance line"; "deafened by the roar"; "all that noise." But although Pigman seems to base his reluctance here on an empirical issue—what can we know about literary relations, and on what evidence can we know it?—we are provided with merely his "guess" that the results of an experiment never conducted would leave us dubious about conscious appropriation of models.

The reluctance shown here is defensive, as if Pigman were anxious that a mechanical procedure (such as a computer program) could produce information that would exceed any single critic's control. Of course, his "massive print-out of similar and identical phrases" need not have been tied so closely to technology. Equally massive lists of possible sources exist for a variety of Renaissance authors, and these lists were produced long before the advent of computers. They are, as Pigman hints, intimidating. And this may be the larger cause of his anxiety: With prolific authors, source study is a humbling experience. Studying Shakespeare's sources, for example, requires a critic to read not only the works of Shakespeare and works that he might have read but also the works of other critics who have published on the subject. This extensive course of study leaves us in a position where we are not guessing whether an undifferentiated printout might be trustworthy. It means, instead, that we must proceed on a case-by-case basis in an attempt to ascertain the relation between a literary text and a possible source. Pigman is right to say that we need to be careful in this endeavor: Two texts can indeed share a resemblance that does not derive from material contact. But this does not, and should not, preclude our noticing a resemblance that does.

In using the terms "imitation" and "model," Pigman takes us away from the core of source study, which is at heart a forensic practice—one that seeks material relationships among texts and their specific sources. The more we move away from the specific, the more difficult it is to identify these relations with any precision. Hence the seventh criticism on our list: that the greatest influences *on* a text may not themselves appear *in* that text.[13] Like Pigman's reluctance, this one also involves questions of evidence and protocol: How are we to prove an influence, when the very word "influence" (from the Latin *influĕre*, "to flow in") suggests an amorphous fluidity? Here we can turn to Laurence Lerner for a strong version of this potential criticism of source study. In an essay titled "Ovid and the Elizabethans," Lerner notes: "There is one preliminary problem in discussing the presence of Ovid in sixteenth-century poetry: the difficulty of detecting it. If you absorbed Ovid, not perhaps with your mother's milk, but at any rate with your schoolmaster's rod, you—and your readers—might not know when you were using him."[14] When Lerner identifies the critic's job with that of the detective ("the difficulty of *detecting* it"), he reveals a valid concern with the "how" of ascertaining literary relations. However, like Pigman's reservation, that of Lerner here risks jeopardizing a mode of criticism because it cannot produce perfect results. Surely all writers (critics included) are not always conscious of when they are using particular sources or of when they are being influenced by an author or tradition. Lerner's recourse to metaphors of embodiment—taking in Ovid not "with your mother's milk, but . . . with your schoolmaster's rod"—aptly characterizes the way in which words, phrases, stories, even language itself, can seep into one's mind without one's awareness.

The unknown worries these two critics, both in terms of what an author does not know and what critics do not discover. This situation is, I would argue, something that we not only must live with but something that we can live with. To be sure, whether authors are conscious of what they do is sometimes important. We could take numerological structures in texts as a good example of this: Much depends on whether an author appears to have consciously arranged a text in a numerologically significant manner. The calendrical structures of Spenser's *Epithalamion* (1595) are a familiar instance here.[15] But in many other cases, an author's consciousness of a particular source or textual formation does not seem as crucial. For instance, an author could reproduce Ovidian phrases or situations without realizing she was doing so, and what could be more important than her realization is the fact of reproduction itself. The fear that there may be textual borrowings and influences that, in Lerner's point of view, readers could not recognize is well founded; there is always more about literary relationships that we do not know than that we do. But, like Pigman's worry concerning unrelated resemblances, this should be only a spur to greater and more careful attention to questions of source.

The two criticisms just examined also display an uneasiness over scale: too many resemblances leading to potentially meaningless coincidence, and too great an acquaintance with a particular author, text, or tradition producing an unverifiable "influence" on an author and work. This concern brings us to our final criticism of source study, which is that it is made possible only by the large holdings of established libraries and archives. This is a more than trivial criticism, in part because it reveals that scholarship is a luxury obtained through access to books. We can observe this potential disparity between the haves and have-nots of academic inquiry even in the price difference between, say, an inexpensive, pared-down, "thrift" edition of a Shakespeare play and an edition that includes copious notes, commentary, and appendixes. Even in paperback, the latter—which, depending on the series, could include a section on the work's sources—could be expected to cost up to ten times what the former does. The differences in format in this example reflect a larger distinction between modes of reading—one in which the "text itself" is mainly sufficient, the other in which ancillary texts are indispensable to our understanding of the text. Until fairly recently, this distinction was pressed home to scholars lacking ready access to large libraries and archives. The situation has begun to change, of course, with the introduction of both microfilmed texts and electronic databases, both of which can provide access to texts that once required extensive travel to consult. These changes, along with computerized search programs that help to identify verbal overlap among texts, mean that source study has become a more "open" critical mode.

SHAKESPEARE AND SOURCE STUDY: NASHE AND *Henry V*

I have argued that source study is related in significant ways to historicism and cultural criticism. I have explored some of the charges commonly leveled against source study, giving reasons these criticisms should not prevent us from taking this mode seriously. To make a practical case for its usefulness, I would like to offer an example of source study. The paragraphs that follow address the relationship be-

tween the Chorus of Shakespeare's *Henry V* (1599) and Thomas
Nashe's *The Unfortunate Traveller* (1594).

As the research of J. J. M. Tobin has demonstrated, Shakespeare
almost certainly had various of Nashe's manuscripts and printed texts
before him as he wrote many of his plays, using them for names,
words, and phrases the way one would dip one's quill in fresh ink.[16]
This borrowing stretches at least from *The Two Gentlemen of Verona*
(1593) to *Macbeth* (1606) and includes such plays as *Titus Andronicus* (1593), *Love's Labor's Lost* (1595), *Romeo and Juliet* (1596), *1
Henry IV* (1597), *As You Like It* (1599), *Hamlet* (1601), *Measure for
Measure* (1604), *Othello* (1604), and *King Lear* (1605). The texts
from which Shakespeare borrowed range throughout Nashe's career,
from *Pierce Penniless* (1592) and *Summer's Last Will and Testament*
(1592), through *Christ's Tears over Jerusalem* (1593), *Have With You
to Saffron-Walden* (1596), and *Lenten Stuffe* (1599). Tobin has identified an extremely close relation among certain passages in these two
writers' texts; the overlap is so strong that it seems clear that Shakespeare routinely turned to Nashe's work for verbal matériel. That one
writer borrowed from the other's manuscripts prior to publication,
and did so over the course of many years, hints that the authors may
have been on close terms as well.

The borrowing in question here occurs in the Chorus of *Henry V*,
which, I will argue, was fashioned in part from material in Nashe's
The Unfortunate Traveller. It is no exaggeration to call *The Unfortunate Traveller* one of the most important pieces of prose fiction in
English before the rise of the novel. From one point of view a Menip-
pean satire in its heterogeneity of incidents and materials, Nashe's
story is, from another perspective, a remarkably copious "history" of
the sixteenth century. Indeed, *The Unfortunate Traveller* remains a
virtual encyclopedia of the Renaissance and Reformation in presenting figures both classical and contemporary, continental and domestic, and various centers of thought and activity. Having so much
material to include, Nashe needs to maintain the audience's attention
to the episodes at hand and to take them from one place and time to
another, with no more than the authority of Jack Wilton, a roguish
Vice figure, justifying the travel.

Jack's stories thus are cast as tales told to an interested but potentially unforgiving audience, one that needs its attention focused—
particularly in the moments of transition between *The Unfortunate
Traveller*'s episodes. Two instances of this focusing are given below.
The first excerpts sentences from within a single paragraph; the second, several complete sentences a few pages later in the narrative. In

these passages, Jack refers to Henry VIII's military campaign in the summer of 1513, a campaign in which the English king led an army across the channel, captured the French cities of "Turney and Turwin," and returned victoriously to England. Jack tells his audience to follow his narrative with their imaginations:

> You must think in an Army . . .
>   Well, suppose he was . . .
>   Suppose out of the parings of a pair of false dice I appareled both him and my self . . .
>   I must not place a volume in the precincts of a pamphlet: sleep an hour or two, and dream that Turney and Turwin is won, that the King is shipped again into England, and that I am close at hard meat at Windsor or at Hampton Court. What, will you in your indifferent opinions allow me for my travel no more signory over the Pages than I had before? yes, whether you will part with so much probable friendly suppose or no, I'll have it in spite of your hearts.[17]

Here "You must think"—a supposition of Jack's, rather than a command—quickly turns into imperative *suppose*s: "Well, suppose," "Suppose." Jack gains the authority for his narrative by taking it; he pleasantly commands his audience to imagine. By the second excerpt, he acknowledges that "probable friendly suppose" may not be given freely yet he assumes it anyway. Condensing over three months' worth of military action and travel into a sentence ("sleep . . . and dream that Turney and Turwin is won, that the King is shipped again into England"), he instructs his audience to suppose, by dreaming, two victories and a triumphant Henry VIII crossing the Channel back to England.

I believe that the passages here formed a material source for Shakespeare's well-known Chorus in *Henry V*, which delivers the Prologue and the Epilogue as well as the choric prefaces to acts two, three, four, and five. Throughout the play, this Chorus begs the audience to be patient and imaginative while it apologizes for the inadequacies of the playhouse and its laborers and for violating the unities of time and place: "Carry them here and there, jumping o'er times, / Turning th' accomplishment of many years / Into an hour-glass" (Pro. 29–31).[18] It is worth observing that in the chronicle histories Shakespeare wrote before the publication of *The Unfortunate Traveller*, such dramatic "travel" had never been a problem. Critics, in fact, have long been puzzled as to why this play's choruses exist. As Samuel Johnson related, early on: "The lines given to the chorus have many admirers; but the truth is, that in them a little may be praised, and much must be forgiven; nor can it be easily discovered why the intelligence given by the chorus is more necessary in this play than in many others where it is omitted."[19] More recently, Anthony Brennan has held that "It is odd . . . that Shakespeare, who had already written many plays without resort to these old-fashioned devices, should employ a formal chorus in the play which brings to a close his preoccupation with the history of England."[20]

These positions represent a general uncertainty about why *Henry V* has a chorus at all. Read alongside Shakespeare's earlier chronicle histories, *Henry V* is indeed anomalous in using a presenter. But these positions do not acknowledge that Shakespeare had employed a chorus in *Romeo and Juliet*, some three years before *Henry V*. I have argued elsewhere that the Prologue and Chorus in *Romeo and Juliet* are "necessary" (in Johnson's words) from the demands of genre: What initially appears to be a romantic comedy—the son and daughter of rival houses meeting, falling in love, marrying, and thereby reconciling their parents—takes a tragic turn that could, without ample warning, shock its audience.[21] With *Henry V*, it is more difficult to say why Shakespeare felt it necessary to provide a chorus. Perhaps in this case, "necessity" is the wrong way to approach the problem. That is, what if we see Shakespeare not compelled by his materials to employ this Chorus but enticed by them to do so? Holding opportunity rather than necessity to be central, what if we see Shakespeare writing this Chorus for *Henry V* not because he should but because he could? In Nashe's work, Shakespeare found a device—that is, an author's apology for episodic leaps across time and space—and words on which he could capitalize to aesthetic effect in *Henry V*. As we will see, what may have been a choice motivated by aesthetics turns out to have implications of a political texture as well.

Having asked, in the Prologue, "Can this cockpit hold / The vasty fields of France? Or may we cram / Within this wooden O the very casques / That did affright the air at Agincourt?" (11–14), the Chorus precedes act three with the following:

> *Suppose* that you have seen
> The well-appointed king at Hampton pier
> Embark his royalty . . .
> . . . .
> . . . . *O, do but think*
> You stand upon the rivage and behold
> A city on th' inconstant billows dancing . . .

> . . . .
> *Suppose* th' embassador from the French comes back
> . . . .
> . . . . Still be kind,
> And eche out our performance with your mind.
>
> (3.0.3–35; emphasis added)

Shakespeare appears to have turned Wilton's casual storytelling tools—"You must think," "Well, suppose," "Suppose"—into the Chorus's decidedly more formal directions: "Suppose," "O, do but think," "Suppose." The problem of space and time in Nashe occupies Shakespeare as well. Jack excuses his narrative compression by saying that "I must not place a volume in the precincts of a pamphlet" ("precinct" from Latin *praecingére*, "to gird or encircle"). Similarly, as we have seen, Shakespeare's Chorus worries about what may be crammed within the circle of the wooden O, about what a cockpit can hold.

Jack tells his audience to "sleep an hour or two, and dream that Turney and Turwin is won, that the King is shipped again into England, and that I am close at hard meat at Windsor or at Hampton Court." The dreaming imagination he asks for not only condenses events but floats Henry and Jack home across the channel. Narrative *travail* and geographical *travel* join in a pun—"allow me for my travel"—no less central to Nashe's narrative than to its title. In Shakespeare, such condensed travel becomes important in passages like those above and in lines like "Now we bear the King / Toward Callice; grant him there; there seen, / Heave him away upon your winged thoughts / Athwart the sea" (4.0.6–9). Nashe's passages seem to have provided many of the building blocks for Shakespeare's Chorus: Jack's acknowledgment of the smallness of his medium, his request for a dreamlike imagining by his audience, and his admission of their potential powers; the compression of time and space; the return of a triumphant King Henry across the channel from France; and the imperative *supposes*. I would offer that Shakespeare saw in Jack's otherwise minor remarks the basis for his Chorus.[22]

Perhaps the first thing to say about these two literary texts, and the passages I have quoted, is that any relationship between them must be alleged rather than proven. This holds for every instance of source study. We can "know," in the strong sense of that word, nothing further than that certain texts have resemblances and/or verbal overlap. Even when authors of imaginative literature cite their sources, or when we possess authors' personal copies of other writers' books (copies that sometimes annotate particular words and passages that occur in these authors' own writings), there is always room for skepticism about what seems a certain borrowing. If source study at times appears to present itself as a quasi-scientific mode of scholarship, its rhetoric always must remain in the suasive mode: "It seems probable, for X reason, that author Y borrowed from text Z." So strong do such probabilities seem in many cases that an author's "sources" harden into the appearance of fact. We could take Shakespeare's reliance on Holinshed's *Chronicles* for his history plays as an example of the latter; here the sentence structure given above is truncated to read " . . . author Y borrowed from text Z," without the introductory phrase. But in most cases, even when authors declare what their sources are, the question of source remains less fact than likelihood.

Given a relationship between these two texts, however, we may ask what they have to say to and about each other. We could start by noting that the dialogue between Shakespeare and Nashe here is telling, for the differences in their "voices" are significant. While Nashe notices what Shakespeare calls the issue "Of time, of numbers, and due course of things" (5.0.4), Nashe names it "travel" and sees it merely as a reason to make a transition. Shakespeare, on the other hand, uses it to justify the Chorus's recurrent and striking poetry. In doing so, he changes the tenor of the remarks in important ways. Nashe has Jack seem to relish the medium he works in, as the pun here on "Page"—coupled with similar puns throughout the work—goes to show. In contrast, Shakespeare's Chorus exaggerates the inadequacies of the playhouse to support poetic *occupatio*. Where Jack's storytelling is roguish and homely, Shakespeare's Chorus is lofty, even priggish in its continued apologies and obsequiousness. Where Jack is grounded in the cozening tradition of the cony-catching pamphlets of the early 1590s, the Chorus of *Henry V* has what Brennan has aptly described as a "priest-like" function.[23] In his edition of the play, Andrew Gurr refers to the Chorus as "coercive," and observes that instead of offering itself as a "humble servant" or representing a "humble author," it transfers the epithet "with some malignancy" by praying for the *audience*'s "humble patience."[24]

If this act of borrowing comes as an assent or repetition with qualification—a kind of "Yes, but . . ."—that qualification speaks to the cultural and political positions of Shakespeare's Chorus. But before we consider what these positions are, it is advisable to begin by noticing what the borrowing does not do. It does not, for instance, contradict a critical tradition that places the Chorus (and, often, the play itself) alongside the epic.[25] Neither does it discount arguments that

Shakespeare's concern with the issues of time and place here responds to Sidney's thoughts on these topics in the *Apology*.[26] It does not disprove a recent argument that Chapman's *Seven Books of the Iliads of Homer* (1598) provided material for both the Chorus and the play.[27] Nor, finally, does it prevent us from seeing the Chorus as related to Essex's ambitions and activities in Ireland. But the borrowing from Nashe by Shakespeare here does tell us about a choice Shakespeare made.

This borrowing indicates, for instance, that he was aware of other possibilities for a chorus. Nashe's Jack is a strong presenter—a Pistol figure, almost, with narrative authority. We observe Nashe's fondness for such a traditionalistic *homo gloriosus* in Will Summers in *Summer's Last Will and Testament*. Nashe endorses, that is, a boisterous and aggressive character who satisfies his and our appetites alike through his wit and linguistic facility. Shakespeare, on the other hand, confines his Pistol to the underplot and elevates the language and ideology of his presenter. Exposed to one model for such a figure—that of Jack Wilton—Shakespeare instead gives the choric words of his play to an anonymous, priestlike Chorus that apologizes in blank verse for the theater and its laborers' efforts. However much he is a part of the physical world of the playhouse, the Chorus puts himself above that world. The implications of this elevation become apparent when we realize that not only is this Chorus not from the tavern world of *Henry V*, he does not show that he knows this world exists. Indeed this sober Chorus never mentions or describes these lower orders and their environment—even when, as at the beginning of act two, the following scene takes place in just such an environment. The Chorus prepares us there for Southampton and the King, but we see instead the Eastcheap world. This Chorus has no language or time for Bardolph, Pistol, Quickly, or Nim; his is an idealizing, even aristocratic vision that does not include their world.

We can begin to see this as typical of Shakespeare when we note that Shakespeare often revised his sources so as to push agency and authority up the social ladder. In his revision of Plautine comedy, for example, aristocrats, not slaves, resolve his plays.[28] Something very similar occurs in this revision in *Henry V*. In writing his Chorus, Shakespeare appears to have drawn on Nashe but changed his presenter in important ways. One could offer many reasons for this, from the reigning tastes of Shakespeare's audiences and the abilities and traditions of the Lord Chamberlain's Men to the competing "pull" of other literary traditions and texts, such as Chapman's *Iliad* translation, and even Essex's ambitions in Ireland. It is also quite possible that we see in the changes some of Shakespeare's own political orientation: that part of Shakespeare that chose Hal over Falstaff and Prospero over Caliban.

This said, I should point out that it is possible that the similarities in language, phrasing, and situation between *The Unfortunate Traveller* and *Henry V* are merely coincidental. They could be, that is, the product of two authors of roughly the same age, schooled in the same texts, writing for similar audiences at roughly the same time, and faced with a similar narrative problem. This is a legitimate consideration, although I believe that, in the context of Shakespeare's use of Nashe's works in other of his plays, the similarities we have observed are much more likely to indicate a material relation between the two texts. Tobin has argued convincingly, for instance, that *The Unfortunate Traveller* provided material for Shakespeare in *Henry V,* act four, scenes 3 to 5, when Shakespeare was writing lines for both Pistol and Bourbon.[29]

Let us consider for a moment, though, what we may take away from this alignment of texts even if we do not believe there is a line of borrowing from one to the other. A comparison of the "presenters" in these two texts, regardless of our feelings about any material indebtedness, leaves us with almost the same findings that were suggested in the reading above. Even when it fails fully to persuade readers of a link between texts, that is, source study succeeds in putting similar things into temporary, and often productive, alignment. More than an arbitrary exercise in comparison and contrast, however, such an examination is based on likeness among objects—objects that, as we have seen, invariably disclose important differences as well.

When it succeeds in persuading readers of a material linkage of texts, source study enriches the narrative through which we understand the past. If a close comparison of *The Unfortunate Traveller* and *Henry V* would tell us some of the same things even if we had not noticed that Shakespeare borrowed from Nashe's text, the possibility that Shakespeare used this text gives us good reason to ask searching questions about differences between them—questions that might otherwise have floated above the works as contrived and extraneous, or not been asked at all. Knowing that Shakespeare made frequent recourse to Nashe identifies for us an important source of his raw materials. In this way source study can ground, in history, our queries and claims about what lies beyond the margins of Shakespeare's plays: By understanding writing as production, it allows us to concentrate on the material relations among texts; by understanding texts as made in time, it helps us explore the differences among them as historically contingent. By scrutinizing the sources of his plays, and how he transformed them, we can learn much about the choices Shakespeare had available to him and the political implications of the decisions he made.

CONCLUSION

The value of a source study concerned with the relations among books is that it allows us to trace the threads of ordinary borrowing, borrowing such as that I have alleged between *Henry V* and *The Unfortunate Traveller*. As currently practiced, the new historicism probably would not take up such a moment for an essay on cultural poetics, for Shakespeare's borrowing in this passage seems only a matter of words—not social energy, power, or authority. Too, the borrowing here is much less provocative than the anecdotes that the new historicism typically chooses to engage. Neither would a vein of criticism interested in "high" literary relations be likely to expend much effort exploring the significance of such borrowing, for Nashe and his earthy narrative seem intrinsically "low," not part of the grand tradition such criticism typically studies.[30] Also working against our notice of this moment of borrowing is the fact that it is not deeply conflictive. Critics interested in divisive struggle between authors—struggle in which authors even devour their forbears—would find little of interest in this low-key, conversational act.[31] In contrast to these methodologies, a source study interested in the seemingly ordinary relations among books and authors provides a way of reading that helps elucidate the various positions of these books and authors in their time and culture, and over time as well.

As we have seen, source study allows us to eavesdrop on literary "conversations." Such conversations may not always be a formal series of well-considered meditations on issues of high merit but, instead, a casual, sometimes chaotic mix of utterances that includes false starts, half-sentences, and wandering thoughts. Talk, that is, that resembles less the polished dialogue of *The Courtier* than it does the meandering remarks of Ben Jonson's *Conversations*. There is no reason to see authors as godlike makers in total control of their sources. The conversations they enter into with their source texts and authors are, much like our own conversations, less rational and controlled than we may wish. As Hans-Georg Gadamer has pointed out, our control over dialogue is partial, at best: "We say that we 'conduct' a conversation, but the more genuine a conversation is, the less its conduct lies within the will of either partner. Thus a genuine conversation is never the one that we wanted to conduct. Rather, it is generally more correct to say that we fall into conversation, or even that we become involved in it."[32] The analogy to literature sticks, of course, on the word "genuine," for many literary works undergo a process of revision before they reach anything like their final form. Authors talk back to works: listen to them, respond to them, and perhaps listen again before responding once more. And surely parody, burlesque, à clef narratives, and topical stories depend on an intending, purposive author. Initially, then, nothing could seem less "genuine" than literature. But there is much about the role of accident in Gadamer's observation that holds true for literary conversation. Authors fall into conversations only partly in their control and conduct these conversations through and with texts made up of parts and forms of other texts. The larger historical and cultural conversations they become involved in are unavoidably literary situations—eras, schools, patronage and marketplace relations—not of their devising.

Since the cultural turn in literary studies, we have expanded our definition of the sources of literary texts to include these larger conversations. So rich are the plays of Shakespeare and his contemporaries that the entire world around them seems to have been actively engaged as a source of their heterogeneity. Although the epic is sometimes held to be the most capacious of all literary forms, plays composed for the theaters of early modern England are arguably even more varied in their makeup. Written, often, by diverse hands, for many actors, and for presentation in multiple venues, they typically are composed of an astonishing array of materials. In this, they deserve to be seen as thoroughly composite texts.

The new historicism has prompted us to see that social and cultural materials form a significant part of these plays—that these materials are "sources" of the plays, even as the plays themselves can be seen as sources of the larger cultural text that new historicism asks us to examine. It has been my contention here and throughout this book that recent modes of criticism interested in the cultural aspects of these plays can benefit from a more studied consideration of the bookishness of these dramatic texts. Playwrights were, for the most part, voracious readers, and they drew significantly on printed matter in composing their plays. Although source study can seem an anachronistic mode of reading, it not only underlies much of what is currently practiced under the name of cultural criticism but also offers us a powerful tool with which to examine the materials—cultural and otherwise—that make up every text. Source study that asks questions beyond the margins of texts can offer a solution to some of these shortcomings traditionally ascribed to it. Far from diverting our attention from these plays' relationships to their environment, source study that acknowledges the profoundly composite nature of early modern plays gives us deeper knowledge of the various ways these dramatic texts are positioned in their culture.

CHAPTER 8

THE NEW MATERIALISM IN
EARLY MODERN STUDIES

> *Today Marxist (and other radical) approaches to Shakespeare are staged by what we may call Reaganite and Thatcherite literary criticism as a kind of cultural Soviet Union, whose collapse is evident to everybody. Conservatives thus need not argue their case, but take it for granted; while by the same token the Left must offer theirs on both levels at once, as the defence of new local interpretations which is at one and the same time a whole social and cultural programme, a whole new defence of the radical agenda as such.*
>
> —Fredric Jameson, "Radicalizing Radical Shakespeare"[1]

Beginning in the early 1990s, a materialism that neither Karl Marx nor Fredric Jameson would be likely to recognize achieved an important place in early modern studies. Indeed, I call this a "new" materialism not only because of its momentum as a critical genre but because it comes as a disciplinary answer to a question that the epigraph asks us to ask: What future can materialist criticism of early modern texts have after Marx? I mean the "after" in this sentence to be attached not to Karl Marx or even to the literary criticism that followed in the wake of his theories. By "after," instead, I mean after a constellation of events during the late twentieth century that worked to lessen the attraction of materialist political theory, events familiar to anyone who has read the newspaper during the past several decades.

What happens in the world does not force us, of course, to alter theoretical practice, much less to paint radical literary criticism as "a kind of cultural Soviet Union, whose collapse is evident to everybody." Yet insofar as the worldly success of any theory affects our confidence in that theory's application, the incontrovertible dissolution of left politics in the late twentieth century appears to have put us in a difficult position relative to critical materialism. How far should we take the insights of Marx and marxist thinkers when these insights, and the theories germinated thereby, have proven impractical in the very world they address? How can we reconcile the "radical agenda" to which Jameson refers with the fact that, for better or worse, and however unevenly, the market has triumphed over Marxism in our time, supplanting class struggle as the apparent motor or logic of modern history?

To some commentators, the decline of left politics has not lessened the explanatory value of materialist philosophy and criticism. "There is no link between theory and practice," goes one line of thought. And another: "Now, more than ever, we need a theory critical of market forces." As Jean Howard and Scott Shershow put it, in the introduction to their anthology, *Marxist Shakespeares,* "The present volume joins others in suggesting that the fall of communist governments around the world does not signal the ignoble end of Marxist thought, but rather the possibility of its renewal."[2]

To be sure, most arguments for a socially conscious criticism are in good faith, and worth our consideration. At the same time, however, it does not seem wrong to pardon the reluctance, over traditional materialism, of many who have turned elsewhere for theories of how the world, and the world of texts, function. What does seem worth questioning is what it could mean to practice critical materialism outside the traditions of political and philosophical materialism. What, for instance, would be involved in a materialist criticism absent "a political commitment to the historical originality of late capitalism," a commitment that, Jameson argues, "is most likely to spur contemporary readers of 'Shakespeare' in new and exciting directions"?[3]

The "new materialism" I describe here answers Jameson, but not in a way that he would expect. By "materialism," this critical genre understands an attention to physical things—"matter," that is, interpreted literally. In place of class struggle, hegemony, or ideology, the new materialism attends to objects in the world: clothing, crockery, sugar. It often does so with "culture" (rather than "society") as its organizing concept. As with any critical mode, this new materialism has advantages and disadvantages. After briefly surveying what "materialism" meant in the study of early modern English literature during the nineteenth and twentieth centuries, I take up in this chapter specific instances of the new materialism to explore what it has to offer the field as well as how it usefully could be changed. It is my contention that the new materialism stands to evolve as a mode of cultural criticism only by more carefully incorporating the history of materialism itself.

EARLIER MATERIALIST CRITICISM

Marx himself was the first "marxist" or materialist critic of English Renaissance literature, if we can take as critically valuable his scattered uses of Shakespeare's works in texts like *The Eighteenth Brumaire of Louis Bonaparte* (1852) and *Capital* (pub. 1867–94).[4] But while Marx's allusions to and quotations of Shakespeare's works have drawn increasing attention of late, arguably the first substantive piece of materialist criticism of early modern English literature was Karl Kautsky's *Thomas More and His Utopia*, originally published in 1888, and still relatively little known.[5] Kautsky, born in Prague in 1854, was a German-Austrian political activist and writer, a leading intellectual of the Second International, and a lifelong popularizer of Marx's theories. His study of Thomas More is perhaps more accurately described as a three-part examination of, respectively, the political and economic features of More's England, of More's life and intellectual allegiances, and of the "communism" of More's most famous work, *Utopia*.

The division of this work into three sections follows Kautsky's deepest convictions. In classic marxist fashion, he sees a chain of influences beginning with the grand sweep of History, proceeding from there to more local environmental influences on an individual writer, and from there to that writer's production of a text. Kautsky explains his approach in the following way: "Like every other Socialist, More can only be understood in the light of his age, to comprehend which a knowledge of the beginnings of capitalism and the decline of feudalism, of the powerful part played by the Church on the one hand, and of world commerce on the other, is necessary. These influences had a profound effect on More, and before we can sketch his personality and estimate his writings, it is incumbent on us to indicate, at least in outline, the historical situation whose product he was."[6] Thus although the study's longest section is Kautsky's reading of *Utopia*, the book's first two parts—comprising, respectively, political and economic history, and intellectual biography—are equally substantive, and held by Kautsky to be prolegomena to the criticism that follows.

It is worth dwelling on this assumption if only because such is so rarely assumed today. For instance, Kautsky's materialist approach to *Utopia* (first looking at the historical background of the work, then at the writer's life, then at the work) stands in stark contrast to much criticism of the late twentieth century. Many historicist treatments that seek to read the world by performing readings of literary texts, for example, can be said actually to *reverse* the procedure that Kautsky followed. That is, where Kautsky started with the world and proceeded to Thomas More and More's *Utopia*, we have seen that many new historicist critics begin with a literary text or brief anecdote and use it as a springboard from which to leap into the cultural world outside the text. And, as we will see, a newer form of materialist criticism begins with neither history nor texts but from the (nontextual) physical objects themselves.

There have been many materialist treatments of English Reformation and Renaissance literature subsequent to Kautsky, and in the paragraphs that follow I have space to mention only a few. Much of the noteworthy materialist criticism of the twentieth century has, like Kautsky's work, treated the Renaissance or early modern era as transitional. It is important to note, however, that this later work generally has been more attentive than Kautsky was to the tensions and ambivalences voiced by writers caught up in these broader currents of change. One thinks inevitably of Robert Weimann, whose work has proven foundational to the field. In what follows, I ask Weimann's writings to stand in for the scholarship of a variety of marxist critics. I do this conscious, of course, of the diversity of approach even within this genre of scholarship. Weimann's work, which both inherits and refines the historical paradigms that Kautsky deployed, seems to me especially representative of a tradition of materialist criticism concerned with the momentous transition to the modern, proto-capitalist world.

Weimann's status as a formidable critic of early modern literature was inaugurated with the 1958 publication of his revised dissertation (1955). Titled *Drama und Wirklichkeit in der Shakespearezeit: ein Beitrag zur Entwicklungsgeschichte des Elisabethanischen Theaters*, this study heralded a line of influential analyses, by Weimann, of early modern literature in England.[7] Among his English-language works that have shaped criticism of early modern literature are, in addition to numerous scholarly essays, *Shakespeare and the Popular Tradition in the Theater: Studies in the Social Dimension of Dramatic Form and*

Function (1978) and *Authority and Representation in Early Modern Discourse* (1996).[8] More recently, Weimann's *Author's Pen and Actor's Voice: Playing and Writing in Shakespeare's Theatre* (2000) has continued the examination of authority and representation in early modern discourse that he began in the study of that title.[9]

Weimann's scholarship ranges widely over texts of the English Reformation and Renaissance; yet an organizing theme in his studies is the importance of the folk practices that have left their traces in the performative imagination of the day. Along with Bakhtin's *Rabelais and His World*, in fact, Weimann's *Shakespeare and the Popular Tradition in the Theatre* has proven seminal to later treatments of popular energies and forms in literature of this time.[10] The linkage here with Bakhtin has been made by John Drakakis, who is responsible for the most sustained analysis of Weimann's scholarly career; Drakakis points out that Weimann's book (as *Shakespeare und die Tradition des Volkstheaters : Soziologie, Dramaturgie, Gestaltung* [1967]) actually preceded the publication of English translations of Bakhtin.[11] And although Drakakis is surely correct to stress a complex pattern of engagement, on the part of Weimann, with poststructuralist theories of society, textuality, and agency, it could be argued that what most basically characterizes Weimann's work is a continuing interest in the changefulness of the sixteenth and seventeenth centuries, with those printed testaments to the sometimes fractious transformations that ushered in the modern era.

Weimann's early modern England resembles Kautsky's in that both scholars focus on a world in transition and on writings that resist, chronicle, or otherwise give voice to tensions associated with that transition. But Weimann's work differs from Kautsky's in democratizing its objects of inquiry. Where Kautsky saw More as privy to a special insight relating to issues of property and social justice through his education and political status (reading, as it were, as More arranges his Utopia, from the top down), Weimann understands literature of this time as representing a charged variety of forces. Some of these forces are authoritarian in nature; others represent resistance to that very authority; still others indicate an attempt to invent new forms of authority. From *Drama und Wirklichkeit* through *Playing and Writing*, Weimann's work can be seen as engaging a single question: In what fashion, and with what effect, have the turbulent social changes of the sixteenth and seventeenth centuries made themselves felt in texts of the time?

The notion of an epochal divide, an intensive break from feudalism to early capitalism, seems a sine qua non for materialist criticism devoted to this period of English history and its literature. We learn of this division in both the title and the essays of Arnold Kettle's influential anthology of materialist criticism, *Shakespeare in a Changing World* (1964).[12] There the lead essay is by Weimann: "The Soul of the Age: Towards a Historical Approach to Shakespeare." Weimann begins his argument by stating that "The age into which Shakespeare was born was, to an extent that only the twentieth century can surpass, an epoch of transition."[13] Significantly, the majority of Kettle's anthology focuses on one-half of what can be called a transitional divide in Shakespeare's career itself—that is, plays written in or after 1599, implicitly connecting the playworld struggles of the second "half" of Shakespeare's dramatic output with the social critiques that are so much a part of materialist criticism. One can see this emphasis throughout materialist criticism of Shakespeare. In *Drama and Society in the Age of Jonson* (1937), for instance, L. C. Knights concerns himself with the Elizabethan inheritance of Jacobean drama, but frames Shakespeare's works in the context of such seventeenth-century dramatists as Middleton, Heywood, and Massinger.[14] Likewise Jameson's turn to Shakespeare in his landmark volume, *The Political Unconscious,* is to *The Winter's Tale* (1610) and to "the twilight of Shakespearean spectacle" in the romances generally.[15]

So durable has this tendency proven in subsequent instances of materialist criticism that we may take it as a given that a materialist Shakespeare is a *later* Shakespeare, the Shakespeare of such problem plays as *Troilus and Cressida* (1602) and *Measure for Measure* (1604), of the major tragedies from *Hamlet* (1601) forward, and of the romances. Materialist criticism has thus been oriented both temporally—to Jacobean literature—and formally—to satirical and tragedic literature. *King Lear* (1605), in particular, stands out as a play that has attracted the special attention of materialists. This is largely because the play so self-consciously stages a "break" or division between times and between modes of life; this division often has struck critics as representing in miniature the larger transition between what can broadly be called, on one hand, "medieval" or "feudal," and, on the other, "Renaissance" or "early modern" England. Most of the major works of materialist criticism devoted to Shakespeare thus give *King Lear* extensive scrutiny. A *Lear* of epochal nature has found its fullest articulation, perhaps, in Paul Delany's "*King Lear* and the Decline of Feudalism" (1977), but a similarly resonant *Lear* also appears in Annabel Patterson's *Shakespeare and the Popular Voice* (1990), Richard Halpern's *The Poetics of Primitive Accumulation: English Renaissance Culture and the Genealogy of Capital* (1991), and Hugh Grady's

Shakespeare's Universal Wolf: Postmodernist Studies in Early Modern Reification (1996).[16] However much these studies are intended to contribute to meaningful change in the present, each points back to the early modern world and makes arguments about the way in which literary texts arc "thick" with the social themes of their own day.

A very different orientation characterizes cultural materialism, which can be defined as a critical practice concerned with the cultural embeddedness of aesthetic objects—from plays to piano concertos to pop music—and the inescapably political nature of all cultural production and interpretation.[17] "Cultural materialism," as used in reference to criticism of early modern English literature, almost invariably describes work by British critics—even as "new historicism" almost always describes the work of American ones. The nationalistic distinctions made here are not wholly arbitrary, however, as many British academics concerned with early modern literature share a family resemblance in their theories and critical strategies, as do their American counterparts with each other. Like Raymond Williams, who coined the phrase "cultural materialism" in his 1977 book, *Marxism and Literature,* cultural materialists seek to read culture with a small "c." Given an emphasis on the complex realities of cultural production, it seems no coincidence that some of the more popular texts of cultural materialism in this field are collaborative ones, or anthologies: Witness the greatly influential *Political Shakespeare* of 1985, an anthology edited by Jonathan Dollimore and Alan Sinfield, and, that same year, *Alternative Shakespeares,* an anthology edited by John Drakakis.[18] Clearly, these and other instances of cultural materialism share a common heritage with earlier marxist criticism of early modern literature. But the differences between cultural materialism and marxist criticism proper are significant, and largely pertain to the "direction" of their critical vision.

Cultural materialism has a contemporary orientation. Persuaded that we can have no pure or disinterested access to the past, cultural materialists are primarily concerned with how present-day culture uses the past: how individuals and institutions employ early modern words and myths for political, ideological, or commercial advantage. If cultural materialism shares marxist criticism's interest in ideology and practice, it inflects that interest with an abiding concern less for the early modern past than for the here-and-now of the critic's present. Where a traditionally marxist critic would be interested in describing a historical truth about, say, John Webster's plays and the relationship of these plays to their historical moment, a cultural materialist would be just as likely to take up the historical reception of

Webster, or the contemporary use of Webster's words in an extra-academic context. Cultural materialists, like Williams before them, tend to be interested in intensively popular forms and in demystifying the sacred aura attached to many canonical works. It is no accident that the cover of Alan Sinfield's *Faultlines: Cultural Materialism and the Politics of Dissident Reading* (1992) features a series of panels from what appears to be a comic book version of *Macbeth* (1606). Where traditional (that is, marxist) materialist criticism seems, with its sometimes profound and grave tone, to be tragic in nature, the cultural materialism of the 1980s and after is more like analytical farce in its attraction to humorous modes of demystification.

Yet there is, even in this contemporary orientation, a conviction that the present is shaped the way it is because of what has come before it. That is, cultural materialism's desire to display and deflate monumental objects often is predicated on a marxist concern with the larger sweep of history, and our place in it. Cultural materialism recognizes the false monumentality of literary objects, for instance, because it knows that those objects have not always been monuments but have been given that status by human actors in and over time.

THE NEW MATERIALISM

Since the early 1990s, cultural materialism has ceded ground to a newer materialism. This "new materialism" has even begun to erode new historicism's dominance over the field. And although it is perhaps too early to speak of this materialism as an instantly recognizable school or a sharply defined practice, it seems to be a growing, and loosely coherent, genre of criticism.

What I call a new materialism here has been given another name by Patricia Fumerton, one of the scholars whose work may be identified with this emergent critical practice. In the introduction to an anthology she co-edited with Simon Hunt, *Renaissance Culture and the Everyday* (1999), Fumerton speaks of a "new new historicism" or, in a less cumbersome phrase, a "newly emergent new historicism."[19] Fumerton describes this "new breed of '90s new historicism" as one that "focuses primarily on the common, but the common in both a class and cultural sense: the low (common people), the ordinary (common speech, common wares, common sense), the familiar (commonly known), the customary or typical or taken-for granted (common law, commonplace, communal), etc. A new new historicism sites particular clusters of such myriad commonality within the context of the manifold details of cultural practice and representation—what we might

call, evoking Michel de Certeau and Henri Lefebvre, the '*everyday.*'"[20]
Fumerton's introduction here has the burden of all anthology introductions, lending the semblance of unity to sometimes disparate
pieces. But her insistence on the everyday accurately describes a growing body of critical work published in the 1990s and early 2000s and
represented in the anthology in question. Much of this criticism focuses on the "common," especially common *objects,* and objects that
had for various reasons proved to be outside the mainstream of critical
attention.

It is worth noting that many instances of the new materialism are
anthologies, collections. We have seen that the cultural materialism of
the 1980s also tended to appear in anthologies. This tendency is even
more evident in the new materialism. The emphasis on fragments in
many of the essays in these collections is recuperated in what we
could call the "fragmented" nature of the publications themselves—
as if a compilation is the form that best fits the critical genre of the
new materialism. Instances of the new materialism include books like
Fumerton's own *Cultural Aesthetics: Renaissance Literature and the
Practice of Social Ornament* (1991); Jeffrey Knapp's *An Empire
Nowhere: England, America, and Literature from "Utopia" to "The
Tempest"* (1992); Lena Cowen Orlin's *Private Matters and Public
Culture in Post-Reformation England* (1994) and her anthology
Elizabethan Households (1995); *Subject and Object in Renaissance
Culture* (1996), an anthology edited by Margreta de Grazia, Mau-
reen Quilligan, and Peter Stallybrass; David Hillman and Carla
Mazzio's anthology, *The Body in Parts: Fantasies of Corporeality in
Early Modern Europe* (1997); *Renaissance Culture and the Everyday*
(1999); Orlin's most recent anthology, *Material London, ca. 1600*
(2000); Ann Rosalind Jones's and Peter Stallybrass's *Renaissance
Clothing and the Materials of Memory* (2000); and Juliet Fleming's
Graffiti and the Writing Arts of Early Modern England (2001).[21]

To an extent unprecedented in criticism concerned with the English Renaissance, each of these works boasts an investment in *things.*
Such objects, for instance, as mirrors, beards, stitchery, rings, household goods, feet, tobacco, and graffiti earn the critics' attention.
Where an anthology of critical articles published, say, in the 1950s,
1960s, or 1970s took literary texts as its object of concern, these
more recent monographs and anthologies testify to the ways in which
studying the early modern era no longer means reading its books
alone. It means, instead, reading a variety of objects and people's relationship to them. We get in these critical works not only a fresh approach to a distant culture but also an approach that seems to ground

us in the *realities* of that culture by reading material objects and the practices associated with them.

The critical genealogy of the new materialism is worth remarking on. One of the clearest distinctions between the new materialism, as I have called it, and traditional materialisms (under which term we could group historical materialism, dialectical materialism, even cultural materialism) is the new materialism's break with Marx. That is, the new materialism that is engaged with early modern literature and culture does not begin with marxist assumptions about history, class, or labor. Indeed, sometimes this criticism's starting point is the market and the expanding contours of consumer culture. Although such topics can be equated to earlier materialist criticism's concern with the epochal divide between the feudal and early capitalist eras, the new materialism's sense of historical division tends to be positive. For where in—if I may be forgiven the phrase—marxist materialism the rise of capitalism is a highly negative, even tragic phenomenon, in the new materialism it is part and parcel of the transition to the "early modern" era.

Thus while Marx may be recoverable in this criticism's analytical heritage (at the very least in the influence that his theory of commodity fetishism has had on various disciplines of thought concerned with objects), the primary sources of the new materialism are intellectual currents from France, not Germany. Thus Orlin's *Private Matters and Public Culture* begins by quoting Philippe Ariès and makes reference to such figures as Henri Lefebvre, Claude Lévi-Strauss, and Marcel Maus. Maus's theory of the gift is important to Fumerton in her *Cultural Aesthetics* as well, and in the introduction to *Renaissance Culture and the Everyday* Fumerton invokes Michel de Certeau and Henri Lefebvre for the notion of the "everyday" employed in that study.

This break with Marx, and an attempted emphasis on the real, form the center of what is to date the most cogent description and critique of the new materialism. In an essay entitled "The New New Historicism's *Wunderkammer* of Objects," Jonathan Gil Harris holds that while this "newer scholarship is self-consciously and defiantly a historicism of the *object*," it is nonetheless a materialism that Marx would scarcely recognize.[22] Harris notes that, for example, the anthology Fumerton co-edited uses the word "material" in a deliberately nontraditional way: "Its residual Marxist baggage has been more or less emptied: the 'cultural materialism' of the eighties, with its vestiges of the dialectic of social struggle and transformation, has given way in the nineties to 'material culture,' with its whiff of the dialectic of renunciation and allure." By "renunciation and allure" here Harris means, I take it, something like the renunciation of marxism and the allure of commodity culture, the extralogical attraction to objects that characterizes consumerist behavior in modern life. Harris suggests that the "everyday" in Fumerton functions as a "mark of synchronic cultural plenitude" and an index of "cultural totality."[23] That is, rather than a set of practices that constitute and transform society and culture (as in de Certeau's formulations), the everyday is, much like anecdotal snapshots of new historicism, that which gives the reader the impression of a "reassuring, synchronically conceived totality."

We can see how sharply the new materialism diverges from traditional materialism—from marxist criticism, that is—in an extract from Debora Shuger's essay in *Renaissance Culture and the Everyday*. The following selection comprises the entire first paragraph of her essay, "The 'I' of the Beholder: Renaissance Mirrors and the Reflexive Mind":

> This essay began as an attempt to document an hypothesis that turned out to be false. While preparing a course on early modern autobiography, I ran across an intriguing essay by Georges Gusdorf which hypothesized that the invention of the clear glass mirror in the sixteenth century gave rise to modern, reflexive self-consciousness, which, in turn, led to the sudden proliferation of autobiographical genres. I thought it might be worthwhile to trace the role this novel everyday artifact played in the emergence of early modern selfhood; at the time it seemed a plausible and suitably materialist alternative to current narratives of the modern self as a capitalist epiphenomenon.[24]

This passage is worth our attention because it is extremely puzzling and also because it is representative of a larger, and no less puzzling, set of assumptions in recent materialist criticism.

The passage is puzzling for several reasons. First, Shuger's honesty in setting out her procedure here does not lessen the curious nature of that procedure itself. That is, she tells us that she began her inquiry into Renaissance mirrors—the central object of her essay—after encountering a patently eccentric claim regarding the glass mirror's sponsorship of "modern, reflexive self-consciousness." I call this claim "patently eccentric" from the way it is represented, perhaps unintentionally, in Shuger's description. Given this description of Gusdorf's thesis, one imagines Renaissance persons buying new mirrors and instantly discovering their selfhood—only to proceed, from that point, to write autobiographies celebrating this bonus acquisition, the self. (Two for the price of one, clearly.) This is, of course, a comic scenario, a parody of deterministic or vulgar materialism, and certainly one worth a skeptical resistance. However, instead of asking "Is this true?" Shuger goes on (again, in her description) to assume that a link between mirrors and reflexive self-consciousness indeed exists; witness the way she phrases her topic of investigation: "*the role this novel everyday artifact played in the emergence of early modern selfhood.*" By the beginning of the essay's third sentence, Shuger has already assumed—at least rhetorically—that this "everyday artifact" did play a role in a large historical development. The grounds on which this assumption is based are never given. Is it necessarily true that mirrors had *any* role in this development? Shuger does not pause to consider this question. One feels that, as the principal assumption on which her essay is based, it is the question that her essay cannot answer and still exist *as* an essay.

Yet what makes this paragraph truly exceptional is not primarily the assumption just examined. What makes it so worth close examination is the sentence that follows, closing out the paragraph: "*at the time it seemed a plausible and suitably materialist alternative to the current narratives of the modern self as a capitalist epiphenomenon.*" This sentence is worth lingering over, if for no other reason than that it stunningly overturns conventional definitions of materialism and conventional assumptions about materialist practice. With twenty-three words, Shuger dispenses of almost two centuries of materialist philosophy and criticism. She suggests here that reading Renaissance mirrors is a "suitably materialist alternative" to seeing the modern self as "a capitalist epiphenomenon," but does not inform her readers about a sticky bit of nomenclature. That is, studies that focus on the epiphenomena of capitalism are, of course, marxist works, works traditionally defined as "materialist" criticism. But in Shuger's formulation, it is her own study of mirrors and subjectivity that is materialist and marxist accounts that are not. For Shuger simultaneously to euphemize materialist criticism as "current narratives" and lend her inquiry any prestige and solidity attached to materialism ("a plausible and suitably materialist alternative") is remarkable; for her to accomplish this in one and the same sentence remains a piece of breathtaking if mischievous prestidigitation.

I have paid this paragraph so much attention because it contains within it something like the whole project of the new materialism. We have, in this sentence, not only the separation from Marx and an implicit argument that marxist criticism is not truly materialist at base; we also have the assumption that only things that can be held or touched are the legitimate focus of "materialism." Like Shuger, many critics have taken the word and practice of "materialism" to depend strictly on concrete "matter" as its ultimate ground. Scholars who "read" mirrors and other physical objects, Shuger implies, are doing materialism. Those who talk about seemingly abstract entities like "capitalism" are not. This is an untenable assumption. It is, unfortunately, an assumption that characterizes not only Shuger's essay but many new materialist works of criticism. Not that there is not a great deal to learn from examining the material culture of early modern England. There is, surely, and what the anthologies and monographs mentioned above have done is bring home to us with new force both the difficulty and the delight of learning about past cultures. But in the break with Marx and with the traditions of philosophical and critical materialism, much stands to be lost.

NEW DIRECTIONS

The new materialism can be described most positively as a mode of criticism that has explored little-known aspects of early modern culture in England and that has shed light on the growing relationship between subject and object in the sixteenth and seventeenth centuries. Also worth noting is the new materialism's emphasis on the "hard facts" of concrete objects and the role of the physical in shaping the culture of the time. Yet, as we have observed, this mode of criticism also can be faulted for promoting a vulgar materialism divorced from some of the complex and nuanced analytical traditions of nineteenth- and twentieth-century materialism. If, returning to the filmic analogy that closed chapter 2, Kautsky can be faulted for asking More's *Utopia* to conform to an out-of-scale reading of English Reformation history, its long-distance "framing shots" incommensurate with the detailed textures of *Utopia* itself, the new materialism reverses this procedure, beginning as thick descriptions tend to begin, with "close-ups" of a particular object and then providing out-of-focus glimpses at English culture and history while still centered on discrete objects. To the extent that it succumbs to what Harris calls the "allure" of its objects without justifying its focus on them (by means, for example, of a more comprehensive theory both of objects and object-criticism), the new materialism runs the risk of being seen as tchotchke criticism, its anthologies the belated J. Crew catalogues of the early modern era. Indeed, it seems significant that the "docent" impulse in new historicism—by which I mean, once again, the impulse to lecture on an object or anecdote in a masterful, controlling way—marks so many new materialist essays. This impulse is perhaps at the root of Fumerton's description of this practice as a "new new historicism." In any case, it hints at the critical fetishism that pervades the new materialism. This is a fetishism that, in replacing large with small and the intangible with what is capable of being touched or held, threatens to restrict the new materialism's usefulness as cultural and historical explanation.

Where do we go from here? Perhaps back to the English Renaissance itself. Earlier in this chapter I claimed that Marx was the first materialist critic of early modern English literature—a claim that is true, of course, only if we qualify it by saying that he was the first materialist critic of the era's literature *after* the early modern era itself. For writers in the sixteenth and seventeenth centuries were the first, and sometimes most penetrating, critics of each other's works, and they were also "critical" of the world itself in a materialist way. Their criticism—and with this term I mean to refer to a range of responses, from brief remarks to more leisured accounts—was often materialist in nature, for several reasons.

The first reason is that early modern writers (as many writers have been, at many times) were deeply immersed in the realities of literary production and reception, from the expense of paper and ink and the vagaries of printing shops to the crowded spaces of booksellers' stalls and peddlers' packs. The works of Renaissance authors often display a reflexive materialism, in which they talk openly about their own works as objects and about the medium of their craft. This openness is linked to the second reason that early modern authors were often materialist in their own right, and that is because writers of this time were familiar with, when they were not thoroughly schooled in, materialist doctrines of science, nature, and behavior (to be sure not, at that time, separate categories). Whether the source was Aristotle, alchemical treatises, proverbs, popular songs, or utilitarian handbooks, educated persons in early modern England would have been exposed to a rich vein of materialist texts and traditions.

Tapping into this vein can likewise enrich our own criticism. The best thing the new materialism can do, I believe, is to begin taking sixteenth- and seventeenth-century materialist thought seriously. The apparent "discovery" of these everyday objects is only that: apparent. When we think, for instance, of the intensive focus on the material world in such writers as Thomas Nashe, Ben Jonson, John Donne, and Thomas Middleton—to name only a few—we are forced to admit that these authors "theorized" objects, and people's relationship to them, in quite complicated and compelling ways. Theirs was a culture that thought almost constantly of the material, even when in the midst of its greatest imaginative leaps: "[M]ay we cram / Within this wooden O the very casques / That did affright the air at Agincourt?" (*Henry V,* Pro. 12–14).

It is a return to this very materialism, in fact, that characterizes one of the most interesting materialist essays to appear in recent years. Henry S. Turner's "Nashe's Red Herring: Epistemologies of the Commodity in *Lenten Stuffe* (1599)" takes Nashe's materialism seriously, reading this notoriously unusual text as "an exercise in epistemology" and "an extended satire of many different modes of Elizabethan writing, all of which sought in some way to derive 'scientific' knowledge from physical objects."[25] The infamous "red herring" praised so humorously in Nashe's text, Turner argues, serves as a means by which Nashe, like Marx after him, theorized the commodity form. As Turner relates, "Nashe's red herring is finally much more than a particular object of knowledge: it is the trope that stands for the many possible methodological gestures of 'taking an object of knowledge' and of the multiple discursive strategies and interarticulations which result."[26] Turner's essay exemplifies what we stand to learn from augmenting our own interest in materialism with a sympathetic reading of the materialism of sixteenth- and seventeenth-century England.

It is for this more comprehensive relationship to "materialism," I believe, that the new materialism in early modern studies needs to strive. Materialism has too rich a heritage, and too firm a hold on the early modern imagination itself, to be neglected as we press forward, and are pressed forward by, the fascination of our own time regarding the objects of the material world. The future of materialist criticism will benefit from being mindful of the past of materialism, including the materialism of the cultures it examines.

SHAKESPEARE AFTER
THE "CULTURAL TURN"

Shakespeare and the Question of Culture has offered "thin" descriptions of various literary topics as a supplement to thick description, the most prevalent and compelling mode of cultural analysis practiced today. To these thinner descriptions, it has joined an analysis of criticism itself, especially recent critical genres concerned with early modern literature. In all of these chapters, my goal has been to heighten awareness of the way in which form structures critical inquiry. By "form" in this study I have meant not only such larger units of patterning as genre and mode but also things like key words and phrases, the very repetition of which can help to create a genre in the first place.

Where this book began with difficulties posed by the word "culture" in criticism of Shakespeare and early modern literature, it concludes by hazarding that a cultural analysis of early modern literature is virtually impossible. As I claimed in the preface, culture remains too extensive a thing to be commensurate with the small sampling of literary evidence typically offered to represent it. Given this incommensurability—the lack of fit between our few books and the totality of the culture we often invoke—cultural analysis is likely to exist only in the aggregate. That is, studies of selected early modern texts, objects, beliefs, symbols, or practices can indeed claim to be isolating elements of particular cultures. But even as these elements remain merely components of a larger whole, so too are critical studies of individual elements "cultural" only in relation to their contribution to the composite project of critical studies of a particular culture. The

208 SHAKESPEARE AND THE QUESTION OF CULTURE

cultural study of early modern England exists, therefore, not "in" any particular study, but only as the sum of various and multiple studies of that culture.[1]

This is more than semantics. As our essays become more and more sophisticated, more and more ambitious, they reveal increasing expectations for them to present something they cannot, as essays, present. We are past the days when an antiquarianism allowed scholars to produce knowledge for its own sake, laboring away at a small part of something—a phase in an author's career; a particular trope, image, or mental habit; a short-lived literary scandal or fashion—that was itself only part of something much larger in scope. We are past the days, it seems, of modest claims. For various reasons, studies that seek mainly to add to our knowledge of a particular work or author (even Shakespeare) resonate less than studies that announce more ambitious implications to their findings. Often critics advertise these implications in terms of culture.

As I confessed in the preface, I am guilty of most, perhaps all, the charges that I level at cultural criticism. One of the things that I am guilty of, along with many others in the field, is being influenced by that particularly modern genre, the brand name. Branding has perfused the academy, of course, and shapes what we do as critics. For instance, to call oneself a "cultural" critic, or one's criticism "cultural" in nature, is to announce a desirable product. Like "the cultural"—to which it has always been linked—"new historicism" has proven a popular label under which various commodities have been sold. In their introduction to *Practicing New Historicism,* Catherine Gallagher and Stephen Greenblatt relate their "incredulity" over its rise as a novel brand in the field:

> When years ago we first noticed in the annual job listing of the Modern Language Association that an English department was advertising for a specialist in new historicism, our response was incredulity. How could something that didn't really exist, that was only a few words gesturing toward a new interpretative practice, have become a "field"? When did it happen and how could we not have noticed? If this was indeed a field, who could claim expertise in it and in what would such expertise consist? Surely, we of all people should know something of the history and the principles of new historicism, but what we knew above all was that it (or perhaps we) resisted systematization.[2]

It is difficult for me to read this paragraph without feeling some incredulity that Gallagher and Greenblatt were actually so surprised to find others hawking the phrase "new historicism." From coining the term himself to founding and editing a prestigious series at the University of California Press ("The New Historicism: Studies in Cultural Poetics"), Greenblatt has done a great deal to foster new historicist products. His own publication under this brand, *Shakespearean Negotiations: The Circulation of Social Energy in Renaissance England,* the fourth entry in the series, anticipated its thirty-first, *Nobody's Story: The Vanishing Acts of Women Writers in the Marketplace, 1670 - 1820,* written by Catherine Gallagher. If Gallagher and Greenblatt were indeed incredulous about "new historicism," each found a way to live with, and profit in spite of, that disbelief.

By pointing out the academic entrepreneurship of these two professors, I do not mean to invoke a stale paradigm of "selling out," whatever that could mean in today's academy. Instead, I wish to point out how, to a surprising degree, selling itself has come to structure what we do as scholars. One could make the case that it has always been this way—for instance, that Great Authors functioned, in the past, in much the same way that such current academic brands as "new historicism" and "cultural studies" have done. Although such an argument could be made, I do not know that I would be entirely persuaded by it—at least, when phrased in such a strong form. For better or worse, I believe that there are qualitative differences between scholarship as practiced prior to the 1980s and criticism produced after that time. Just in the labels I have given them here—"scholarship" and "criticism"—we can sense the potential distinctions that can be drawn between what are arguably varied research modes. Such distinctions underlie our very conceptions of the academic worker. Within the past generation the model of the literature professor has gone from scholarly drudge to intellectual entrepreneur, from laborer to capitalist.

This change has accompanied culture's lessening status as a thing valuable in and of itself. We have seen that, over the past century, "culture" has gone from being primarily a "vertical" concept suggesting hierarchy and degree, to being primarily a "horizontal" concept suggesting variety and difference without invidious distinction. In chapter 1 I speculated as to some of the influences on this change, influences that included transformations to the academy itself. To these influences I would add the increasing role of market forces within the academy. Although they may seem far afield from the changing senses of the word "culture" referred to here, things like the business model of higher education, the bureaucratic emphasis on productivity and on its *doppelganger,* the assessment of research through quantitative formulas, the decline in library funds for the purchase of journals and scholarly monographs, the concomitant need to publish "marketable" books, even the academic "star system" itself—all these speak to the way in which market forces increasingly shape research and its presentation.

Having found its older label, that of "the humanities," appealing to a dwindling demographic, this commercialized academy finds in "culture" an attractive brand that it can market to a wide range of consumers. University presses today routinely circulate catalogues of "literary and cultural studies." Friendlier, for various reasons, than "the humanities," culture is a commodity that by definition excludes no one. And because everyone participates in this kind of culture, cultural analysis can be sold to everyone. In fact, under this definition culture remains a capitalist's dream: an appealing and all-purpose product that the consumers themselves produce.

Lest I finish on a cynical note, I will close with some positive remarks about "culture" as it relates to Shakespeare and early modern literature. I believe that cultures are open unities: open in the sense that their boundaries are porous, unities in the sense that they hold together through shared patterns of belief and behavior. I have argued in this book that, while the world-picturing faculties of early modern plays—including, perhaps especially, Shakespeare's—lead us to trust their sufficiency as repositories and conveyors of early modern English culture, they are first and foremost entities of literary culture and bring us the world outside the playhouses in a forceful but mediated way. Such is not to say that these plays do not have a special place in the history of representation, certainly where it concerns the environment that contributed to their existence. We stand to learn—to continue to learn—about these documents from studying their "culture," just as we stand to learn about their "culture" from studying these documents. Yet however much we may feel that these plays constitute the "abstract and brief chronicles of the time," as Hamlet referred to the itinerant players, we need to advance our arguments about the relationship between text and culture in a more studied manner.

Appendix

"Culture"

Perhaps the only thing we can safely say about "culture" is that it is a word.[1] After that simple statement comes disagreement. Such disagreement, in fact, may have been behind Raymond Williams's characterization of "culture" as "one of the two or three most complicated words in the English language."[2] Williams's characterization is well known, has often been repeated, and may seem uncontroversial. But this way of putting it risks confusing things, for, contrary to Williams's claim, could it not be argued that "culture" is actually a simple word? If it did not strike so many users as simple—in the sense of its meaning seeming transparent, even obvious—how could so many people use it in so many different ways?[3] I do not mean for this last to be a facetious question; I hope, instead, that it points at a simple truth. A word's ability to produce "complicat[ions]" of meaning can be inversely related to its surface difficulty: The more complicated a word, the less likely it may be to figure into complex interpretive situations. We could offer, therefore, that "culture" can be used in complicated ways, ways that produce ambiguity and disagreement, precisely because it is so simple. Although he was only following William Empson in seeing as complex or "complicated" those words which facilitate ambiguity, Williams confuses a material thing (a word) with the ways in which that thing has been used.[4] What Williams could have said, in the pursuit of accuracy, is that culture is a short word whose simplicity has enabled it, over time, to be used in extremely complicated ways.

Williams was of course as well aware as anyone of the various and competing uses of words. His celebrated book *Keywords,* in fact, begins with an anecdote about the various senses of "culture" he encountered when returning to Cambridge after World War II. Williams relates how the "formations of the 1930s" had changed while he was away, and how surprised he was to meet those who did not "speak the same language" that had been spoken before the war. As Williams tells it:

> I found myself preoccupied by a single word, *culture*, which it seemed I was hearing very much more often: not only, obviously, by comparison with the talk of an artillery regiment or of my own family, but by direct comparison within the university over just those few years. I had heard it previously in two senses: one at the fringes, in teashops and places like that, where it seemed the preferred word for a kind of social superiority, not in ideas or learning, and not only in money or position, but in a more intangible area, relating to behaviour; yet also, secondly, among my own friends, where it was an active word for writing poems and novels, making films and paintings, working in theaters. What I was now hearing were two different senses, which I could not really get clear: first, in the study of literature, a use of the word to indicate, powerfully but not explicitly, some central formation of values (and *literature* itself had the same kind of emphasis); secondly, in more general discussion, but with what seemed to me very different implications, a use which made it almost equivalent to *society:* a particular *way of life*—"American culture," "Japanese culture."[5]

Whereas Williams elsewhere describes "culture" as a complicated word, here he explains his entry into the subject that became *Keywords* by recounting his equally complicated personal relationship to and experience of a word. Biographical details given earlier in his introduction convey the pervasive dislocations of those years, including the movement of a youth from his place of upbringing in Wales to Cambridge University, his subsequent service in an artillery regiment of the British Army on the Kiel Canal, and his return to school at Cambridge in 1945. Yet in this paragraph it is perhaps not Williams who is his story's protagonist but the word "culture." Indeed, we could note that his initial description of the word comes close to personifying it. When he describes the first two "senses" of the word that he heard, for instance, he does so by painting a dramatic scene: "one at the fringes, in teashops and places like that . . . yet also, secondly, among my own friends, *where it was an active word* . . ." (emphasis added). As if a companion that he knows and trusts, "culture" was at this time vital and energetic ("relating to behaviour . . . working in theatres"), a word connected with certain locations ("at the fringes, in teashops and places like that") and persons ("among my own friends").

If "culture" becomes the lead actor of this biographical story, however, we need to recognize that the traditional narrative pattern is reversed: We know less and less about its protagonist as we go along. Williams's comfortable notions of "culture" were shattered when he returned to Cambridge after the war. Gone is the "culture" of the "fringes," the "teashop[s]," and the "theatres" of the 1930s. What replaces it is a somewhat globalized "culture" that strikes him as strange if not uncanny ("two different senses, which I could not really get clear"). This "culture" is no longer a friendly and close lad but a thing of the printed page ("the study of literature") and of "general discussion" that seems to take place in no specific location, and among unidentifiable parties. It is also not English. That the paragraph turns for its definition to two nations that took a prominent role in the war Williams had just fought ("'American culture,' 'Japanese culture'") hints that, like Williams himself and like so many of his contemporaries, the word "culture" has been dislocated from its home and absorbed into an unanticipated world dynamic.

With the word "culture" as its protagonist, this remarkable paragraph reads like a miniature history of the mid-twentieth century. Its narrative of change asks us to acknowledge that the weight Williams puts on "culture" has if anything been increased by our own time—an increase that is by no means peculiar to Shakespeare studies. As we have seen, the close of the twentieth century produced an abundance of "culture talk." So widely has the discourse of culture spread, in fact, that writers of very different political orientations have recently called for its restriction. For instance, in *Culture: The Anthropologists' Account,* Adam Kuper confesses that "the more one considers the best modern work on culture by anthropologists, the more advisable it must appear to avoid the hyper-referential word altogether."[6] Likewise, in a stimulating essay titled "What We Talk About When We Talk About Culture," Matthew Greenfield offers "the perhaps counterintuitive suggestion that the concept of culture no longer does the work that literary critics want it to, and that in fact the concept exists in an uneasy tension with much of our thinking about literary texts and historical processes."[7] Terry Eagleton comes to a similar conclusion, but for other reasons, when he ends *The Idea of Culture* by saying, of his title subject, that "It is time, while acknowledging its significance, to put it back in its place."[8] Similarly, Jacques Barzun pauses in the prologue of *From Dawn to Decadence: 500 Years of Western Cultural Life* to let out the rhetorical equivalent of a sigh: "Culture—what a word! Up to a few years ago it meant two or three related things easy to grasp and keep apart. Now it is a piece of all-purpose jargon that covers a hodge-podge of overlapping things."[9] As we will observe, Barzun is mistaken to claim that "culture" has ever had meanings "easy to grasp and keep apart." But he is right in suggesting, with Kuper, Greenfield, and Eagleton, that we have witnessed a remarkable proliferation of the word's use. This proliferation has had consequences. As is the case with all inflationary situations, for instance, abundance can diminish value: The more that "culture" is used, the more that it is asked to mean, the less it actually seems to mean in any single instance of its use. To the scholars quoted above, as well as to others, "culture" has been used to the point of abuse. How did we get to this point? "Culture" is a word, after all, that does not appear in the Shakespeare concordance between "culpable" and "culverin." Where did this piece of "all-purpose jargon" come from, and how has it come to serve so many purposes?

Investigating a word's origins means inquiring about a history that may or may not have relevance for its current usage.[10] Certainly we need to keep in mind the ways in which words can stray greatly from their onetime range of meanings. Yet care of another sort is called for as well, as one of the problems with examining earlier patterns of word usage is the urge to see previous moments, and other languages, as simpler than they actually were. Perhaps we are tempted to do so because this allows us to explain the complications of the present through a narrative of accumulated difficulty. (Here we could note Barzun's exaggerated "Up to a few years ago it meant two or three related things easy to grasp and keep apart"). Whatever the cause, critics who have talked about the history of "culture" have tended to simplify that history by concentrating almost solely on its English contexts. While some critics acknowledge its various forms and senses as a Latin word, few make anything of that variety. Thus although Williams admits, in *Keywords*, that Latin *cŏlĕre* "had a range of meanings," he devotes scarcely two sentences to those meanings, and more than five pages to the many valences that "culture" has assumed in English.[11] That proportion could easily have been reversed. For one of the things that we find out when we scrutinize the shapes of *cultŭra* and its root *cŏlĕre* is that Latin speakers had a relationship to this word and its various forms that was equally as rich, and equally as complicated, as our relationship to "culture." While we should stop short of implying that Latin *cultŭra* and its community of terms were used so variously because the Romans had the same concerns that we do, it *is* clear that they were faced with similar situations and that they complicated their language accordingly.

"Culture" always seems to have revolved around the sense of disciplined raising and tending that survives in the English word "agriculture." The Latin verb *cŏlo,* for instance, followed the Greek stem κολ; in Greek, a κολος was a herdsman, and its root is there in our word "bucolic."[12] Latin *cŏlo* took some of the following senses: "to cultivate, till, tend, take care of a field or garden"; "to abide, dwell, stay in a place, to inhabit"; "to bestow care upon a thing, to care for." Hence *agrĭcŏla* meant "a cultivator of land" and *cŏlōnus* "a farmer or colonist." (It is from the Latin *cŏlōnĭa* ["farm, estate, dwelling; a colony"], of course, that we take the English "colony" and Spanish "colonia.") The idea of disciplined care, of being devoted to a place or thing (for instance, crops or animals), led to a further meaning for *cŏlo* of "to honor, respect, reverence, worship (a deity, etc.)." From *cŏlo,* Latin had such words as *culta,* a neuter noun meaning "tilled, cultivated land; gardens; plantations," and *cultus,* a participial adjective with a surprisingly wide range of meanings, among them: "cultivated, tilled"; "the action of dwelling (in a place)"; "the training or education (of a person, his or her faculties)"; "personal care and maintenance"; "the management or care (of a house or similar thing)"; "the adorning (of anything), especially the decking or attiring (or a person, his or her body, etc.)"; "style of dress or ornament"; "the state of being adorned, trimness, smartness"; and, in a predecessor to our English word "cult" (but without its negative implications), "an honoring, reverence, adoration, veneration, worship."[13] Significantly, what we see in *cŏlo* and *cultus* is the journey down a common semantic path: an expansion of reference from the *doing* of a thing—the cultivation or tending of something: a field, livestock, the body, one's mind—to the *results or means of that action:* the tended garden, care given to one's body, mind, or home, the particular style of dress or ornamentation that evidences the careful cultivation of fashion.[14] Hence did the adverb *cultē* mean "elegantly," as in *cultē dicere,* "to speak elegantly." And thus also the feminine noun *cultŭra,* which could mean: "a cultivating, care, cultivation"; as an absolute, "agriculture, tillage, husbandry"; and, figuratively, "care, culture, civilization" and "the training or improvement (of the faculties)."

Disciplined tending, continuous care, careful cultivation, as well as the sites, goals, and results of such activity: These remain the core meanings of the *cultŭra* complex in Latin. They are also the core meanings of "culture" in the English language. Although its range of meanings in English often has been discussed, it is helpful to rehearse some of the basic senses that the word has taken over the centuries.

Like Latin, English has (and has had) various forms of "culture" in which the word means (and has meant) the tending to or improving of land, minds, persons; it can also mean, in a biological context, the rearing of microorganisms. There is a related adjectival sense of "culture" that refers to the development, maintenance, and/or improvement of microorganisms or plants, or the minds or manners of persons.

As a noun, "culture" has at times been a variant spelling (along with "coultur," "culter," "coulter," and so forth) of the iron blade fixed in front of the share in a plow. When Absolon smites Nicholas with a hot instrument in "The Miller's Tale," it is with a "cultour" borrowed from the Oxford blacksmith. Another, somewhat rare usage of "culture" as a noun parallels the Latin *cultus* by referring to homage or worship. "Culture" also can refer to the cultivation of the soil, to husbandry, and, as in Latin, to the results thereof; to the cultivation or rearing of a plant or crop; to the raising or rearing of certain animals (fish and oysters, for instance) or natural products (pearls, crops); to the artificial rearing of certain microorganisms (such as bacteria); to the training of the human body; and to the cultivation or development of the mind, faculties, or manners, and the improvement or refinement thereof by education or training.

NOTES

CHAPTER 1

1. Michael Bristol, *Big-time Shakespeare* (London and New York: Routledge, 1996), 1. On Shakespeare's cultural function in an American context, see also Bristol's *Shakespeare's America, America's Shakespeare* (London and New York: Routledge, 1990).
2. Marjorie Garber, "Shakespeare as Fetish," *Shakespeare Quarterly* 41.2 (1990): 242–50; quotations at 242, 243.
3. See Harold Bloom, *Shakespeare: The Invention of the Human* (New York: Riverhead Books, 1998).
4. The phrase is that of Samuel Taylor Coleridge. See R. A. Foakes, ed., *Coleridge's Criticism of Shakespeare* (Detroit: Wayne State University Press, 1989). From Lecture 9 in the 1811–12 series, delivered December 16, 1811: "He appeals to the imagination, to the reason, and to the noblest powers of the human heart. He is above the iron compulsion of space and time . . ." (48).
5. As Nancy Armstrong points out, the "cultural turn" is "a permutation of the linguistic turn" that affected the humanities and social sciences during the latter half of the twentieth century. See Nancy Armstrong, "Who's Afraid of the Cultural Turn?" *differences: A Journal of Feminist Cultural Studies* 12.1 (2001): 17–49; 18. On the "cultural turn," see also Kevin Sharpe, "Celebrating a Cultural Turn: Political Culture and Cultural Politics in Early Modern England," *Journal of Early Modern History* 1 (1997): 344–68; David Chaney, *The Cultural Turn: Scene-Setting Essays on Contemporary Cultural History* (London: Routledge, 1994); Victoria E. Bonnell and Lynn Hunt, eds. *Beyond the Cultural Turn: New Directions in the Study of Society and Culture* (Berkeley: University of California Press, 1999); Chris Rojek and Bryan Turner, "Decorative Sociology: Towards a Critique of the Cultural Turn," *The Sociological Review* 48.4 (2000): 629–48; and Kate Nash, "The 'Cultural Turn' in Social Theory: Towards a Theory of Cultural Politics," *Sociology* 35.1 (2001): 77–92. The "linguistic turn" refers, of course, to the widespread influence of linguistic paradigms and questions on various fields from the humanities to the social sciences; in the humanities, the linguistic turn

most often involved addressing problems by treating ostensibly nonlinguistic phenomena as "languages"—hence the unconscious being structured like a language in Lacanian psychoanalysis and society working as a language works in the anthropology of Levi-Strauss. The inadequacy of my simplification here will be apparent to those who consult Geoff Eley's "Is All the World a Text? From Social History to the History of Society Two Decades Later," in *The Historic Turn in the Human Sciences*, ed. Terrence J. MacDonald (Ann Arbor: University of Michigan Press, 1996), 193–243; and Christopher Norris, "On the Discrimination of Discourse-Theories: The 'Linguistic Turn' in Philosophical Perspective," *REAL: Yearbook of Research in English and American Literature* 10 (1994): 355–426.

6. On the emergence of cultural studies, see, among other works, Patrick Brantlinger, *Crusoe's Footprints: Cultural Studies in Britain and America* (New York: Routledge, 1990); and Toby Miller, ed., *A Companion to Cultural Studies* (Malden, MA: Blackwell, 2001). For a critique of some of cultural studies' excesses, see J. E. Elliott's review of *Cultural Studies and the New Humanities: Concepts and Controversies*, by Patrick Fuery and Nick Mansfield, in *Comparative Literature* 51.1 (1999): 76–80. Studies of early modern culture are numerous, and I can refer here, and in the following notes, to only a few. One of the more thoughtful collections of essays on the topic is *The Production of English Renaissance Culture*, ed. David Lee Miller, Sharon O'Dair, and Harold Weber (Ithaca, NY: Cornell University Press, 1994); see esp. the editors' introduction, 1–12. My thinking about English culture of this period has also benefited from Bruce Boehrer's *Shakespeare Among the Animals: Nature and Society in the Drama of Early Modern England* (New York: Palgrave, 2002); Deborah Kuller Shuger, *Habits of Thought in the English Renaissance: Religion, Politics, and the Dominant Culture* (Berkeley: University of California Press, 1990; rpt. 1998); and Peter Burke, *Varieties of Cultural History* (Ithaca, NY: Cornell University Press, 1997). Burke describes the practice of writing cultural history as "rather like trying to catch a cloud in a butterfly net" (1). On the larger role of "culture" in contemporary thought, see also Gary Taylor, *Cultural Selection* (New York: Basic Books, 1996).

7. This search was originally performed in the summer of 2001 using the JSTOR database and search engine, which, when this manuscript was completed, provided access to issues of the journal published from 1950 through 1995, inclusive. The figures for 1995 to 1999 here were generously supplied by Ms. Aimee Pyle, User Services Assistant of JSTOR, in an electronic communication to the author dated February 14, 2002. I am extremely grateful to Ms. Pyle for her assistance in this matter.

8. David Harris Sacks, "Searching for 'Culture' in the English Renaissance," *Shakespeare Quarterly* 39 (1988): 465–88.

9. Stephen Greenblatt, *Shakespearean Negotiations: The Circulation of Social Energy in Renaissance England* (Berkeley: University of California Press, 1988), 5.

10. Leah S. Marcus, *Puzzling Shakespeare: Local Reading and its Discontents* (Berkeley: University of California Press, 1988), 219. The phrase quoted in Marcus's remark is taken from Alvin Kernan, *Printing Technology, Letters & Samuel Johnson* (Princeton, NJ: Princeton University Press, 1987), 313. Appearing the year Marcus's book went to press, it must have seemed like a timely and irresistible phrase.

11. Albert H. Tricomi, *Reading Tudor-Stuart Texts Through Cultural Historicism* (Gainesville: University Press of Florida, 1996), ix, 1–22.

12. Meredith Anne Skura, "Recent Studies in Tudor and Stuart Drama," *Studies in English Literature, 1500–1900* 40.2 (2000): 355–86; 356–57.

13. Shakespeare Association of America, *Bulletin* (January 2002); this refers to the meeting in Minneapolis, March 21–23, 2002.

14. See Michael Dobson, *The Making of the National Poet: Shakespeare, Adaptation and Authorship, 1660–1769* (Oxford: Clarendon Press, 1992), 1 ff., where Dobson adapts the phrase from Joseph C. Hart; see also Gary Taylor, *Reinventing Shakespeare: A Cultural History, from the Restoration to the Present* (New York: Weidenfeld & Nicolson, 1989).

15. I have discussed the new historicism at some length in "New Light on the Old Historicism: Shakespeare and the Forms of Historicist Criticism," *Literature and History* 5.1 (1996): 1–18; and *Quoting Shakespeare: Form and Culture in Early Modern Drama* (Lincoln: University of Nebraska Press, 2000), esp. 3–6, 7–8, 10–11, 27–38.

16. See, for example, Francis Mulhern, *Culture/Metaculture* (London: Routledge, 2000), xvi; and Adam Kuper, *Culture: The Anthropologists' Account* (Cambridge, MA: Harvard University Press, 1999), 9.

17. Matthew Arnold, "Culture and Anarchy: An Essay in Political and Social Criticism," in *"Culture and Anarchy" and "Friendship's Garland"* (New York: Macmillan and Co., 1883), xi.

18. This is the word (that is, "company") that Arnold uses, in fact, in an arresting story that invokes the value of Shakespeare's works by assuming their qualities in Shakespeare himself: "Notwithstanding the mighty results of the Pilgrim Fathers' voyage, they and their standard of perfection are rightly judged when we figure to ourselves Shakspeare or Virgil,—souls in whom sweetness and light, and all that in human nature is most humane, were eminent,—accompanying them on their voyage, and think what intolerable company Shakspeare and Virgil would have found them!" Arnold, *Culture and Anarchy*, 7.

19. "But a lover of perfection, who looks to inward ripeness for the true springs of conduct, will surely think that . . . Shakspeare has done more for the inward ripeness of our statesmen than Dr. Watts . . ." Arnold, *Culture and Anarchy*, xvi.

20. See, for only one example, *The Dictionary of Cultural Literacy*, 2nd ed., rev., ed. E. D. Hirsch, Jr., Joseph F. Kett, and James Trefil (Boston: Houghton Mifflin, 1993).

21. A. L. Kroeber and Clyde Kluckhohn, *Culture: A Critical Review of Concepts and Definitions* (1952; New York: Vintage Books, 1966), 357. This definition, again, is a condensed and revised version of that written by Charles A. Ellwood for H. Fairchild's *Dictionary of Sociology* (New York: Philosophical Society, 1944). See Kroeber and Kluckhohn, *Culture*, 65–66.

22. Kuper, *Culture*, 5.

23. For early assessments of Kluckhohn's contributions to anthropology—assessments that include discussion of his famous study with Kroeber—see *Culture and Life: Essays in Memory of Clyde Kluckhohn*, ed. Walter W. Taylor, John L. Fischer, and Evon Z. Vogt (Carbondale, IL: Southern Illinois University Press, 1973).

24. This search was run at the same time as the search for "culture" given above, and under the same conditions. Here the term searched for is the word "society":

Year	Items Containing the Word "Society"
1950–1954	112
1955–1959	147
1960–1964	155
1965–1969	121
1970–1974	125
1975–1979	145
1980–1984	172
1985–1989	193
1990–1994	145

25. See Francis E. Merrill, *Society and Culture: An Introduction to Sociology*, 4th ed. (Englewood Cliffs, NJ: Prentice-Hall, 1969), 80.

26. I owe this suggestion to Mary Blockley.

27. Louis Montrose, "The Work of Gender in the Discourse of Discovery," *Representations* 33 (1991): 1–41; quotations at 5, 2. Emphasis in the original.

28. Geraldo U. de Sousa, *Shakespeare's Cross-Cultural Encounters* (New York: St. Martin's Press, 1999), 5.

29. Jyotsna G. Singh, "History or Colonial Ethnography? The Ideological Formation of Edward Terry's *A Voyage to East-India* (1655 and

1665) and *The Merchants and Mariners Preservation and Thanksgiving* (1649)," in *Travel Knowledge: European "Discoveries" in the Early Modern Period,* ed. Ivo Kamps and Jyotsna G. Singh (New York: Palgrave, 2001), 197–207; quotation at 203–4.

30. Indeed, in essays published in the same volume in which Singh's contribution appears, various authors extend the metaphor of psychic tension touched on but largely undeveloped in the passage just quoted ("subjects struggling to interpret"). To Gerald MacLean, for instance, Britain can best be read as an acquisitive and envious national psyche: "The British wanted an empire and devoted the seventeenth century . . . to sorting out how to get theirs. . . . To a divided Christian Europe, this crucial moment of territorial loss created not an absence but a lack; and in consequence of that lack, a desire that, among the British at least, most often took shape as what I call imperial envy." Gerald MacLean, "Ottomanism Before Orientalism? Bishop King Praised Henry Blount, Passenger in the Levant," in Kamps and Singh, *Travel Knowledge,* 85–96; quotation at 87. See also Daniel Vitkus: "In this picture of imperial sexuality, and throughout Sandys's description of the Turkish nation, there is a condescending and superior tone that thinly veils a deeper sense of imperial envy, sometimes exacerbated by an anxious feeling of competition with the other Europeans in the Levant." Vitkus, "Trafficking with the Turk: English Travellers in the Ottoman Empire during the Early Seventeenth Century," in Kamps and Singh, *Travel Knowledge,* 35–52; quotation at 48.

31. See n. 18 above.

32. In addition to de Sousa, *Shakespeare's Cross-Cultural Encounters,* see, for example, Stephen Greenblatt, "Invisible Bullets: Renaissance Authority and its Subversion," *Glyph* 8 (1981): 40–61.

33. For an account of the role that institutionalized genres of inquiry play in academic narratives—an account that sheds useful light on the possessive instincts I am describing about "cultural" discourse—see Marjorie Garber, *Academic Instincts* (Princeton, NJ: Princeton University Press, 2001).

34. Christopher Pye, *The Vanishing: Shakespeare, the Subject, and Early Modern Culture* (Durham, NC: Duke University Press, 2000), 13.

35. On "lumping" and "splitting," see J. H. Hexter, *On Historians* (Cambridge, MA: Harvard University Press, 1979): 241–43; and Charles Kindleberger, "Lumpers and Splitters in Economics, A Note," *American Economist* 44 (Spring 2000): 88–92.

36. It is worth noting that the comprehensive definition of culture here possesses, in its emphasis on totality, an affinity with Althusser's definition of ideology; see, in particular, "Ideology and Ideological State Apparatuses (Notes towards an Investigation)" in Althusser, *Lenin and Philosophy and Other Essays* (New York: Monthly Review Press, 1971), 127–86.

37. For a recent study that actively multiplies the objects of cultural inquiry, see Juliet Fleming, *Graffiti and the Writing Arts of Early Modern England* (London: Reaktion Books, 2001); Fleming's argument takes up such objects and practices as pots and graffiti.

38. See, for instances of criticism that examine these social objects alongside early modern plays, Lena Cowen Orlin, "The Performance of Things in *The Taming of the Shrew*," *YES* 23 (1993): 167–88; and Natasha Korda, "Household Kates: Domesticating Commodities in *The Taming of the Shrew*," *Shakespeare Quarterly* 47 (1996): 109–31.

39. To my mind, some of the more compelling accounts of what one could describe, in terms that simplify the issue, the relationship between literature and society include those of Pierre Macherey, *A Theory of Literary Production*, trans. Geoffrey Wall (London and Boston: Routledge & Kegan Paul, 1978); Fredric Jameson, *The Political Unconscious: Narrative as a Socially Symbolic Act* (Ithaca, NY: Cornell University Press, 1981); Janet Wolff, *Aesthetics and the Sociology of Art*, 2nd ed. (Ann Arbor: University of Michigan Press, 1993); and Pierre Bourdieu, *The Rules of Art: Genesis and Structure of the Literary Field*, trans. Susan Emanuel (Stanford, CA: Stanford University Press, 1996).

40. Douglas Bruster, *Drama and the Market in the Age of Shakespeare* (Cambridge: Cambridge University Press, 1992), 64.

41. John Lyly, *Midas*, Prologue, ll. 1–22, in the edition of Lyly's *Gallathea* and *Midas* prepared by Anne Begor Lancashire (Lincoln: University of Nebraska Press, 1969).

42. Robert Weimann, "From 'Hodge-Podge' to 'Scene Individable,'" chapter 3 in Robert Weimann and Douglas Bruster, *Prologues to Shakespeare* (tentative title; forthcoming). See also Weimann's "Scene Individable, Mingle-Mangle Unlimited: Authority and Poetics in Lyly's and Shakespeare's Theatres," *European Journal of English Studies* 1.3 (1997): 310–28.

43. I have discussed some of the factors that contributed to early modern drama's heterogeneity in *Quoting Shakespeare*, esp. 15–16, 44–45. For Hegel's arguments concerning drama's representational status, see G. W. F. Hegel, *Aesthetics: Lectures on Fine Art*, trans. T. M. Knox, 2 volumes (Oxford: Clarendon Press, 1975). Hegel believed in the expressive power of drama to such an extent that he called it "the most perfect totality of content and form," going on to say that "it must be regarded as the highest stage of poetry and of art generally" (vol. 2, 1158). To Hegel, drama combined lyric's satisfaction of the need "for self-expression and for the apprehension of the mind in its own self-expression" with epic's "objective presentation of a self-grounded world, made real in virtue of its own necessity" (vol. 2, 1047, 1113).

44. See Ann Moss, *Printed Commonplace-Books and the Structuring of Renaissance Thought* (Oxford: Clarendon Press, 1956), vi, viii, 211.

45. Quoted and translated in E. K. Chambers, *The Elizabethan Stage*, 4 vols. (Oxford: Clarendon Press, 1923), vol. 2, 364–66.

46. Robert Dallington, "A Method for Travell," prefaced to his *A View of France* (London: Thomas Creede, 1605?) [STC 6203], B3ᵛ, B3ʳ.

47. Louis Montrose, *The Purpose of Playing: Shakespeare and the Cultural Politics of the Elizabethan Theatre* (Chicago: University of Chicago Press, 1996), xii.

48. Louis Montrose, "*A Midsummer Night's Dream* and the Shaping Fantasies of Elizabethan Culture: Gender, Power, Form," in *Rewriting the Renaissance: The Discourses of Sexual Difference in Early Modern Europe,* ed. Margaret W. Ferguson, Maureen Quilligan, and Nancy J. Vickers (Chicago: University of Chicago Press, 1986), 65–87.

49. George Puttenham, *The Arte of English Poesie*, ed. Gladys Doidge Willcock and Alice Walker (Cambridge: Cambridge University Press, 1936), 185, 195–96.

50. Kenneth Burke, *A Grammar of Motives* (New York: Prentice-Hall, 1945), 508.

CHAPTER 2

1. In describing a transition from book-length to essayistic treatments of early modern culture, I am thinking of such earlier studies as, for example, Louis B. Wright's *Middle-Class Culture in Elizabethan England* (Chapel Hill: University of North Carolina Press, 1935); E. M. W. Tillyard's *The Elizabethan World Picture* (London: Chatto & Windus 1943); H. S. Bennett's trilogy, *English Books and Readers 1475 to 1557* (Cambridge: Cambridge University Press, 1952), *English Books and Readers 1558 to 1603* (Cambridge: Cambridge University Press, 1965), and *English Books and Readers 1603 to 1640* (Cambridge: Cambridge University Press, 1970); and John Buxton's *Elizabethan Taste* (New York: St. Martin's Press, 1963). One might take a harbinger statement of the essay's growing role in cultural studies from Clifford Geertz's *The Interpretation of Cultures* (New York: Basic Books, 1973): "the essay, whether of thirty pages or three hundred, has seemed the natural genre in which to present cultural interpretations and the theories sustaining them" (25). One can of course see the rise of the cultural-studies essay in the field of early modern studies in Louis Montrose's influential body of work. See, in addition to his "Shaping Fantasies" essay, Montrose, "Celebration and Insinuation: Sir Philip Sidney and the Motives of Elizabethan Courtship," *Renaissance Drama* 8 (1977): 3–35; "The Purpose of Playing: Reflections on a Shakespearean Anthropology," *Helios* 7.2

(1980): 53–74; and "Gifts and Reasons: The Contexts of Peele's *Araygnement of Paris*," *ELH* 47 (1980): 433–61. In early modern studies, the journal *Representations* (first issued in 1983) and the influential anthology *Representing the English Renaissance* (1988) that derived from essays published in that journal jointly functioned to establish a kind of watershed between the book and essay forms of cultural inquiry in the field.

2. In a review of *Subject and Object in Renaissance Culture* (1996), Elizabeth Harvey relates that "That there are no new, young, or alternate voices represented here is slightly disturbing, for it has the effect either of representing new historicism (and cultural materialism) as hegemonic, as a closed circle of insiders, or as serving as a kind of retrospective for a moment in critical history that, in its very memorializing gesture, is seen to be passing." Harvey, in *Journal of English and Germanic Philology* 100.1 (2001): 133–36; 134. A short, anonymous review of Gallagher and Greenblatt's *Practicing New Historicism* (2000) is more blunt still about the apparent datedness of new historicism: "The problem with this book is that it speaks to and of a form of cultural and literary criticism that no one practices today except the founders, Gallagher and Greenblatt. This book strikes one as a vanity publication, full of self-referentiality and marked with a refusal to engage the serious criticisms that have been lodged against new historicism over the last fifteen years. This book is best described as a swan song. It is very unlikely to have any impact on literary or cultural studies, which seem to have moved beyond the kind of criticism espoused here." *Virginia Quarterly* 77.1 (2001): S12.

3. Edward Pechter, review of Judy Kronenfeld, *King Lear and the Naked Truth: Rethinking the Language of Religion and Resistance*, in *Journal of English and Germanic Philology* 99.1 (2000): 132–35; 134.

4. Jane Donawerth, "Teaching Shakespeare in the Context of Renaissance Women's Culture," *Shakespeare Quarterly* 47.4 (1996): 476–89; 477.

5. Meredith Anne Skura, *Studies in English Literature, 1500–1900* 40.2 (2000): 355–86; 356.

6. See Gilbert Ryle, "Thinking and Reflecting" (1967) and "The Thinking of Thoughts: What Is 'Le Penseur' Doing?" in Ryle, *Collected Papers*, 2 vols. (London: Hutchinson & Co., 1971); "Thinking and Reflecting" can be found in vol. 2, 465–79; and "The Thinking of Thoughts: What Is 'Le Penseur' Doing?" in vol. 2, 480–86.

7. Ryle, "The Thinking of Thoughts: What is 'Le Penseur' Doing?" in *Collected Papers*, vol. 2, 480–86; 480.

8. Ryle, "The Thinking of Thoughts," vol. 2, 496.

9. Clifford Geertz, *The Interpretation of Cultures* (New York: Basic Books, 1973), 9–10, emphasis added.

10. Geertz, *Interpretation of Cultures*, 10.
11. Geertz, *Interpretation of Cultures*, 5.
12. Geertz, *Interpretation of Cultures*, 412.
13. Geertz, *Interpretation of Cultures*, 452; see also his statement that "cultural forms can be treated as texts, as imaginative works built out of social materials," 449.
14. On the tension between intuition and rigor in thick description, see Thomas J. Scheff, "Toward Resolving the Controversy over 'Thick Description,'" *Current Anthropology* 27.4 (1986): 408–9; Scheff writes to defend Geertz's practice on the basis of "counterfactual variants" (409).
15. Kenneth A. Rice, *Geertz and Culture* (Ann Arbor: University of Michigan Press, 1980).
16. Paul A. Roth, "Ethnography Without Tears," *Current Anthropology* 30.5 (1989): 555–61; 561.
17. Alan Tongs, "Interpretive Anthropology and Thick Description: Geertz and the Critics," *The Eastern Anthropologist* 50.3–4 (1997): 215–32; 215.
18. S. P. Reyna, "Literary Anthropology and the Case Against Science," *Man* n.s. 29.3 (1994): 555–81; 576.
19. Paul Shankman, "The Thick and the Thin: On the Interpretive Theoretical Paradigm of Clifford Geertz," *Current Anthropology* 25.3 (1984): 261–79; 270.
20. William Roseberry, "Balinese Cockfights and the Seduction of Anthropology," *Social Research* 49 (1982): 1013–28.
21. Stephen Foster, review of Geertz's *Negara*, in *American Anthropologist* 84 (1982): 221–22; 222.
22. For criticisms of new historicist practice within the field of early modern studies, see Jean E. Howard, "The New Historicism in Renaissance Studies," *English Literary Renaissance* 16.1 (1986): 13–43; Lynda E. Boose "The Family in Shakespeare Studies; or—Studies in the Family of Shakespeareans; or—The Politics of Politics," *Renaissance Quarterly* 40.4 (1987): 707–42; Edward Pechter, "The New Historicism and Its Discontents: Politicizing Renaissance Drama," *PMLA* 102.3 (1987): 292–303; Albert H. Tricomi, *Reading Tudor-Stuart Texts Through Cultural Historicism* (Gainesville: University Press of Florida, 1996); and Bruster, *Quoting Shakespeare: Form and Culture in Early Modern Drama* (Lincoln: University of Nebraska Press, 2000), esp. 27–36.
23. Stephen Greenblatt, *Renaissance Self-Fashioning: From More to Shakespeare* (Chicago: University of Chicago Press, 1980), 5; emphasis in original.
24. Stephen Greenblatt, "Shakespeare and the Exorcists," in *Shakespeare and the Question of Theory,* ed. Patricia Parker and Geoffrey Hartman (New York: Methuen, 1985), 163–87; and "Fiction and Friction," in

Reconstructing Individualism: Autonomy, Individuality, and the Self in Western Thought, ed. Thomas C. Heller et al. (Stanford, CA: Stanford University Press, 1982), 30–52.

25. Greenblatt, "Shakespeare and the Exorcists," 163.

26. Steven Mullaney, "Strange Things, Gross Terms, Curious Customs: The Rehearsal of Cultures in the Late Renaissance," in *Representing the English Renaissance*, ed. Stephen Greenblatt (Berkeley: University of California Press, 1988), 65–92; 65.

27. Lena Cowen Orlin, "Women on the Threshold," *Shakespeare Studies* 25 (1997): 50–58; 50.

28. Bruce Boehrer, "Shylock and the Rise of the Household Pet: Thinking Social Exclusion in *The Merchant of Venice*," *Shakespeare Quarterly* 50.2 (1999): 152–70; 152.

29. For an insightful critique of new historicism that parodies such beginnings, see Frank Grady, "Gower's Boat, Richard's Barge, and the True Story of the *Confessio Amantis*: Text and Gloss," *Texas Studies in Language and Literature* 44.1 (2002): 1–15.

30. I explore this new materialism at more length in chapter 8 of the present study.

31. Stephen J. Greenblatt, *Learning to Curse: Essays in Early Modern Culture* (New York: Routledge, 1990), 161–83.

32. Greenblatt, *Learning to Curse*, 162.

33. Wendy Wall, "Why Does Puck Sweep?: Fairylore, Merry Wives, and Social Struggle," *Shakespeare Quarterly* 52.1 (2001): 67–106. Recently Wall has published a version of this essay in her *Staging Domesticity: Household Work and English Identity in Early Modern Drama* (Cambridge: Cambridge University Press, 2002).

34. Wall, "Why Does Puck Sweep?" 67.

35. Wall, "Why Does Puck Sweep?" 106.

36. Henry S. Turner, "Nashe's Red Herring: Epistemologies of the Commodity in *Lenten Stuffe* (1599)," *ELH* 68.3 (2001): 529–61; 529.

37. On the "paradigm exhaustion" of thick description, see Foster's review in *American Anthropologist* 84 (1982): 221–22; 222.

38. See, for example, Joel Fineman, "The History of the Anecdote: Fiction and Fiction," in *The New Historicism*, ed. H. Aram Veeser (New York: Routledge, 1989), 49–76.

39. See Carolyn Porter, "Are We Being Historical Yet?" *South Atlantic Quarterly* 87 (1988): 743–86, quotation at 779. Porter points out that "the use of cultural anecdotes is one of the techniques most often remarked upon by the more skeptical members of new historicism's audience" (778, and see her bibliography 785 n. 51).

40. Burke, *Grammar of Motives*, 508.

41. On the "allure" of the object in thick description, see Jonathan Gil Harris, "The New New Historicism's *Wunderkammer* of Objects," *European Journal of English Studies* 4.2 (2000): 111–23.

42. Stephen Greenblatt, in Catherine Gallagher and Stephen Greenblatt, *Practicing New Historicism* (Chicago: University of Chicago Press, 2000), 46. I cite Greenblatt alone here because this chapter of their book has been published previously under Greenblatt's name.

43. It seems worth remarking here that new historicism often has been drawn to the analysis of paintings and other works of art. One could note, for example, Greenblatt's "Murdering Peasants: Status, Genre, and The Representation of Rebellion," which begins with an analysis of Albrecht Dürer's plans for a triumphal column. This essay is reprinted in *Representing the English Renaissance*, 1–29.

44. *Northern Securities Co. v. U.S.*, 193 U.S. 197, 400–01 (1904) (Justice Holmes, dissenting).

45. Nelson Goodman, *Ways of Worldmaking* (Indianapolis, IN: Hackett Publishing, 1978), 135–36.

46. Raymond Williams, "The Analysis of Culture," reprinted in *Culture, Ideology and Social Process: A Reader*, ed. Tony Bennett et al. (London: Batsford, 1981), 43–52; 47.

47. Madeleine Doran, *Endeavors of Art* (Madison: University of Wisconsin Press, 1964), 4.

48. As Matthew Greenfield observes: "Although some anthropologists have developed powerful accounts of migrancy and hybridity in the postcolonial world, the conceptual apparatus of anthropology still carries with it a family of metaphors that imagine communities as homogeneous entities with clearly demarcated boundaries. Literary critics, on the other hand, now follow Ernst Gellner, Benedict Anderson, Eric Hobsbawm, and Liah Greenfeld in seeing the borders drawn around communities as ideological fictions." Greenfield, "What We Talk About When We Talk About Culture," *Raritan* 19.2 (1999): 95–113; 105. For a philosophical meditation on the role of variety in cultural analysis, see Louis Dupré, "Cultural Variety in Metaphysical Unity," in *The Practice of Cultural Analysis*, ed. Mieke Bal (Stanford: Stanford University Press, 1999), 255–67. One could take, as an instance of variety's growing role in cultural analysis concerned with the early modern period, the preference of textual critics for multiple and varying texts, including, famously, three *Hamlet*s and two *Lear*s. A brief for such textual variety can be found in Leah Marcus, *Unediting the Renaissance: Shakespeare, Marlowe, Milton* (London and New York: Routledge, 1996).

49. Quoted (from Harvey's marginalia in his copy of Speght's edition of Chaucer) in *The Riverside Shakespeare*, 2nd ed., at 1965.

50. Doran goes on to say, however, that the chief distinction we need to make is between the assumptions of our time and those of the Elizabethan era: "The best we can hope to do through learning more about Shakespeare's age is to try to induce a sufficiently sympathetic frame of mind to see his plays in a new perspective which will reveal

new meanings and modify those we may have anachronistically assumed" (4).

51. Anne Barton, "Perils of Historicism," *The New York Review of Books* 38.6 (March 28, 1991): 53–55; at 53.

52. Wall, "Why Does Puck Sweep?" She continues "For elite audiences they signified the exotic or vulgar hominess of serving women; for the middle part of the population they enabled a critique of elite neglect for life's basics; and for general audiences they simply marked the threat or comfort of a 'familiarity' inscribed in the rural roots of Londoners, native traditions, or the mythological space of childhood itself" (80–81).

53. Wall, "Why Does Puck Sweep?" 88, 90.

54. On the history of the Mummers' play, see E. K. Chambers, *The English Folk-Play* (Oxford: Clarendon Press, 1933); and Alex Helm, *The English Mummers' Play* (Woodbridge, Suffolk: D. S. Brewer, 1980).

55. In R. J. E. Tiddy, *The Mummers' Play* (Oxford: Clarendon Press, 1923), 162.

56. Cited in Alan Brody, *The English Mummers and Their Plays: Traces of Ancient Mystery* (Philadelphia: University of Pennsylvania Press, 1970), 60.

57. *Tarltons newes out of Purgatorie. Onely such a iest as his Iigge, fit for Gentlemen to laugh at an houre, &c. Published by an old Companion of his, Robin Goodfellow* (London: Printed for T. G. and T. N. 1590), 6.

58. Vivien Brodsky Elliott notes that apprenticeship records for fifteen London companies—records containing over 8,000 entries—do not record a female apprentice between 1580 and 1640. Elliott, "Single Women in the London Marriage Market: Age, Status, and Mobility, 1598–1619," in *Marriage and Society: Studies in the Social History of Marriage*, ed. R. B. Outhwaite (New York: St. Martin's Press, 1981), 81–100; 91. I am indebted, for much of my knowledge of this topic, to a presentation by Natasha E. Korda entitled "Single Women and the Properties of Poverty in *Measure for Measure*" at the New Orleans meeting of the Modern Language Association, December 28, 2001.

59. On Ariel's status as boy actor in *The Tempest*, see Bruster, *Quoting Shakespeare*, 117–42.

60. *Masterworks of the British Cinema: "Brief Encounter," "Henry V," "The Lady Vanishes"* (London: Faber and Faber, 1990), 197.

61. Tillyard's book reminds us that, just as not every book that invokes "culture" strives to address culture, some books that do not invoke the term aspire to comment on it. With all its faults, *The Elizabethan World Picture* seems an instance of the latter. A useful corrective to Tillyard's univocal model of Elizabethan ideology can be found in Deborah Kuller Shuger, *Habits of Thought in the English Renaissance:*

Religion, Politics, and the Dominant Culture (Berkeley: University of California Press, 1990; rpt. 1998).

62. Peter S. Donaldson, "Virtual and Tragic Spaces: Julie Taymor's *Titus*," paper read at the annual conference of the Modern Language Association; New Orleans, December 28, 2001.

63. On "deep focus," see David Bordwell, Janet Staiger, and Kristen Thompson, *The Classical Hollywood Cinema: Film Style and Mode of Production to 1960* (New York: Columbia University Press, 1985), 341–52; and Patrick L. Ogle, "Technological and Aesthetic Influences Upon the Development of Deep-Focus Cinematography in the United States," *Screen Reader* 1 (London: Society for Education in Film and Television, 1977).

64. See my argument about the industrial role of the early modern playhouses in Bruster, *Drama and the Market in the Age of Shakespeare* (Cambridge: Cambridge University Press, 1992), and in "Entertainment: The Birth of an Industry," in the early modern volume of *The Cambridge History of English Drama*, ed. Peter Thompson (Cambridge: Cambridge University Press, forthcoming).

65. See Paul Yachnin, *Stage-Wrights: Shakespeare, Jonson, Middleton, and the Making of Theatrical Value* (Philadelphia: University of Pennsylvania Press, 1997), and, more recently, Anthony B. Dawson and Paul Yachnin, *The Culture of Playgoing in Shakespeare's England: A Collaborative Debate* (Cambridge: Cambridge University Press, 2001).

66. See Bruster, *Quoting Shakespeare*, esp. 15–51; and chap. 7 in the present study.

CHAPTER 3

1. The expressive individual has, of course, been crucial to definitions of the Renaissance from Burckhardt forward. See Jacob Burckhardt, *The Civilization of the Renaissance in Italy*, 2 vols. (1860; New York: Harper & Row, 1958), esp. vol. 1, "The Development of the Individual" and "The Perfecting of the Individual," 143–50; and vol. 2, "The Discovery of Man—Spiritual Description in Poetry," and "Biography," 303–33. For more recent examinations of the self in works of this era, see Thomas Greene, "The Flexibility of the Self in Renaissance Literature," in *The Disciplines of Criticism: Essays in Literary Theory, Interpretation, and History*, ed. Peter Demetz et al. (New Haven, CT: Yale University Press, 1968), 241–64; Anne Ferry, *The "Inward" Language: Sonnets of Wyatt, Sidney, Shakespeare, Donne* (Chicago: University of Chicago Press, 1983); Katharine Eisaman Maus, *Inwardness and Theater in the English Renaissance* (Chicago: University of Chicago Press, 1995); and Elizabeth Hanson, *Discovering the Subject in Renaissance England* (Cambridge: Cambridge University Press, 1998). Stephen Greenblatt describes

print's increasing openness to the self in the following remarks on Tyndale's *Obedience of a Christian Man:* "In seventeenth-century spiritual autobiography, the inner life is *represented* in outward discourse; that is, the reader encounters the record of events that have already transpired, that have been registered and brought from the darkness within to the clear light of the page. In the early sixteenth century there is not yet so clearly a fluid, continuous inner voice—a dramatic monologue—to be recorded." Greenblatt, *Renaissance Self-Fashioning: From More to Shakespeare* (Chicago: University of Chicago Press, 1980), 86.

2. Gabriel Harvey, from the *Second Letter* of *Four Letters and Certain Sonnets* (London: 1592; reprinted in the Bodley Head Quartos, London: John Lane, 1922), 15.

3. My understanding of the relationship between print and the body in early modern England has benefited from a number of studies, including the foundational essay by Mary Claire Randolph, "The Medical Concept in English Renaissance Satiric Theory: Its Possible Relationships and Implications," *Studies in Philology* 38.2 (1941): 125–57. I also have profited from John G. Norman's unpublished manuscript, "Literature After Dissection in Early Modern England." See also Gail Kern Paster, *The Body Embarrassed: Drama and the Disciplines of Shame in Early Modern England* (Ithaca, NY: Cornell University Press, 1993); Jonathan Sawday, *The Body Emblazoned: Dissection and the Human Body in Renaissance Culture* (London: Routledge, 1995); and Norman's extended review of Sawday's work in *Medievalia et Humanistica* n.s. 23 (1996): 176–80. Kristen Elizabeth Poole has argued that the Marprelate tracts' "polyvalency of competing, overlapping, and interactive voices" opened "a space for the reader's internal participation," thus altering the relations among reader, author, voice, and page. Poole, "Talking Back: Marprelate and His Readers," paper delivered at the annual meeting of the Renaissance Society of America, April 5, 1997.

4. Nashe uses the coinage "body-wanting" to refer to various "venereal" quotations from Ovid in *The Unfortunate Traveller;* McKerrow, ed., *Works of Thomas Nashe,* vol. 2, 271.

5. See, for representative studies along these lines, Douglas Bush, *Mythology and the Renaissance Tradition in English Poetry* (Minneapolis: University of Minnesota Press, 1932), esp. chapter 4, section 2, "The New Ovid," 72–85; et passim. Acknowledging the strong influence of "the dogma *ut pictura poesis,*" Bush writes that "mythological poets vied with painters in rich ornamentation and warm flesh tints. The body had come into its own, although in mythological verse it often seems to be under glass" (78). See also Bush's bibliography of English mythological poems to 1680, 301–23. For other approaches to these traditions, see Alvin Kernan,

The Cankered Muse: Satire of the English Renaissance (New Haven, CT: Yale University Press, 1959); John S. Coolidge, "Martin Marprelate, Marvell, and *Decorum Personae* as a Satirical Theme," *PMLA* 74 (1959): 526–32; Roma Gill, "The Renaissance Conventions of Envy," *Medievalia et Humanistica* n.s. 9 (1979): 215–30; and Ritchie D. Kendall, *The Drama of Dissent: The Radical Poetics of Nonconformity, 1380–1590* (Chapel Hill: University of North Carolina Press, 1986), who grounds Elizabethan religious satire in a diverse but cohesive aesthetic, a "poetics of dissent" stretching back to the Lollard preachers. For the influence of the flyting and *débat*, see C. L. Barber, *Shakespeare's Festive Comedy: A Study of Dramatic Form and Its Relation to Social Custom* (Princeton, NJ: Princeton University Press, 1959), 5–6, 60, 80, 116. Concerning the influence of Petrarch upon the lyric in early modern England, see Roland Greene, *Post-Petrarchism: Origins and Innovations of the Western Lyric Sequence* (Princeton, NJ: Princeton University Press, 1991), 63–108. Greene argues that Sidney's *Astrophel and Stella* "distinctly plays down the temporal process passed on from the *Canzoniere* in favor of a still more person-oriented scope and order" (107). See also Nancy J. Vickers, "Diana Described: Scattered Woman and Scattered Rhyme," *Critical Inquiry* 8 (1981): 265–79, who speaks of Petrarch's "legacy of fragmentation" as it relates to "the development of a code of beauty, a code that causes us to view the fetishized body as a norm" (277). H. Davison is only one of many critics who have explored the importance of Old Comedy for Jonson and other playwrights of this era; see "*Volpone* and the Old Comedy," *Modern Language Quarterly* 24 (1963): 151–57. On the voyeuristic quality of many early modern texts, see Wendy Wall, "Disclosures in Print: The 'Violent Enlargement' of the Renaissance Voyeuristic Text," *Studies in English Literature 1500–1900* 29.1 (1989): 35–59.

6. Still standard introductions to the issues and chronology of the Marprelate controversy can be found in McKerrow, ed. *The Works of Thomas Nashe*, vol. 5, 34–65; and William Pierce, *An Historical Introduction to the Marprelate Tracts* (London: A. Constable & Co, 1908). See also the entry by Joseph Black in *The Dictionary of Literary Biography*, vol. 132: 'Sixteenth-Century British Nondramatic Writers.' First Series, ed. David A. Richardson (Detroit: Gale Research, 1993), 240–44; Black's doctoral thesis, *Pamphlet Wars: The Marprelate Tracts and 'Martinism,' 1588–1688* (University of Toronto, 1996), and Black's "The Rhetoric of Reaction: The Martin Marprelate Tracts (1588–1589), Anti-Martinism, and the Uses of Print in Early Modern England," *The Sixteenth-Century Journal* 28.3 (1997): 707–25 (I am indebted to Black for sharing this with me prior to its publication); and Leland Carson, *Martin Marprelate, Gentleman* (San Marino, CA: Huntington Library, 1981).

7. Robert Weimann, *Authority and Representation in Early Modern Discourse*, ed. David Hillman (Baltimore, MD: Johns Hopkins University Press, 1996), 90. My remarks in this chapter come as a kind of footnote to Weimann's foundational arguments, in the above text and various essays, concerning the changing shapes of authority in early modern England.

8. For insightful surveys of early Tudor polemic, see Louis A. Schuster, "Thomas More's Polemical Career, 1523–1533," in *The Complete Works of St. Thomas More*, ed. Schuster et al., vol. 8, Part III (New Haven, CT: Yale University Press, 1973), 1137–268; and John M. Headley's Introduction to More's *Responsio ad Lutherum*, vol. 5, Part II (New Haven, CT: Yale University Press, 1969), 715–831, esp. "Form and Style in the *Responsio*," 803–23. Headley discusses More's use of Lucian, Horace, Juvenal, Terence, and Plautus in fashioning his abusive satire (814–20). Exploring the intensively *ad hominem* nature of the controversy between More and Luther, Schuster notices that More's *Confutation of Tyndale's Answer* contains "more than sixty references" to the potentially incriminating fact of Luther's marriage (to Katherine von Bora, a former Cistercian nun) (1477).

9. In William Pierce, ed. *The Marprelate Tracts 1588, 1589* (London: James Clarke & Co., 1911), 262–63. This passage refers to William Gravet (d. 1599), vicar of St. Sepulchre in London since 1566, and from the following year prebendary of Willesden in St. Paul's. "[D]umb John" here is John Aylmer (1521–1594), Bishop of London; "T. C." is, of course, Thomas Cooper.

10. Thomas Nashe, *A Countercuff Given to Martin Junior: By the Virtuous, Hardy, and Renowned Pasquil of England, Cavaliero* ([London:] 1589); in McKerrow, ed. *Works*, vol. 1, 57.

11. John Dover Wilson, "The Marprelate Controversy," in *The Cambridge History of English Literature*, ed. A. W. Ward and A. R. Waller (New York: Macmillan, 1939), vol. 3, 436; qtd. in Weimann, *Authority and Representation*, 90.

12. The author of *The Return of the Renowned Cavaliero Pasquill of England* (1589) relates "Me thought *Vetus Comædia* began to prick him at London in the right vein, when she brought forth *Divinity* with a scratcht face, holding of her heart as if she were sick." See McKerrow, ed. *The Works of Thomas Nashe*, vol. 1, 92. For other references to possible stagings of the Marprelate controversy, see McKerrow, *Works*, vol. 4, 44, notes to lines 13, 15. See also Kristen Poole, "Saints Alive! Falstaff, Martin Marprelate, and the Staging of Puritanism," *Shakespeare Quarterly* 46 (1995): 47–75. On the influence of Old Comedy (figured, above, in the phrase "*Vetus Comædia*") as both form and concept, see n. 5 above and *Ben Jonson*, vol. 8, 644; vol. 9, 421, n. 232.

13. Allan Holaday, ed., *The Plays of George Chapman: The Comedies* (Urbana: University of Illinois Press, 1970), 235–36, ll. 13–19.
14. *Ben Jonson*, vol. 5, ll. 52–74. Compare also Marston's prologue to *The Fawn*, published in 1606; there he boasts that in his play "no rude disgraces / Shall taint a public, or a private name" (ll. 5–6). John Marston, *The Fawn*, ed. Gerald A. Smith (Lincoln: University of Nebraska Press, 1965). As James Bednarz points out, Jonson had a special reason to be concerned over embodied writing, for his "swarthy, pock-marked face afforded his critics an easy and constant opportunity for satire." Bednarz, "Representing Jonson: *Histriomastix* and the Origin of the Poets' War," *Huntington Library Quarterly* 54 (1991): 1–30. See 4–5 for various references, usually unflattering, to Jonson's face.
15. E. D. Pendry, ed., *Thomas Dekker: Selected Prose Writings* (Cambridge, MA: Harvard University Press, 1968), 101.
16. See *OED* "flirt," v. 1–7.
17. Here I disagree with Richard A. McCabe's belief that the terms of the Bishops' Ban "show quite clearly that its primary target . . . was neither eroticism nor lewdness but satire itself." McCabe, "Elizabethan Satire and the Bishops' Ban of 1599," *Yearbook of English Studies* 11 (1981): 188–93; 189. The presence of works that were, variously, primarily misogynistic, politically *à clef*, privately controversial, and satirical cannot be covered by any current or early modern understanding of "satire." I would argue that satire, eroticism, lewdness, misogyny (of the kind evidenced in *The Fifteen Joys of Marriage* and *Of Marriage and Wiving*) were objectionable because they too openly brought the human body—both generally and particularly—onto the printed page. Lynda E. Boose also departs from McCabe's position, suggesting that to see pornography and satire in an "either-or context . . . is not only unnecessary but misses something vital." ("The 1599 Bishops' Ban, Elizabethan Pornography, and the Sexualization of the Jacobean Stage," in *Enclosure Acts: Sexuality, Property, and Culture in Early Modern England,* ed. Richard Burt and John Michael Archer [Ithaca, NY: Cornell University Press, 1994], 185–200; 196.) However, Boose's solution—"as the Muse labored, it brought forth a monstrously hybrid creature which combined the salaciously erotic with the violent, misogynistic excoriations of the Juvenalian satiric speaker" (196)—remains unpersuasive, as it cannot account for the otherwise wide range of materials included in the Ban, including prose controversy and the "English historyes" not allowed by the Privy Council. See Boose, 199 n. 7. Cyndia Susan Clegg has argued that the Bishops' Ban is not "representative of a widespread, long term, and efficient cultural practice," but is instead "an improvisational play of competing personal interests" related to Essex's activities in the closing years of the century.

Clegg, *Press Censorship in Elizabethan England* (Cambridge: Cambridge University Press, 1997), 217, and chapter 9, "The 1599 Bishops' Ban: 'Shreud Suspect of Ill Pretences'," 198–207, passim. Obviously my argument would dovetail with Clegg's interest in the intensive personalism of many of the works covered by the Ban—especially those that may be linked with Essex himself.

18. Ian Frederick Moulton, "'Printed Abroad and Uncastrated': Marlowe's Elegies with Davies' Epigrams," in *Marlowe, History, and Sexuality: New Essays on Christopher Marlowe*, ed. Paul Whitfield White (New York: AMS Press, 1997), 77–90. Moulton continues: "Given an understanding of corruption which does not draw strong distinctions between a 'private' realm of the erotic and a 'public' political realm, I believe that Marlowe's translations of Ovid may well have been perceived as socially disorderly." I am grateful to Moulton for sharing this material with me prior to its publication. See also Moulton's insightful, recent study, *Before Pornography: Erotic Writing in Early Modern England* (Oxford: Oxford University Press, 2000).

19. *The Poems of Robert Southwell, S. J.*, ed. James H. McDonald and Nancy Pollard Brown (Oxford: Clarendon Press, 1967), "St. Peter's Complaint," ll. 355–357, 361.

20. *Virgidemiae* (1598), in *The Poems of Joseph Hall, Bishop of Exeter and Norwich*, ed. Arnold Davenport. English Texts and Studies (1949; Liverpool: Liverpool University Press, 1969), Book I, Satire VIII, ll. 9–11, 19.

21. See William Keach, *Elizabethan Erotic Narratives: Irony and Pathos in the Ovidian Poetry of Shakespeare, Marlowe, and Their Contemporaries* (New Brunswick, NJ: Rutgers University Press, 1977), 231. Keach speaks of "the conflict and convergence of satire and erotic poetry at the turn of the century," as evidenced in Weever, and in Marston's *Pygmalion's Image* (188). On the subversive nature of these narratives' Ovidian inheritance, see also Jonathan Bate, "Sexual Perversity in *Venus and Adonis*," *Yearbook of English Studies* 23 (1993): 80–92.

22. Christopher Marlowe, *Hero and Leander*, from *The Complete Poems and Translations*, ed. Stephen Orgel (Harmondsworth, Middlesex: Penguin Books, 1971), ll. 175–91; ll. 188–91.

23. *Venus and Adonis*, ll. 229–40. With Shakespeare's blazon one might compare Spenser's erotic description of the Temple of Venus in *The Faerie Queene*, Book 4, Canto 10, stanzas 21 ff.

24. Thomas Freeman, "*To Master W: Shakespeare*," *Run and a Great Cast* (1614), K2ᵛ-K3ʳ, ll. 7–8. The *Short-Title Catalogue* cites this work by its first title, *Rub and a Great Cast*; "*Run*" describes a second part subsumed into the first.

25. See Hilton Kelliher, "Unrecorded Extracts from Shakespeare, Sidney and Dyer," *English Manuscript Studies 1100–1700* 2 (1990): 163–87.

Kelliher examines a hitherto unnoticed transcription of two stanzas of *Venus and Adonis* (ll. 229–240) in the hand of one Henry Colling from around the period 1593 to 1596—what may be "the earliest extract in manuscript yet to be discovered from any poem [of] Shakespeare's" (167). Colling was not the only reader to be especially taken by these stanzas: Kelliher points out that they are also quoted in Thomas Heywood's *Fair Maid of the Exchange* (1602) and in Gervase Markham's and Lewis Machin's *The Dumb Knight* (1608).

26. On the early modern libel, see Pauline Croft, "Libels, Popular Literary and Public Opinion in Early Modern England," *Historical Research: The Bulletin of the Institute of Historical Research* 68, no. 167 (1995): 266–85. Croft relates that "The fifteen-nineties saw a proliferation of libels, the result of the strains imposed both by disastrous harvests and by an apparently endless international war which disrupted trade" (269). Libels concerning the Essex uprising and concerning the trials of Walter Ralegh and those involved in the Bye and Main plots of 1603 demonstrated the continuing unease in the political sphere of early modern England (274–75). For studies of libelous material during the Stuart era, see Alastair Bellany, "'Raylinge Rymes and Vaunting Verse': Libelous Politics in Early Stuart England, 1603–1628," in *Culture and Politics in Early Stuart England*, ed. Kevin Sharpe and Peter G. Lake (Basingstoke, England: Macmillan, 1994), 285–310; and Tom Cogswell, "Underground Verse and the Transformation of Early Stuart Political Culture," in *Political Culture and Cultural Politics in Early Modern England*, ed. Susan D. Amussen and Mark Kishlansky (Manchester, England: Manchester University Press, 1995), 277–300.

27. The publication figures in the following paragraphs are derived from research by this writer, using information in *The Short-Title Catalogue*. They form part of a chronological, year-by-year analysis of publications by topic and by frequency of imprint tentatively titled "What They Read: English Books in the Early Modern Era." Concerning publication in early modern England, see Edith Klotz, "A Subject Analysis of English Imprints for Every Tenth Year from 1480 to 1640," *Huntington Library Quarterly* 1 (1937/38): 417–19; and H. S. Bennett, *English Books and Readers 1475 to 1557* (Cambridge: Cambridge University Press, 1952); *English Books and Readers 1558 to 1603* (Cambridge: Cambridge University Press, 1965); and *English Books and Readers 1603 to 1640* (Cambridge: Cambridge University Press, 1970).

28. As Jesse Lander suggests, in a private communication to the author, the fact that the 1590s were a period of retrenchment for London printers and publishers—then feeling the effects of a severe inflation—might have led them to experiment with inexpensive forms like the pamphlet and to commit themselves to proven texts and authors.

29. The epithet was coined by Nashe in *Pierce Penniless* (1592); see McKerrow, *Works,* vol. 1, 192–93.

30. Arthur Marotti, "Southwell's Remains: Catholicism and Anti-Catholicism in Early Modern England," in *Texts and Cultural Change, 1520–1700,* ed. Arthur Marotti and Cedric C. Brown (New York: St. Martin's Press, 1997).

31. As Tyler Smith has pointed out to me in a private communication, the multiplication of numbers for Harrington's text here is artificially inflated from its preparation in various forms as "gift" copies.

32. Here and with *Greene's Groatsworth of Wit* I follow the attribution of the original title pages in including these texts of divided authorship with the figures for works of less controversial origin.

33. John Weever, *Epigrammes—Epigrammes in the Oldest Cut and Newest Fashion,* ed. R. B. McKerrow (Stratford-upon-Avon, 1911; reissued 1922), v.

34. E. A. J. Honigmann, *John Weever: A Biography of a Literary Associate of Shakespeare and Jonson, Together with a Photographic Facsimile of Weever's 'Epigrammes' (1599)* (Manchester, England: Manchester University Press, 1987), 27.

35. Harvey, *Four Letters,* 52. It should be pointed out that Nashe returned the favor here, and did so in kind. In the "Epistle Dedicatorie" to *Have With You to Saffron-Walden,* he mocks Harvey's style with the following: "Spend but a quarter so much time in mumping upon *Gabrielism,* and I'll be bound, body and goods, thou wilt not any longer sneakingly come forth with a rich spirit and an admirable capacity, but *an enthusiastical spirit & a nimble entelechy.*" McKerrow, ed., *Works,* vol. 3, 16–17. The italicized phrase—what Nashe calls "Gabrielism"—draws, of course, on Harvey's own works. See McKerrow, ed., vol. 4, 310, note to 17, line 4.

36. On Tarlton's "celebrity image" in early modern England, see Alexandra Halasz, "'So beloved that men use his picture for their signs': Richard Tarlton and the Uses of Sixteenth-Century Celebrity," *Shakespeare Studies* 23 (1995): 19–38. Halasz charts the development and shapes of Tarlton's celebrity and explores the "appropriation of [Tarlton's] reputation by the book trade in its effort to expand and create a market for printed texts" (20). See also Robert Weimann, *Shakespeare and the Popular Tradition in the Theater* (Baltimore, MD: Johns Hopkins University Press, 1978), 186–89.

37. Georges Louis Leclerc, Comte de Buffon, *Discours sur le Style* (Paris: Librairie Hachette, 1901), 25. The general sentiment was not new with Buffon, of course (see n. 2 in this edition of the *Discours* for classical precedents), but his has been the most succinct and lasting expression.

38. Dekker, *The Gull's Horn-Book,* ed. Pendry, 102.

39. J. J. Jusserand, *The English Novel in the Time of Shakespeare* (1894), 105; quoted in R. Warwick Bond, ed. *The Complete Works of John Lyly*, vol. 1 (Oxford: Clarendon Press, 1902), 160.

40. G. K. Hunter, *John Lyly: The Humanist as Courtier* (Cambridge, MA: Harvard University Press, 1962), 259.

41. Harvey, *Four Letters*, 11.

42. Jonson apostrophizes Vulcan after the burning of his library, suggesting that he would have gladly substituted "many a ream / To redeem mine," works that would include "Nicholas Pasquil's *Meddle with your Match*, / And the strong lines, that so the time do catch" (ll. 62–63, 77–78). Two manuscript copies of *The Underwood* read "Nicholas *Breton's Meddle with your Match*" (my emphasis). Ben Jonson, "An Execration upon Vulcan," *The Underwood* xliii, in *Ben Jonson*, vol. 8, 205–6.

43. Robert Joyner, *Itis, or Three Severall Boxes of Sporting Familiars* (London: Thomas Judson, 1598), A9^v-B1^r.

44. See Epigram 93, "*Against* Itis *a Poet*," in Norman Egbert McClure, ed., *The Letters and Epigrams of Sir John Harington* (Philadelphia: University of Pennsylvania Press, 1930), 185.

45. On the implications of the unique form here, see Honigmann, ed., *John Weever*, 90–92. Another instance of an author being identified with one of his characters involved Christopher Marlowe, whom Harvey refers to as "Tamberlaine" in the sonnet ("*Gorgon, or the wonderfull yeare*") appended to *A New Letter of Notable Contents* (London: 1593).

46. Honigmann, ed., *John Weever*, reproduction of E6a of Weever's *Epigrammes* (1599), ll. 13–14.

47. "Public sphere" is a phrase and concept advanced by Jürgen Habermas in *The Structural Transformation of the Public Sphere* (1962) to describe the bourgeois sphere of rational political and intellectual exchange that thrived temporarily in the world of the eighteenth-century, European "town." The public sphere was demarcated, on one side, by the more intimate realm of private activity that includes the family, commodity exchange, and social labor, and, on the other, by the realm of the state, a realm defined by public authority, police, court, and courtly nobility. According to Habermas, places in which the public sphere unfolded had "a number of institutional criteria in common": (1) "they preserved a kind of social intercourse that, far from pre-supposing the equality of status, disregarded status altogether"; (2) "discussion within such a public presupposed the problematization of areas that until then had not been questioned"; (3) "the same process that converted culture into a commodity . . . established the public as in principle inclusive." *The Structural Transformation of the Public Sphere: An Inquiry into a Category of Bourgeois Society*, trans. Thomas Burger and Frederick Lawrence (Cambridge,

MA: MIT Press, 1989), 36–37. For later reflections by Habermas on this concept, see "The Public Sphere: An Encyclopedia Article," trans. Sara Lennox and Frank Lennox, in *Critical Theory and Society: A Reader*, ed. Stephen Eric Bronner and Douglas MacKay Kellner (New York: Routledge, 1989) 136–42, and "Further Reflections on the Public Sphere," in *Habermas and the Public Sphere*, ed. Craig Calhoun (Cambridge, MA: MIT Press, 1993), 421–61.

48. See, for example, David Norbrook, "*Areopagitica*, Censorship, and the Early Modern Public Sphere," in Richard Burt, ed., *The Administration of Aesthetics: Censorship, Political Criticism, and the Public Sphere*. Cultural Politics 7 (Minneapolis: University of Minnesota Press, 1994). Norbrook works consciously against the cumulative efforts of revisionist and certain new historicist paradigms, which tend to envision "a pre-Enlightenment world of bodily submission" (6–7). Both Steven Pincus (in "'Coffee Politicians Does Create': Coffeehouses and Restoration Political Culture," *The Journal of Modern History* 67.4 [1995]: 807–34), and Sharon Achinstein ("Women on Top in the Pamphlet Literature of the English Revolution," *Women's Studies* 24 [1994]: 131–63, and *Milton and the Revolutionary Reader* [Princeton, NJ: Princeton University Press, 1994]) join Norbrook in suggesting that a public sphere existed in English political life earlier than Habermas's chronology would allow. Where Pincus might be said to interpret Habermas too literally, however—overidentifying the public sphere with the physical place of the coffeehouse—Achinstein provides a more supple reading of the situation, speaking of "a cultural milieu in which the material conditions were in place for affordable, accessible printing, and an intellectual climate of public debate: all these might be said to anticipate Habermas's scheme by a century or so" ("Women on Top," 155). For an account of the ways in which such critics as David Lawton and Anne Middleton have explored a fifteenth-century public sphere, see Joyce Coleman, *Public Reading and the Reading Public in Late Medieval England and France* (Cambridge: Cambridge University Press, 1996), 93–97. For a recent argument concerning satire's relation to the public sphere in the early eighteenth century, see Christian Thorne, "Thumbing Our Nose at the Public Sphere: Satire, the Market, and the Invention of Literature," *PMLA* 116.3 (2001): 531–44.

49. Norbrook, "*Areopagitica*, Censorship, and the Early Modern Public Sphere," 7. See, for a critique of Habermas's idealism that stresses the entrenched hierarchies of early modern Europe, Robert Darnton, "An Enlightened Revolution?" *New York Review of Books*, October 24, 1991, 34. For this reference I am indebted to Annabel Patterson's "Rethinking Tudor Historiography," *South Atlantic Quarterly* 92 (1993): 185–208, an essay that contributes to but is not superseded by Patterson's *Reading Holinshed's "Chronicles"* (Chicago:

University of Chicago Press, 1994). There Patterson suggests that we can read the *Chronicles* as a "*textual* space . . . in which the public's right to information could to some extent be satisfied" (21). My argument with Patterson's claim concerning the public implications of the *Chronicles*—a claim that dovetails in many ways with my own—is that it replicates Habermas's rational emphasis on information and communication. In contrast, I would suggest, the late Elizabethan public sphere often entertained the irrational and the ludic.

50. Habermas, *The Structural Transformation of the Public Sphere,* 36.

51. It is something like this pressure on the established order of things that Joseph Loewenstein ascribes to the rogue printer John Wolfe's "tradition of practical assault on control and privilege" in relation to print and the licensing of print. "For a History of Literary Property: John Wolfe's Reformation," *English Literary Renaissance* 18 (1988). 389–412, 411. For relevant arguments about literary property and "possessive authorship" during the early modern era, see also two of Loewenstein's recent publications: *The Author's Due: Printing and the Prehistory of Copyright* (Chicago: University of Chicago Press, 2002); and *Ben Jonson and Possessive Authorship* (Cambridge: Cambridge University Press, 2002).

52. On the shapes of decorum in relation to courtly practice in the Elizabethan era, and the ways in which, as vehicles of exclusion, decorum handbooks were used by these growing ranks of the meritorious to gain power and prestige, see Frank Whigham, *Ambition and Privilege: The Social Tropes of Elizabethan Courtesy Theory* (Berkeley: University of California Press, 1984).

53. That is, Robert Wilson's *Fair Em the Miller's Daughter of Manchester, with the Love of William the Conqueror* (1590), apparently owned by Strange's Men. On Shakespeare's probable connections with this company, see E. A. J. Honigmann, *Shakespeare: The 'Lost years'* (Manchester, England: Manchester University Press, 1985), 59–76.

54. Richard Corbett, "Iter Boreale," ll. 343–52, in *The Poems of Richard Corbett,* ed. J. A. W. Bennett and H. R. Trevor-Roper (Oxford: Clarendon Press, 1955).

55. For a theoretical meditation on the relationships among actors, writers, audience members, and readers in the early modern era, see Robert Weimann, *Author's Pen and Actor's Voice: Playing and Writing in Shakespeare's Theater* (Cambridge: Cambridge University Press, 2000).

56. James Shapiro, *Rival Playwrights: Marlowe, Jonson, Shakespeare* (New York: Columbia University Press, 1991), 8.

57. Shapiro, *Rival Playwrights,* 8.

58. D. Allen Carroll, ed., *Greene's Groatsworth of Wit: Bought With a Million of Repentance* (Binghamton, NY: Medieval & Renaissance Texts & Studies, 1994), preface. For convenience, in what follows I will

speak of *Groatsworth* without naming the author; as Caroll indicates in his unpaginated preface, much recent scholarship shows that "the case for a serious participation by Henry Chettle" in the writing of this text "is much stronger than has been generally thought. Greene *may* have had something to do with the writing of *Groatsworth,* Chettle *certainly* did."

59. Carroll, ed., *Greene's Groatsworth,* 85, ll. 938–43.
60. For an extended meditation on the relationship between such intensively self-conscious language—evident in the notorious puns on "Will" in Sonnets 135 and 136—and developing forms of poetic subjectivity in the era, see Joel Fineman, *Shakespeare's Perjured Eye: The Invention of Poetic Subjectivity in the Sonnets* (Berkeley: University of California Press, 1986); and, more recently, Lisa Freinkel, *Reading Shakespeare's Will: The Theology of Figure from Augustine to the Sonnets* (New York: Columbia University Press, 2002).
61. George Puttenham, *The Arte of English Poesie,* ed. Gladys Doidge Willcock and Alice Walker (Cambridge: Cambridge University Press, 1936; rpt. 1970), "*Of Stile,*" Book 3, chapter v, 148.
62. Here I am adopting the translation of Thomas Phaer and Thomas Twynne in *The Whole XII Books of the Æneidos of Virgil* (London: 1573), C4ᵛ·
63. Hall, *Virgidemiae,* in *The Poems of Joseph Hall,* ed. Davenport, IV.ii.79–84, 57.
64. Edward Arber, ed., *An Introductory Sketch to the "Martin Marprelate" Controversy, 1588–1590.* The English Scholar's Library of Old and Modern Works, no. 8 (London: 1879), 176.
65. Arber, ed., *Introductory Sketch,* 178, 179. At least two other instances of "stylistic" identification came out of the Marprelate controversy. In "The Deposition of Henry Sharpe, a bookbinder at Northampton, on the 15th October 1589," the following is recorded: "When this Second Booke came out, then this Examinate [that is, Henry Sharpe], as he sayth, began to suspect Penry to be the Author of it and talking with him told him as much, alleging this reason, 'Surely,' sayth this Examinate, 'I think this Book (the *Epitome*) to be of your making, because there are two or three Phrases in the *Epistle* of it, which are yours certainly.' Whereunto Master Penry gave no answer but laughed" (in Arber, *Introductory Sketch,* 96). Likewise in "Summary of the information in the hands of the Queen's Government as to the Martinists on the 22nd September 1589," it is related that "The author of the written copie [that is, the manuscript of *More Work for Cooper*], that was taken by the Earl of Derby, taketh upon him to be the same, that made the first. 3. Libels, and the Styl doth not vary. That his last [that is, the manuscript work] was contrived by Penrie besides the former presumptions (gathered of his owne speeches and dealinges in providinge a printer &c after Waldgrave his

departure) the two hands used in the same do seem to be, the one Penry's and the other his man's hand; as by a collation of such their writings (as have been heretofore taken) may appear. The style of it and spirit of the man (where he is out of his scoffing vein) doth altogether resemble such his writings, as he hath published with his name to them" (Arber, *Introductory Sketch,* 117). I am grateful to Joseph Black for bringing these instances to my attention.

66. See Harvey, *Four Letters,* 19.

67. Francis Bacon, *Sir Francis Bacon his Apology, In Certain Imputations Concerning the Late Earl of Essex* (orig. publ. 1604; London: 1642), 10.

68. Bacon's remembrance of the Elizabethan era also helps place this phenomenon in its historical context. His anecdote here follows immediately upon similar mention of John Hayward's (Haywood's) politically controversial *The First Part of the Life and Reign of King Henry the IV* (1599)—a work not named in the Bishops' Ban of 1599, yet certainly pertinent to the climate that produced the ban. Elizabeth, according to Bacon, "being mightily incensed with that book which was dedicated to my Lord of *Essex* . . . thinking it a seditious prelude to put into the people's heads boldness and faction, said she had good opinion, that there was treason in it, and asked me if I could not find any places in it that might be drawn within case of treason." To which Bacon answered, his *Apology* tells us, "for treason surely I found none, but for felony very many," as "the Author had committed very apparent theft, for he had taken most of the sentences of *Cornelius Tacitus,* and translated them into English, and put them into his text." Bacon, *Sir Francis Bacon his Apology,* 10.

69. Here I should point out that this chapter suggests an earlier chronology to the shift, from manuscript to print, of certain energies connected with political and obscene topics in early modern England than is seen by Marotti (who discusses the emergence of these topics in relation to the 1630s and 1640s) in his *Manuscript, Print, and the English Renaissance Lyric* (Ithaca, NY: Cornell University Press, 1995), esp. chap. 2, "Sex, Politics, and the Manuscript System," 75–133.

70. My argument here about the pivotal nature of the 1590s draws on a number of recent studies, including John Guy, ed., *The Reign of Elizabeth I: Court and Culture in the Last Decade* (Cambridge: Cambridge University Press, 1995); Steve Rappaport, *Worlds within Worlds: Structures of Life in Sixteenth-Century London* (Cambridge: Cambridge University Press, 1989); *The European Crisis of the 1590s,* ed. Peter Clark (London: George Allen and Unwin, 1985); Eric Mallin, *Inscribing the Time: Shakespeare and the End of Elizabethan England* (Berkeley: University of California Press, 1995); Peter C. Herman, "'O, 'tis a gallant king': Shakespeare's *Henry V* and the Crisis of the 1590s," in *Tudor Political Culture,* ed. Dale

Hoak (Cambridge: Cambridge University Press, 1995), 204–25; Mark Thorton Burnett, "Apprentice Literature and the 'Crisis' of the 1590s," *The Yearbook of English Studies* 21 (1991): 27–38; and Margreta de Grazia, "Fin-de-Siècle Renaissance England," in *Fins de Siècle: English Poetry in 1590, 1690, 1790, 1890, 1990*, ed. Elaine Scarry (Baltimore, MD: Johns Hopkins University Press, 1995), 37–63. For a study that focuses on the effects of urbanization and the dialectic of "court" and "town" cultures within London as portrayed in the drama of the late sixteenth and early seventeenth centuries, see Janette Dillon, *Theater, Court and City, 1595–1610: Drama and Social Space in London* (Cambridge: Cambridge University Press, 2000).

71. See Debra Belt, "The Poetics of Hostile Response, 1575–1610," *Criticism* 33 (1991): 419–59; 436. See also Wall, "'Violent Englargement.'"

72. Lawrence Manley, *Literature and Culture in Early Modern London* (Cambridge: Cambridge University Press, 1995), 372.

73. Weimann, *Authority and Representation*, 10.

74. Christopher Hill, *The English Bible and the Seventeenth-Century Revolution* (London: Penguin Books, 1993), 439.

75. For the Reformation as "the story of great books," see John E. Booty, ed., *The Godly Kingdom of Tudor England: Great Books of the English Reformation* (Wilton, CT.: Morehouse-Barlow Co., 1981), 8.

76. John Foxe, *Actes and Monuments of the Christian Church* (London: 1576), ii.

77. [R. Wilson?], *Martine Mar-Sixtus* (London: 1591), A3ᵛ, and Address to the Reader from Florio's *World of Words* (1598), reproduced in Appendix I of Frances A. Yates, *John Florio: The Life of an Italian in Shakespeare's England* (Cambridge: Cambridge University Press, 1934), 337.

78. Matthew Greenfield, "The Strange Commodities of Pamphlet Culture," paper delivered at the annual meeting of the Renaissance Society of America, April 5, 1997.

79. Anthony Esler, *The Aspiring Mind of the Elizabethan Younger Generation* (Durham, NC: Duke University Press, 1966), xvi. For more comprehensive accounts of the issue of "age" during the transition to the modern period, see Keith Thomas, "Age and Authority in Early Modern England," *Proceedings of the British Academy* 62 (1977 for 1976): 205–48; Ilana Krausman Ben-Amos, *Adolescence and Youth in Early Modern England* (New Haven, CT: Yale University Press, 1994); and Paul Griffiths, Adam Fox, and Steve Hindle, eds., *The Experience of Authority in Early Modern England* (London: Macmillan, 1996). We still lack a comprehensive study of the University Wits and their influence on the literary scene of early modern England. But for the marked rise of educational opportunities in sixteenth-century

England, see Lawrence Stone, "The Educational Revolution in England 1560–1640," *Past and Present* 28 (1964): 41–80.

80. For the importance of Latin, and Latin literary models to the late Elizabethan era, see J. W. Binns, *Intellectual Culture in Elizabethan and Jacobean England: The Latin Writings of the Age*, ARCA Classical and Medieval Texts, Papers and Monographs 24 (Leeds, England: Francis Cairns Publications Ltd., 1990). Binns notes "the pervasive nature of the Latinate culture of Elizabethan England at the zenith of the Queen's reign," and relates that the "age of greatest popularity of the new Latin books is perhaps the fifty-year stretch from 1570–1620" (xv, 3). On the role of the epigram—popular with this generation, and arguably the building block of many larger textual forms—see Hoyt Hopewell Hudson, *The Epigram in the English Renaissance* (1947; rpt. New York: Octagon, 1966); and Mary Thomas Crane, *Framing Authority: Sayings, Self, and Society in Sixteenth-Century England* (Princeton, NJ: Princeton University Press, 1993), 136–161. On the relationship of humanism's agonistic basis to the activities of its scholar-authorities, see Charles Nisard, *Les gladiateurs de la république des lettres aux XVe, XVIe et XVIIe siècles* (Paris: Michel Levy frères, 1860). For the roles of discipline in the early modern schoolroom, see Rebecca Bushnell, *A Culture of Teaching: Early Modern Humanism in Theory and Practice* (Ithaca, NY: Cornell University Press, 1996), esp. chap. 2 "The Sovereign Master and the Scholar Prince," 23–72. On the "discipline" of Latin language instruction, see Walter J. Ong, "Latin Language Study as a Renaissance Puberty Rite," *Studies in Philology* 56 (1959): 103–24. Ong sees Latin learning in the Elizabethan grammar schools as a "Renaissance puberty rite"; the sexual segregation of the schools, their strict corporal discipline, insistence upon obedience and imitation, and emphasis on such epic/heroic values, in classical literature, as courage and bravery, led to a hardening of the individual student "for the extra-familial world in which he would have to live" (123). A useful qualification of Ong's thesis, however, may be found in Marjorie Woods' "Boys Will Be Women: Musings on Classroom Nostalgia and the Chaucerian Audience(s)," in *Speaking Images: Essays in Honor of V. A. Kolve*, ed. Charlotte C. Morse and Robert F. Yeager (Asheville, NC: Pegasus Press, 2001), 143–66.

81. For the influence, on embodied writing, of the Inns of Court, see Philip Finkelpearl, *John Marston of the Middle Temple: An Elizabethan Dramatist in His Social Setting* (Cambridge, MA: Harvard University Press, 1969); and Arthur F. Marotti, *John Donne, Coterie Poet* (Madison: University of Wisconsin Press, 1986), 3–95, who explores the social conditions of Donne's early verse. Kenneth Alan Hovey also has explored the lingering influence of Francis Bacon's tenure at the

Inns of Court, and its hospitality to "parabolic" dramas, for our un-
derstanding of his later works and politics. See "Bacon's Parabolical
Drama: Iconoclastic Philosophy and Elizabethan Politics," in *Francis
Bacon's Legacy of Texts: The Art of Discovery Grows With Discovery*, ed.
William A. Sessions (New York: AMS Press, 1990), 215–36.

82. For the early modern "commonwealth of wit" as a "social institution
in Vosskamp's and Luhmann's sense," see Eckhard Auberlen, *The
Commonwealth of Wit: The Writer's Image and His Strategies of Self-
Representation in Elizabethan Literature*. Studies and Texts in English 5 (Tübingen: Narr, 1984).

83. I include in the former number an entry of 35 for Marlowe, his age
in 1599 had he lived. I follow received estimates of birth dates for
Marston (1575?), Middleton (1580?), and Whitgift (1530?).

84. On the decline of patronage during the 1590s, see Alistair Fox, "The
Complaint of Poetry for the Death of Liberality: The Decline of Literary Patronage in the 1590s," in *The Reign of Elizabeth I*, ed. Guy,
229–57. The "paranoia of the establishment" is described by Guy in
the introduction to this study, 11.

85. *Hamlet*, quotations from 2.2.524–5, 5.1.139–41.

86. Nashe, Preface to *Astrophel and Stella* (1591), in McKerrow, ed.,
Works, vol. 3, 329.

87. See Paul Yachnin, "The Powerless Theater," *English Literary Renais-
sance* 21 (1991): 49–74; reprinted in revised form in his book *Stage-
Wrights: Shakespeare, Jonson, Middleton, and the Making of Theatrical
Value* (Philadelphia: University of Pennsylvania Press, 1997).

CHAPTER 4

1. Aristotle ranks recognition by means of external tokens as the least
artistic method of anagnorisis. See the *Poetics*, 1454b24–30.

2. See, for examples of criticism that relate stage objects to the traditions of iconography, Bridget Gellert, "The Iconography of Melancholy in the Graveyard Scene in *Hamlet*," *Studies in Philology* 67
(1970): 57–66; Katherine A. Rowe, "Dismembering and Forgetting
in *Titus Andronicus*," *Shakespeare Quarterly* 45 (1994): 279–303;
Michael Neill, "'What Strange Riddle's This?' Deciphering '*Tis Pity
She's A Whore*," in *John Ford: Critical Re-Visions*, ed. Michael Neill
(Cambridge: Cambridge University Press, 1988), 153–81; Houston
Diehl, "Inversion, Parody, and Irony: The Visual Rhetoric of Renaissance English Tragedy," *Studies in English Literature 1500–1900* 22
(1982): 197–209; Samuel Schuman, "*The Theatre of Fine Devices*":
The Visual Drama of John Webster (Salzburg: Inst. fur Anglistik &
Amerikanistik, Univ. Salzburg, 1982); and Brownell Salomon, "Vi-
sual and Aural Signs in the Performed English Renaissance Play," *Renaissance Drama* n.s. 5 (1972): 143–69. Stating that "Certain hand

properties have a metaphoric value matching that used in Renaissance iconography," Salomon goes on to discuss the bleeding heart in *'Tis Pity* and describes the human skull in revenge tragedy as a *memento mori* emblem (161).

3. Alan S. Downer, "The Life of Our Design: The Function of Imagery in the Poetic Drama," *The Hudson Review* 2 (1949): 242–60; reprinted in Leonard F. Dean, ed., *Shakespeare: Modern Essays in Criticism* (New York: Oxford University Press, 1975), 19–36; at 28. Downer's lone example of this "language of props" involves Macbeth and his borrowed robes, which he relates to the imagery studies of Caroline Spurgeon and Cleanth Brooks, respectively. Downer's connection of props to language has since found expression, of course, in semiotic analysis of the theater. See, for example, Jiří Veltruský, "Man and Object in the Theater," in Paul L. Garvin, trans. and ed., *A Prague School Reader on Esthetics, Literary Structure, and Style* (Washington, DC: Georgetown University Press, 1964), 83–91; and Ruth Amossy's relating of stage objects to verbal systems in "Toward a Rhetoric of the Stage: The Scenic Realization of Verbal Clichés," *Poetics Today* 2.3 (1981): 49–63.

4. Psychoanalytic readings of stage props include Lynda E. Boose, "Othello's Handkerchief: 'The Recognizance and Pledge of Love,'" *English Literary Renaissance* 5 (1975): 360–74; Barbara Freedman, "Errors in Comedy: A Psychoanalytic Theory of Farce," in *Shakespearean Comedy*, ed. Maurice Charney (New York: New York Literary Forum, 1980), 233–43; and Edmund Wilson, "Morose Ben Jonson," *The Triple Thinkers* (New York: Oxford University Press, 1948), 213–32, who remarks on the significant *absence* of a certain property in a Jonson play: "in *Volpone*, where real gold is involved, we are never allowed to see it" (227). Wilson's insistence on the reality of this unseen stage gold speaks to the power of theatrical properties, even in their absence.

5. See, for example, Linda Austern, "'Sing Againe Syren': The Female Musician and Sexual Enchantment in Elizabethan Life and Literature," *Renaissance Quarterly* 42 (1989): 420–48; Jean E. Howard, "Sex and Social Conflict: The Erotics of *The Roaring Girl*," in *Erotic Politics: Desire on the Renaissance Stage*, ed. Susan Zimmerman (New York: Routledge, 1992), 170–90; Douglas Bruster, chaps. 5 ("The Objects of Farce: Identity and Commodity, Elizabethan to Jacobean") and 6 ("The Farce of Objects: *Othello* to *Bartholomew Fair*") in *Drama and the Market in the Age of Shakespeare* (Cambridge: Cambridge University Press, 1992), 63–80, 81–96; and Steven Mullaney, *The Place of the Stage: License, Play, and Power in Renaissance England* (Chicago: University of Chicago Press, 1988), 128–29. Mullaney suggests that Macbeth's severed head "doubles the stage it bloodies" by reminding the viewer of the

similarities between the platform stage and the scaffolding which authorities would erect for a public execution (129).

6. One of the most extensive studies of hand props in the early modern era focuses on Shakespeare. Frances Teague's *Shakespeare's Speaking Properties* (Lewisburg, PA: Bucknell University Press, 1991), to which this chapter later refers, provides valuable information on Shakespeare's use of hand props but without placing his use in the context of others' uses of hand props. See also Felix Bosonnet, *The Function of Stage Properties in Christopher Marlowe's Plays*. The Cooper Monographs on English and American Language and Literature, "Theatrical Physiognomy Series," vol. 27 (Bern: Francke, 1978).

7. Shoshana Avigal and Shlomith Rimmon-Kenan, "What Do Brook's Bricks Mean? Toward a Theory of the 'Mobility' of Objects in Theatrical Discourse," *Poetics Today* 2.3 (1981): 11–34, 12–13. Avigal and Rimmon-Kenan acknowledge this list's debt to the approach of Anne Ubersfeld. See her *Lire le Théâtre*, 4th ed. (Paris: Messidor, 1982), esp. the appendix to chapter 4, "L'objet théâtral," 177–85.

8. For the role of objects in certain dramatic constructions of the "human" in early modern England, see Margareta de Grazia, "The Ideology of Superfluous Things: *King Lear* as Period Piece," in *Subject and Object in Renaissance Culture*, ed. de Grazia, Maureen Quilligan, and Peter Stallybrass (Cambridge: Cambridge University Press, 1996), 17–42.

9. See n. 1 above.

10. Avigal and Rimmon-Kenan, "What Do Brook's Bricks Mean?" 13 ff.

11. Brownell Salomon, "Visual and Aural Signs in the Performed English Renaissance Play," *Renaissance Drama* n.s. 5 (1972): 143–69; at 160. Teague cites alternate definitions of *property* as well: "appurtenances worn or carried by actors" (David Bevington, *Action Is Eloquence* [Cambridge, MA: Harvard University Press, 1984], 35); "Any portable article of costume or furniture, used in acting a play" (Bosonnet, *Function of Stage Properties*, 10). See Teague, *Shakespeare's Speaking Objects*, 15.

12. For exceptions to this, see Lena Cowen Orlin, "The Performance of Things in *The Taming of the Shrew*," *YES* 23 (1993): 167–88; and Natasha Korda, "Household Kates: Domesticating Commodities in *The Taming of the Shrew*," *Shakespeare Quarterly* 47 (1996): 109–31.

13. "SUMMA of all the Wages in December, January, and ffebruary *anno Regni Reginæ* Elizabeth *prædictæ* Xv^to," in *Documents Relating to the Office of the Revels in the Time of Queen Elizabeth*, ed. Albert Feuillerat (Louvain: A. Uystpruyst, 1908), 175. The plays involved in the Christmas Revels that year are no longer extent, but those associated with the objects described here have been tentatively identified as *Chariclea* (*Theagenes and Chariclea*), and *A Double Mask* [*of Fish-*

erman and Fruit-wives?]. See *Annals of English Drama 975–1700,* 3rd ed., ed. Alfred Harbage, rev. S. Schoenbaum and Sylvia Stoler Wagonheim (London and New York: Routledge, 1989).

14. *Documents Relating to the Office of the Revels,* 175.
15. *Henslowe's Diary,* ed. R. A. Foakes and R. T. Rickert (Cambridge: Cambridge University Press, 1961), 319–21. On Henslowe's inventory, see Lena Cowen Orlin's essay, "Things with Little Social Life," in *Staged Properties in Early Modern English Drama,* ed. Natasha Korda and Jonathan Gil Harris (forthcoming: Cambridge University Press).
16. See, for example, Ann Rosalind Jones and Peter Stallybrass, *Renaissance Clothing and the Materials of Memory* (Cambridge: Cambridge University Press, 2001); Stallybrass's "Worn Worlds: Clothes and Identity on the Renaissance Stage," in *Subject and Object,* 289–320; and Stallybrass's "Properties in Clothes" in *Staged Properties in Early Modern English Drama,* ed. Korda and Harris.
17. *Henslowe's Diary,* 319–20.
18. Neil Carson, *A Companion to Henslowe's Diary* (Cambridge: Cambridge University Press, 1988), 53. I am indebted, for this reference, to Natasha Korda's "Household Property/Stage Property: Henslowe as Pawnbroker," *Theatre Journal* 48 (1996): 185–95.
19. Korda, "Household Property/Stage Property," 194. See also Korda's and Harris's introduction to *Staged Properties* as well as Korda's essay, "Women's Theatrical Properties" in that volume.
20. These references are quoted in Teague, *Shakespeare's Speaking Properties,* 9.
21. *A Warning for Fair Women* (London: 1598). Quoted in Andrew Gurr, *Playgoing in Shakespeare's London* (Cambridge: Cambridge University Press, 1987), appendix 2, "References to Playgoing," 213.
22. Bodkins were short, pointed instruments used, variously, for weapons, to pierce cloth, and to curl and fasten up women's hair. Perhaps in relationship to the latter usages, and to their diminutive status as weapons, bodkins were commonly represented as "feminine" objects. In the *New Arcadia,* for example, Sidney has Pamphilius attacked by a group of nine women, all of whom "held bodkins in their hands wherewith they continually pricked him." Sidney, *The Countess of Pembroke's Arcadia,* ed. Maurice Evans (Harmondsworth: Penguin Books, 1977), 334. Jonathan Gil Harris relates to me (in private communication) the relevance here of Arden's rebuke to Mosby in *Arden of Faversham,* 1.310–14. Depriving Mosby of his sword, Arden remarks "So, sirrah, you may not wear a sword. / The statute makes against artificers, / I warrant that I do. Now use your bodkin, / Your Spanish needle, and your pressing iron, / For this shall go with me." *Arden of Faversham,* ed. Martin White (New York: Norton, 1982).

23. Quoted in Gurr, *Playgoing*, 213, 218, 235.
24. Quoted in Gurr, *Playgoing*, 246. For sexual play on a fool's "bauble," see *Romeo and Juliet* 2.4.91–3, and *All's Well That Ends Well* 4.5.30–31.
25. For an extended study of the social and psychological valences of hands and manual agency in literature, see Katherine Rowe, *Dead Hands: Fictions of Agency, Renaissance to Modern* (Stanford, CA: Stanford University Press, 1999).
26. R. A. Foakes, *Illustrations of the English Stage 1580–1642* (Stanford, CA: Stanford University Press, 1985). As Foakes reminds us, we need to exercise considerable caution in evaluating visual records of the early modern stage (xvi). Illustrations published with dramatic texts do not necessarily represent the plays in question or any actual performance. Printers often used "stock" pictures to illustrate dramatic texts. So while the woodcut on the title page of Robert Wilson's *The Three Lords and Three Ladies of London* (1590), for instance, appears to represent a dramatic performance of some kind, the fact that it had appeared in a text published over two decades prior to Wilson's play, and comes from an earlier illustration still, should give us pause (164). But such representations can nonetheless provide evidence relating to "stage practices, costumes and properties" that might otherwise escape us (xvi). Even illustrations of a non-theatrical origin, once selected to accompany a play text when printed, speak to contemporary notions of the appropriate. What does it mean, we could ask, that those responsible for bringing out Wilson's play chose *this* illustration rather than another? And that readers of *The Three Lords and Three Ladies of London* had an illustration (in which one figure holds a pointing stick, apparently lecturing or directing another figure) that they might associate with the play? It is certainly not the case, as Foakes alleges, that the illustration "has no reference to Wilson's play," for the prominent position of the woodcut on the title page makes it something like the primary visual reference to and of Wilson's play as originally published. There is thus a literalism about "the" theater in Foakes's collection that detracts from his analysis of the illustrations.
27. On the historical era of Falstaff's costume in this illustration, see T. J. King, "The First Known Picture of Falstaff (1662). A Suggested Date for His Costume," *Theatre Research International* 3 (1977–78): 20–23.
28. Reproduced in Foakes, *Illustrations*, 141.
29. Thomas Rymer, "A Short View of Tragedy," in *The Critical Works of Thomas Rymer*, ed. Curt A. Zimansky (New Haven, CT: Yale University Press, 1956), 160.
30. Compare Aristotle's observation, cited in n. 1 above.
31. Cyril Tourneur, *The Revenger's Tragedy*, ed. Lawrence J. Ross (Lincoln: University of Nebraska Press, 1966).

32. Shoshana Felman, "Turning the Screw of Interpretation," *Literature and Psychoanalysis; The Question of Reading: Otherwise, Yale
French Studies* 55/56 (1977): 94–207; at 101 (emphasis in the original). The passage quoted is part of a larger argument about the relationship between the critical history of *The Turn of the Screw* and
James's text itself. On the notion of a "reading effect," see also Barbara Johnson, *The Critical Difference* (Baltimore, MD: Johns Hopkins University Press, 1985), esp. chap. 6, "Melville's Fist: The
Execution of *Billy Budd*," 79–109. Johnson describes two tendencies in criticism of *Billy Budd* and points out that the dichotomy they
fall into "is already contained within the story . . . it is obviously one
of the things the story is *about*" (85). Johnson expands on the concept further in her comments on a series of critical texts devolving
from Poe's "The Purloined Letter," where she remarks that "no
analysis . . . can intervene without transforming and repeating other
elements in the sequence, which is thus not a stable sequence, but
which nevertheless produces certain regular effects. It is the func-
tioning of this regularity, and the structure of these effects, which
will provide the basis for the present study." Barbara Johnson, "The
Frame of Reference: Poe, Lacan, Derrida," in *The Purloined Poe:
Lacan, Derrida, and Psychoanalytic Reading*, ed. John P. Muller and
William J. Richardson (Baltimore, MD: Johns Hopkins University
Press, 1988), 213–51; 213–14.
33. Teague, *Shakespeare's Speaking Properties*, Table B: "Frequency of
Properties in the Folio," 197. The data in Teague's appendixes come
as a welcome revision of more subjective estimations of hand props,
such as that of Mary Crapo Hyde—who, in *Playwriting for Elizabethans, 1600–1605* (New York: Columbia University Press, 1949),
calls "love tokens" (that is, rings, and so forth) "The most common
dramatic properties." (147). Hyde discusses properties at 146–49.
Nevertheless, I should point out that Teague's tabulations in *Speaking Properties* have been the subject of critical remarks in a review by
C. E. McGee; see *Shakespeare Quarterly* 48 (1997): 353.
34. See T. J. King, *Casting Shakespeare's Plays: London Actors and Their
Roles* (Cambridge: Cambridge University Press, 1992), chap. 2,
"Eight Playhouse Documents," 27–49.
35. I borrow this telling phrase from the work of Scott Cutler Shershow.
See, esp., his essay "'The Mouth of 'hem All:' Ben Jonson, Authorship, and the Performing Object," *Theatre Journal* 46 (1994):
187–212.
36. The most "typical" play in regard to distribution and number is
Richard III, which has close to this distribution of props but over
more lines (3,887) than is usual for a Shakespeare play.
37. In addition to Peele's *The Battle of Alcazar*—discussed later in this
chapter—one might look to Nashe's *The Unfortunate Traveller* for a

parodic salute to the ostentation of neo-chivalric display. See his extended and loving mockery of the "lists" before the Duke of Florence. Thomas Nashe, *The Unfortunate Traveller and Other Works*, ed. J. B. Steane (London: Penguin, 1985), 316–23.

38. See, for example, Jonathan Goldberg, "Rebel Letters: Postal Effects from *Richard II* to *Henry V*," *Renaissance Drama* 19 (1988): 3–28, and "Hamlet's Hand," *Shakespeare Quarterly* 39 (1988): 307–327. Even Teague's index to *Shakespeare's Speaking Properties* replicates this tendency, indexing pages dealing with documents in history plays and in tragedies but not in the comedies.

39. Lists of properties here are taken from Teague, *Shakespeare's Speaking Properties*, Appendix A, "Property Lists for Shakespeare's Plays," 157–93.

40. Daniel called these masques "Punctillos of Dreams and shows." Samuel Daniel, Epistle prefaced to *The Vision of the Twelve Goddesses*, l. 269. In *The Complete Works in Verse and Prose of Samuel Daniel*, ed. Alexander B. Grosart, 5 vols. (1885; New York: Russell & Russell, 1963), vol. 3, 196. I have made a similar observation about this shift, from verbal to visual, in "Local *Tempest*: Shakespeare and the Work of the Early Modern Playhouse," *Journal of Medieval and Renaissance Studies* 25 (1995): 33–53.

41. Andrew Gurr, *Playgoing in Shakespeare's London* (Cambridge: Cambridge University Press, 1987), 93.

42. Because it is a widely available text, Fraser and Rabkin's two-volume anthology—*Drama of the English Renaissance (Vol. I: The Tudor Period; Vol. II: The Stuart Period)*—was employed for the following plays in this survey: *The Spanish Tragedy, The Jew of Malta, A King and No King, The Roman Actor,* and *Perkin Warbeck*. For the Jonson plays (*Every Man in His Humour* [Quarto], *Sejanus, Catiline,* and *The Devil is an Ass*), the texts employed were those in *Ben Jonson*, 11 vols., ed. C. H. Herford, Percy Simpson, and Evelyn Simpson (Oxford: Clarendon Press, 1925–1950). For the Middleton plays (*A Trick to Catch the Old One, The Revenger's Tragedy,* and *Women Beware Women*), the texts used were those in *Thomas Middleton: Five Plays*, ed. Bryan Loughrey and Neil Taylor (London: Penguin Books, 1988). Peele's *The Battle of Alcazar* was edited by John Yoklavich in *The Dramatic Works of George Peele* (New Haven, CT: Yale University Press, 1961). *Woodstock* comes from the edition of A. P. Rossiter (London: Chatto and Windus, 1946). George Chapman's *All Fools* was edited by Frank Manley in the Regents Renaissance Drama series (Lincoln: University of Nebraska Press, 1968). The anonymous *Edmund Ironside* was edited by Eric Sams (Aldershot, Hants: Wildwood House, 1986). Massinger's *The Picture* comes from *The Plays and Poems of Philip Massinger*, ed. Philip Edwards and Colin Gibson, 5 vols. (Oxford: Clarendon Press, 1976), vol. 3. G. Blakemore Evans'

edition of Cartwright's works (*The Plays and Poems of William Cartwright* [Madison: University of Wisconsin Press, 1951]) was used for *The Royal Slave*. Carey's *The Tragedy of Mariam* was edited by Barry Weller and Margaret Ferguson (Berkeley: University of California Press, 1994). And *Philotas* comes from Alexander Grosart's edition of *The Complete Works in Verse and Prose of Samuel Daniel*, 5 vols., vol. 3 (1885; New York: Russell and Russell, 1963). The tabulation of total lines for each play here includes stage directions, as it is in such stage directions that many references to props occur.

43. See Andrew Gurr, *The Shakespearian Playing Companies* (Oxford: Clarendon Press, 1996), 40, 43, 47, 48, 59–60; David Bradley, *From Text to Performance in the Elizabethan Theatre: Preparing the Play for the Stage* (Cambridge: Cambridge University Press, 1992); T. J. King, *Casting Shakespeare's Plays: London Actors and Their Roles, 1590–1642* (Cambridge: Cambridge University Press, 1992); and Scott McMillin, *The Elizabethan Theatre and the "Book of Sir Thomas More"* (Ithaca, NY: Cornell University Press, 1987).

44. See Gurr, *The Shakespearian Playing Companies*, 59–60.

45. Gurr, *The Shakespearian Playing Companies*, 131, 150.

46. Quotation from *Ben Jonson*, vol. 9, 240. Ian Donaldson aptly characterizes the drama's reception when he refers to *Catiline* as "disastrously unsuccessful." Donaldson, *Jonson's Magic Houses: Essays in Interpretation* (Oxford: Clarendon Press, 1997), 42.

47. *Ben Jonson*, vol. 5, 432.

48. Jonas Barish, *The Antitheatrical Prejudice* (Berkeley: University of California Press, 1981), 135.

49. *Doctor Faustus* from the A-text in *Doctor Faustus*, ed. David Bevington and Eric Rasmussen (Manchester, England: Manchester University Press, 1992), 5.1.91–92. On the politics of the poetic blazon, see Nancy J. Vickers, "Diana Described: Scattered Woman and Scattered Rhyme," *Critical Inquiry* 8 (1981): 265–79, who explores Petrarch's "legacy of fragmentation" and its relationship to "the development of a code of beauty, a code that causes us to view the fetishized body as a norm" (277).

50. Bruster, *Drama and the Market in the Age of Shakespeare*, 64–65.

CHAPTER 5

1. See Gordon Williams, *A Dictionary of Sexual Language and Imagery in Shakespearean and Stuart Literature*, 3 vols. (London: Athlone Press, 1994).

2. See James Holstun, "'Will you rent our ancient love asunder?': Lesbian Elegy in Donne, Marvell, and Milton," *ELH* 54 (1987): 835–67; Janel Mueller, "Troping Utopia: Donne's Brief for Lesbianism," in *Sexuality and Gender in Early Modern Europe: Institutions,*

Texts, Images, ed. James Grantham Turner (Cambridge: Cambridge University Press, 1993), 182–207; Paula Blank, "Comparing Sappho to Philaenis: John Donne's 'Homopoetics,'" *PMLA* 110.3 (1995): 358–68; Elizabeth D. Harvey, *Ventriloquized Voices: Feminist Theory and English Renaissance Texts* (New York: Routledge, 1992), 116–39; Nadia Rigaud, "L'homosexualité féminine dans *A Mad Couple Well Match'd* (1639) de Richard Brome," *Bulletin de la société d'études anglo-américaines des XVII* et *XVIII* siècles 20 (1985): 23–36; and Harriette Andreadis, "The Sapphic-Platonics of Katherine Philips, 1632–1664," *Signs* 15 (1989): 34–60, and *Sappho in Early Modern England: Female Same-Sex Literary Erotics 1550–1714* (Chicago: University of Chicago Press, 2001). For further bibliography on female-female eroticism in the literature and culture of the early modern era, see Valerie Traub, *The Renaissance of Lesbianism in Early Modern England* (Cambridge: Cambridge University Press, 2002). I am extremely grateful to Traub for sharing a copy of this work with me prior to its publication; I regret not being able to acknowledge its argument more fully in the following pages.

3. Laurie Shannon, *Sovereign Amity: Figures of Friendship in Shakespearean Contexts* (Chicago: University of Chicago Press, 2001).
4. The phrase "anxieties of anachronism" is that of Claude J. Summers. For this reference I am indebted to Winfried Schleiner, "'That Matter Which Ought Not to Be Heard of': Homophobic Slurs in Renaissance Cultural Politics," *Journal of Homosexuality* 26.4 (1994): 41–75.
5. We can see this most clearly, perhaps, in relationship to a work of history. Here I am referring to Rudolph Bell's extended review of *Immodest Acts*—Judith Brown's history of Benedetta Carlini, a "lesbian" nun. Bell demonstrates that an affirmative tendency in Brown's account not only obscures Carlini's particularities but distorts the authorities' responses to Carlini. Brown, for instance, imagines a melodramatic scene of interrogation in which the testimony of Carlini's lover both made the scribe's hand shake and "must have stunned" the officials in attendance—officials who "entirely lacked either an intellectual or an imaginative schema that would incorporate the kind of behavior she described." "To anyone's knowledge," Brown asserts, "there had been nothing like it in any Italian convents" (qtd. in Bell, 497). In contrast, Bell, having reviewed the archival materials that Brown consulted, is struck by "how lightly the visiting friars treated the entire matter"; he points out that Brown herself quotes, only to lose sight of, the recommendation of (Saint) Charles Borromeo that a woman fornicating with another woman should do two years' penance (497, 499). See Judith C. Brown, *Immodest Acts: The Life of a Lesbian Nun in Renaissance Italy* (New York: Oxford University Press, 1985); and

Rudolph M. Bell and Judith C. Brown. "Renaissance Sexuality and the Florentine Archives: An Exchange," *Renaissance Quarterly* 40 (1987): 485–511. It should be noted as well that a common motif in pornography of the Italian Renaissance involved the sexual license of convents and other religious houses—a recurrent theme in Western pornography at least through Diderot's *La religieuse*. See David O. Frantz, *Festum Voluptatis: A Study of Renaissance Erotica* (Columbus: Ohio State University Press, 1989), 63–67. In one instance Aretino has a nun penetrate another nun with a glass dildo (71). Brown's exciting historical narrative depends on alternately exaggerating and downplaying the evidence at hand. But it also depends on refashioning historical awareness of female homosexuality to create ignorant authority figures who, as the straight men of this scenario, are stunned by it. As Bell's review suggests, overemphasizing the affirmative aspects of the erotic can produce an incomplete picture of the past.

6. Andreadis, *Sappho in Early Modern England,* 101.
7. Moore's remarks come in a review of the film *She Must Be Seeing Things* (1987) and discussion of the controversy it occasioned. Suzanne Moore, "Missionary Sex," *New Statesman & Society* 16 (September 1988): 47.
8. See B. Ruby Rich's still-relevant review essay on these debates: "Feminism and Sexuality in the 1980s," *Feminist Studies* 12 (1986): 525–61. Likewise Cherríe Moraga inveighs against a "transcendent" definition of sexuality that underwrote a "'perfect' vision of egalitarian sexuality, where we could magically leap over our heterosexist conditioning into mutually orgasmic, struggle-free, trouble-free sex. . . . Who can really live up to such an ideal?" Amber Hollibaugh and Cherríe Moraga, "'What We're Rollin Around in Bed With': Sexual Silences in Feminism: A Conversation toward Ending Them," *Heresies* 12 (1981): 58–62; at 58.
9. Compare the "for-others" eroticism of sex among women in much modern pornography, where, as Linda Williams points out, such sex "is not presented *as* lesbian." Williams, *Hard Core: Power, Pleasure, and the "Frenzy of the Visible"* (Berkeley: University of California Press, 1989), 256. In an early modern context, we could bring to bear Barbara Hodgdon's remark on a particular moment in *The Taming of the Shrew.* Hodgdon suggests that at one point *Shrew* "evokes the classic pornographic repertoire": "The image of Bianca tied and bound, at the mercy of Kate the torturer (2.1), hints at a mild 'sadie-max' lesbian fantasy." Hodgdon, "Katherina Bound; or, Play(K)ating the Strictures of Everyday Life," *PMLA* 107 (1992): 538–53, at 539. Is there, as Hodgdon holds, an erotic charge to the spectacle of a female character with another female character she has bound? If so, was this charge there for Shakespeare's audiences? Certainly when

Kate enters with Bianca and the Widow "As prisoners to her womanly persuasion" at this farce's end (5.2.120), we are asked to think about the drama's economy of pleasure and how it comes to depend on these scenes of female-female bondage.

10. Nadia Rigaud, "L'homosexualité féminine," 24.

11. Erica Rand, "Diderot and Girl-Group Erotics," *Eighteenth-Century Studies* 25 (1992): 495–516, at 496. See also Lisa L. Moore, *Dangerous Intimacies: Toward a Sapphic History of the British Novel* (Durham, NC: Duke University Press, 1997).

12. Mueller, "Troping Utopia," 187, 192.

13. Donne from *The Poems of John Donne*, ed. Herbert J. Grierson, 2 vols. (Oxford: Oxford University Press, 1912).

14. Arthur F. Marotti, *John Donne, Coterie Poet* (Madison: University of Wisconsin Press, 1986), xi.

15. For the history of the Sappho tradition in the English Renaissance, see Mueller, "Troping Utopia," 184–91; and Andreadis, *Sappho in Early Modern England*. Joan E. DeJean's study confines mention of Donne's poem to a footnote. However, she says that the French "obsession with Sappho" might never "have been initiated if the *Heroides* had not suddenly succeeded in capturing the collective literary imagination of the age that prepared the way for French neoclassicism." DeJean, *Fictions of Sappho, 1546–1937* (Chicago: University of Chicago Press, 1989), 42.

16. For the attribution of this otherwise anonymous masque to Thomas Pestell, see Philip Finkelpearl, "The Authorship of the Anonymous 'Coleorton Masque' of 1618," *Notes and Queries* 238 (1993): 224–26. Among the evidence that Finkelpearl advances in his persuasive case is the fact that Pestell's poetry is characterized by feminist themes and positions like that of the Coleorton masque and that Pestell was closely involved in the Beaumont circle.

17. David Norbrook, *Poetry and Politics in the English Renaissance* (London: Routledge, 1984), 250.

18. Rudolf Brotanek, *Die Englischen Maskenspiele* (Wien: Braumüller, 1902), 333.

19. Brotanek, *Die Englischen Maskenspiele*, 334.

20. See Brotanek, *Die Englischen Maskenspiele:* "A maske presented on Candlemas nighte at Coleoverton, by the earle of Esex, the lorde Willobie, Sr Tho. Beaumont, Sr Walter Devereux, Mr Christopher Denham, Mr Walter T. . . .., Mrs Ann R. . . .., M^{rs} An Burnebye, Mrs Susann Burnebye, Mrs Elizabeth Beaumont, Mrs Katherine Beaumont, Mrs Susann Pilkingetun, to Sr William Semer and the ladie Francis Semer" (328).

21. See Morris Palmer Tilley, *A Dictionary of the Proverbs in England in the Sixteenth and Seventeenth Centuries* (Ann Arbor: University of Michigan Press, 1950), B166; and R. W. Dent, *Proverbial Language*

in English Drama Exclusive of Shakespeare, 1495–1616 (Berkeley: University of California Press, 1984), B177.

22. George Sandys, trans., *Ovid's Metamorphosis: Englished, Mythologized, and Represented in Figures,* ed. Karl K. Hulley and Stanley T. Vandersall (Lincoln: University of Nebraska Press, 1970).

23. Laurens J. Mills, *One Soul in Bodies Twain: Friendship in Tudor Literature and Stuart Drama* (Bloomington, IN: Principia Press, 1937), 239, 430 n.254.

24. See T(homas) Washington, trans., *The Navigations, Peregrinations and Voyages, Made into Turkey by Nicholas Nicholay* (London: 1585), 60; and [Busbequius, Augerius Gislenius], *The Life and Letters of Obgier Ghiselin de Busbecq,* trans. Charles Thornton Forster and F. H. Blackburne Daniell, 2 vols. (London: C. Kegan Paul, 1881), vol. 1, 231. As Winfried Schleiner points out, Robert Burton owned a copy of the Turkish letters and used material from it on same-sex relationships for the *Anatomy of Melancholy.* Schleiner, "Burton's Use of *praeteritio* in Discussing Same-Sex Relationships," in *Renaissance Discourses of Desire,* ed. Claude J. Summers and Ted-Larry Pebworth (Columbia: University of Missouri Press, 1993), 159–78, at 164. I am indebted to Mario DiGangi and to Valerie Traub for bringing de Nicolay's text to my attention.

25. Myra Reynolds, *The Learned Lady in England, 1650–1760* (Boston: Houghton, 1920), 258.

26. Carroll Smith-Rosenberg, "The Female World of Love and Ritual" in her *Disorderly Conduct: Visions of Gender in Victorian America* (Oxford: Oxford University Press, 1985), 53–76.

27. James T. Henke, *Gutter Life and Language in the Early "Street" Literature of England: A Glossary of Terms and Topics, Chiefly of the Sixteenth and Seventeenth Centuries* (West Cornwall, CT: Locust Hill, 1988).

28. *Erotopolis: The Present State of Betty-Land* (London, 1684), 148–49.

29. Andrew Marvell, *The Poems and Letters of Andrew Marvell,* ed. H. M. Margoliouth, 2 vols. (Oxford: Clarendon Press, 1927), 200.

30. On the potentially threatening eroticism of this celebrated lyric, see Bruster, *Quoting Shakespeare: Form and Culture in Early Modern Drama* (Lincoln: University of Nebraska Press, 2000), 52–87.

31. These "vices" are justified with the assumption that nothing that did not change the status of virginity would threaten their salvation. Compare Traub's reading of Heywood's *The Golden Age,* where the Nymphs' otherwise erotic sporting among themselves seems chaste, outside the circuit of sexual reproduction that seems to demarcate the potentially sinful. Traub, "The (In)Significance of 'Lesbian' Desire in Early Modern England," in *Erotic Politics: Desire on the Renaissance Stage,* ed. Susan Zimmerman (New York: Routledge, 1992), 150–69; 159–61.

32. Traub, "(In)Significance," 158.
33. Traub, "[In]Significance," 158–63.
34. G. E. Briscoe Eyre and Charles Robert Rivington, eds., *A Transcript of the Registers of the Worshipful Company of Stationers from 1640–1708 A.D.*, 3 vols. (London, 1913), vol. 2: 271.
35. Traub, "[In]Significance," 165.
36. Traub, *Desire and Anxiety: Circulations of Sexuality in Shakespearean Drama* (London: Routledge, 1992), 107.
37. Compare Mueller: "'Mutuall feeling' will register in retrospect as a richly multivalent pun that signalizes the acts as well as the emotions of lesbian erotics." "Troping Utopia," 197.
38. However authorial, a remarkable example of the male gaze fantasizing spectacles of female-female eroticism occurs in Richard Brome's drama *The Queen's Exchange* (1631). The sequence in question concerns a conversation between a king and his favorite, in which the king has been comparing pictures of their beloveds. After contrasting the pictures, the king returns both to Theodrick and says: "Phew, This is all too sweet for mortal sense, / Here, take't again, and keep mine for me with it. / Lay 'em together, th'one may mend the other." To which Theodrick responds: "I have known women oft marry one another. / Their Pictures may perhaps have greater virtue" (2.1, sig. C2). Brome, *The Queenes Exchange* (London, 1657). See Rigaud, "L'homosexualité féminine," 24.
39. Tessa Watt, *Cheap Print and Popular Piety, 1550–1640* (Cambridge: Cambridge University Press, 1991), 119.
40. The story of Callisto was not unfamiliar to writers in early modern England: Spenser and Milton, among others, mention her myth. Prince Charles was offered Titian's *Diana and Callisto* as part of Philip IV's wooing in the Spanish Match. See Arthur MacGregor, ed. *The Late King's Goods: Collections, Possessions and Patronage of Charles I in the Light of the Commonwealth Sale Inventories* (London: Oxford University Press, 1989), 210. And for a list of the many representations of Callisto in Europe from the early sixteenth through the eighteenth centuries, see A. Pliger, *Barockthemen*, 3 vols. (Budapest: Kiado, 1974), vol. 2: 145–47.
41. Traub, "(In)Significance," 159–61.
42. Thomas Middleton and Thomas Dekker, *The Roaring Girl*, ed. Paul A. Mulholland (Manchester, England: Manchester University Press, 1987). A typographical error (?) in the edition quoted reads "make him to as much."
43. Lady Margaret Hungerford was the daughter of William Hollidaie (or Haliday), an alderman and Lord Mayor of London; sometime after February 26, 1619/20, she married Sir Edward Hungerford (1596–1648), eventually a parliamentary commander, surviving him until 1672.

44. Henry Neville (?), *Newes from the New Exchange, Or the Common-wealth of Ladies, Drawn to the Life, in their Several Characters and Concernments* (London: 1649/50), 7.

45. See Henke, *Gutter Life,* 6–7, 294.

46. It is this friction that the term "tribade" (ultimately from the Greek for "to rub") seems most often meant to explain in Renaissance usage, this despite several well-known associations of "tribade" with penetration of another woman by an unnaturally enlarged clitoris or dildo. See Stephen Greenblatt, *Shakespearean Negotiations: The Circulation of Social Energy in Renaissance England* (Berkeley: University of California Press, 1988), 74; Traub, "(In)Significance," 153–54.

47. See Marcus Tullius Cicero, "De Provinciis Consularibus," in *The Speeches,* 2 vols., trans. R. Gardner. Loeb Classical Library (Cambridge, MA: Harvard University Press, 1958), vol. 2: 523–610, 4.9; and compare Jonson in *Epicoene,* where Morose laments that "She is my regent already! I have married a Penthesilea, a Semiramis, sold my liberty to a distaff!" (3.4.51–52). Ben Jonson, *Epicoene: or, The Silent Woman,* ed. R. V. Holdsworth (New York: Norton, 1990). Shakespeare could have been familiar with the Semiramis legends from any of a number of sources. The fullest narrative is that of Diodorus, who chronicles her rise to power, military exploits, and architectural achievements. Her private life, however, would be remembered more than her political achievements—perhaps a way of discrediting or repressing the latter. Diodorus tells us two things that later writers would repeat. First, when called on by her husband to come to him at the site of a siege, she invented a special costume: "since she was about to set out upon a journey of many days, she devised a garb which made it impossible to distinguish whether the wearer of it was a man or a woman"; this invention, which Diodorus tells us was later taken up by the Medes and the Persians, prefigures her assumption of agency typically reserved for men. For, after becoming queen, "she passed a long time and enjoyed to the full every device that contributed to luxury; she was unwilling, however, to contract a lawful marriage, being afraid that she might be deprived of her supreme position, but choosing out the most handsome of the soldiers she consorted with them and then made away with all who had lain with her." Diodorus, *Diodorus of Sicily,* Loeb Classical Library, 12 vols. (Cambridge, MA: Harvard University Press, 1933–67), at 2.6.6 and 2.13.4. Pliny, Valerius Maximus, and Justinus also added elements to the myth, the last contributing incest to Semiramis's story in his *Historiae Philippice,* 1. 1–2—a detail that many later accounts would emphasize. Her military, administrative, and civic achievements thus were subordinated to her image as an insatiable, sexually aggressive cross-dresser with desires that included incest and as a killer of her

lovers. Semiramis was a popular figure in the late sixteenth and early seventeenth centuries, then again during the Enlightenment. Cristóbal de Virués, the sixteenth-century Spanish playwright, composed the first dramatic treatment of the Semiramis legend in *La gran Semíramis*, written between 1579 and 1590. (It is probably more than coincidence that Virués's plays, all written during a time of political tensions with Elizabeth's England, feature strong female figures like Semiramis.) Lope de Vega and Calderón also penned plays on Semiramis; Lope's treatment is lost, but Calderón's *Hija del aire, Parte I* and *Parte II*, survives. On these dramas see Cecilia Vennard Sargent, *A Study of the Dramatic Works of Cristóbal de Virués* (New York: Instituto de las Españas, 1930). On the myth of Semiramis generally, see François Lenormant, *La legende de Semiramis—mythologie comparative* (Bruxelles: 1873), and Anna Maria G. Capomacchia, *Semiramis: Una femminilita ribaltata*, Storia delle Religioni 4 (Roma: Bretschneider, 1986).

48. Eric Partridge, *A Dictionary of Slang and Unconventional English*, rev. ed. (New York: Macmillan, 1967).

49. On Howard's possible influence on *The Witch* (1612), see Anne Lancashire, "*The Witch*: Stage Flop or Political Mistake?" in "*Accompaninge the players*": *Essays Celebrating Thomas Middleton, 1580–1980*, ed. Kenneth Friedenreich (New York: AMS, 1983), 161–81.

50. See Thomas Bayly Howell, ed., *A Complete Collection of State Trials and Proceedings for High Treason and Other Crimes and Misdemeanors from the Earliest Period to the Year 1783*, 21 vols (London: T.C. Hansard, 1816), vol. 2, 802–3.

51. Anthony Weldon, *The Court and Character of King James* (London: 1650), 79–81.

52. For a strongly topical reading of *The Changeling*, see A. A. Bromham and Zara Bruzzi, *The Changeling and the Years of Crisis, 1619–1624: A Hieroglyph of Britain* (London: Pinter Publishers, 1990).

53. See Eric Partridge, *Shakespeare's Bawdy: A Literary and Psychological Essay and a Comprehensive Glossary*, rev. 3rd ed. (London: Routledge, 1968), and James T. Henke, *Courtesans and Cuckolds: A Glossary of Renaissance Dramatic Bawdy (Exclusive of Shakespeare)* (New York: Garland, 1979).

54. Marjorie Garber, *Symptoms of Culture* (New York: Routledge, 1998), 217–35.

CHAPTER 6

1. Joseph Burckhardt, *The Civilization of the Renaissance in Italy*, trans. S. G. C. Middlemore (London: Harmondsworth: Penguin, 1990). On this work's influence, as well as on the concept of "the Renaissance" generally, see William Kerrigan and Gordon Braden, *The Idea*

of the Renaissance (Baltimore, MD: Johns Hopkins University Press, 1989).

2. Jules Michelet, *Histoire de France jusqu'au XVIe siècle*, 17 vols. (Paris: 1852–67). See Wallace Ferguson, *The Renaissance in Historical Thought: Five Centuries of Interpretation* (Cambridge, MA.: Houghton Mifflin Co., 1948), 173 ff.

3. Hippolyte Taine, *Histoire de la littérature anglaise*, 5 vols. (Paris: 1863–64); J. J. Jusserand, *Histoire littéraire du peuple anglaise* (Paris: 1894, 1904).

4. Mandell Creighton, *The Early Renaissance in England*. Rede Lecture (Cambridge: Cambridge University Press, 1895).

5. H. E. Rollins, ed., *Old English Ballads, 1553–1625, Chiefly from Manuscripts* (Cambridge: Cambridge University Press, 1920).

6. D. C. Allen, "Symbolic Color in the Literature of the English Renaissance," *Philological Quarterly* 15 (1936): 81–92; at 81.

7. I have discussed twentieth-century constructions of the English Renaissance in "A Renaissance of Quotation," chapter 6 of *Quoting Shakespeare: Form and Culture in Early Modern Drama* (Lincoln: University of Nebraska Press, 2000), 171–208. Part of this section summarizes material examined at more length there.

8. See Thornton Graves, "Notes on the Elizabethan Theaters," *Studies in Philology* 17 (1920): 170–82; "Recent Literature of the English Renaissance," *Studies in Philology* 19 (1922): 249–91; and "Some References to Elizabethan Theaters," *Studies in Philology* 19 (1922): 317–27.

9. See Louis B. Wright, "Variety-show Clownery on the Pre-restoration Stage," *Anglia* 52 (1928): 51–68; "Handbook Learning of the Renaissance Middle Class," *Studies in Philology* 28 (1931): 58–86; "The Reading of Renaissance English Women," *Studies in Philology* 28 (1931): 671–88.

10. Louis B. Wright, *Middle-Class Culture in Elizabethan England* (Chapel Hill: University of North Carolina Press, 1935), viii.

11. J. William Hebel and Hoyt H. Hudson, eds., *Poetry of the English Renaissance 1509–1660* (New York: F. S. Crofts & Co., 1929); Martha Hale Shackford, *Plutarch in Renaissance England* (N.p.: Wellesley? MA: 1929); Lily B. Campbell, "Theories of Revenge in Renaissance England," *Modern Philology* 28 (1930/31): 281–96; Israel Baroway, "The Bible as Poetry in the English Renaissance," *JEGP* 32 (1933): 447–80; and H. O. White, *Plagiarism and Imitation during the English Renaissance* (Cambridge, MA.: Harvard University Press, 1935).

12. See Michael D. Bristol, *Shakespeare's America, America's Shakespeare* (London: Routledge, 1990).

13. Joan Shelly Rubin, *The Making of Middlebrow Culture* (Chapel Hill: University of North Carolina Press, 1992).

14. See Hugh Grady, *The Modernist Shakespeare: Critical Texts in a Material World* (Oxford: Clarendon Press 1991); and Richard Halpern, *Shakespeare Among the Moderns* (Ithaca, NY: Cornell University Press, 1997).
15. William Shakespeare, *Julius Caesar* with Maxwell Anderson's *Elizabeth the Queen* (New York: Noble and Noble, 1935), 291–93.
16. F. O. Matthiessen, *American Renaissance: Art and Expression in the Age of Emerson and Whitman* (London: Oxford University Press, 1941).
17. See Charlene Avallone, "What American Renaissance? The Gendered Genealogy of a Critical Discourse," *PMLA* 112 (1997): 1102–20. On the decline of "Renaissance" as a period label in German scholarship, see Eckhard Bernstein, "What Happened to the Renaissance in the German Academy: A Report on German 'Renaissance' Institutes," *Renaissance Quarterly* 52.4 (1999): 1118–31.
18. F. O. Matthiessen, *Translation: An Elizabethan Art* (Cambridge, MA: Harvard University Press, 1931).
19. This thesis was published as *The Triumph of Realism in Elizabethan Drama, 1558–1612* (Princeton, NJ: Princeton University Press, 1928).
20. Heather Dubrow, "The Term *Early Modern*," *PMLA* 109 (1994): 1025–26; at 1026. On "early modern," see also Randolph Starns's forthcoming essay, "The Early Modern Muddle," *JEMH* 6.3 (August 2002).
21. Margreta de Grazia, "World Pictures, Modern Periods, and the Early Stage," in *A New History of Early English Drama*, ed. John D. Cox and David Scott Kastan (New York: Columbia University Press), 7–21; 10–11.
22. de Grazia, "World Pictures," 12.
23. Fernand Braudel, "Histoire et sciences sociales: la longue durée," *Annales Economies Sociétés Civilisations* 13.4 (1958): 725–53.
24. Braudel, *La Méditerranée et le Monde Méditerranéen à l'époque de Phillippe II* (Paris: Colin, 1949); *Civilization and Capitalism, 15th–18th Century*, 3 vols. (New York: Harper and Row, 1981–84).
25. Quoted in Peter Burke, *The French Historical Revolution: The 'Annales' School 1929–89* (Stanford, CA: Stanford University Press, 1990), 50.
26. Lawrence Stone, "Social Mobility in England, 1500–1700," *Past and Present* 33 (1966): 16–55; Alan Everitt, "Social Mobility in Early Modern England," *Past and Present* 33 (1966): 56–73.
27. Lawrence Stone, "The Educational Revolution in England, 1560–1640," *Past and Present* 28 (1964): 41–80.
28. Everitt, "Social Mobility in Early Modern England," 72–73.
29. Stone, "Social Mobility in England," 17.
30. Keith Thomas, "Rule and Misrule in the Schools of Early Modern England" (Reading: University of Reading, 1976); Joan Thirsk, *Eco-*

nomic Policy and Projects: The Development of a Consumer Society in Early Modern England (Oxford: Clarendon Press, 1978); J. A. Sharpe, *Defamation and Slander in Early Modern England: The Church Courts at York* (York: Bothwick Institute of Historical Research, University of York, 1980).

31. Annabel Patterson, *Censorship and Interpretation: The Conditions of Writing and Reading in Early Modern England* (Madison: University of Wisconsin Press, 1984).

32. Barbara K. Lewalski, *Protestant Poetics and the Seventeenth-Century Lyric* (Princeton, NJ: Princeton University Press, 1979).

33. Kerrigan and Braden, *The Idea of the Renaissance*, x.

34. Patterson, *Censorship and Interpretation*, 3.

35. Stephen Greenblatt, *Renaissance Self-Fashioning: From More to Shakespeare* (Chicago: University of Chicago Press, 1980), and *Representing the English Renaissance* (Berkeley: University of California Press, 1988); and Jean Howard, "The New Historicism in Renaissance Studies," *English Literary Renaissance* 16 (1986): 13–43.

36. Greenblatt, *Learning to Curse: Essays in Early Modern Culture* (London: Routledge, 1990); and Howard, "Crossdressing, the Theater, and Gender Struggle in Early Modern England," *Shakespeare Quarterly* 39 (1988): 418–40.

37. Howard, *The Stage and Social Struggle in Early Modern England* (London: Routledge, 1994).

38. Leah Marcus, "Renaissance/Early Modern Studies," in *Redrawing the Boundaries: The Transformation of English and American Literary Studies*, ed. Stephen Greenblatt and Giles Gunn (New York: MLA, 1992), 41–63; at 41.

39. Dolan's original essay was titled "Taking the Pencil Out of God's Hand: Art, Nature, and the Face-painting Debate in Early Modern England," *PMLA* 108 (1993): 224–39. Her essay was responded to by Crystal Dowling in a "Reply" published the next year: *PMLA* 109 (1994): 119–20.

40. Dowling, "Reply," 119.

41. Dolan, "Reply" (to Crystal Dowling), 120.

42. Heather Dubrow, "The Term *Early Modern*," *PMLA* 109 (1994): 1025–26.

43. Frances Dolan, "Reply" (to Heather Dubrow), *PMLA* 109 (1994): 1026–27.

44. Michael Dobson, "Cold Front in Arden," *London Review of Books* 18 (1996): 24–25; at 24.

45. Marjorie Garber, "Roman Numerals," in *Symptoms of Culture* (New York: Routledge, 1998), 179–97; at 181.

46. See, for only one recent work of medievalist criticism that calls into question common assumptions about periodicity and "modern" forces, Patricia Clare Ingham, *Sovereign Fantasies: Arthurian Romance*

and the Making of Britain (Philadelphia: University of Pennsylvania Press, 2001).

47. Albert C. Baugh and Thomas Cable, *A History of the English Language*, 3rd ed. (Englewood Cliffs, NJ: Prentice-Hall, 1978), 250.

48. Arvid Gabrielson, "Early Modern English I/r (+ cons.)," *Studia Neophilologica* 3.1–2 (1930): 1–10; E. J. Dobson, "Early Modern Standard English," *Transactions of the Philological Society* (1955): 25–54.

CHAPTER 7

1. On what I am calling the "thickness" of early modern texts, see Linda Woodbridge, "Patchwork: Piecing the Early Modern Mind in England's First Century of Print Culture," *English Literary Renaissance* 23 (1993): 5–45. I have discussed this phenomenon at more length in *Quoting Shakespeare: Form and Culture in Early Modern Drama* (Lincoln: University of Nebraska Press, 2000); see, esp., 13–51, 203–12.

2. On "cultural historicism," see Albert H. Tricomi, *Reading Tudor-Stuart Texts Through Cultural Historicism* (Gainesville: University Press of Florida, 1996).

3. Heather Dubrow, *A Happier Eden: The Politics of Marriage in the Stuart Epithalamium* (Ithaca, NY: Cornell University Press, 1990), 266.

4. Robert S. Miola, "Othello *Furens*," *Shakespeare Quarterly* 41 (1990): 49–64; 49. On the changing face of source study, see also Miola's "Shakespeare and His Sources: Observations on the Critical History of *Julius Caesar*," *Shakespeare Survey* 40 (1988): 69–76.

5. See Andrew Gurr, "Intertextuality at Windsor," *Shakespeare Quarterly* 38 (1987): 189–200; Claire McEachern, "Fathering Himself: A Source Study of Shakespeare's Feminism," *Shakespeare Quarterly* 39 (1988): 269–90; G. Harold Metz, ed., *Sources of Four Plays Ascribed to Shakespeare: The Reign of King Edward III, Sir Thomas More, The History of Cardenio, The Two Noble Kinsmen* (Columbia: University of Missouri Press, 1989); Robert S. Miola, *Shakespeare and Classical Tragedy: The Influence of Seneca* (Oxford: Oxford University Press, 1992) and *Shakespeare and Classical Comedy: The Influence of Plautus and Terence* (Oxford: Oxford University Press, 1994); Eric S. Mallin, *Inscribing the Time: Shakespeare and the End of Elizabethan England* (Berkeley: University of California Press, 1995); Frank Whigham, *Seizures of the Will in Early Modern English Drama* (Cambridge: Cambridge University Press, 1996), esp. 67–74; Heather James, *Shakespeare's Troy: Drama, Politics, and the Translation of Empire* (Cambridge: Cambridge University Press, 1997); Stephen J. Lynch, *Shakespearean Intertextuality: Studies in Selected Sources and*

Plays (Westport, CT: Greenwood Press,1998); Richard Knowles, "Cordelia's Return," *Shakespeare Quarterly* 50 (1999): 33–50; Grace Tiffany, "Shakespeare's Dionysian Prince: Drama, Politics, and the 'Athenian' History Play," *Renaissance Quarterly* 52 (1999): 366–83; John Klause, "New Sources for *King John:* The Writings of Robert Southwell," *Studies in Philology* 98 (2001): 401–27.

6. Gurr, "Intertextuality at Windsor," 189.

7. See Raymond Williams, *Keywords: A Vocabulary of Culture and Society,* rev. ed. (New York: Oxford University Press, 1985), 11–13.

8. *The Norton Shakespeare,* ed. Stephen Greenblatt (New York: Norton, 1997), 46–49.

9. *The Norton Shakespeare,* 46.

10. I have discussed the "old historicism" more extensively in "New Light on the Old Historicism: Shakespeare and the Forms of Historicist Criticism," in a special issue, "Shakespeare and History," *Literature and History,* third series, 5.1 (1996): 1–18; see, esp., 2–6.

11. Barry Gaines, review of John Wilders, ed., *Antony and Cleopatra, Shakespeare Quarterly* 50 (1999): 207.

12. G. W. Pigman III, "Neo-Latin Imitation of the Latin Classics," in *Latin Poetry and the Classical Tradition: Essays in Medieval and Renaissance Literature,* ed. Peter Goodman and Oswyn Murray, Oxford-Warburg Studies (Oxford: Clarendon Press, 1990), 199–210; 199, 200.

13. For a cogent articulation of this position, see the anonymous reader cited in Annabel Patterson, *Hermogenes and the Renaissance: Seven Ideas of Style* (Princeton, NJ: Princeton University Press, 1970), vi.

14. Laurence Lerner, "Ovid and the Elizabethans," in *Ovid Renewed: Ovidian Influences on Literature and Art from the Middle Ages to the Twentieth Century,* ed. Charles Martindale (Cambridge: Cambridge University Press, 1988), 121–35; 122.

15. On these structures, see A. Kent Hieatt, *Short Time's Endless Monument: The Symbolism of the Numbers in Spenser's "Epithalamion"* (New York: Columbia University Press, 1960); and Alastair Fowler, *Triumphal Forms: Structural Patterns in Elizabethan Poetry* (Cambridge: Cambridge University Press, 1970).

16. See, for example, J. J. M. Tobin, "Texture as Well as Structure: More Sources for *The Riverside Shakespeare,*" in *In the Company of Shakespeare: Essays on English Renaissance Literature in Honor of G. Blakemore Evans,* ed. Thomas Moisan and Douglas Bruster (Madison, NJ: Fairleigh Dickinson University Press, 2002), 97–110; "*Hamlet* and *Christ's Teares over Jerusalem,*" *The Aligarh Journal of English Studies* 6 (1981): 158–67; "Nashe and *The Two Gentlemen of Verona,*" *Notes and Queries* 28 (1981): 122–23; "*Macbeth* and *Christ's Teares over Jerusalem,*" *The Aligarh Journal of English Studies* 7 (1982): 72–78; "Nashe and *Richard II,*" *American Notes & Queries* 24 (1985): 5–7;

and "Nashe and Shakespeare: Some Further Borrowings," *Notes and Queries* 39 (1992): 309–20.

17. Thomas Nashe, *The Unfortunate Traveller,* in McKerrow, ed. *Works,* vol. 2, 217, 227.

18. The reference to "an hour-glass" here connects this Prologue to the figure of Time in *The Winter's Tale;* see 4.1.16 in that play for Time's reference to his "glass."

19. Samuel Johnson, from his 1765 *Works of Shakespeare,* quoted in *Shakespeare: "Henry V,"* ed. Michael Quinn (London: Macmillan, 1969), 34.

20. Anthony Brennan, "That Within Which Passes Show: The Function of the Chorus in *Henry V,*" *Philological Quarterly* 58 (1979): 40–52; 42. The opposite point of view was taken by Peter Alexander, who in *Shakespeare's Life and Art* (London: James Nisbit and Co., 1939) called the play "a thing of rags and patches, held together by the Choruses" (128).

21. See Douglas Bruster, "Teaching the Tragi-comedy of *Romeo and Juliet,*" in *Approaches to Teaching Shakespeare's "Romeo and Juliet,"* ed. Maurice Hunt (New York: MLA, 2000), 59–68; at 60.

22. A minor piece of supporting evidence can be taken from Gary Taylor's argument about the play's indebtedness to Nashe—and perhaps to *The Unfortunate Traveller*—for one of its unusual words. See Taylor, "Shakespeare's Leno: *Henry V,* IV.v.14.," *Notes and Queries* n.s. 26 (1979): 117–18.

23. Brennan, "That Within Which Passes Show," 47.

24. Andrew Gurr, ed., *King Henry V* (Cambridge: Cambridge University Press, 1992), 6–16; 15.

25. On the epic tenor of the play—and, especially, of the Chorus—see Albert H. Tolman, "The Epic Character of *Henry V,*" *Modern Language Notes* 34 (1919): 7–16; John Dover Wilson, ed., *King Henry V,* The New Cambridge Shakespeare (Cambridge: Cambridge University Press, 1947); and Edward I. Berry, "'True Things and Mock-'ries': Epic and History in *Henry V,*" *JEGP* 78 (1979): 1–16.

26. See, for example, Alwin Thaler, *Shakespeare and Sir Philip Sidney: The Influence of "The Defense of Poesy"* (Cambridge, MA: Harvard University Press, 1947), and J. H. Walter, ed., *Henry V,* The Arden Shakespeare (London: Methuen, 1954), xv-xvi.

27. See Gary Taylor, ed., *Henry V* (Oxford: Oxford University Press, 1994), 52–58.

28. See chapter 3 of *Quoting Shakespeare,* "The Agency of Quotation in Shakespearean Comedy," 88–116. An earlier version of this chapter was published as "Comedy and Control: Shakespeare and the Plautine Poeta," *Comparative Drama* 24 (1990): 217–31.

29. Tobin remarks on "the influence of Jack Wilton's adventure with the murdering rapist Esdras, whose forcing of Heraclide Shakespeare had

already adopted for use as early as *Titus Andronicus*. The threatening of and forcing of Heraclide by Esdras and the rape of Jack Wilton's mistress by Bartol have provided material for Pistol's threatening of the captured French soldier and for Bourbon's imagining the fleeing soldiers as bawdy panders. The French soldier plays the role of the threatened Heraclide, with the brutally comic Pistol in the role of the bandit rapist Esdras." Tobin, "Nashe and Shakespeare: Some Further Borrowings," 315. See also Gary Taylor's "Shakespeare's Leno" (n. 22, above).

30. Here I am thinking about a tradition of scholarship best evidenced, perhaps, by Thomas Greene's *The Light in Troy: Imitation and Discovery in Renaissance Poetry* (New Haven, CT: Yale University Press, 1982). Greene's influential book concentrates too exclusively, I believe, on prestigious authors and texts and fails to take into account the enormous range of reading and borrowing in the early modern period. Greene, for instance, mentions Nashe once in *The Light in Troy*, but only in a list of authors who inherited a *mundus* of "semiotic reserves" (20).

31. For the *locus classicus* of "conflict" theories of literary relations, see Harold Bloom's *The Anxiety of Influence: A Theory of Poetry* (New York: Oxford University Press, 1973); for criticism of early modern drama based on such a model, see Bruster, *Quoting Shakespeare*, 38–40, 221–22 n. 60.

32. Hans-Georg Gadamer, *Truth and Method* (New York: Crossroad Publishing, 1991), 383.

CHAPTER 8

1. Fredric Jameson, "Radicalizing Radical Shakespeare: The Permanent Revolution in Shakespeare Studies," in *Materialist Shakespeare: A History*, ed. Ivo Kamps (London: Verso, 1995), 320–28; at 323.

2. Jean E. Howard and Scott Cutler Shershow, "Introduction: Marxism now; Shakespeare now," in *Marxist Shakespeares*, ed. Howard and Shershow (London: Routledge, 2001), 1–15; at 15.

3. Jameson, "Radicalizing Radical Shakespeare," 328.

4. See Karl Marx, *Capital*, vol. 1 (New York: International Publishers, 1967), where he quotes or alludes to, variously, *1 Henry IV* (54), *Much Ado About Nothing* (87), *Timon of Athens* (132), and *The Merchant of Venice* (272, 457); and *The Eighteenth Brumaire of Louis Bonaparte*, in Marx and Friedrich Engels, *Selected Works* (New York: International Publishers, 1968), 170, where he paraphrases Hamlet. On Marx's use of Shakespeare, see Johanna Rudolph, "Karl Marx und Shakespere," *Shakespeare-Jahrbuch* (East) 105 (1969): 25–53; and Marjorie Garber, *Shakespeare's Ghost Writers* (New York: Methuen, 1987), 195–96 n. 89.

5. Karl Kautsky, *Thomas More und seine Utopie* (Stuttgart: J.H.W. Dietz, 1888); published in English as *Thomas More and His Utopia*, trans. H. J. Stenning (New York: International Publishers, 1927).

6. Kautsky, *Thomas More and His Utopia*, 3.

7. Robert Weimann, *Drama und Wirklichkeit in der Shakespearezeit: ein Beitrag zur Entwicklungsgeschichte des Elisabethanischen Theaters* (Halle: VEB Max Niemeyer Verlag, 1958).

8. Robert Weimann, *Shakespeare and the Popular Tradition in the Theater: Studies in the Social Dimension of Dramatic Form and Function*, ed. Robert Schwartz (Baltimore, MD: Johns Hopkins University Press, 1978).

9. Robert Weimann, *Authority and Representation in Early Modern Discourse*, ed. David Hillman (Baltimore, MD: Johns Hopkins University Press, 1996); *Author's Pen and Actor's Voice: Playing and Writing in Shakespeare's Theatre*, ed. Helen Higbee and William West (Cambridge: Cambridge University Press, 2000).

10. See, for an example of such work, Michael Bristol's *Carnival and Theater: Plebeian Culture and the Structure of Authority in Renaissance England* (New York: Methuen, 1985).

11. John Drakakis, "Discourse and Authority: The Renaissance of Robert Weimann," *Shakespeare Studies* 26 (1998): 83–104; 84. See Weimann, *Shakespeare und die Tradition des Volkstheaters : Soziologie, Dramaturgie, Gestaltung* (Berlin: Henschelverlag, 1967).

12. Arnold Kettle, ed., *Shakespeare in a Changing World* (New York: International Publishers, 1964).

13. Robert Weimann, "The Soul of the Age: Towards a Historical Approach to Shakespeare," in *Shakespeare in a Changing World*, ed. Kettle, 17–42; at 20.

14. L. C. Knights, *Drama and Society in the Age of Jonson* (London: Chatto and Windus, 1937).

15. Fredric Jameson, *The Political Unconscious: Narrative as a Socially Symbolic Act* (Ithaca, NY: Cornell University Press, 1981), 103, 136, 148; quotation at 136.

16. Paul Delany, "*King Lear* and the Decline of Feudalism," *PMLA* 92 (1977): 429–40; Annabel Patterson, *Shakespeare and the Popular Voice* (Cambridge, MA: Basil Blackwell, 1990); Richard Halpern, *The Poetics of Primitive Accumulation: English Renaissance Culture and the Genealogy of Capital* (Ithaca, NY: Cornell University Press, 1991); and Hugh Grady, *Shakespeare's Universal Wolf: Postmodernist Studies in Early Modern Reification* (Oxford: Oxford University Press, 1996).

17. It should be pointed out here that the phrase "cultural materialism" registers quite differently in literary criticism than in sociology and anthropology, where "cultural materialism" describes an approach

popularized by Marvin Harris in *The Rise of Anthropological Theory* (New York: Thomas Y. Crowell, 1968). On this "cultural materialism," which seeks to lend the rigor of science to the explanatory goals of anthropology, see also Eric B. Ross, ed. *Beyond the Myths of Culture* (New York: Academic Press, 1980), and Martin F. Murphy and Maxine L. Margolis, eds. *Science, Materialism, and the Study of Culture* (Gainesville: University Press of Florida, 1995).

18. Jonathan Dollimore and Alan Sinfield, eds. *Political Shakespeare: New Essays in Cultural Materialism* (Ithaca, NY: Cornell University Press, 1985); John Drakakis, ed., *Alternative Shakespeares* (London: Methuen, 1985).

19. Patricia Fumerton and Simon Hunt, eds., *Renaissance Culture and the Everyday* (Philadelphia: University of Pennsylvania Press, 1999), 3.

20. Fumerton, "Introduction: A New New Historicism," in *Renaissance Culture and the Everyday*, ed. Fumerton and Hunt, 1–17; at 3–4.

21. Patricia Fumerton, *Cultural Aesthetics: Renaissance Literature and the Practice of Social Ornament* (Chicago: University of Chicago Press, 1991); Jeffrey Knapp, *An Empire Nowhere: England, America, and Literature from "Utopia" to "The Tempest"* (Berkeley: University of California Press, 1992); Lena Cowen Orlin, *Private Matters and Public Culture in Post-Reformation England* (Ithaca, NY: Cornell University Press, 1994), and Orlin, ed., *Elizabethan Households: An Anthology* (Washington, DC: The Folger Shakespeare Library, 1995); Margreta de Grazia, Maureen Quilligan, and Peter Stallybrass, eds., *Subject and Object in Renaissance Culture* (Cambridge: Cambridge University Press, 1996); David Hillman and Carla Mazzio, eds , *The Body in Parts: Fantasies of Corporeality in Early Modern Europe* (New York: Routledge, 1997); and Orlin, ed., *Material London, ca. 1600* (Philadelphia: University of Pennsylvania Press, 2000); Ann Rosalind Jones and Peter Stallybrass, *Renaissance Clothing and the Materials of Memory* (Cambridge: Cambridge University Press, 2000); and Juliet Fleming, *Graffiti and the Writing Arts of Early Modern England* (Philadelphia: University of Pennsylvania Press, 2001).

22. Jonathan Gil Harris, "The New New Historicism's *Wunderkammer* of Objects," *European Journal of English Studies* 4.3 (2000): 111–123; at 111.

23. Harris, "The New New Historicism's *Wunderkammer*," 113, 115.

24. Debora Shuger, "The 'I' of the Beholder: Renaissance Mirrors and the Reflexive Mind," in *Renaissance Culture and the Everyday*, ed. Fumerton and Hunt, 21–41; at 21.

25. Henry S. Turner, "Nashe's Red Herring: Epistemologies of the Commodity in *Lenten Stuffe* (1599)," *ELH* 68.3 (2001): 529–61; at 530.

26. Turner, "Nashe's Red Herring," 551.

CONCLUSION

1. This totality, of course, will not be seamless but full of contradiction and conflict. Like the early modern culture such studies seek to revive and describe, the aggregate "fantasy" of culture among these critical works generates contestations and may even operate dialectically in terms of them.
2. Catherine Gallagher and Stephen Greenblatt, *Practicing New Historicism* (Chicago: University of Chicago Press, 2000), 1.

APPENDIX

1. With apologies to Willem de Kooning. "Nothing is positive about art except that it is a word" (quoted by Richard Wollheim, *Art and Its Objects: An Introduction to Aesthetics* [1968; New York: Harper and Row, 1971], vii).
2. Raymond Williams, *Keywords: A Vocabulary of Culture and Society* (New York: Oxford University Press, 1976), 76–77.
3. To my mind, words like "Pleistocene," "electrocardiograph," and "diarthrosis" are complicated—complicated in their components and in resisting easy understanding. As such, they are rarely if ever used in complicated ways. Their very complicatedness as words ensures that when people use them, they mean just one thing. Two "hard" words in Shakespeare—Holofernes's "honorificabilitudinitatibus" and Macbeth's "incarnadine" come immediately to mind in this context, although they are complicated in a different way.
4. See William Empson, *The Structure of Complex Words* (1951; Cambridge, MA: Harvard University Press, 1989). There Empson explores, famously, the multiple valences of such words as "fool" in *King Lear,* "all" in *Paradise Lost,* "honest" in *Othello,* and "wit" in the "Essay on Criticism." We could take as quintessentially Empsonian the following remarks about "honest" in *Othello:* "The fifty-two uses of honest and honesty in *Othello* are a very queer business; there is no other play in which Shakespeare worries a word like that. *King Lear* uses fool nearly as often but does not treat it as a puzzle, only as a source of profound metaphors. In *Othello* divergent uses of the key word are found for all the main characters . . ." (218). It is from this book (*The Structure of Complex Words*) that Williams may have borrowed his title for *Keywords,* as the phrase "key word[s]" appears frequently in Empson's text.
5. Williams, *Keywords,* 12.
6. Adam Kuper, *Culture: The Anthropologists' Account* (Cambridge, MA: Harvard University Press, 1999), x.
7. Mathew Greenfield, "What We Talk About When We Talk About Culture," *Raritan* 19.2 (1999): 95–113; at 95. As will be apparent

to those familiar with Greenfield's essay, I have benefited greatly from
his insights throughout this book.

8. Terry Eagleton, *The Idea of Culture* (London: Verso, 2000), 131.

9. Jacques Barzun, *From Dawn to Decadence: 500 Years of Western Cultural Life* (New York: HarperCollins, 2000), xiv.

10. Along these lines Derek Attridge has criticized the "romance of etymology" that supposes a word's origins (and here, we could add, its history of use) necessarily shed light on its implications hundreds, even thousands of years later. See Derek Attridge, "Language as History/History as Language: Saussure and the Romance of Etymology," in *Poststructuralism and the Question of History,* ed. Derek Attridge, Geoff Bennington, and Robert Young (Cambridge and New York: Cambridge University Press, 1987), 183–211.

11. Williams, *Keywords,* 87–93.

12. Definitions for Latin terms in this paragraph and the ones that follow are taken from both Lewis and Short's *Latin Dictionary* and *The Oxford Latin Dictionary.* I have also benefited from consulting the *Thesaurus Linguae Latinae.*

13. On "cultus" in Latin literature, see L. C. Curran's reading of Propertius 1.2. ("Quid iuvat ornato procedere") in "Nature to Advantage Dressed: Propertius 1.2," *Ramus* 4 (1975): 1–16. Curran argues that "Artifice itself becomes the central theme of the poem as its value is radically reinterpreted" (2), and goes on to say, of the poem's Cynthia, that "her *cultus* is artificial, foreign, and bought, the landscape's beauty is natural, native, and spontaneous." In contrast, Ovid delivers an unexpected endorsement of *cultus* in his *Ars Amatoria;* see Patricia Watson, "Ovid and *Cultus,*" *Transactions and Proceedings of the American Philological Association* 112 (1982): 237–44. There Watson explores Ovid's use of the term to examine themes of artifice, beauty, and nature and points out that, in an argument that covers lines 101 to 128 of the work, Ovid explains that he prefers the present age because of the splendid nature of the *puella*'s *cultus,* which "has a specific application to women's dress, hair-style, etc." (241).

14. On "cultus" and cosmetology in Latin, see Peter Green, "*Ars Gratia Cultus:* Ovid as Beautician," *American Journal of Philology* 100 (1979): 381–92.

INDEX

Kendall, Ritchie D., 231n5
Kettle, Arnold, 196
Kernan, Alvin, 219n10, 230n5
Kerrigan, William, 158, 258n1,
  261n33
Kindleberger, Charles, 221n35
King, T. J., 107, 114, 248n27,
  249n34, 251n43
Klause, John, 171, 263n5
Klotz, Edith, 235n27
Kluckhohn, Clyde, 11, 220n21
Knapp, Jeffrey, 199, 267n21
Knights, L. C., 12, 196, 266n14
Knowles, Richard, 171, 263n5
Korda, Natasha, 101, 222n38,
  228n58, 246n12, 247n18
Kronefield, Judy, 224n3
Kroeber, A. L., 11, 220n21
Kuper, Adam, 213, 219n16,
  268n6
Kyd, Thomas, 73
  The Spanish Tragedy, 114

Lake, Peter, 235n26
Lancashire, Anne, 258n47
Lawton, David, 238n48
Leclerc, Georges Louis, 236n37
Lennox, Frank, 238n47
Lennox, Sara, 238n47
Lenormant, François, 258n47
Lerner, Laurence, 179, 263n14
Lewalski, Barbara K., 158, 261n32
Lodge, Thomas, 71, 73, 75
Loewenstein, Joseph, 239n51
Lyly, John, 24, 71, 75, 222n41
  Gallathea, 126–27
Lynch, Stephen J., 171, 262n5

Macherey, Pierre, 222n39
Machin, Lewis, 235n25
MacLean, Gerald, 221n30
Magnusson, Lynne, 170
Mallin, Eric, 170, 241n70, 262n5
Manley, Lawrence, 11–12, 242n72
Manningham, John, 102

Mansfield, Nick, 218n6
Marcus, Leah S., 5, 159, 219n10,
  227n48, 261n38
Markham, Gervase, 70, 235n25
Marlowe, Christopher, 70, 71,
  234n22
  Doctor Faustus, 103
  The Jew of Malta, 114
Marsh, Henry, 104
Marotti, Arthur F., 74, 123,
  236n30, 243n81, 254n14
Marprelate, Martin, 67–71
Marvell, Andrew, 129, 255n29
Marx, Karl, 193, 265n4
Massinger, Phillip, 113
Matthiessen, F. O., 154, 260n16,
  n18
Maus, Katharine Eisaman, 229n1
Mazzio, Carla, 11, 199
McCabe, Richard A., 233n17
McEachern, Claire, 170, 262n5
McGee, C. E., 249n33
McKerrrow, R. B., 75
McMillin, Scott, 114, 251n43
Merrill, Francis E., 220n25
Metz, G. Harold, 170
Michelet, Jules, 149, 259n2
Middleton, Anne, 238n48
Middleton, Thomas, 93, 256n42
  A Game at Chess, 139
  The Revenger's Tragedy, 139
  The Roaring Girl, 96
  Women Beware Women, 113, 139
  —with William Rowley
    The Changeling, 96, 139–41,
    144
Mills, Laurens J., 127, 255n23
Miola, Robert S., 170, 262n4, n5
Montrose, Louis, 13, 27, 220n27,
  223n48
Moore, Lisa L., 254n11
Moore, Suzanne, 121, 253n7
Moraga, Cherrie, 253n8
Moseley, Humphrey, 130
Moss, Ann, 170, 223n44